The Legend of
Red Clydeside

To the memory of three honest men:
Christopher Addison (1869-1951)
David Kirkwood (1872-1955)
John MacLean (1879-1923)

The Legend of Red Clydeside

Iain McLean

Professor of Politics,
Oxford University

JOHN DONALD PUBLISHERS LTD
EDINBURGH

Published by
John Donald Publishers Limited
an imprint of Birlinn Limited
8 Canongate Venture
5 New Street
Edinburgh EH8 8BH

Reprinted 1999

ISBN 0 85976 516 4

British Library Cataloguing in Publication Data
A catalogue record for this book is available from the British Library

Cover design by Barrie Tullett
Cover images:
Tanks in the Saltmarket, 1919 and Raising the Red Flag, George Square, 1919
Reproduced with permission from Scottish Media Newspapers

Printed in Great Britain by Bell & Bain Ltd., Glasgow

Acknowledgements

This book has been thirteen years in the making. Over these years I have accumulated a huge pile of intellectual debts which I can at last acknowledge in public.

The Warden and Fellows of Nuffield College, Oxford, generously elected me to a Junior Research Fellowship from 1969 to 1971, and thus made possible the doctoral thesis on which this book is based. Philip Williams was a peerless supervisor, with an uncanny ability to take my paragraphs apart and reassemble them to make better sense in fewer words. My examiners, James Kellas and Roderick Martin, made a number of helpful suggestions which I have tried to incorporate.

Thereafter, the project was crowded out for several years by the demands of the cheerful, stimulating, but grievously understaffed Department of Politics at the University of Newcastle-upon-Tyne. Its revival is due in the first instance to two grants from the Research Fund of Newcastle University and to the kindness of my colleagues in covering my teaching for a short time during which I restarted the work and secured a grant from the Social Science Research Council (HR 4535) to collect and process the statistics and other materials needed to take the story beyond 1922. Colin Gordon was a model research assistant, who found out far more than I asked him to look for, and he helped to throw light in many dusty corners. Ann Turner and the late John Leece initiated me quickly and efficiently into the mysteries of SPSS; John Leece was a teacher of genius whose tragic death was a dreadful shock to all who knew him. A number of my students worked carefully and accurately on coding my data and preparing it for deposit in the SSRC's Data Archive at Essex University.

When I changed jobs in 1978 the project nearly died again as I arrived in Oxford with sheaves of cards that the Newcastle computer could read but the Oxford one couldn't. Chris Harvie, who was present at the birth on Bletchley station platform all those years ago, brought the patient back to life by introducing me to John Tuckwell of

John Donald Ltd, without whose enthusiasm and commitment the work would have remained incomplete. In the final stages I had very welcome help from Alan McKinlay, Ken Morgan and John Rowett, whose comments were all very valuable.

My thanks go also to all the libraries listed in the Bibliography where relevant records are held. On several occasions I toiled through old newspapers for weeks at a time in the Glasgow Room of the Mitchell Library. I could not have wished for a better place, itself redolent of the ghosts of the Clydesiders and their great meetings in the St Andrew's Halls next door. A number of people kindly gave their time and recollections to Colin Gordon or myself; these also are listed in the Bibliography. John Foster of Strathclyde University generously let me listen to his tapes of other veterans' memories. The staff of the Scottish Record Office and of the General Register Office (Census Branch) were helpful beyond the call of duty. My parents offered me hospitality, sandwiches, a much-prized link with Scotland, and much, much more. Like all other workers in this field, I was assisted by the tireless and selfless work of Ian MacDougall, the Secretary of the Scottish Labour History Society, and congratulate him on his monumental *Catalogue of some Labour Records in Scotland.* If only it had been available when I started!

For ten years some of the arguments in this book have been circulating in increasingly battered *samizdat.* To everybody I have mentioned and all the many others who have helped to drag them into the full light of day, I owe my most grateful thanks.

Iain McLean,
Oxford, 1983

Contents

Abbreviations

Trade unions rank below only the Civil Service and the EU in the quantity of alphabet soup they produce. Hence this necessarily long list of bodies referred to in the text by the initials.

AEU   Amalgamated Engineering Union
AOH   Ancient Order of Hibernians
ASE   Amalgamated Society of Engineers

BCM   Beveridge Collection on Munitions (at British Library of Political and Economic Science, London)
BSP   British Socialist Party

CO   conscientious objector
CPGB   Communist Party of Great Britain
CWC   Clyde Workers' Committee

DC   District Committee
DNB   *Dictionary of National Biography*
DORA   Defence of the Realm Act(s)

EC   Executive Committee (or Council)
ETU   Electrical Trades Union

GOC   General Officer Commanding

HMM   *History of the Ministry of Munitions*

ILP   Independent Labour Party
IWGB   Industrial Workers of Great Britain

MEA   Municipal Employees' Association

NDP	National Democratic Party
NEC	National Executive Committee
NFDSS	National Federation of Discharged Sailors and Soldiers
PC	Parliamentary Committee
RILU	Red International of Labour Unions
SCWS	Scottish Co-operative Wholesale Society
SDF	Social Democratic Federation (in 1911 renamed BSP, *q.v.*)
SED	Scotch Education Department
SLP	Socialist Labour Party
SNP	Scottish National Party
SPGB	Socialist Party of Great Britain
STUC	Scottish Trades Union Congress
TCM	Minutes of the Glasgow Trades Council
TP	(nickname of Thomas Power O'Connor, MP (Irish Party) for Liverpool Scotland 1885-1929)
TUC	Trades Union Congress
UF	United Free (church)
UIL	United Irish League
WMV	War Munitions Volunteers

All prices are quoted in pre-decimal pounds, shillings (s. or /-), and pence(d.)

Introduction to the Paperback Edition

This Book and Its Sources[1]

I am delighted that *The Legend of Red Clydeside* is now available in paperback, fully 30 years after I started work on the doctoral dissertation that was the heart of this book. The first edition of this book came out in 1983. But what happened, and didn't happen, and nearly happened, and might have happened, in the streets and munitions factories of Glasgow between 1914 and 1922, was already legendary long before I chose my title. Legends have continued to grow, and the controversies into which I pitched my ha'porth have continued unabated. In this Introduction I will try to summarise how the debate has moved on since the main text of the book was written; where I would now concede ground to my (many and vociferous) critics; and where I dig in. A little intellectual history may help to set the scene.

When I started work on Red Clydeside, in 1969, the scholarly reassessment had already started. The 30-year rule was a 50-year rule then. So government documents about the home front during the First World War were only just coming into the public domain. I was not the first in the field. I was intrigued and spurred on by such pioneer scholarly discussions as Terry Brotherstone's 'The suppression of the "Forward" '; Walter Kendall's *Revolutionary Movement in Britain 1900–21*; and James Hinton's Ph.D. thesis, which gave rise to first a book chapter then an entire book on *The First Shop Stewards' Movement*.[2]

These predecessors helped me to find the rich source material in the archives of Government departments, especially the Ministry of Munitions, and in the papers of politicians. I think we were all equally astonished to come on such a mine of candid information about politicians' and civil servants' attitudes to Clydeside industrial politics between 1910 and 1922. The most important single source was the partly predigested Ministry of Munitions records under classmark MUN 5 at the Public Record Office. They were in a series of wartime Nissen huts in the grounds of Ashridge College in deepest Hertfordshire. A researcher with no car had a struggle to get there and had to walk a mile to the nearest pub for lunch. But once inside the Nissen huts, what a bonanza! Here were politicians' and administrators' candid thoughts about the troublemakers on Clydeside, uncensored, and brought to me by helpful staff who even plied me with cups of tea. I also had access to a set of the very scarce *History of the Ministry of Munitions*. This was compiled just after the war for internal use. It was never published, and I have never found out exactly why the successor departments went to so much trouble to record its history. Was it to remind themselves of the lessons the Civil Service had learnt should there be another world war? At all events, this *History* is on a vast scale. There are twelve volumes in parts, each part separately paginated. Volume 4, which contains most of the material on labour relations in the Clyde munitions area, comprises four parts each of between 100 and 200 pages.

The set I used had once belonged to G.D.H. Cole, the Guild Socialist academic who was a participant-observer of these events. As a founding fellow of Nuffield College, Oxford, he had left both his rich collection of trade union archives, and a tradition of continuing to collect such material, to the college on his death. Because it is so scarce, this *History is* still an under-exploited source. I hope this new edition may spur people to have another look at it. Few of the 250 copies of the original version are known to survive, but there are some in research libraries. A microfiche edition was published by Harvester Press in 1976, with a typescript introduction by Cameron Hazlehurst, but unfortunately it seems to have been very little used.

Were the records truly uncensored? That is a question that has troubled me, on and off, since then. MUN 5 was a small part of the material the official historians used in preparation of the *History of the Ministry of Munitions*. Gerry Rubin has found *Yes, Ministerial* evidence of censorship of Vol. IV. Part 2 of the printed *History*: 'I have substituted "the principles of the Munitions of War Act" for "their policy of repressive action" – an innocuous phrase which means the same thing!'[3] This makes it all the more remarkable that in places the *History* is quite critical of its Ministry (see, e.g., p. 58 below). The self-censors did not censor out all criticism. But it shows that the scholar must get beyond the *History* to its source documents. Were they themselves weeded or censored before reaching the public records? I do not think so.

Here, for instance, is the chairman of the Clyde Dilution Commissioners, Lynden Macassey, writing to the Ministry of Munitions on 'The industrial situation on the Clyde' on 9 February 1916:

> It [the Clyde Workers' Committee] is ostensibly a Socialist Organisation if indeed it is not something worse. Its primary object is to overthrow all official Trades Unions on the Clyde and to supplant such effete organisations by a revolutionary propaganda of an international Anarchist type . . . I have been convinced for some days that the only effective way of handling the situation is to strike a sharp line of cleavage between the loyal workmen, who undoubtedly compose the great majority of Munition Workers, and the disloyal Socialist minority who are pawns of the Clyde Workers' Committee, and those whoever they may be behind the Committee. The means of effecting this was wanting until yesterday February 8th.[4]

Those who wish to see the hand of the censor at work may note that this document is incomplete. They may also observe that not all the public records on Red Clydeside fell into the researcher's hands as neatly as MUN 5. The Scottish Office Records are much more meagre than those of the Ministry of Munitions. The records kept by the Scottish prison service on John MacLean have always intrigued researchers. I was refused permission to see them despite appealing to the Secretary of State for Scotland.[5] B.J. Ripley and J. McHugh (see their *John Maclean*, Manchester: Manchester University Press 1989) were the first to get access to these records, although I shall argue below that they do not materially alter our picture of MacLean. (They were opened to public inspection in January 1994). But the case against regarding the Ministry of Munitions records as censored is strong. A competent censor would have taken out the passage just quoted and a great deal more.

Government anxieties about Red Clydeside emerge in many other documents. The Cabinet records (CAB 23 and 24) and Cabinet committees have discursive minutes for this period, and I use them extensively.[6] A collection of papers on munitions made by William Beveridge, and the ministerial papers of Lloyd George and Christopher Addison, also contain a great deal of frank material about ministers' and civil servants' intentions. Employers' records, which I do not use to any great extent, have been a goldmine for others.[7] The official side of trade unionism has naturally left more records than the unofficial side, but some of both are in what was my most voluminous unpublished primary source, the Minutes of the Glasgow Trades Council.

The 'Revisionist' Case on Red Clydeside

In 1969, the established picture of Red Clydeside was of a heroic episode of labour struggle against both capital and government. This picture was set out in the many memoirs of participants, of which the best-known are William Gallacher's *Revolt on the Clyde* (London: Lawrence & Wishart, 1936) and David Kirkwood's *My Life of Revolt* with a foreword by Winston Churchill (London: Harrap, 1935).[8] It was sharpened rather than challenged by Kendall and Brotherstone. From 1971 onwards, there emerged what Joseph Melling has called a 'new orthodoxy on the myth of Red Clydeside', which he summarises as follows:

> [A] number of recent studies of workers' campaigns have stressed the defensive conservatism of industrial labour and the extremely limited support enjoyed by such marxists as John MacLean. It is now almost conventional to dismiss the claims for class struggle on the Clyde and document the poverty of marxist politics.[9]

I attempt to list the claims made by the 'new orthodoxy'. Although sometimes I wonder whether I am supposed to be its only member, the following notes attempt to incorporate arguments made by Alastair Reid, Jonathan Zeitlin, and James Hinton (especially in his more recent work), as well as mine.[10] I give first the summary, and then a short expansion of each heading.

Most of the Red Clydesiders were driven less by socialist ideology than by material concerns.

Those who were driven by socialist ideology got a sympathetic hearing, but only on those matters where ideology and material interests coincided.

Wartime Red Clydeside was not a class struggle but a collection of sectional interests.

So was post-war Red Clydeside; but the sectional interests were different.

Therefore there never was a revolutionary situation on Red Clydeside, although both revolutionaries and some people in government thought there was.

However, Red Clydeside had a highly significant impact on housing and planning policy, in Glasgow and nationwide.

Most of the Red Clydesiders were driven less by socialist ideology than by material concerns.

Deskilling and dilution were touchy points among engineering and shipbuilding workers on the Clyde long before 1914 (see chapter 1 below). Dilution of labour meant the substitution of unskilled or semi-skilled workers for skilled ones, and could be implemented in various ways. Craft jobs could be split up, and the parts that could be done by a less skilled person hived off. During the war, employers saw that introducing women as well as unskilled men could speed up dilution. Craft unionists suspected, with justification, that employers were trying to erode their position. The unions, led by the Amalgamated Society of Engineers (A.S.E.), had been buffeted by the employers' counter-offensive against craft unionism since 1897: the A.S.E., whose members had relatively transferable skills, suffered worse during the war than unions in the shipyards whose members had more job-specific skills. In March 1915, the A.S.E and the other engineering unions signed a corporatist bargain called the Treasury Agreement with Lloyd George, who at the time was Chancellor of the Exchequer, and would shortly become Minister of Munitions. The Treasury Agreement pledged the unions to accept dilution and ensure that their rank-and-file members accepted it. In return they got representation on official committees on labour supply and a promise of legislation to restore pre-war practices after the war (which was kept). The A.S.E. Executive actually obstructed dilution by all means it could, but its shop stewards and local members were not necessarily aware of this. They regarded their leaders' action as a sell-out, and became involved with unofficial strikes, which brought them into conflict with wartime emergency legislation, and sometimes with their own unions.

During 1915 the Ministry of Munitions tried to enforce labour flexibility in the shipyards and failed. Industrial relations were further worsened by an unrelated attempt to raise rents, which led to a rent strike (involving both refusal to pay rents and some strikes) and to legislation to control rents. Both the shipyard employers and the

Ministry of Munitions, which had a common interest in making the labour market work smoothly, wanted the rent strike to be settled, on the strikers' terms if necessary.

The Ministry of Munitions did not try to enforce dilution across the whole of the Clyde munitions industry until October 1915. The campaign had two spectacular highlights: the suppression of the *Forward* for its accurate report of Lloyd George's unsuccessful attempt to woo an audience of munition workers on Christmas Day 1915 (chapter 5 below), and the deportation of leading opponents of dilution to Edinburgh and other non-revolutionary places in March 1916 (chapter 7 below). After March 1916 there was no further organised opposition to dilution in Glasgow.

The language used by many of the opponents of dilution was socialist and favoured workers' control of industry, but socialist language was neither necessary nor sufficient to the campaign.

Those who were driven by socialist ideology got a sympathetic hearing, but only on those matters where ideology and material interests coincided.

Various socialist groups had been preaching Marxism and/or syndicalism since before the war; they now had a sympathetic audience. The best-known socialist in Glasgow, John MacLean, attracted massive audiences with his anti-war speeches outside the Corporation Tramways offices in Bath Street (a site chosen because James Dalrymple, the tramways manager, was an exceptionally aggressive recruiter for the military). However, there is no evidence that the audience were pacifist. John MacLean and the Socialist Labour Party were either unconditionally pacifist (the war was a capitalist war, and the workers should take no part), or revolutionary defeatist (the war was an opportunity for socialist revolution). Their audience was neither. Pacifism was strongest not when the war was going worst (July 1916 and March 1918[11]) but when the first (Kerensky) Russian Revolution appeared to offer a chance of a negotiated peace, in the summer of 1917.

Wartime Red Clydeside was not a class struggle but a collection of sectional interests.

Dilution necessarily set trade against trade, sex against sex, and skilled against unskilled. The struggle against it was confined to skilled male trade unionists. These comprised less than half of the Clydeside working class. In the first anti-dilution unofficial strike of 1915, the toolmakers who went on strike resolved 'That no woman shall be put to work a lathe, and if this was done the men would know how to protect their rights'.[12] The rent strike had significantly more female involvement, but was geographically concentrated south of the river.

So was post-war Red Clydeside; but the sectional interests were different.

The Forty Hours' Strike of January 1919 was an attempt to regain control over working conditions by trying to enforce a reduction in the working week. If successful, this would have increased the bargaining power of skilled unionists. It failed to attract unskilled support, and the tramcars kept running. A mass meeting in George Square on 31 January 1919 was read by the authorities, probably wrongly, as an insurrectionary attempt to stop the cars and seize the City Chambers. It was violently broken up and the strike leaders were arrested (chapter 11). This made no difference to the progress of the strike, which would have collapsed anyhow because of the hardline opposition to it by official unions. The Government, who were being fed exceptionally bad military intelligence, ludicrously overestimated the revolutionary potential of the situation.

Contrary to local expectations, Labour had won only one seat in Glasgow in the 1918 General Election. In 1922 it won ten out of fifteen and came close even in the remaining Conservative strongholds. There were fervent mass rallies in the St Andrews Halls and St Enoch Station to see the new Clyde MPs off on the night train to London. Both *The Red Flag* and Psalm 124 (Scotland's Psalm of Deliverance'[13]) were sung.

The red Clydeside of 1922 was very different from that of 1916. As long as it had been a movement of the male skilled working class, it could never have been electorally successful. The failure of the 1919 strike was a precondition for the success of 1922, which was built on a new Labour coalition. The new elements were a widely supported campaign for controlled rents and public housing, which scored a significant court victory on the eve of the 1922 General Election, and the recruitment of the local Irish Catholic community to the Labour Party after the collapse of the Irish Party. This was still a sectional alliance, but numerically a much larger one than that of 1915–16.

Therefore there never was a revolutionary situation on Red Clydeside, although both revolutionaries and some people in government thought there was.

Lenin appointed John MacLean Bolshevik Consul in Glasgow in 1918. Both William Gallacher and Andrew Bonar Law thought that Glasgow was on the brink of revolution in January 1919. They were all wrong in their evaluation of Glasgow's revolutionary potential, for the reasons given in the previous subsection. John MacLean's influence declined, a decline made sadder and more bitter by the development of the paranoia that had afflicted him in prison as early as 1917.[14] However, this was not the root reason for the decline in his influence. He no longer had common concerns with any sizeable fraction of the working class, although they gave him substantial electoral and emotional support.

However, Red Clydeside had a highly significant impact on housing and planning policy, in Glasgow and nationwide.

The Clydesider John Wheatley became Minister of Health, responsible for housing, in the 1924 Labour Government. Here he built British council housing policy on foundations laid by the Coalition Liberal Christopher Addison (previously one of the ministers involved in the enforcement of dilution, and later a Labour Cabinet minister) and the Conservative Neville Chamberlain. The Wheatley Housing Act gave more generous subsidies for council housing than any of its predecessors. It led to the construction of high-quality, low-density council housing which is still generally popular with tenants and in good condition. However, the policy of building at low density stored up problems for later in Glasgow, and led to a perverse pattern of development after slum clearance in the 1950s and 1960s, whereby the highest density housing, with the fewest facilities, was in peripheral estates such as Easterhouse and Drumchapel.

Rent control was introduced in 1915 in response to the rent strikes in Govan. Though nominally introduced by McKinnon Wood, the Secretary for Scotland, it was actually forced through the Coalition Cabinet by Lloyd George as a nationwide policy in the face of extreme reluctance from his Tory colleagues, who feared that once imposed it would be difficult to remove.[15] How right they were. No government of any party found it politically possible to remove rent control until the Housing Acts 1980 and 1988. Nor did any find it possible to force local authorities to charge market rents, or rents which covered costs, on council housing. Thus the two cardinal features of British housing policy from 1919 to 1979 were laid down in Red Clydeside.

Some Modifications to the 'Revisionist' Case

I now think that this book, and the preceding doctoral thesis, have two main weaknesses: failure to look sufficiently at the Labour movement as a whole; and underestimation of the repressive intentions of government.

The Labour Movement as a Whole

Some aspects of the Labour movement on Clydeside between 1914 and 1922 make almost no appearance below. I could defend myself by saying that I wrote about what I wrote about and did not write about what I did not write about. But Hugh Roberton and the Glasgow Orpheus Choir were as much a part of the movement as David Kirkwood or Willie Gallacher. Indeed, to pursue this particular example, they contributed much more to civilisation as we know it. For instance, the Scottish metrical version of Psalm 23, to the tune Crimond, was little known until popularised by Roberton.[16] And his settings of Negro spirituals are unbearably beautiful. Michael Tippett's equally powerful settings in *A Child of Our Time* are very like Roberton's, although I do not know whether Roberton was a conscious influence on Tippett. Unlike David Kirkwood, Hugh Roberton can reduce me to tears (and usually does, for example as I write this). 'Steal away' and Let my people go' may be read as Roberton's updatings of Psalm 124.[17]

I paid too little attention to issues of gender. Craft conservatism was hostile to women in the workplace, and so was John Wheatley. But other aspects of Red Clydeside, especially the Rent Strike, were more inclusive:

> Well, we were young you see, and it was great fun! . . . And it gets hold of you, when you've been used to it. When you've been a member of a thing like that, it just never leaves you . . . They werenae just labourers' wives that were on strike against the factors . . . In fact, you were on strike against the whole blooming thing.[18]

In sharp contrast to the dilution struggle, the rent strike campaign united male with female, skilled with unskilled, and not least Catholic with Protestant – the organiser, Andrew McBride, was a Catholic.

Hugh Roberton and Jessie Barbour were part of the same movement as Kirkwood and MacLean. Of course, they did not stand for the same things, and I stand by everything I have written about the differences among the various strands in Clydeside socialism. But they were part of what was recognisably, at the time, one movement. They surely all read the *Forward,* whose mix of socialism, pacifism, nationalism, temperance, and faintly religiose culture is uniquely of its time and place.

Government Repression

In his review of the first edition of this book, James Hinton wrote:

> Dr McLean has always had it in for my own account of these events. In *The First Shop Stewards Movement* (1972), I did a good deal of debunking of the revolutionary myth myself. But, being young and ignorant, I was taken aback by the nastiness, ruthlessness, and mendacity revealed by some of the agents of the state in their dealings with the Clydesiders. By comparison, the founders of the British Communist Party appeared mere amateurs in class war . . . Rereading some of these documents nearly twenty years since I first saw them I think I was right to be taken aback. What they record is a vital moment in the decay of British liberalism. (*Albion* 17 (1985) p. 127).

Rereading some of these documents nearly thirty years since I first saw them I think I was wrong not to be taken aback. I do not believe that capitalists were any more capitalist, nor authoritarians any more authoritarian, during the First World War than before or since. But they had new avenues to exercise their authority, which they exploited. The official papers certainly reveal instances of ruthlessness and of mendacity. The other side of both corporatism and labour shortage is that they also empowered working men and women more than previous policy. I cannot be sure which side gained a relative advantage as a result.

What about a Ministry of Munitions conspiracy against the Clyde Workers' Committee? I stand by my evidence that any such conspiracy was patchy, episodic, and (until March 1916) incompetent. But I am persuaded by Jose Harris's review of the whole controversy[19] that I went too far in denying the extent to which the CWC was one of the Ministry's targets.

Open Issues

Some of the issues that I believe are still open in the study of Red Clydeside are already apparent from previous sections. I think there is considerable scope for further work in, for instance, gender politics and workplace politics. The latter should be illuminated by the growing volume of business archives for the period, some of them in the Business Archives Centre at Glasgow University. I wish to examine four open questions in a little more detail.

A Revolutionary Situation?

There was no revolution', said Emanuel Shinwell in a Radio 4 interview in 1983, commenting on this book when it was first published. It may be said

1. that Shinwell in 1983 may have misremembered Shinwell in 1919;

2. that until the phrase 'a revolutionary situation' is satisfactorily defined, we cannot say what is and is not one.

If there was a revolutionary moment, it was in 1919. Not in 1915–16 because the anti-dilution struggle was too narrowly based and the Ministry of Munitions was in control. Not in 1922, because Labour politics were by then firmly in a parliamentarian mould. But some people on both sides perceived 1919 as a revolutionary situation. On the side of the strikers, we have to beware of hindsight. The contemporary record shows that both Gallacher and Kirkwood were appalled by the police attack on the strikers in George Square on 'Bloody Friday' (not very bloody, actually), and tried to move the crowd out of harm's way. The evidence on Shinwell is more mixed. He had been the main organiser of Scargillite flying pickets and Gallacher later dropped dark hints that Shinwell was up to something insurrectionary. However, Gallacher is an untrustworthy witness.

The case that Bloody Friday could have sparked off a Glasgow socialist revolution rests on either or both of two arguments. 1) A revolution may just happen spontaneously, as did the February 1917 Revolution in Russia. 2) The government was in such a jittery state that it might have sent the tanks in the Saltmarket to break the strike, which might have resulted in deaths, which might have resulted in general insurrection. For my part, I think the string of 'might haves' is too conjectural to make a plausible counterfactual, but 1 can see how others might disagree.

Corporatism and the Decline of Liberalism

James Hinton is the most eloquent, though not the only, writer to expound the argument that something irreversible happened to government in 1914. As we have seen, he described the campaign to enforce dilution as 'a vital moment in the decay of British liberalism'. But the progress of tripartite corporatism has not all been in one direction. It took a step backwards after the war, not least with the Restoration of Pre-war Practices Act 1919. After the nadir (for corporatism) of the General Strike, it cautiously edged forward with the Mond-Turner talks but did not again become established until the Second World War. From then on, it progressed steadily until the abrupt reversal of 1979. It has shown no signs as yet of reviving from this new slump.[20]

Alternatively, the mendacity and ruthlessness of government may not be connected with the degree of corporatism. Recent events, such as the Scott inquiry on the use of public interest immunity certificates to attempt to block the defence of the Matrix Churchill defendants, and the disgrace of former ministers Neil Hamilton and Jonathan Aitken, suggest that mendacity and other unethical behaviour may have as much to do with unchallenged single-party government as with corporatism. A sort of reverse Whiggism maintains that the standard of public life reached its highest under Mr Gladstone, began a sharp decline under Lloyd George, revived somewhat under Churchill and Attlee, and has now reached its lowest post-1841 level. I do not know whether this is true; I am not sure that I even know how one would investigate it; but it remains an open and important question.

Ecology, Regression, and the Spread of the Labour Vote

The claims I make about the spread of the Labour vote, in chapters 14 and 16 below, are based on statistical evidence. For the period 1920–22 I present a simple bivariate association between class and Labour vote, listing wards in ascending order of deviance. Thus for 1920 Cowcaddens had the lowest Labour vote compared to expectations, and North Kelvin the highest. For 1922 Kinning Park (where John

MacLean stood) had the lowest, and Fairfield the highest.[21] By inspection of these lists of residuals, I argue that the deviantly anti-Labour wards in 1920 were largely those with a substantial Irish and/or unskilled population, and the deviantly pro-Labour wards were those with a substantial artisan, 'labour-aristocratic' population. I later repeated the exercise for the Census years 1921, 1931, 1961, 1966, and 1971 (chapter 16). This time I performed a multiple regression in which I attempted to predict the Labour vote from measures of class, Catholicism, (militant) Protestantism, and prohibitionism. The results showed that class and Catholicism were always predictors of a Labour vote, and that they ran in the direction we would now expect for all Census years including 1921: the more working-class and/or Catholic a ward, the higher its Labour vote. Nothing surprising there, but a definite change from the position before 1921. The measures of militant Protestantism and of dry voting ran the other way – the more of either of these (after controlling for everything else tested), the lower the Labour vote. Thus already by 1921 the ideology of Tom Johnston and David Kirkwood – the Presbyterian activists who ensured that there were no pubs in Kirkintilloch and that the 1922 send-off meeting sang Psalm 124 – was a vote-loser for Labour.[22]

Statistical analysis has moved on since the 1970s. I had to grapple with home-made programs and with feeding thousands of punched cards into the Newcastle University mainframe, all for admittedly modest results which one reviewer complained 'erupt . . . somewhat incomprehensibly into the text'.[23] My data are in the ESRC Data Archive at the University of Essex. It would now be a relatively trivial task, occupying a few nanoseconds of processing time on a desktop computer, to reanalyse them more rigorously, in order to evaluate the claims I and others have made about the spread of electoral socialism in Glasgow.

Election results are an example of aggregate rather than survey data. For a long time, social scientists were wary of using them because of the risk of falling into the 'ecological fallacy'. The ecological fallacy is the fallacy of making inferences about individuals when data are available only for aggregates such as ward electorates. From the fact that a high incidence of Catholic baptisms is associated, other things being equal, with a high Labour vote we cannot strictly infer that Catholics voted Labour. However, powerful multiple regression now means that this problem is minimised and ecological analysis is becoming much more popular. For an era before opinion polls it is all there is.[24] Not everybody accepts my story; I hope they will test their counter-arguments against the evidence.[25]

Trends and Interpretations

My most formidable critic, John Foster, makes many points, only one of which I accept.[26] That is that this book gives a misleading impression of industrial unrest on Clydeside between 1915 and 1922 because

1. it is too narrowly restricted to Glasgow;

2. it does not point out just how much bigger was the wave of strikes in early 1919 than everything that had gone before.

I plead guilty on both counts and readers should look at the figures in his article for a corrective. But what would follow if I had defined Red Clydeside more inclusively and/or said more about the sheer size of the 1919 strike wave? Nothing, I submit, that would reinstate anything like the traditional view. The most important fact about the strike of January 1919 is not that it had radical objectives, but that it utterly failed to achieve them (chapter 11) – a conclusion Foster does not dispute. Attempts to spread its political objectives beyond Glasgow got nowhere. And (as Foster points out), 'it must be remembered that all stoppages in war-related industries were illegal'.[27] Therefore mere numbers are not the whole story. The strikes of 1915 and 1916 were a challenge to the state in a sense that the much bigger strike of 1919 was not. The wartime strikers took more personal risks and incurred higher costs. In 1919, with their personal costs much reduced, a section of the Glasgow trade union movement struck to regain some of that very control over the workplace that they and their predecessors had got during the war and lost with the peace. They lost; probably the only thing that could have saved them would have been the incompetence and panic of the military and some of the lower reaches of the Coalition government. But had the tanks in the Saltmarket fired on anybody, it would not have been long before Lloyd George returned to control his underlings. A man who could make peace in Ireland in 1921 would have had no trouble in Glasgow in 1919.

Several critics have pointed out that this book itself contains an explanation of the poor Labour performance in the 1918 General Election in Glasgow. The explanation (pp. 154–7 below) is that registration was chaotic and turnout low. Then, it is said, there is nothing to be explained. With proper registration and a high turnout,

Labour would have polled its 'true' strength in the General Election. Then it would have seemed all of a piece with the 1919 strike and the 1922 General Election: the break between wartime and postwar Red Clydeside does not really exist.

The trouble with this argument is that it treats Glasgow in isolation. Registration and low turnout were national factors. If they depressed the Labour vote (as they probably did), there is no reason to suppose that they depressed it more in one place than another. But Labour did worse in Glasgow than in the English conurbations in the 1918 election (Tables 13.1 and 13.2). So there is something to be explained, after all. I remain content with my explanation.

Let me conclude with a plea for tolerance and for dialogue based on the evidence. Many of the attacks on this book have been sweeping and general.[28] I can live with that. They have said what they say; what they say, let them say. But unsubstantiated attacks get us nowhere. There is still work to be done on Red Clydeside, and still questions that have not been settled. Disagreement is the lifeblood of enquiry. But let those who disagree at least do their readers the courtesy of saying what they disagree with, on what grounds, and with what counter-evidence.

Notes

1. Parts of this introduction appeared previously in my 'Red Clydeside after 25 years', *Scottish Labour History Society Journal* 29 1994, pp. 98–111. With grateful thanks to the editor for permission to reproduce this material.

2. T. Brotherstone, 'The suppression of the "Forward"', *Scottish Labour History Society Journal* 1, 1969, pp. 5–23; W. Kendall, *The Revolutionary Movement in Britain, 1900–21* (London, Weidenfeld & Nicolson 1969); J. Hinton, 'The Clyde Workers' Committee and the Dilution Struggle' in A. Briggs and J. Saville ed., *Essays in Labour History 1886–1923* (London, Macmillan, 197 1), pp. 152–84; J. Hinton, *The First Shop Stewards' Movement* (London, Allen & Unwin 1973).

3. A.J. Jenkinson to G.I.H. Lloyd, Public Record Office MUN 5/328/160/R.2, cited in G. R. Rubin, *War, Law, and Labour: the Munitions Acts, State Regulation, and the Unions 1915–1921* (Oxford, Clarendon Press 1987), p. 18.

4. MUN 5173, 324/15/7. See p. 74 below.

The Legend of Red Clydeside

5. The fact of the records' existence, as well as their contents, was supposed to be secret. I was therefore in the position of having to ask to see documents I officially did not know existed (and I was probably in breach of the Official Secrets Act by knowing what I wanted to ask permission to see). This curious situation exists elsewhere. For instance, according to 1. Linn (*Application Refused: employment vetting by the state*, London, Civil Liberties Trust 1990, p.32), civil servants who have been refused positive vetting clearance have a right of appeal, but they have no right to know that they have been refused positive vetting clearance in the first place. It is only fair to add that access to the records of government departments is much easier now than in the early 1970s.

6. At the height of the Red Scare of 1919, some of the Cabinet minutes were typed into a separate 'A series' because ministers suspected that their printers might not be loyal. CAB 23/15; I. McLean, 'Popular Protest and Public Order, Red Clydeside 1915–19', in P. Thane and A. Sutcliffe ed, *Essays in Social History Vol.* 2 (Oxford, Clarendon Press, 1986), p. 311.

7. Notably Rubin, *War, Law, and Labour*; Alastair Reid, 'Dilution, Trade Unionism and the State in Britain during the First World War' in S. Tolliday and J. Zeitlin (ed.), *Shop Floor Bargaining and the State* (Cambridge, Cambridge University Press 1985), pp. 46–74; A. McKinlay, 'Employers and Skilled Workers in the Inter-war Depression: Engineering and shipbuilding on Clydeside 1919–39', unpublished D.Phil. thesis, Oxford University, 1986.

8. There were rumours that Kirkwood's autobiography was 'ghosted' by Rosslyn Mitchell, a fringe Clydesider and lawyer who was best known for his role in the parliamentary defeat of the revised Church of England Prayer Book in 1928 (a matter on which it might be thought Scottish MPs had no business to vote). This may account for its occasionally religiose tone. But there is independent evidence that Kirkwood held similar religious views to Mitchell's. Messrs Harrap were unable to confirm or deny that Mitchell was Kirkwood's ghost when I contacted them in the early 1970s.

9. J. Melling, 'Work, culture and politics on "Red Clydeside": the ILP during the First World War' in A. McKinlay and R.J. Morris ed., *The ILP on Clydeside 1893–1932, from foundation to disintegration* (Manchester, Manchester University Press 1991), pp. 83–122, quoted at p. 83. See also Melling's review article, 'Whatever happened to Red Clydeside – industrial-conflict and the politics of skill in World War I', *International Review of Social History*, 35, 1990, pp.3–32.

10. See especially A. Reid, 'Glasgow socialism', *Social History* 11, 1986, pp. 89–97; Reid, 'Dilution, trade unionism and the state in the First World

War'; J. Zeitlin, 'From labour history to the history of industrial relations', Economic History *Review* 40, 1987, pp. 159–84; J. Zeitlin ' "Rank and filism" in British labour history, a critique', *International Review of Social History* 34, 1989, pp. 42–61. As far as I know, Hinton has not published any modification of his views since 1985, but he and I have disappointed at least two radio producers by appearing together in programmes on Red Clydeside and agreeing on all main points in the story.

11. Cf Tom Johnston, editor of *Forward*, writing in the journal at the time of the German offensive of March 1918, 'What is happening on the Western Front makes a peace propaganda impossible . . . One cannot indulge even in the customary amenities of criticism at a time like this' (*Forward*, 30 March 1918, p. 1). If the circulation of their respective newspapers is any guide, Johnston was closer to working-class opinion than was MacLean.

12. A.S.E. *Monthly Journal and Report*, October 1915, p. 13. See further H. Benenson, 'The family wage and working women's consciousness in Britain, 1880–1914', *Politics and Society* 19, 199 1, pp. 71–108.

13. D. Kirkwood, My *Life of Revolt* (London, Harrap 1935), p. 192. For a discussion of the iconography of Psalm 124, see pp. 98–9 below. It was written to celebrate the deliverance of the Jews from Babylonian captivity. It was taken up by Calvinists in the 16th and 17th centuries – the tune 'Old 124th', which was certainly that sung in 1922, was written in mid-sixteenth-century Geneva, and the verse translation used comes from the mid-seventeenth-century *Scottish Metrical Psalter*. Specifically, the late 17th-century Covenanters sang it as a Calvinist and nationalist battle-hymn against their repression under Charles II and James II. Thus its subtext is nationalist and Calvinist, but not socialist.

14. For new evidence on this, see T. Royle and R. Clancy, 'Secrets dull a martyr's image', *Scotland on `Sunday*, 2 January 1994, p.3.

15. Ch.2 below passim.

16. I. Bradley, *The Book of Hymns* (Woodstock, NY, Overlook Press 1989), p. 414.

17. For a good survey, more oriented to 'movement' politics than this book, see the relevant chapters of McKinlay and Morris, *The ILP on Clydeside*

18. Jessie Barbour, recorded in 1978. In J. Melling, 'Clydeside rent struggles and the making of Labour politics in Scotland, 1900–39', in R. Rodger ed., *Scottish Housing in the Twentieth Century* (Leicester, Leicester University Press 1989), pp. 54–88, quoted at pp. 79, 80.

19. J. Harris, *William Beveridge, a biography* (Oxford, Clarendon Press 1977), pp. 206–31.

20. On this, see also R. Davidson, 'Government Labour Policy, 1914–16, a reappraisal', *Scottish Labour History Society Journal* 8, 1974, pp. 3–20. For a UK/USA comparative review, see L.G. Gerber, 'Corporatism in comparative perspective – the impact of the First World War on American and British labor relations', *Business History Review* 62 (1988), pp. 93–127.

21. Table 14.1 below (p. 179).

22. Table 16.6 below (p.227). William Knox says, in 'Religion and the Scottish Labour Movement 1900–39', *Journal of Contemporary History* 23, 1988, pp. 609–30, that he has refuted this claim of mine. I am puzzled, because in his source for this claim – his own *Scottish Labour Leaders 1918–39* (Edinburgh, Mainstream, 1984), pp. 25–6, he agrees with me.

23. Hinton, in *Albion* 17 (1985), p. 128.

24. See Gary King, A *Solution to the Ecological Inference Problem: reconstructing individual behavior from aggregate data* Princeton, N.J., Princeton University Press, 1997.

25. Reid, in 'Glasgow Socialism', stresses (as I do) that the Labour-Irish alliance was not made anew in 1920 but was revived from the period before the Third Home Rule Bill. Yes; but I do not see how that invalidates the inferences I make from the ward electoral data.

26. See especially J. Foster, 'Strike action and working-class politics on Clydeside 1914–1919', *International Review of Social History* 35, 1990, pp. 33–70.

27. Ibid., p. 47.

28. For instance, Royden Harrison, reviewing J. D. Young's *John Maclean, Clydeside Socialist* in *Scottish Labour History Society Journal* no. 28 (1993), p. 106, commends the 'pardonable severity' with which I and others are 'put down', but does not explain why I merit humane execution. There are references in a similar tone on pp. 7 and 87 of that issue. Of course, I am pleased and honoured that contributors to that *Journal* still find what I say in this book provocative enough to be worth attacking.

Introduction

On Christmas Day 1915, Lloyd George was shouted down by an angry hall-full of munitions workers in Glasgow, and he promptly suppressed the socialist newspaper *Forward* for reporting the fact. On 3rd December 1918, a Marxist revolutionary called John MacLean, who had just been released from Peterhead Jail after serving only seven months of a sentence of five years' penal servitude for sedition, was drawn through cheering crowds in a triumphal procession from Buchanan Street Station to Carlton Place. On 31st January 1919 — 'Bloody Friday' — a vast demonstration of unofficial strikers in front of the City Chambers in George Square was very roughly broken up by the police, and the next day six tanks lay in the Saltmarket with their guns pointing at the citizens of Glasgow. In the 1922 General Election, Labour won ten out of the fifteen seats in Glasgow, and the new M.P.s, several of them colourful leftist rebels, were given a tumultuous send-off from St. Enoch Station: 'The singing of the *The Red Flag* was general'.[1]

From these famous scenes, and many others like them, springs the legend of Red Clydeside. It is a powerful legend, which entranced many in its own time and has continued to do so ever since. It records how Clydeside was ripe for revolution throughout the First World War; how the revolution just failed to occur in January 1919; and how some of the revolutionaries entered Parliament four years later, still determined to wipe capitalism out. It is a stirring story, which impressed frightened members of the 1918-22 Coalition Government as much as it did the revolutionaries themselves. Nevertheless, it *is* a legend. If Glasgow really was ripe for revolution in January 1919, why had it just sent fourteen Coalition M.P.s to Westminster, only one Labour, and none from any point further left? Throughout the war, some people on Clydeside were calling for a revolution (though not as many as later claimed to have done so); groups of workers sometimes listened to them, but only in order to protect their own group. In its first phase,

1

Red Clydeside was not a class movement; it was an interest-group movement. That phase ended in January 1919. The second phase began with Labour gains on Glasgow Corporation starting in 1920, and culminated in the famous scenes of joy on the night of the 1922 General Election. Some actors in these scenes had also played in the wartime drama; but it was a different play. The second Red Clydeside was much more nearly a class movement than the first. Indeed, the failure of the first Red Clydeside was almost a precondition for the success of the second. The issues raised during the war did not unite the Glasgow working class; they intensified its already deep divisions.

This book is in three parts. Part I, 'Clydeside in Wartime', looks at the causes and effects of the first Red Clydeside. Part II, 'From George Square to St. Enoch Square', proceeds from its last throes, in George Square on Bloody Friday, to the dispatch of the Clyde M.P.s from St. Enoch Square in November 1922. Since the first phase of Red Clydeside cannot have been the cause of the second, this first part of the book tries to establish what was. Part III examines the impact of Red Clydeside on Glasgow and on Parliament: an impact smaller than has sometimes been claimed, but nevertheless substantial, for good and ill. John Wheatley's Housing Act of 1924 was a product of Red Clydeside; but so are Glasgow's awful council house ghettos.

Throughout, I use 'Glasgow' and 'Clydeside' as virtual synonyms. Careful readers will protest against this slapdash practice; my defence is that I merely follow contemporary ways. Glasgow Labour politics were very introverted. Even when socialists in Glasgow were appealing to the workers of the world, they rarely tried, and never succeeded, in getting the workers of Motherwell, nor of Paisley, to act with them. For forty miles, from Wishaw to the mouth of the Clyde, the industrial towns in the river valley are either contiguous or separated only by narrow strips of mostly indifferent farmland. Several of them had common boundaries with Glasgow and the whole conurbation was knit together by road and rail routes. (Until only a couple of years before the last tram ran in 1962, a poor man with plenty of time could still ride from Airdrie to beyond Clydebank for sixpence (2½p)). But none of the neighbouring towns except Clydebank was ever sucked in to the politics of Red Clydeside before 1922. After that the 'Clydesiders', broadly defined, represented seats scattered all over the West of Scotland, but of the half-dozen men who comprised the core Clyde group, five represented inner Glasgow seats and the sixth sat for Clydebank and Dumbarton.

Like Christopher Harvie's classic sombre history of twentieth-century Scotland,[2] this is a tale with no gods and precious few heroes. Some men and women in it, however, had an honesty and a singleness of purpose that marks them out from the crowd. This book is dedicated to the memory of three of them.

Part I

Clydeside in Wartime

1

The Industrial Environment

The industrial militancy of wartime 'Red Clydeside', which centred round the Clyde Workers' Committee, originated among a small section of the industrial workers: mostly engineering craftsmen employed in the munitions industry. During the first two years of the war, these men found themselves under increasing pressure to admit unskilled men to jobs which had been open only to duly time-served craftsmen. In their resistance to this 'dilution' they were covertly, and at times openly, supported by the executive of their union, the Amalgamated Society of Engineers (A.S.E.).

For twenty years before the outbreak of war, 'militancy' in the A.S.E. had been a rather ambiguous mixture of conservatism and aggressive political radicalism:

> Among the Engineers . . . the socialists had increased their influence by putting themselves in the forefront of an aggressive industrial movement to resist technical and organisational change. Thus socialists intent on pursuing the class war to end all privilege allied themselves with members anxious to preserve their ancient privileges against the inroads of machines, piecework and unskilled workers.[1]

This ambiguously revolutionary impulse produced a change in the Executive of the society at the quadrennial elections in 1896, when the old apolitical leadership was succeeded by the socialist George Barnes, who stood, *inter alia*, for 'increased militancy in trade policy'.[2]

Many observers shared the view of the liberal economist F. W. Hirst, who wrote:

> The masters have fought . . . against interference in regard to machinery and the claim of Trade Unionist officials to 'boss' their workshops . . . The further development of a system of this sort would of course be ruinous, and one cannot wonder that the masters were alarmed at what seemed to be only the beginning of a new policy.

These recent developments are due to the success of the Independent Labour Party in this particular society . . . [3]

Later in the same article he described the economic 'fallacies' which so pained him:

'Lower the productive capacity of labour in order to absorb the unemployed!' is the socialist idea . . . Mr Barnes for example . . . is a declared socialist, and has given himself up not only to abstract aspirations for a future millennium, but also to the advocacy of the policy involved in the special economic fallacy which we have been discussing . . . There is no doubt that there has been a marked change for the worse in the spirit and conduct of the engineers since the election of Mr Barnes as secretary.[4]

The employers were becoming more militant and better organised. During the 1890s, the Employers' Federation of Engineering Associations came into being. One of its objects was:

to protect and defend [its] interests against combinations of workmen seeking by strikes or other action to impose unduly restrictive conditions upon any branch of the engineering trades.[5]

For many employers, new unionism, socialist militancy and craftsmen's restrictionism were all the same (disagreeable) thing. As a large Tyneside employer said:

the degrading doctrines of the new unionism have so poisoned the A.S.E. as to make them as a class fully 20 per cent less valuable than they ought to be.[6]

In 1897, Barnes displayed his 'new militancy' by trying to get employers nationwide to agree to a settlement of the 'machine question' that the union had negotiated after a long strike in Hull: namely that machines which displaced fully skilled men should be manned by fully skilled men. The new Employers' Federation counter-attacked fiercely by threatening to lock out all the men who made this demand. The threat was renewed later in the year when the union started a campaign for an eight-hour day. This time it was carried out. The Employers' Federation was much more united than the unions, a number of which found various excuses for not taking any action which might harm their own members. The employers, on the other hand, showed what Clegg *et al* delicately call a 'lack of fastidiousness' in coercing firms which did not want to lock out their employees by, for instance, threatening to refuse sub-contracts to them.

In early 1898 the union had to surrender. Thereafter, Barnes and his Executive were forced to become less militant on the 'machine

question', only to be harried by their suspicious and resentful membership. The events of 1896 were repeated in 1912, when rebels against
Barnes' regime, later confirmed in office, actually besieged and forced
an entry into the union's headquarters in Peckham.[7] The new regime
found the cycle moving faster still: they were seriously threatened by
their rebellious members on the machine question in 1915 and had to
face the tiger on which they had ridden in 1912 against Barnes, just as
he had against his own predecessors in 1896.

Rank-and-file craftsmen not unnaturally were even more bitter and
hostile to mechanisation after 1898 than before. Technical change was
making A.S.E. members' position much less secure by comparison with
that of the unskilled and semi-skilled men in the industry. Partly as a
result of the Great Depression of the 1880s and in an attempt to
emulate foreign competitors, manufacturers were turning away from
the production of one-off jobs depending on the skill of engineers'
precision work, towards something more like mass-production
methods where much more sophisticated machine tools could enable a
job to be done by men with less well-trained precision skills. Allied
with this was a growing interest in the new 'science' of work-study and
increased emphasis on planning of process and line production:

> The most desultory reader of our technical journal cannot fail to be struck with the
> great and increasing interest which has, of late years, been taken in the internal
> economy of our engineering workshops . . . The interest which is spreading in
> regard to workshop economies is one of the most hopeful signs that an awakening
> of the new order of things is taking place . . . The first and greatest of all these
> influences is the introduction of the Premium System.[8]

Engineering employers also admired the new machine tools:

> The main object of these modern methods . . . was that of reducing as far as
> possible the number of highly trained workmen, that is, the fitters, from the
> modern mechanical engineering workshop.[9]
>
> Those engineers who saw . . . a lathe running at a high speed with a tool with its
> point red-hot removing a dark blue chip felt that they were witnessing the
> beginning of a revolution in Tool-steel and in machines fitted for its use. This
> revolution has now taken place.[10]

The machines most responsible were the capstan or turret lathe, the
universal milling machine, and the grinding machine,[11] all of which
tended to devalue the skills of the fitters and turners who comprised the
core of the A.S.E. The threat to craftsmen came from many quarters at
once: 'if privileges were to be preserved they must be defended against
all comers, whether employers, unskilled workers, or other crafts'.[12]

As shopfloor activists in the A.S.E. saw it, 'the introduction of unskilled labour on lathes and machines . . . seems to be of far too frequent occurrence'.[13]

In 1906 the Executive Committee (E.C.) suspended the whole Manchester District Council for supporting an unofficial strike against the introduction of 'handymen' to man a new lathe. A very full report of the District Committee's case, and the E.C.'s reply, complete with a photograph of the offending machine, was produced. *Inter alia*, the District claimed:

> The time has arrived when the engineering industry shall cease to be the happy hunting grounds of the handyman,

and the E.C. retorted,

> Council do not accept the soft impeachment (sic) that they have adopted a peace-at-any-price policy, and strongly resent same, which the progress made during the past few years fully disproves.[14]

In engineering most unskilled and semi-skilled workers who became unionised joined the Workers' Union, a 'New Union' founded in 1898; in Glasgow another general union catering for them was the National Amalgamated Union of Labour.[15] The rank and file of the A.S.E. actively resented the unskilled men and their unions. During a strike in 1913, the local A.S.E. delegate reported:

> The workers' union[16] is not so much directing the strikes as following them, and is making members by the thousand. Men who have resisted all inducements to join the skilled unions for which they are eligible are paying their shilling entrance fee and consider themselves Trade Unionists as soon as they can get a button in their coats.

He went on to criticise undercutting fitters, turners and smiths who:

> having been thrown into a struggle they did not seek expect to be hailed as valiant warriors and to purchase their place among the elect for a shilling entrance fee and 3d a week contribution.[17]

The 1901 Delegate Meeting (the four-yearly supreme legislative body of the union at that time) decided to open a Machinists' Section for men who had been in the trade for at least two years and received at least 75% of the standard district rate. But resolutions from branches opposing this flooded into the Delegate Meeting while it was still sitting, and

> the new rule . . . while not withdrawn was largely inoperative. Only 4,000 had been recruited into this section by 1904.[18]

In 1912, 'Section F' of the A.S.E. was formed for unskilled labourers in the industry, but it met with similar opposition, and was abolished in 1917.[19]

During the First World War, all the stresses inherent in this position were vastly increased. The pressure of war conditions accelerated innovation, and greatly enlarged the amount of mass production of armaments. The greatest single fear of the engineers was that it would not be possible to restore the previous ascendancy of skilled workers after the war, and many were therefore deeply suspicious of the 'Treasury Agreement' negotiated between the Government and the Executives of the A.S.E. and the other engineering unions in March 1915. In this agreement the unions promised to ban all strikes for the duration of the war, and added:

> the workmen's representatives at the Conference are of opinion that during the war period the relaxation of the present trade practices is imperative, and that each union be recommended to take into favourable consideration such changes in working conditions or trade customs as may be necessary with a view to accelerating the output of war munitions or equipments.[20]

But this concession was to be offered on the strict understanding that the government would legislate to restore pre-war practices at the end of the war. J. T. Murphy, the most percipient of the wartime shop stewards, recalled his suspicious reception of this in a discussion with F. S. Button, a member of the A.S.E. Executive:

> Did he not think that the Executive Council and the Government were regarding us as very credulous beings when they asked us to believe that all the new machinery, all the new processes of production, and all the new labour which we have trained to work at cheaper rates than ourselves, would be discarded, and the shops reorganised on the 1914 pattern?
>   He replied most adroitly that 'it was not good to try to look too far ahead and we had better let the future look after itself. The immediate fact was that we had the pledged and written signature of the Government that the pre-war conditions of the skilled workers should be restored, and to that pledge we must hold them.'[21]

Furthermore, the insecurity felt by the skilled men was supplemented through the disparity between piece and time rates. Another Sheffield veteran recalled:

> Men came in and were put on repetition jobs. They smashed the machinery. Nothing mattered, only their huge wage at the weekend. The skilled men had to keep the machinery going and all for the weekly daywork rate. We said we were entitled to something apart from the ordinary daywork rate.[22]

The machine-tool revolution, speeded up by the war, accentuated the role of the skilled man as the one who set up jobs for others to do.

Much of the wartime industrial unrest thus concerned the private interests of the skilled engineers in competition with other sections of the workforce, including the unskilled in the same trade. To become a revolutionary movement, it needed to have grafted on a separate political ideology which far transcended these conservative aims. The evidence for the existence of such an ideology needs to be carefully scrutinised.

A number of descriptions of the course of industrial unrest on the Clyde in the First World War have appeared in print. Those offered by prominent participants[23] suffer from the authors' natural desire to stress both their own roles and the revolutionary credentials of the movement. They also frequently contradict each other on factual details. Reference to the contemporary Press is not always as helpful as might be supposed, for reasons of wartime censorship, or the fear of reprisals. The principal socialist journal in the West of Scotland, the *Forward*, was very reluctant to comment on industrial affairs, justifying itself by reference to the Defence of the Realm restrictions introduced in December 1914:

> Now the net has been drawn still tighter we must cut our cloth accordingly. The alternative to that is suspension of publication and confiscation and destruction of our printers' plant, plus penal servitude for life. The living dog is of more use to the working class than the dead lion. Verb. sap.[24]

When the first major strike of the war took place, the *Forward* proceeded very cautiously:

> For reasons which seemed sufficient and wise to us, we took no part whatever in urging the engineers in the West of Scotland either to strike, or when once they had struck to persist in striking . . . We originally took up the position that however much we disagreed with, and would criticise, the policies and practices of our capitalist governors which eventuated in this war, we would not give any excuse for the suppression of such criticism by the publishing of anything that would affect the military defence of this country. The engineers' strike clearly came into such a category of forbidden subjects.[25]

The *Forward* actually had less to say about the strike than Glasgow's two daily papers, the *Glasgow Herald* and the *Daily Record*, and they did not have a great deal.

When war broke out, discussions between the engineering employers and the A.S.E. were actually in progress on renegotiation of the district time rates. On 7th December 1914 the A.S.E., together with the Allied Trades Committee representing the other unions in engineering, presented a demand to the employers for 2d an hour on the basic rate for all engineers in the north-west of England and in Scotland.[26] In February 1915 the employers and the union executive jointly offered a war bonus of ¾d an hour and 7½% on piece rates. This was widely regarded as unsatisfactory in view of the abrupt rise in food prices which had already occurred. In addition William Weir, the most anti-union of the big Glasgow engineering employers, was a keen exponent of work-study and American speeding-up techniques labelled 'Taylorism'.[27] Early in 1915, he introduced to his Cathcart works a number of American engineers at a bonus of 6/- per week as part of an open campaign against his own craftsmen and their union. An A.S.E. member at Cathcart complained to Lloyd George on Christmas Day 1915 that in the previous twelve years the following catalogue of operations had been 'taken from turners':

> pump rods, roughing piston rods, rocking levers, shafts, columns, glands, neck rings, pump lever and washers, valve chest end and bottom doors, locks for piston valves, and some chest covers.[28]

Taylorism had been resisted by local representatives of the A.S.E. in most places where it had been introduced, one delegate calling it 'one of the last stages of lunacy'.[29] The Weir's men had eventually swallowed Taylorism, but were not prepared to swallow the American engineers, and about 2000 of them struck in mid-February 1915. Ultimately they were joined by engineers from about twenty plants to a total of between 8000 and 10,000[30] striking for the original 2d an hour wage claim. While the strike was in progress the A.S.E. members in the district voted, on a ballot conducted by the Executive, by 8926 votes out of 9755 to reject the ¾d an hour offer.[31] The A.S.E., both locally and nationally, refused to recognise the strike:

> the Glasgow District Committee of the A.S.E. have expressed their entire disapproval of the course which their members have taken,[32]

and it paid no strike benefit. Nevertheless, the position was very confused, and William Gallacher later claimed that the strike was official because he, an official of his union, took part.[33] This sort of un-certainty was inherent in the nature of unionism in the industry at this time. Three sorts of unions were involved: first, the A.S.E., a large national organisation; secondly, a number of specialist national organisations such as the Steam Engine Makers' Society; and thirdly, some small local craft unions, such as Gallacher's West of Scotland

Brassfinishers and the United Ironmoulders of Scotland. In all of these, there was tension between a militant membership and the demand from above for co-operation in the war effort, but it was resolved in different ways. The A.S.E., for which the Clyde had previously been a troublesome district whose District Committee had had to be suspended,[34] possessed at this time a very co-operative group of local officials. These naturally provoked the fury of the militants,[35] and eventually the compromising Sam Bunton was replaced by the militant Harry Hopkins as full-time District Secretary.[36] This lessened the tension between local officials and members at the cost of reopening it between local officials and Executive, and the District Committee was again suspended in 1919.[37]

In the small Scottish unions, however, it was easier for militants to attain positions of real responsibility. Thus Tom Bell became President of the Scottish Iron Moulders' Union.[38] The constraint on these unions, however, was financial. They were much less able than the A.S.E. to weather a local strike because a higher proportion of their membership would be demanding strike pay. They had not the resilience of large unions in adversity, and most of them were swallowed up in the enlargement of the A.S.E. in 1920. It is very doubtful whether they actually had the resources to pay strike benefits to their members in the February 1915 strike.

From the beginning of March the men started to drift back to work, perhaps 'inflamed by the strength of public opinion against them'.[39] For the first of many times during the war, the Clydeside engineers were to find that it was very easy for opponents to damn them as unpatriotic. On this occasion Lloyd George led the attack:

> I say here that it is intolerable that the lives of Britons should be imperilled for a matter of ½d an hour . . . Drink is doing us more damage in this war than all the German submarines put together.[40]

The allegation that production was being lost because of excessive drunkenness caused a great deal of resentment among the engineers and especially their (almost all teetotal) leaders: by the middle of 1915 it had been quietly dropped.[41]

On a later ballot, on 17th March, the men agreed by 5616 votes to 1522 to abide by the verdict given by Sir George Askwith, who had been appointed arbitrator. They accepted an advance of 1d an hour on time rates and 10% on piece rates, 'the advances to be . . . recognised as due to and dependent on the existence of abnormal conditions then prevailing in consequence of the War'.[42]

The leaders of the February 1915 strike had joined together as the Central Labour Withholding Committee — not calling themselves the strike committee for fear of prosecution under the Defence of the Realm regulations — and after the strike they decided to meet on a permanent basis to protect living standards and seek advances in wages and conditions.[43] The need for such a committee was dictated by the common interests of men working in the same industry but belonging to different craft unions and working in different plants. For all, however, the aim was the safeguarding of the position of craftsmen in engineering against the threats to it inherent in the vast new munitions industry.

Munitions, of course, involved much more than general engineering. Ships and railway engines are materials of war just as much as shells and howitzers, and Whitehall departments responsible for munitions — in this wide sense — took broad powers of control over all sorts of plants. It has been persuasively argued that 'What *made* a munitions worker in late 1915 was not the work on his bench or hull, but the coercion of the state and his struggle against it'.[44] But, as we shall see, 'the state' was no monolith. Neither the War Office nor the Admiralty actually used most of the sweeping powers they had taken. Only the Ministry of Munitions consistently tried to 'coerce' munitions workers. Naturally only those who felt themselves coerced could respond by 'struggling' against the coercer, and not all of them did. When the Ministry of Munitions was thought to be using the Munitions of War Act to restrict workers' freedom to move from one job to another, it provoked unrest in a wide variety of trades. But the most important conflict, that over dilution, was much more narrowly based. It was restricted to general engineering works, and primarily to a small number of those, where individual militants happened to work. 'Munitions' workers in the broader sense were not involved in the dilution struggle because nobody tried to force them to dilute. The shipyards were on the fringe of wartime 'Red Clydeside', and one of the world's greatest concentrations of railway engineering plants, at Springburn and Govanhill, was scarcely affected at all.

Figures have been compiled of A.S.E. membership in Glasgow which show that, although the militant-dominated plants showed an above-average rate of growth of union membership, nevertheless even after the wartime expansion they formed a smallish proportion of total membership:

Table 1.1.   A.S.E. membership, Glasgow, 1914 and 1919

Area	A.S.E. membership June 1919	% of total A.S.E. membership in Glasgow	% of 1914 figure
1. *East End*	2069	10.4	358
2. *Scotstoun*	863	4.3	266
3. Springburn	2368	11.9	197
4. *Dalmuir*	497	2.5	176
5. Cathcart	564	2.8	159
6. Central	7072	35.5	153
7. Clydebank & Renfrew	2521	12.6	146
8. Govanhill	2526	12.7	132
9. Miscellaneous	1451	7.3	128
Total	19931	100.1	163

Source: Appendix to J. Hinton, 'Rank and File Militancy in the British Engineering Industry, 1914-1918', London Ph.D. thesis, 1969. Compiled from A.S.E. *Monthly Journal and Report* June 1914 and June 1919. Slightly adapted. Column 2 adds up to 100.1 because of rounding error.

Only the areas italicised in the Table 1.1 contained plants that were dominated in 1915 and 1916 by the militants, and of these four, Scotstoun contained a number of 'non-militant' plants as well. Many large plants had not the vestiges of a militant organisation. Later, in 1917, the A.S.E. sent a circular to 31 large plants in the Glasgow area to find out what forms of shop-floor organisation existed. Of the 31, 17, including such giants as the Barclay Curle and Lobnitz shipyards, had not so much as a Shop Committee — and this was after the 1916 Dilution Commissioners had given official encouragement to the formation of a shop committee to supervise dilution in every works.[45] Of course, one cannot extrapolate with confidence from A.S.E. membership to membership of the craft unions as a whole, but there is no reason to suppose that the balance of their membership would have been fundamentally different from that of the A.S.E. When we speak of 'Red Clydeside' in the war, we should be clear that we are speaking of Weir's of Cathcart and James Messer and Arthur McManus; the Albion Motor Works, Scotstoun, and William Gallacher; Barr and Strouds, instrument makers, of Anniesland, and John Muir; the works of Messrs. Beardmore at Parkhead and Dalmuir and Thomas Clark and David Kirkwood. This group of factories and men formed the core of the Clyde Workers' Committee, into which the Labour Withholding

Committee transformed itself. And within this group the largest single works — Beardmore's Parkhead Forge, in the East End district — stood somewhat apart. Here the leading A.S.E. shop steward was David Kirkwood, a highly skilled instrument maker — 'not just a craftsman, an engineer'[46] — who had in the past acted as chief engineer in a small steelworks. He had left that job after an argument with his employer because he wanted a trade union closed shop. After many years of what he regarded as exile,[47] he returned in 1910 to Parkhead Forge, from which he had been excluded in 1898 after the engineering lock-out. His return coincided with the great growth of the forge, which was in 1910 just setting up the machinery for the production of munitions; and it is possible that the expertise of Kirkwood, an engineer trained in both steam and electrical engineering, overrode Sir William Beard-more's ideological objections to him in a plant which adapted to technical change with great difficulty.[48]

This may have contributed to the extraordinary relationship between Beardmore and Kirkwood[49] in which paternalism and militancy co-existed, short-circuiting both middle management and the trade-union apparatus. In 1915 this arrangement was at the height of its success, and Kirkwood had got for the Parkhead engineers an increase of 1½d an hour over the district rate, as well as improvements in conditions for the semi-skilled and unskilled men — and all this independently of the February strike and the Central Labour Withholding Committee. The rift between Parkhead and the rest, and the fall of Kirkwood, which are discussed in Chapters 6 and 7, can only be fully understood in the light of these facts.

The February strike gave the Clyde its popular image as a centre of militant discontent. This image appeared to be thoroughly confirmed by the unrest which began again in June 1915 and lasted until March 1916, to which we must now turn.

2

The Rent Strikes

The unrest on the Clyde between June 1915 and March 1916 was partly a complaint about rents, and partly a complaint about dilution. Dilution (which will be discussed in Chapters 3 to 7) bulked much larger to contemporaries than did the rent strikes, and indeed it caused a great deal more upheaval. But the rent strikes had a much more enduring effect. In the most literal sense, they were to change the face of Britain, and nowhere more than Glasgow.

Furthermore, settling the rent strikes was a matter of munitions policy, not housing policy. The Government department nominally responsible — the Scottish Office — was quite remarkably feeble. From the beginning of 1915 to the end of 1916 the Secretary for Scotland circulated only one paper for discussion in Cabinet, and the Scottish Office records for the period are very thin and uninformative — partly because of defective filing practices, but much more because, when important decisions were to be taken, the Scottish Office was simply bypassed. Christopher Addison, the Parliamentary Under-Secretary at the Ministry of Munitions, told his diary in August 1916 about a brush with H. J. Tennant, the newly appointed Secretary for Scotland:

> I am afraid I was obliged, with a considerable measure of bluntness, to point out to him that the Ministry of Munitions had had to face the music from the start to the finish and to do all the work . . . I might have told him that when originally I had to make the statement in the House on the deportations question, McKinnon Wood [Secretary for Scotland 1915-16] made me take out of the proposed statement the fact that the Scottish Office had agreed to the course proposed, which they had done. He was afraid to face the music; and from start to finish, the Scottish Office have sheltered themselves behind us all the time, and have never been prepared to take any initiative.[1]

And as with dilution in 1916, so over housing in 1915 the Scottish

Office was brushed aside. To see how and why, we need to look at the roots of the crisis of 1915.

The war led to a great influx of men and women to work in the Glasgow munitions factories, and there was soon a severe housing shortage. By Whitsun 1915, under 1% of the houses in the working-class areas of Glasgow were unlet, and in some areas the figure was only one-fifth of 1%, which included a number of uninhabitable houses.[2] Class conflict in Glasgow housing was more acute than anywhere else, to judge by the extraordinarily high incidence of evictions in Glasgow.[3] By 1914, housing in Glasgow was already uniquely bad. The population was crammed in at the highest density in Britain — sometimes over 1000 persons per acre, many of them in notorious 'backlands': that is, tenement blocks erected in the back greens of older ones, with miserably inadequate light or space. The tenement tradition had started on the cramped defensive sites of Edinburgh and Stirling, where multi-storey, multi-dwelling buildings dating back to the 17th century survive in considerable numbers. Glasgow was not physically constricted like Edinburgh or Stirling: so why did the tenement style of building spread there? It was partly a matter of tradition and the easy availability of strong, load-bearing building stone; partly that the existence of tenements elsewhere had encouraged Scots law, unlike English, to make provision for buying and selling of individual houses in multi-dwelling buildings. Most of all, it resulted from a Scots peculiarity called feu-duty. Under Scots law, the seller ('feudal superior') of a piece of land was entitled to an annual payment from the purchaser. As this was levied on the land at a fixed rate per acre, it was obviously in the developers' interest to develop land as densely as possible.[4]

When munition workers were sucked into Glasgow after 1914, people from other parts of the United Kingdom found out the ghastly secrets of Scottish working-class housing for themselves. The *History of the Ministry of Munitions* (a vast official history of the Ministry, printed in twelve volumes soon after the end of the war but never published) recorded:

> The main cause of discontent was the discomfort entailed in the transfer of men to places where the housing, food, and climate were worse than they had grown used to at home. Those suffered most who went from the South of England or the Midlands to the North-East Coast or the Clyde. The inclemency of the weather, the overcrowding, and the indifferent cooking in such lodgings as were available aggravated any weakness of health or temper that might have developed in men already worn by long hours of labour . . .[5]

Another section of the same massive work reviews the effect of Lloyd George's charge that production on the Clyde was being hampered by the excessive drunkenness of the workers. This, it pointed out, only increased the men's 'suspicious and irritable temper' at what they regarded as an unjust charge:

> . . . the root of the trouble was the housing of the people. Nearly half the population of Glasgow in 1911 lived in houses of two rooms. More than one-eighth lived in single rooms. And the housing conditions of the neighbouring towns were no better. Only sordid experience or a strong effort of imagination can realise the significance of these appalling figures . . . And the evil has been aggravated during the War by the influx of munition workers and the stoppage of building. If the Clyde workman has not always done all that he might have done to bring this War to a victorious issue, if he has followed the lure of drink, if he has shown a sullen and suspicious temper and embraced too readily revolutionary ideas and the gospel of class hatred, his Country, which has failed to provide for him the first condition of making a home for his family and himself, cannot with justice or a good conscience cast the first stone.[6]

In similar, though less impassioned, tones, the Report of the Commission of Enquiry into Industrial Unrest (Cd 2669) of 1917 commented that:

> In Scotland there is an immediate need for about 100,000 workers' houses . . . The industrial unrest attributable to this cause, it is strongly represented, can only be allayed by the Government taking steps with a problem that appears to have grown too great for private enterprise now to meet.[7]

Independently of the industrial unrest that had been building up during the year, agitation over rises in the cost of living in general and against rent increases in particular had been one of the principal activities of the 'official' bodies of Labour opinion in the Glasgow area — the Glasgow Trades Council, the Glasgow Central Labour Party, and the Glasgow Federation of the I.L.P.

The first reaction of these bodies to the war was that of many labour organisations at every level; they expected it to produce massive unemployment, hardship, and distress among the working class. Though the unemployment was, in fact, taken up very rapidly as the demand for troops and munitions workers rocketed, the threat to the housing conditions of servicemen, arms workers and their families, remained very real. As early as September 1914 the Trades Council resolved to

> indignantly Protest against the manner in which Agents of the Soldiers' and Sailors' Families Association are prosecuting enquiries into the circumstances of women and children.[8]

From this the next step was to protest against cases in which house factors were threatening service wives or widows with removal to smaller houses or even with eviction. In April 1915 the Trades Council called upon the Government

> to immediately take effective action to prevent property owners raising rents at this unprecedented time, such as passing a prohibition order or establishment of a Fair Rent Court which shall fix rents in every city, large town, or district.[9]

At the same time, housing was the principal concern of the Labour group on Glasgow Corporation. John Wheatley and his main lieutenant, Andrew McBride, had been agitating since before the war for Wheatley's '£8 cottage' scheme. On the eve of the war, Wheatley and Thomas Johnston, the editor of *Forward*, were conducting a vigorous propaganda campaign on its behalf.[10] Cottages were to be built on the fringe of the city for a rental of £8 or £10 a year. Small cottages, Wheatley thought, were both cheaper to build and more attractive to the working-class people who would live in them than the tenement blocks to which they were accustomed. The construction of the cottages was to be paid for out of the city's Common Good Fund, which was in substantial surplus because of the profits being made by the tramway system, which had belonged to the city since 1894. (The system was paying 'possibly £30,000 or more' a year to the Common Good Fund in the years leading up to the first world war.)[11] When Wheatley's scheme was debated by the Corporation, its opponents complained that since it would account for only about 150 houses it would hardly scratch the surface of the housing problem.[12] Even if these 150 became self-financing, as Wheatley argued, this seems a fair criticism. But Wheatley and McBride campaigned vigorously for it, and in February 1915 a Glasgow Labour Party Housing Committee was founded.[13] Its objects were:

> To Establish Branches in Each Ward.
> To Organise Tenants against Increased Rents.
> To support Municipal Housing on an Interest Free Basis by utilising the Tramway Surplus and by means of State Grants.
> To Secure the Return of Labour Candidates who will Support this Policy.[14]

Thus the 'official' Labour movement in the city had housing as the main plank in its platform. The *Forward*, which, as we saw in Chapter 1, was very chary of even supporting industrial disputes, was in the forefront of the housing crusade. It was able to report widespread sympathy with strikers against increased rents from June 1915 onwards: in

Govan, where conditions were worst, even the employers took the tenants' side. The managing director of Harland and Wolff's Govan shipyard wrote:

> We are very pleased to hear that the tenants of Govan propose refusing to pay these increased rents, and we sympathise entirely with them. We trust that the legislature will intervene to annul all the increases which have recently taken place, and to prevent any further increases.[15]

The management of Fairfield's expressed similar sympathies:

> The manager of Fairfield told a deputation that they would allow no workman of theirs to occupy any house of any person victimised for refusing to pay a rent increase.[16]

The sympathy between management and men may seem surprising, especially in the light of the bad industrial relations at Fairfield which we consider in Chapter 4; but the management had, after all, no community of interest with the house factors. The shipyard employers did not want industrial strife on an issue over which they had no control, and they had a positive interest in seeing rents kept down, because this would tend to moderate wage demands.

The Association of House Factors and Property Agents had tried to improve its image by resolving that servicemen's dependants should not have their rents raised during the war, but not all factors held to this decision:

> others, less considerate, had served notices of a 10% advance on their tenants, including soldiers' wives, Belgian refugees, old age pensioners and recipients of outdoor relief.[17]

George Barnes, the Labour M.P. for Blackfriars, appealed to McKinnon Wood to intervene. In reply he confessed his inability to do anything:

> Mr. McKinnon Wood expressed to Mr. Barnes his profound sympathy with the tenants, but felt he could not get sufficient support in the House to move in any direction.[18]

Eventually, in October 1915, McKinnon Wood appointed Lord Hunter, a judge, and W. R. Scott, Professor of Political Economy at Glasgow University, to enquire into changes in rent levels. They found that since May 1914, 33.9% of the rents they sampled (though it was not a random sample in a statistically acceptable sense) had risen by up to 5%; 14.6% had risen by between 5 and 10%; and 7.7% had risen by over 10%. In Govan and Fairfield, the centre of the storm, all the

houses they sampled had suffered rent increases ranging from 11.67%
to 23.08%.[19]

While this was being considered, the rent strike was building up
massively: 15,000 tenants were estimated as refusing to pay increased
rent by the end of October, and 20,000, including five Labour
councillors, by mid-November.[20] On 17th November McKinnon Wood
submitted a memorandum to the Cabinet calling for a bill to limit
working-class rentals to the level obtaining at the outbreak of war.
Quoting from the report submitted by Hunter and Scott, he said that
'the great fear of the tenants is that, eventually, monopoly rents may be
exacted from them' and quoted, as an example of the many representa-
tions asking for action which he had received, a resolution from
Cambuslang Parish Council:

> The population of the parish is 25,000; at May 1915 there were 17 empty houses
> . . . No houses have been built for years; none are in course of erection; none are
> likely to be built in the immediate future. There is thus an actual house famine,
> which grows more acute.[21]

It was only the 'monopoly' question which justified action in defiance
of market forces:

> It seems to me that the justification for dealing with the question as a war
> emergency matter is that there has been in such districts a large influx of workmen
> . . . while new building has ceased, and that a condition of monopoly has thus
> been created, which, if nothing is done to check the rise in rents, will lead to much
> larger increases of rent than have yet taken place.[22]

As the existing conditions, especially on the Clyde, were 'abnormal,
artificial, and temporary', the proposed legislation should be strictly
confined to the duration of the war. McKinnon Wood rejected the
proposal for fair rent courts (which, as we have seen, were strongly
advocated by labour bodies) as unworkable, and added that such
courts would be 'difficult to abolish after the restoration of peace'. The
Bill should be confined in its operation to large burghs and other
congested areas, which could be specifically designated. Rents should
be restricted as from the Martinmas term, 1915 (11th November) to the
level at which they stood on 1st August 1914. As a corollary the
interest rate on bonds secured on working-class houses would have to
be frozen, and the bonds themselves statutorily protected against
recall, until the end of the war.

These proposals show that McKinnon Wood (who himself
represented the Glasgow working-class constituency of St. Rollox) was

broadly sympathetic to the pleas of working-class organisations, as he had in fact shown in his letter to Barnes some months earlier. But we may presume that it was only his accompanying comments on the political scene which persuaded Conservative members of the Coalition Cabinet to entertain his views at all. After reproducing the findings of the Hunter-Scott committee, the memorandum comments:

> The Committee was not directed to make any proposals for legislation, but . . . I find that both members are impressed, as a result of their enquiry, with the necessity of action being taken to stop increases of rent. I understand that the Minister of Munitions attaches considerable importance to the agitation as contributing to the unrest which exists throughout the Clyde districts, where . . . labour difficulties have caused him much anxiety.

In conclusion, McKinnon Wood says,

> The agitation is growing, and I think it is necessary that a prompt decision should be taken by the Government, otherwise there are signs that demands for interference will become more clamant and will expand in scope and character.[23]

We have already noted the unimportance of the Scottish Office. In seeking the reason why McKinnon Wood, having failed to 'move the House in any direction' in June, should be able to persuade the Cabinet to take action in November, the above sections of the memorandum are clearly important. Action on the rents issue was brought about, and brought about rapidly, when the voice of Lloyd George, who mattered, was added to that of McKinnon Wood, who did not.

Lloyd George's correspondence shows that for some months he had been aware of the importance of the question of rents in munitions areas. In July, Austen Chamberlain had sent him a cutting from a Birmingham paper about rent increases, together with a petition from 'The Greater Birmingham Residents', who wanted the Government 'to establish a Pre-War Rent on all dwelling houses'. Chamberlain wrote to Lloyd George,

> I do not know whether you have similar complaints from elsewhere, but it may be necessary to deal with the matter.[24]

To this Lloyd George replied,

> The complaints I have had about rents have almost invariably come from the Glasgow area. There is a great scarcity of houses in all the munitions areas, and I have no doubt rents will be inflated as a result; I think we ought to take decisive action on the subject at an early date.[25]

Chamberlain in turn suggested that the Local Government Board
should make enquiries

> as to the state of affairs in the munitions areas from the local authorities. The
> reports so obtained would show us the extent of the evil and strengthen the hands
> of the Government for dealing with it.[26]

Three months later, Lord St. Davids wrote to Lloyd George
proposing rent control as a specific remedy for the ruffled feelings of
trade unionists:

> You have had lately to pitch into the Trade Unionists a good deal and to point out
> the ways in which they and their rulers have been damaging the National Cause.
> They have put up with it from you in a way they would not have done from any-
> body else because of your championing them on so many previous occasions. It is
> most important, however, at the present time not only that you should be fair but
> that you should be ostentatiously fair and impartial. Rents have been greatly
> raised for cheap houses and workmen's dwellings in different parts of the country
> and there have been strikes of rent payers here and there. Could you make an
> occasion to speak against this or to write a letter against it? You understand that it
> is your own position and power for good that I am anxious about. Now and again
> you have accepted a little hint from me and I throw you out this one which is, in
> my judgment, well worth thinking about from the position of your highest
> efficiency in your present office.[27]

Though St. Davids had ended, 'Don't *of course* bother to answer',
Lloyd George replied,

> You are quite right. It is an admirable suggestion. I am collecting all the material,
> and shall say something about it.[28]

Thus it was that when McKinnon Wood eventually took his request
for rent control to the Cabinet, he had the powerful support of Lloyd
George against the resentment of the Conservatives and the obstruc-
tionism of the Local Government Board. On 23rd November, Walter
Long, who was President of the Local Government Board, circulated
with obvious reluctance a draft bill to apply to the whole country. In
the accompanying memorandum he said:

> I still prefer my original proposals, which, I think, would have been more
> appropriate to the actual difficulty, particularly as it is experienced in this
> country,[29] but, in accordance with the promise I made to the Cabinet, I have
> abandoned that position, and the Bill which I now circulate adopts the principle
> advocated by the Secretary for Scotland and makes it applicable to the United
> Kingdom . . .
>   It cannot be pretended that the Bill is other than an emergency measure. It is
> drastic in its proposals, and will, I fear, arouse a good deal of opposition in

various quarters . . . and it is impossible to make it altogether equitable in its application. It is very difficult to make a forecast now; all I desire to do is to warn my colleagues that there may be trouble from those who consider that legislation of this kind is too drastic, and is calculated to interfere with national credit.[30]

The Bill was introduced on 25th November, and met opposition from expected and unexpected quarters. A number of backbench Tories expressed their surprise and resentment that a party colleague should be introducing such a Bill, and Sir Frederick Banbury complained, not unexpectedly, that 'in my opinion, this Bill violates all the principles of political economy'.[31] W. M. R. Pringle, the radical Liberal who sat for North-East Lanarkshire, somewhat quixotically styled it an unjust and a necessary Bill'.[32] Two other Glasgow M.P.s, one Liberal and one Unionist (MacCallum Scott and Halford Mackinder), spoke in favour of the Bill. The Bill was thereafter hurried through all its stages in less than a month and received the Royal Assent on 23rd December (5 & 6 Geo V ch 97).

While legislation was being discussed by the Cabinet, the agitation reached its peak in Scotland. On 17th November, the same day that the Cabinet considered McKinnon Wood's memorandum, an insistent factor, having failed to evict defaulting tenants because of organised resistance, summoned eighteen of them to the Sheriff Court with a request for the arrestment of their wages.[33] The response was a strike and demonstrations of munitions and shipyard workers who marched on the court, threatening an indefinite strike if the summoned men were evicted or fined. Opinions differ as to how many demonstrators, from how many plants, were present. The *Forward* estimated 4000,[34] while W. C. Anderson, speaking on the introduction of the Rent Restriction Bill to the Commons, put it as high as 15,000, including all the employees of Albion Motors and the Coventry Ordnance Works.[35] According to two sources, the men at Barclay Curle's, Fairfield, Harland & Wolff, D. & W. Henderson and A. Stephen were involved;[36] while Gallacher cites also Beardmores (Dalmuir), Parkhead Forge, Weir's, Hyde Park Locomotive Works, and Yarrow's and Meechan's shipyards.[37] In the court, the eighteen men summoned received sympathetic treatment from Sheriff Lee. He complained that, although Parliament was at that moment considering the question, the factor before him had ignored a plea from the Secretary for Scotland to stay his hand, and 'intimate(d) in open court' that insistence on the increase in rent 'would produce serious national consequences'.[38] The cases were withdrawn; the tone of the sheriff's remarks suggests that he would have brought pressure to have them withdrawn even without what the normally sympathetic Pringle called 'apparently the exercise of mob law'.[39] No prosecutions followed against the strikers because the strike had lasted only one day and the matter did not directly concern the production of munitions.

The rent strike marks the appearance in the forefront of affairs for the first time of John MacLean, a Govan primary schoolteacher who had been dismissed by the School Board the day before the eviction cases. (He was dismissed not because of his political opinions, but after an intemperate series of letters between him and the Board over a row between himself and Mr. Hugh Fulton, his former headmaster.)[40] On the 17th he chaired a meeting which sent to Asquith the following resolution:

> That this meeting of Clyde munitions workers requests the Government to definitely state, not later than Saturday first,[41] that it forbids any increase in rent during the period of the war, and that this failing a general strike will be declared on Monday, 22nd November.[42]

We cannot be certain what influence the rent strikers in general, and John MacLean in particular, had on the action taken by the Government; we cannot now reconstruct what may have happened in the Cabinet between 17th and 23rd November, just over a year before the 1916 crisis led to the introduction of a full and rational system of keeping Cabinet records — for instance, we cannot guess what might have been Long's 'promise made to the Cabinet' (p. 24 above).[43] As the *History of the Ministry of Munitions* comments, 'The Government were slow to deal with the matter'[44] of the rents agitation. But Lloyd George, it appears, had been convinced of the need for action since at least July, and it was his backing of McKinnon Wood's proposal which ensured its passage through the Cabinet. No doubt the alarming down-tools of 17th November was instrumental in securing for the Bill the approval of the Unionist members of the Cabinet, including Long, whose job it was as President of the Local Government Board to pilot the Bill through. Doubtless also the strike encouraged the quick and relatively trouble-free passage of the Bill through the Commons, in spite of the controversial nature of the proposal to freeze mortgage money and the rate of interest on it. Many speakers supported the view of Pringle that it was unfair but necessary, and Barnes said on the Second Reading:

> It is a matter for congratulation that the House has, almost with one accord, agreed to the demise of political economy.[45]

To all this the action of the strikers may have made its contribution, but in an important way it was secondary. At best it was necessary but not sufficient. The salient fact was the conversion of Lloyd George. If an important minister had not been already convinced of the need for action, then a strike, however alarming, could not on its own have precipitated a Bill so hasty and arbitrary that it perturbed not only the Conservatives but also Radicals. There were no real grounds for MacLean's optimistic belief that

> the rent strike on the Clyde is the first step towards the Political Strike so frequently resorted to on the Continent in times past.[46]

The rent strike movement was not the sole property of John MacLean, and it was hardly at all the property of the Clyde Workers' Committee. The C.W.C. leaders did bring their men out on 17th November in support of the defendants. But it was not primarily a munitions workers' issue. The most congested areas were Govan and Fairfield wards, south of the river, which housed shipyard employees rather than munitions workers in the narrow sense. And it seems to have been in a spontaneous movement that, in the early stages of the rent strike, the women of Govan, led by Mrs. Barbour,[47] formed posses to prevent sheriff's officers from evicting tenants who refused to pay increased rents. To the support of the movement came not only the C.W.C. and the militants but also the 'official' section of the local Labour movement headed by Wheatley, McBride, and the *Forward*, all primarily housing reformers in the past.

The rent strike heightened the tension and increased the mutual suspicion and bloody-mindedness that 'stained the good name of the men on the Clyde in the months that followed'.[48] In other words, it set the scene for the struggle over dilution which began at the same time as the rent strike and lasted till March 1916. To this we must now turn.

3

The Ministry of Munitions,
July-December 1915

The events which gave wartime 'Red Clydeside' its reputation all took place within a very short period. Craft resistance to dilution was the central issue. The government did not try to enforce the Treasury Agreement until it was made mandatory in July 1915; by April 1916 it had broken all resistance in Clydeside (though not elsewhere).

But even these terms can be misleading, if they imply a monolith (government-and-employers) looming over, and eventually crushing, the Clyde Workers' Committee. All the actors in the drama had different interests; and the Clyde Workers' Committee was not one of the principals. (Until February 1916, nobody at the Ministry of Munitions regarded it as more than a trivial irritant.) The full cast list in the Scottish Dilution Play reads something like this:

'The Government'
> The Ministry of Munitions
> The War Office
> The Admiralty
> The Board of Trade
> The Scottish Office

'The Employers'
> William Weir, an Aggressive Employer
> William Beardmore, a Conservative Employer

'The Workers'
> The Executive of the A.S.E.
> The Glasgow District Officials of the A.S.E.
> The Workforce of Lang's, Johnstone
> The Clyde Workers' Committee

Soldiers, Leader-writers, Ministry officials, Workers, etc. etc.

The records show that not one of the above wholly agreed with any other. To assume that they lined up in fixed formation is to distort the record; to assume that they all conspired against the C.W.C. is grotesque. In order to elucidate this complex struggle, we will have to go back some months to examine the origins of the Ministry of Munitions.

Prior to the Cabinet crisis of May 1915, labour arbitration and conciliation problems had been handled by the Board of Trade, which was nurturing the first generation of professional conciliators such as Sir George (later Lord) Askwith and Isaac Mitchell (a former A.S.E. official who in 1916 became one of the Clyde Dilution Commissioners). It was Askwith, for instance, who had negotiated a settlement after the February 1915 strike.[1] After May 1915, Lloyd George became Minister of Munitions, and by the Ministry of Munitions Act of June 1915 the Ministry was founded; its first Permanent Secretary was Sir Hubert Llewellyn Smith, on loan from the Board of Trade. Llewellyn Smith brought over William Beveridge as Under-Secretary to deal with labour matters; as he explained to Lloyd George:

> As regards Beveridge I am quite unwilling to dispense with his assistance, and in particular I must have his help and advice on labour matters as to which he is really the technical expert while Girouard and Booth[2] are amateurs. He [Beveridge] would be the officer I should rely on for all matters relating to the Secretariat, and as in this event[3] — I should have to be responsible for labour myself I shall naturally seek his counsel on a subject which he has made his own . . .
>
> I doubt if either Girouard or Booth has any idea of the pitfalls in any new labour policy, and personally I am not prepared to face any such development without having by me an experienced adviser whom I trust.[4]

As this letter might indicate, the first opponents the new Ministry had to face in its 'new labour policy' were the Ministries whose responsibilities it was taking over. The Munitions of War Act of July 1915 gave statutory backing to dilution, and empowered the Ministry to designate munitions factories as 'controlled establishments' on which it could impose rules to regulate both management and labour: it could regulate profits, and it could control the supply of labour by the system of leaving certificates. If a man left a munitions works without a leaving certificate, he could not be re-employed within six weeks of leaving. The Act banned strikes, and made provision for the prosecution of strike leaders, but the ineffectiveness of this was very rapidly shown up by the massive South Wales miners' strike of the same month

(July 1915). The KC sent by Lloyd George to preside over the Munitions Court dealing with that strike wrote:

> I have now carefully considered the Munitions of War Act and the regulations under it. The Act only applies to men employed who have gone on strike. It does not apply to the secretaries and others who have incited the men to strike who may not themselves be actually employed in the collieries. To prosecute only the dupes while the real offenders escape will I am afraid cause great heart burning. It is of course impossible to summon and try 200,000 men, and only a few can at first be dealt with and the length of time before there can be any real enforcement of the sentence will, I fear, only lead the men generally to regard the Act as ineffective.[5]

The behaviour of Lloyd George and his Ministry in labour matters in general and this strike in particular provoked fierce criticism from professional arbitrators, most notably Askwith, whose bitterness may have been in part due to the usurpation of the arbitration powers of his Committee on Production by the Ministry of Munitions:

> The example was set [by the South Wales miners] to strike first and apply to Mr. Lloyd George, whatever the Minister's officials, employers, or union leaders might say, with a view to the allowance of all claims as the reward of violence or pressure.
>
> The activity of the Ministry of Munitions probably appeared in its most unfortunate form in its dealings with Labour. Its Labour Department was very badly organised, or not organised at all in its initial stages, but that fact did not prevent it under the guise of efforts towards control and dilution, from constant interference in labour differences or quarrels. Numbers of young men, without the least knowledge or experience, were scattered over the country without defined authority or under any definite or adequate leadership.[6]

In fact, the relevant Ministry officials were not even agreed among themselves. Beveridge was the most hawkish, Addison the most doveish; and Lloyd George the most inconsistent: one moment complaining that his officials were not tough enough, the next appeasing union executives over their heads and against their advice.[7]

The new Ministry also fought the Scottish Office, the War Office and the Admiralty to gain control of munitions. It beat the first two, and drew with the third. As we have seen, it beat the Scottish Office by simply ignoring it. Kitchener's War Office was bigger game. Even after the new Ministry was formed, it had to struggle for months to wrest control of government munitions factories from the Master General of Ordnance as evidence mounted that some of them were only reaching a fifth of their target production.[8] As to the Admiralty, the Ministry of Munitions had responsibility but not power; it was involved in labour questions in the yards, but it had no control over questions of management or contracts, and no say whatever in the management of naval dockyards. The Ministry of Munitions bitterly resented having, in the first instance, no control over Admiralty affairs and, later, having to do the Admiralty's job for it. Addison complained:

> It was astonishing to those of us behind the scenes that, whilst Balfour[9] had professed that the Admiralty were pressing dilution forward, the self-same evening he was having an interview with the Clyde Commission(er)s for the first time asking them to assist in getting dilution in the shipyards on the Clyde — the first step which has been taken by the Admiralty to do anything in the Clyde area. If the House had known this there would have been much more trouble — as there will be, if it ever comes out.[10]

'The employers' were no more united than 'the government'. A few, like William Weir, were aggressive dilutionists. He had been urging dilution, and breaking craftsmen's power, since long before the war,[11] but he saw the war as a heaven-sent opportunity. Immediately the Munitions of War Act was passed, he became more dilutionist than the Ministry, had himself appointed Director of Munitions for Scotland, and singlemindedly pursued dilution in order both to win the war and to increase the efficiency of G. & J. Weir Ltd.

On the other hand, many Glasgow engineering employers were profoundly conservative and unable or unwilling to manage their own workforce, though sometimes prepared to let somebody else try. A shipbuilder wrote to the Secretary of the Munitions Parliamentary Committee in October 1915:

> The principal trouble in our business is the 'Black Squad' [riveters, platers, and their helpers], and all the Parliamentary Orators that could be sent here will not affect them . . .
> At the time of writing this, 11 a.m., in a Street adjoining our Works, there are no less than about 50 Lads playing Football, and HM ships standing waiting for them to get on with their work — all 'Black Squad' . . .
> Serving [sic] or beseeching this Class of men is of no use whatever and the sooner this is realised the better for our country.[12]

Employers who were too incompetent, or too frightened, to introduce dilution on their own account proved very unreliable allies to a Ministry trying to do it for them.

It was thus against a background of suspicion and obstruction in Whitehall and Clydeside that the new Ministry carried out its 'new labour policy' of increasing the supply of labour available for manufacturing munitions. The policies open to the Ministry, in decreasing order of acceptability to the trade unions, were *firstly*, putting all skilled men on government work, and supplementing British craftsmen with Belgian or Canadian workmen, in addition to securing the release from the Colours of engineering craftsmen; *secondly*, the dilution of labour: and *thirdly*, industrial conscription:

> The government consented to try the policy urged by the Trade Unions first, holding Dilution in reserve and, if that should not be accepted, Industrial Conscription.[13]

The Ministry was, at first, hopeful of the success of the volunteer and Release from the Colours schemes. As many as 100,000 men enrolled as 'War Munitions Volunteers', who would be prepared to move to work in munitions areas, and Addison welcomed the scheme as it prevented discussion of industrial conscription:

> The Volunteer Labour Army promises to be a great success . . . It has knocked the bottom out of labour conscription and bosh of that kind.[14]

By a month later, Release from the Colours was being shown up as a failure:

> The return of skilled men from the Colours so far amounts to very little. Passive obstruction by the Battalion Orderly Rooms has no doubt a good deal to do with it. They don't like parting with good men. Similarly the munitions volunteer movement is not giving us as many men as we want.[15]

In August Addison estimated that 15,000 usable War Munitions Volunteers might be secured; a further month later he estimated that the total available would only be 6,000 W.M.Vs. and 5,000 men released from the Colours.[16] These figures are confirmed by the official history of the Ministry[17] which explained that the W.M.V. scheme failed to take into account the difficulties of moving men from one part of the country to another because of

> (f)amily ties, local connections and prejudices, differences in manners, mode of living, and dialect, the craftman's expectations, and conservative habits[18]

— as well as innumerable minor quarrels over wages and conditions.

With the manifest failure of schemes acceptable to the unions for the supply of labour, the Ministry had to press for those less acceptable, and turn in the first instance to the dilution of labour. The Treasury Agreement had, of course, been signed three months before the foundation of the Ministry but in practice it amounted to very little. With typical asperity Askwith observed that a ballot of A.S.E. members on accepting dilution was taking place at the time, but before its result was out Mr. Lloyd George had come in with the Treasury Agreement imposed without a ballot, but remaining practically a dead letter until a ballot had been taken several months after a conclusion might possibly have been reached.[19]

Subsequent events showed that resistance by A.S.E. members to dilution was far too deeply implanted to be much affected by the presence of a favourable ballot.

Llewellyn Smith urged upon Lloyd George from the beginning the necessity of giving the Treasury Agreement statutory backing:

> My judgement is in favour of immediate legislation as I am convinced that any further attempt on merely voluntary lines unsupported by legislative enactment will only break down and lose valuable time. I am glad to find that these views are shared by Sir George Askwith and by Mr. Mitchell, of the Chief Industrial Commissioner's Department.[20]

As we have seen, this was done in the Munitions of War Act. But no action was taken to impose dilution for some two months after its passing, until the failure of the W.M.V. and Release from the Colours schemes was too obvious to ignore. Anxious meetings on the labour shortage were held in the Ministry in late August,[21] and in September the Committee of the Labour Supply Department, set up to administer the W.M.V. scheme, reported to Lloyd George:

> The Committee desires to impress upon the Minister of Munitions of War the urgency of taking immediate steps to devise a fresh scheme for securing the skilled labour necessary for the manufacture of War Munitions in view of the impracticability for this purpose of the scheme with which they were asked to deal and have been dealing.[22]

Finally it was agreed to make dilution as acceptable as possible by having it supervised by a committee mainly composed of trade unionists, including the refractory A.S.E:

> Last week I put it up to L.G. to let us try to devise a scheme whereby we could secure the co-operation of trade unionists in bringing in unskilled labour. The National Advisory Committee on labour over which [Arthur] Henderson presides has constantly said that they (sic) have never been asked to help and I think there is justice in their complaint . . .
> This week, after a series of conferences with the Trade Union delegates and with the A.S.E., at first separately and then together, they agreed to join a Ministry Committee for the purpose of introducing unskilled labour and spreading skilled labour . . . Ll[ewellyn] Smith and Beveridge threw cold water on the scheme, but I am glad to say that West backed it up heartily, as did Henderson and the Labour Committee.[23]

Thus was the National Advisory Committee transmuted into the Central Munitions Labour Supply Committee: a notable step in the incorporation of trade unions into the ranks of Government. The National Advisory Committee had included Henderson, J. T. Brownlie (Chairman of the A.S.E.) and William Mosses of the Patternmakers Union, and was described as:

> a Committee, representative of the organised workers engaged in production for Government requirements, appointed by the Government to facilitate the carrying out of the Treasury Agreement and for consultation by the Government or by the workmen concerned.[24]

It had not done anything, and the changes of September were designed to make it a more powerful body, representing the Ministry, employers, and labour — the three men listed above being joined on the labour side by W. Dawtry (Steam Engine Makers), J. Kaylor (A.S.E.), Charles Duncan (Workers' Union) and Mary Macarthur (Women's Trade Union League). Addison wrote to Henderson:

> Mr. Lloyd George has given instructions that in regard to all matters within the terms of reference of the Committee its advice should be sought before any steps involving a change of policy are taken.[25]

(Lloyd George ignored his own instructions, against protests from the Committee, when setting up the Clyde Dilution Commission in January 1916.) The main work of the Committee was to issue the 'L' series of circulars on dilution of which the most important were L2 (on the introduction of women), L3 (unskilled and semi-skilled men), and L6 (procedure for introducing dilution). L2 was to cause continual trouble, which we shall examine in later chapters. L6 was couched in surprisingly firm terms. Headed 'Dilution of skilled labour — Notes for the Guidance of Controlled Establishments', it recommended that the workmen in each plant to which it was proposed to introduce a dilution scheme should be consulted 'together with their local Trade Union representatives if they so desire'. But

> It is not intended that the introduction of the change should be delayed until the concurrence of the workpeople is obtained. The change should be introduced after a reasonable time . . . While this is so, the Minister is of opinion that it will be consistent with prudence that every endeavour should be made by employers to secure the co-operation of their workpeople in matters of this description.
>
> Any difficulties experienced either by employers or workpeople should be at once referred to the Ministry in order that an immediate endeavour may be made to find a satisfactory solution.[26]

Writing firm circulars was one thing, enforcing them quite another. The Ministry soon found dilution being obstructed on all sides. At the very outset Addison complained:

> We had a deputation of employers from the Clyde. They wanted all sorts of powers over workmen — a sort of martial law — which they themselves might administer, obviously an impossible demand. They gave us the immediate impression of being a poor lot . . . [27]

Having failed to achieve these 'impossible demands', some employers took to bombarding the Ministry with advice. As Addison again noted wryly on the Clyde:

> It was difficult to disentangle the facts from the excited comments of Weir and our representative there, or even from the less excited comments of the Labour Office. One big employer was bursting with the desire to arrest a lot of people, but he could not mention anybody who ought to be arrested except one man against whom there was no evidence. [28]

Beveridge summarised the situation in a report of the Ministry's Labour Department:

> 1) . . . while a considerable number of firms are making changes, a much greater number reported that they do not need to have any trade union restrictions abolished and have made no attempt to do so.
> 2) . . . a number of firms, though they might be willing to make changes, are still deterred from doing so either by actual or anticipated difficulty with their work people.
>   There is a good deal of conservatism, both on the part of employers and on the part of workpeople, to be faced, and the result is that, generally speaking, while suspension of restrictions and dilution of labour is undoubtedly taking place to some extent, it is taking place too slowly for the necessities of the situation. [29]

A number of hints have already been dropped about the attitude of A.S.E. Executive. For nearly a year it fought a skilful rearguard action against the dilution to which it was nominally pledged. In September 1915 it sent a deputation to the Ministry at which Brownlie expressed concern at Lloyd George's statement that the W.M.V. scheme had failed. 'We have understood you to imply that compulsory powers or industrial conscription will be resorted to,'[30] he added, although this had not been envisaged in the Munitions of War Act. With this fear in the back of their mind the A.S.E. Executive obstructed the progress of dilution at every step. On 21st September 1915, for instance, they wired the Minister:

> Re Tyne Conference A.S.E. resolution that we as an executive council are not

prepared to take part in any Conference either local or national which has as its object dilution of skilled labour until the Minister of Munitions takes steps to render legal and mandatory rates of pay and conditions of labour to those semi-skilled and unskilled men who may take places of those of our members transferred to more highly skilled work.[31]

'The A.S.E.', as Addison remarked, 'had a difficult Executive',[32] and the Ministry's exasperation with it was amply expressed in notes prepared by Llewellyn Smith for Asquith as a result of the situation created by the telegram:

> The serious part of the situation is that we have reached a position in which the nation is being held up by a single Union . . . The negotiations with this union appear to be interminable, and no sooner is one agreement arrived at than it is broken, and new black-mailing conditions are proposed.
>
> These observations may seem strong but I do not think that anyone who has been engaged in the Labour Department of the Ministry during the last few months will think them unjustified.
>
> The Society wish now to add a fresh term to the Treasury Agreement.[33]

When the A.S.E. Executive attended at the Ministry for yet another conference in February 1916, Beveridge endorsed his superior's opinion in notes prepared for Lloyd George. Claiming that the Ministry was 'entitled and bound' to demand the A.S.E. Executive's support, he went on:

> They have continually gone back on their agreements and withdrawn their co-operation at a moment's notice, because of some difference with the Minister — that is to say, have themselves gone on strike.[34]

In a sense, the A.S.E. Executive had the worst of both worlds: condemned by the Ministry for dragging its feet over dilution, it was condemned by its militants for encompassing it at all. As a leaflet put out by the Clyde Workers' Committee claimed:

> The support given to the Munitions Act by the Officials was an act of Treachery. Those of us who refused to be Sold have organised the above Committee . . . to take the first opportunity of forcing the repeal of all the pernicious legislation that has recently been imposed upon us.[35]

Militant opinion was aroused, not only by the proposals for control of labour mobility, compulsory arbitration, and dilution, which were in the Act, but by the spectre of industrial conscription, which was not. Such fears were not entirely groundless. Industrial conscription was seen as a last resort, which Addison and Lloyd George disliked, but did not shrink from admitting they might have to introduce. During the Fairfield strike of October 1915[36] Lloyd George confided to C. P. Scott:

> . . . 90,000 men on the Clyde were threatening to strike because out of 20 men heavily fined for absenting themselves from work 3 had elected to go to prison rather than pay and their release was demanded pending an enquiry into the original grievances which had caused them to absent themselves. 'That would mean', said Lloyd George, 'that the Munitions Act would become a dead letter. Yet it is my last resource *short of Conscription*'.[37]

What the official history refers to as 'the papers read by more thoughtful workmen'[38] were continually raising fears as to what might lie behind the Act. For instance, the *Forward* drew its readers' attention to statements in other papers stressing the advantages to employers of dilution[39] or advocating industrial conscription or the application of military discipline to strikers:

> We must deal as harshly with strikers who throw down their tools as with soldiers who desert in the field.[40]

The attitude of the militants contained elements of both revolutionary socialism and craft conservatism. Other workers — such as those at Lang's machine-tool factory in Johnstone — were conservatives pure and simple. Isaac Mitchell spoke of their

> 'Old trade-union' type of bitterness, narrow and selfish . . . They are not intelligent and are selfishly opposed to any innovations into their trade.

Mitchell complained that there were three points of view on the Clyde: that of the 'narrow old-time trade unionist' which was being upheld by the A.S.E. Executive; that of the Ministry, which was supported by the local officials of the A.S.E; and that of the Clyde Workers' Committee; and that any proposal coming from one of these groups led 'to the other two sections being always ready to frustrate their efforts'.[41]

The stage was set for a complex and bitter conflict.

4

Leaving Certificates and Dilution,
August-December 1915

The first strikes against dilution and against the leaving certificate provisions of the Munitions of War Act took place while the rent strike campaign was still in progress. The two quarrels jointly promoted the Clyde's troublesome image; but they were quite separate.

Lang's of Johnstone, Renfrewshire, were 'one of the principal firms in the country making shell lathes',[1] and in August 1915 they proposed to introduce female labour on some of the simpler processes of lathe-making. The men reacted sharply against this, and with the support of a member of the A.S.E. Executive voted

> That no woman shall be put to work a lathe, and if this was done the men would know how to protect their rights.

The Executive justified its support of the men on the grounds that

> there was strong prima facie evidence that the firm in question was anxious to introduce cheap labour to the detriment of highly skilled labour inasmuch as the skilled labour in their employ was not utilised to its fullest capacity.[2]

But the Ministry took a very dim view of this explanation. The Lang's case was cited, though not by name, by Lloyd George in his speech to the TUC in Bristol in September when he attacked the continuation of restrictive practices.[3] The official history comments:

> The Ministry has been severely criticised for not forcing an issue on this decision without delay . . . for the employers regarded this as a test case. When they saw the men defying the instructions of the Ministry with impunity they refused to risk any similar and probably fruitless trouble in their own works.[4]

The explanation given there for the Ministry's inaction was that the men could not be prosecuted for their strike threat because of a technical misdemeanour by Lang's in failing to post a notice. The real reason was surely the fundamental weakness of the Ministry's position. The South Wales miners' strike had shown that threats of legal action were utterly useless against a large body of strikers, and it was to be three months before the Ministry could draft a regulation enabling it to act against the leaders of strikes. And the A.S.E. was far too big an opponent for a newly established and unpopular Ministry to tackle headlong. There could be no question of its trying to impose dilution against strikers backed by the executive of the largest union in the industry. The Ministry could not possibly take any action at Lang's until it had the A.S.E. Executive, however unwillingly, on its side. The case was discussed at two conferences between the Ministry and the Executive, and finally, on 29th October, Brownlie went to Johnstone, accompanied by the same executive councilman who two months earlier had urged Lang's men to resist dilution. This time their errand was to get the men to accept women on the simpler parts of the process of lathe manufacture. On their return, Brownlie reported that he had spoken of

> the imperative urgency of giving immediate effect to the various clauses of the [Munitions of War] Act so far as it applied to the suspension of established trade customs and practices during the period of war, urging the gravity of the national situation and emphasising the present needs of the Allies.
> The speeches of both speakers were listened to with wrapt (sic) attention, and were well received.[5]

He continued by saying that he and his colleagues had then seen the management and reported that 'the introduction of female labour on the operation desired was in order'.[6]

Even the backing of the Executive, however, made no difference. In a long memorandum prepared for Lloyd George before his Christmas visit to Glasgow the Ministry's chief labour officer for Scotland, J. Paterson, explained what ensued. He stressed that the employers wanted the Ministry to take some action and were not prepared to do so themselves because

> it [the Ministry] knows the hollowness and insincerity of Trade Union Action in waiving — on paper — restrictions which in actual practice have not been waived at all, and which there is no intention of waiving — unless under pressure of a nature that has not hitherto been attempted.[7]

The employers, Paterson continued, regarded the Lang's story as an object lesson in the worthlessness of trade union promises. The meeting with Brownlie had led to agreement that women might be employed on any machine, with a few named exceptions:

> The opinion of the firm, and of other engineering employers in the district is that that meeting did not in any way improve the position in so far as increased output was concerned . . . [The men were permitting women to work] *only when a man left or when a new machine was installed.*[8] [and women were being allowed to work only] the simplest types of lathes which are at present worked by first-year apprentices.[9]

Even this Pyrrhic victory for dilution did not go very far; by mid-November, Paterson continued, fifteen women had been started, and the men threatened to strike if any more women dilutees were introduced, and renewed their threat in December. Lang's was a test case for the employers:

> no engineering firm in the district was willing to take the risk of upsetting its establishment by making similar proposals to the A.S.E.; and when they saw that the Ministry allowed the A.S.E. to dictate the terms of settlement in the Johnstone cause, practically all interest in the question of dilution of labour evaporated — so far as the engineering employers in this district were concerned.[10]

The long drawn out struggle at Lang's over dilution had thus produced almost complete victory for the stay-put attitude of the men by the time of Lloyd George's visit, and had induced an attitude of truculent non-co-operation with the Ministry among the employers. Although it raised the issues which were to be the key to the struggle in the new year, it did not hold the centre of the stage in Glasgow while it was in progress. To the Ministry it was, of course, crucial, and the *History of the Ministry of Munitions* is the only printed source which gives it much coverage. Lang's was at no time under the control of the Clyde Workers' Committee; it was not a plant at which militants could channel craft conservatism into revolutionary agitation. The struggle at Lang's is therefore not discussed in the reminiscences of the leaders of the C.W.C. and thus by those whose accounts derive substantially from them.[11] During 1915, the militants were much more involved in the unrest at Fairfield's shipyard, which centred not on the dilution but on the leaving certificate clauses of the 1915 Act.

We have already noted that the Ministry of Munitions failed to wrest control of the shipyards from the Admiralty. But as 'controlled establishments' they were included in the sections of the Act dealing with labour, and when labour unrest broke out it was the Ministry of Munitions which had to handle it.

One Admiralty observer claimed that Fairfield Shipyard, in Govan, was badly run:

> Bad Time-Keeping.
> The Fairfield Company on the Shipbuilding side, are by a long way the worst timekeepers in the District. I believe it is due largely to methods of management.[12]

And once the dispute was under way Addison was to comment:

> There is no doubt that the men have genuine grievances and that the management of the Fairfield Yard is very bad.[13]

It was, at any rate, at Fairfield that two strikes, themselves originating in trivial issues, broke out. On 27th July a number of coppersmiths struck over a demarcation dispute; on 26th August the shipwrights struck against the allegedly unfair dismissal of two of their workmates for slacking. What gave this commonplace situation urgency and importance was that the men challenged the legitimacy of the leaving certificate system. By failing to give a man a clean certificate, the firm was victimising him, using a weapon provided by the Government for another purpose to settle petty scores. The weakness of the sanctions behind the Act was again shown up when the strike leaders were summoned before a General Munitions Tribunal and seventeen of them were fined £10 each.[14] Matters remained quiet for a short time, until three of the men refused to pay and were imprisoned, whereat the Govan Trades Council urged a sympathetic strike. (Govan, though well within the Glasgow conurbation, was not incorporated into the city until 1912, and its Trades Council remained an independent body until it was amalgamated with the Glasgow Trades Council in 1918. At this time, led by Harry Hopkins, an A.S.E. militant, it was both more activist and more concerned with the engineers than Glasgow Trades Council.)

The Government took the threat very seriously,[15] especially when it was supplemented by gloomy reports from Paterson, the labour officer in Glasgow, on 2nd October, and Isaac Mitchell on 11th October. Both reported that the men were in an angry mood, and especially aggrieved with Section 7 of the Act (the part dealing with leaving certificates). Mitchell added that an eviction decree against rent strikers might be enough to provoke a strike,

> (b)ut the position might be saved if he could receive a telegram stating that such a man as Lord Balfour of Burleigh or Mr. Macassey had been appointed to enquire into the men's grievances.[16]

The Ministry acted quickly to appoint the two men suggested to 'enquire into the causes and circumstances of the apprehended differences affecting munition workers in the Clyde District'.[17] Before reporting, however, Balfour and Macassey announced that they were not competent to recommend the remission of the strikers' sentences. This provoked another storm. The Ministry received a telegram from

> the members of the Executive Councils or District Committees of the 23 Trades Unions connected with the engineering and shipbuilding industry, representing 97,500 workmen in the Clyde Valley,[18]

which urged the remission of the sentences and demanded an answer within three days. (The officials of the industry had been convened by David Kirkwood 'for the purpose of organising the prevailing opposition to the operations of the Act',[19] after a visit to Glasgow by Brownlie which Paterson described as 'a bear garden'.)[20] A deputation from the signatories had a meeting with Lloyd George, McKinnon Wood, and some national union officials which reached no agreement until Lloyd George proposed that the unions concerned should pay the fines.[21] This they did, to the mystification and annoyance of some militants whose vicarious sacrifice was cut short.[22] In the more relaxed atmosphere that followed, the Balfour-Macassey committee continued to take evidence and shortly issued its Report (Cd 8136). This argued that most of the differences which led to friction were not 'disputes of definite principle under the . . . Act' but merely indiscretion or inconsideration on one side or the other: much of the friction was caused by ignorance of the operation of the 'leaving certificate' system by the men, or (more important) its exploitation and abuse by foremen and managements. The Committee made two recommendations of a more general kind:

> 17 . . . We have come to the conclusion that if there was some person of experience in industrial matters appointed by you[23] in the Clyde District to act as a mediator or conciliator, with possibly final power in minor matters accessible with a minimum of delay, the great majority of the disputes we have inquired into would had been prevented, and those not wholly disposed of, localised in their effects.
> 18 . . . Finally we recommend that the imprisonment should be abolished for non-payment of fines inflicted upon a workman by a Munitions Tribunal. In the event of non-payment by the workman of a fine inflicted upon him . . . the Tribunal should have jurisdiction to order the employer . . . to deduct . . . the total amount thereof from the workman's wages by weekly instalments prescribed by the Tribunal.[24]

The first of these recommendations showed the way for the appointment of the Dilution Commissioners, one of whom was Macassey himself. Although the Commission was to have more serious purposes, Macassey obviously enjoyed taking upon himself the role of shop-floor trouble-shooter. Later, when the Dilution Commission was at work, he thus described his activity after dilution schemes had been brought into use:

> ... from time to time thereafter [we] fix and adjust immediately minor inequalities that emerge in the carrying into practice of the scheme . . . That course has avoided numerous strikes.

He added that he personally had gone out to settle points 'at all hours of the day and night'.[25]

The second recommendation was one of a number considered by the Ministry for incorporation into the Amending Bill which was being drafted at the time, and which became law as the Munitions of War (Amendment) Act in January 1916. A number of the Balfour-Macassey committee's recommendations were covered in the Ministry's draft amending bill, especially those relating to the reform of the leaving certificate system aimed at lessening the men's resentment of it. But action on paragraph 18 was not in the Ministry of Munitions' hands:

> The decision to retain the power of imprisonment is a Cabinet decision.[26]

When the Cabinet did decide to abolish imprisonment for non-payment, it did not adopt Balfour and Macassey's proposal to introduce attachment of earnings. But the Ministry was taking steps to strengthen its position vis-a-vis strikers, not through the Munitions Act, but through the Defence of the Realm regulations, an action which we shall examine below.

Many people accused the Ministry of appeasement in its settlement of the rent strike and the Lang's and Fairfield disputes. Weir wrote to Addison on 8th October:

> It is useless to enunciate a policy and then fail to support the carrying out of it . . . I must refuse to be associated with a lack of policy which is doing the greatest possible harm.[27]

Two months later he reiterated these views in notes to Lloyd George, adding that the Ministry's present policy was 'worse than futile'.[28] Weir's view was shared by smaller, more conservative, employers. Their views were passed on in the sometimes plaintive memoranda sent in by Paterson, who found himself stymied between employers who refused to introduce dilution and unionists who would refuse to accept it. One employer wrote to him, flatly refusing to dilute

> as long as the Trade Unions are permitted to flout the Government's instructions and treat their solemn engagements with the Government as so much waste paper.
>
> We can assure you in all seriousness that the fact of Trade Unions being allowed to carry out their policy and the delay on the part of the Government in bringing them to book for their action is having a most serious effect upon the labour question in this district.

Another employer wrote to his local labour exchange, which had offered him a batch of soldiers released from the Colours, that his workmen had refused to work alongside them:

> Our acceptance, therefore, of the men you have offered to us is subject to the Minister of Munitions making satisfactory arrangements with the Trade Union officials.

Paterson had pleaded at a meeting of the North-West Engineering Trades Employers' Association for its members to dilute:

> After I had spoken, the President of the Association made some very pointed remarks as to the employers in the district having no faith in the Ministry of Munitions' securing the removal of the restrictions which were understood to have been waived by the Munitions Act: and it was evident from the applause with which the President's statement was greeted, and the remarks of subsequent speakers, that he was voicing the general sentiment of the meeting.

When he asked these employers to send him schemes of the dilution which could be introduced into their works, they agreed only if they remained identified solely by numbers, to which they refused Paterson the key, because otherwise

> the returns would be made available to the National Labour Advisory Committee, which would transmit these to the local officials of the Trade Unions, who would then proceed to make matters as uncomfortable as possible for the employers who had had the courage to show in what way dilution could be achieved.[29]

The Ministry also received unsolicited advice on how to deal with the revolutionary militants. T. J. Macnamara, Parliamentary Secretary to the First Lord of the Admiralty, passed on to Lloyd George a letter from a Glasgow estate agent, Richard Williamson:

> A great deal of harm is being done by men who are speaking at street corners, in halls, and in all the munition districts on the Clyde, . . . [saying that] as regards Trade Unionists now is the time to be out for 'blood' and demand all the wages they can get — that now is the time to bring not only the masters, but the Government, to their knees.

John McLean . . . is doing a tremendous amount of harm. He distinctly declares whenever he speaks that any man who joins the British Army is a hired assassin and a murderer.

. . . These men must be dealt with at once, Ben Tillett comes down here and makes patriotic speeches and gets hissed, while these men are getting big audiences and doing a great amount of mischief.

Immediate attention is necessary.

Yours faithfully
(sgd)   Richard Williamson

PS. 'Forward', which I enclose, ought to be suppressed. It is doing incalculable harm.[30]

Macnamara added that the defects of the Munitions Act had been 'skilfully magnified by the small band of eager and tireless malcontents' on the Clyde:

They should be taken seriously in hand . . . Your office, our office, the War Office, the Home Office and the Scottish Office should confidentially advise their officers on the spot to keep an eye on the firebrands.

Macnamara went on to advise Lloyd George to indicate his intentions to proceed under the Defence of the Realm Act against any strike or incitement to strike, if need be amending the Munitions Act or Defence of the Realm Act (D.O.R.A.). Finally after endorsing the need for dilution, he claimed that the Advisory Committee had far less appeal among Clyde workmen than had the revolutionaries, and concluded,

On the one hand you must detach the men from them [the revolutionaries] by the sincerity of your administration in the direction of promptly meeting legitimate claims for the removal of grievances; on the other hand you must, if necessary, lay these gentlemen by the heels.[31]

In spite of nagging from the Admiralty and elsewhere, the Ministry failed to 'lay these gentlemen by the heels' during 1915. In late November, from at least four separate sources, it received copies of the C.W.C. manifesto 'To All Clyde Workers' to which reference has been made.[32] The Admiralty's Captain Superintendent on the Clyde remarked,

The Committee proclaims its activities as a conspiracy against the law, and at the present time is undoubtedly traitorous.

To obtain a reasonably smooth working of the Munitions Act this Committee should be smashed.[33]

Paterson, forwarding another copy, commented:

From a perusal of this leaflet . . . it seems very clear that this body is preparing for a big strike . . . and it is doing so in such an open manner in this leaflet that I think the two men[34] who have put their names to paper render themselves liable to action under the Defence of the Realm Act or Regulations.[35]

Beveridge thought it would be 'worthwhile' to try to prosecute the authors under D.O.R.A., and suggested that the Scots Law Officers should be consulted, to which Lloyd George added that he wanted the Attorney-General consulted 'as to the likelihood of a prosecution succeeding'.[36] Consulting the Scots Law Officers was a long-drawn-out business, since the Solicitor-General worked in Edinburgh and the Lord Advocate in London, and meanwhile Macnamara sent Addison a querulous note:

> We sent over some days ago a leaflet from the Clyde Workers' Committee signed by a Mr. Messer and another — I think Mr. Gallagher. I really should like to know what, if anything, your people propose respecting that leaflet.[37]

The Solicitor-General thought a prosecution under D.O.R. Regulation 42 would succeed, but the Lord Advocate said:

> On the question of law . . . I am disposed to share the view of the Solicitor-General though I must own that I do not hold it with such confidence as he.[38]

The subsequent history of the proposal is traced by four subsequent notes all on the same piece of paper pinned to the law officers' reports:

> 1) Beveridge to Llewellyn Smith: 'I am sorry that by an accident the paper had been mislaid for a few days over the Christmas holidays.' 30.12.15
> 2) Llewellyn Smith to [?] Addison: 'I think active steps ought to be taken to deal with these people.' 1.1.16
> 3) Addison to Lloyd George: 'In view of the Lord Advocate's very qualified opinion, the lapse of time, your visit and the amending Bill I cannot advise you to authorise a prosecution in this matter.' 5.1.16
> 4) Addison to Llewellyn Smith: 'I have seen Mr Lloyd George and he agrees with me.'[39] 5.1.16

The response of the Ministry was certainly dilatory. Perhaps this was simply a reaction to the nagging that Addison and his civil service subordinates had been receiving from the Admiralty and employers; or possibly (though the chapter of minor accidents recorded on the final minute-sheet makes this unlikely) it was a matter of policy to ca' canny in dealing with the C.W.C. The simplest explanation, however, is that the Government, and in particular Lloyd George, had much more important things on hand than the C.W.C. Lloyd George was far too preoccupied with the conscription crisis in December 1915 and January

1916 to bother about such a minor aspect of the Clydeside affair. The leaflet had been overtaken by bigger things, even on Clydeside, before it was finally decided to take no action.

The only positive steps taken by the Ministry during 1915 towards securing the imposition of dilution on Clydeside were the continued attrition by conference of the A.S.E; the amendment of D.O.R. Regulation 42; and the planning of Lloyd George's visit to Glasgow. (The first of these will be discussed at the beginning of Chapter 6.) The Ministry officials thought that the Munitions of War Act had two main weaknesses. Its leaving certificate provisions were too harsh on the workers; its treatment of strikers and those who incited workers to strike was too gentle. They were drafting a Munitions of War (Amendment) Bill which relaxed the first provisions and, originally, toughened the second by adding these words:

> If any person commits or attempts to commit or procures or attempts to procure or aids and abets the commission of any act which is an offence under the principal Act he shall be guilty of an offence under the principal Act.[40]

It was thought, however, that this would cause such widespread opposition that the Bill as a whole would be held up for it, and therefore the desired regulation was slipped in as an amendment to Defence of the Realm Regulation 42. This procedure was contemplated by Addison without any qualms:

> We have drafted an amendment of the Defence of the Realm Regulations to suit the occasion, if trouble really arises.[41]

The amendment expanded Regulation 42 by the addition of the words underlined:

> If any person attempts to cause mutiny, sedition, or disaffection among any of His Majesty's forces or among the civil population, <u>or to impede, delay, or restrict the production, repair or transport of war material or any other work necessary for the successful prosecution of the war,</u> he shall by guilty of an offence under these Regulations.[42]

This regulation was brought into force on 30th November. A Ministry memorandum, discussing it, notes:

> A regulation has been made making incitement to strike on all work essential to the prosecution of the war an offence under the Defence of the Realm Act. Clause 5 of the Bill takes away the power to imprison for general munition tribunal offences.[43]

Thus the abolition of imprisonment was to be offered as a sop to ease the passage of the Amending Bill. However, the memorandum just quoted shows that the Ministry, like its radical opponents, linked the questions of imprisonment under the Munitions Acts and the extension of D.O.R.A. When the Munitions Bill came to be debated in the Commons on 4th January 1916, radicals complained bitterly that the Government was taking away with one hand what it was giving with the other. In the debate on Clause 5 of the Bill, a Radical, W. F. Roch, complained that the new D.O.R. Regulation gave the Minister far more comprehensive powers of arrest and imprisonment than those he was preparing to abandon in the new Bill. Lloyd George initially refused to discuss the issue, on the grounds that it was the Act and not the Regulation that was before the House, but on being pressed he explained:

> The workman who turns up late, or breaks regulations, or commits a breach of discipline is dealt with under the Munitions Act, but the cases referred to under the Order in Council are those in which there is incitement to mutiny to prevent workmen doing their best to assist in the production of munitions . . . these regulations . . . are intended to deal with the man who deliberately goes about with the intention and in order to interfere with the output of munitions.[44]

In spite of the fact that W. C. Anderson wrote regularly for *Forward* during 1915 on the progress of munitions legislation, the Scottish socialist press seems not to have noticed the extension of Regulation 42 at all. Ironically, the first time the new powers were mentioned was in Lloyd George's defence, only six days after the debate discussed above, of his action in the suppression of the *Forward*.[45] They were also a substantial aid in the move against the leadership of the C.W.C. in March 1916, and were required for the second trial of John MacLean in the same month.

5

Lloyd George's Visit and the Suppression of the Forward

The other part of the counter-attack which was planned in 1915 was Lloyd George's visit to Glasgow. The initiative for such a visit came from the Central Munitions Labour Supply Committee. An *ad hoc* sub-committee on Dilution of Labour recommended

> that the Minister should be requested to initiate a campaign in certain districts in favour of the scheme. The districts suggested are Sheffield, Newcastle and Glasgow.[1]

The report went on to outline a day's suggested itinerary for the Minister, spending the forenoon in getting the employers interested in the scheme, visiting the works to show the men his interest in the afternoon, and meeting union officials and shop stewards in the evening. This was followed by a letter to Lloyd George from Henderson in his capacity as chairman of the Committee:

> The Labour Supply Committee is exceedingly anxious that you should arrange to visit Sheffield and Newcastle, and if possible Glasgow at an early date for the purpose of promulgating the scheme for the dilution of skilled labour by semi-skilled and women . . . I am to urge the importance of your consenting to address the first conference and of fixing immediately any dates convenient to yourself so that the conference may at once be properly organised.[2]

In the event, Lloyd George did not visit Sheffield, but his real reason for visiting Glasgow was certainly concern over the worsening deadlock over dilution there. A bundle of material was prepared in the Ministry for him to use as background information for his visit;[3] it includes the long memorandum from Paterson, already quoted in part, explaining why dilution was making such slow progress, and also a note by Macassey covering the same ground and also touching on

49

leaving certificates and on ways of getting rid of 'troublemakers'. Macassey advised Lloyd George

> to appoint those two or three local Trade Union officials whom I can name if necessary to some official post remote from Clydeside where their activities, which are immense, could be controlled and diverted to the useful service of their country. It would be impossible to obtain sufficient evidence to dispose of them under the Defence of the Realm Act. Even if possible, their prosecution in the present state of mind of the workmen would be attributed unto them for righteousness sake, and would produce an industrial revolution on the Clyde.[4]

Lloyd George went to the Tyne on 21st December, and to the Clyde on the 23rd. On the Clyde, however, the expedition was badly organised. Lloyd George had arranged to meet local union committee members on 23rd December, but by changing the date to Christmas Day without consulting them he offended them, and they voted to take no part in the proceedings.[5] The Glasgow Trades Council was even more offended, and recorded in an unusually lively minute:

> A discussion followed on the Lloyd George meeting to be held on Thursday, 23rd December, and the manner in which this meeting was called, the Council being ignored in the matter. It was moved by Mr. Heenan that Council take no notice of this meeting. Amendment moved by Mr. Jas Walker that we protest against the manner in which this meeting has been called. No fault should be found with the [Engineering and] Shipbuilding Trades(;) he was quite certain that the fault lay with the Ministry of Munitions. Mr. Shinwell supported the Amendment, and said that in his opinion the only way to counteract the people who were responsible for this meeting was to use plenty of ridicule. He believed they were officials and the Government guided by their so-called experts. We were asked to welcome Lloyd George as a prophet and Arthur Henderson was coming to allay any opposition among Trade Unionists. He hoped the Trade Unions would give these people the welcome they deserved. To protest was carried by a large majority.[6]

Lloyd George and his party in fact held three meetings. On 23rd December they went to Parkhead, and spoke to a meeting of shop stewards chaired by David Kirkwood.[7] On 24th December they met a number of the leaders of the Clyde Workers' Committee, whose demands were presented by John Muir.[8] And on 25th December the mass meeting was held in St. Andrew's Halls.

It had been planned to have the issue of tickets controlled by members of trade union executives.[9] But this plan was frustrated by the doubly chaotic outcome of events: some unions agreed officially to take part[10] but most stood by their earlier decision not to. The Clyde Workers' Committee for its part decided, in the absence of its chairman Gallacher, to reverse its previous policy and to take over a batch of the tickets. Gallacher quotes the explanation given by Sam Bunton, the District Secretary of the A.S.E. and one of his colleagues on the Allied Trades Committee, to Murray of Elibank (who was a member of the Lloyd George party):

> 'My Lord'. A pause, then pointing a finger at me, 'This man has been repudiated by his own colleagues . . . While he was at our meeting last night getting us to turn down the Lloyd George meeting, his own committee met in the Central Hall and decided to carry on with it. A group of them came round to our hall this morning and took away the tickets.' [11]

Gallacher was thus a victim of his own dual position as Chairman of the C.W.C. and a member of the Allied Trades district committee: while he successfully persuaded the latter to take one decision his own committee met and moved in the opposite direction. The confusion with the C.W.C. was thus scarcely less than in any other bodies involved. The C.W.C. had originally intended to boycott Lloyd George altogether. On 23rd December his party visited Weir's at Cathcart, and Gallacher's own factory of Albion Motors, but the shop stewards refused to see him. As the *Forward* reported sarcastically,

> The men at Weir's declined to listen to him, preferring to get on with the production of munitions. [12]

But Parkhead broke ranks. Any revolutionary egalitarianism that David Kirkwood might have possessed was tempered by a large dose of snobbery, or (to put it more generously) self-esteem at the way in which he was accustomed — so he believed — to deal on equal terms with Sir William Beardmore. [13] He was clearly so delighted at receiving a telegraphed summons from Lloyd George addressed to

David Kirkwood,
Parkhead Forge,
Glasgow

and asking the Parkhead shop stewards to meet Lloyd George that he agreed with relish, and took the opportunity to upbraid Lloyd George because

> the Munitions Act had bound the workers to Beardmore as completely as if it had branded 'B' on their brows. [14]

Kirkwood was clearly more worried about leaving certificates (which the Ministry already had in mind) than about dilution. But his reported remarks continued:

They as Socialists welcomed dilution of labour, which they regarded as the natural development in industrial conditions. They were not like the Luddites of another generation, who smashed the new machinery. But this scheme of dilution must be carried out under the control of the workers.[15]

Then, according to Kirkwood's account,[16] it was at his behest that Lloyd George agreed to hold the Christmas Day meeting, and compensate the men for loss of pay. (Christmas Day was not a holiday in Scotland in 1915, nor for many years afterwards.) Kirkwood was asked to organise the meeting: 'I went back to the shop stewards, and we agreed to have the meeting.'[17] If this account is accurate, then clearly Kirkwood and Gallacher were set on opposite courses, and Kirkwood won. (But the account in the suppressed issue of *Forward* makes it clear that Lloyd George had already decided to hold a meeting on Christmas Day and compensate the men for loss of pay before he met Kirkwood, so that Kirkwood does more than justice to himself in suggesting in his account that he was actually responsible for the meeting being held at all.)

Kirkwood was the outsider in the C.W.C., with a principality of his own, and the only I.L.P. member in a committee of British Socialist Party and Socialist Labour Party members. On political matters he was very strongly influenced, even manipulated, by Wheatley: 'Wheatley exercised a strong influence over Kirkwood, a strange phenomenon of the Calvinist succumbing to the Jesuit'[18] in the view of Thomas Bell, who was particularly hostile because Wheatley had poached Kirkwood from the S.L.P. of which Bell was the leading member. John McGovern wrote of the events of 23rd December:

> On the way home he told John Wheatley and me the full story of the Lloyd George episode. Wheatley became interested and asked Kirkwood to write it up for publication in 'Forward'. Davie said, 'I could not write it up, as I am no penman'. Wheatley asked him to come to his house the following evening, and he would take full notes of the whole affair, and then he (Wheatley) would write an article for 'Forward'. The article duly appeared, and Davie Kirkwood became a national leader overnight. Wheatley wrote his articles, his speeches, and decided on meetings and conferences at which Davie would appear.[19]

The events of Christmas Day were perhaps less enduringly important, though much more dramatic, than those of the previous two days. Arthur Henderson spoke to the crowd, talking first about the violation of the neutrality of a brave and independent people ('Oh heavens, how long have we to suffer this? . . . That's enough')[20] and then about the presence of union officials on the Ministry's dilution committee — the Chairman of the A.S.E. (Booing and hissing), Kaylor ('Away with him') and Miss Macarthur ('Miss Macarthur's the best man o' the lot'). He appealed for a hearing for Lloyd George in the name of freedom of speech ('What about the action of the Glasgow Magistrates? You've made a bloomer that time, Arthur!' Great commotion).

Lloyd George's speech was in part drowned altogether by the commotion, although Kirkwood at one point appealed for a hearing for him. Much of his speech, as released in the official text, could not be heard by those at the meeting. He stressed that the new National munitions factories were 'great Socialist factories' (Violent interruption); he appealed to the men through their loyalty to 'one of my greatest personal friends', Ramsay MacDonald; in his peroration on the need for dilution, he stressed that 'the responsibility of a Minister of the Crown in a great war is not an enviable one' ('The money's good', and laughter) and that attempts to hold up the progress of dilution were 'haggling with an earthquake'. The meeting broke up in disorder after Muir had tried to make a statement on behalf of the C.W.C. John MacLean subsequently wrote that he had been largely responsible for organising the disorder at this meeting for revolutionary purposes; but there is no evidence to support his claim.

The aftermath of the meeting is well known. The Press Bureau had authorised the publication of an official report, and in the course of a general instruction on the handling of the Lloyd George visit emphasised that only the official report of the meeting should be carried:

> It is understood that a Trade Union Meeting was held in that Town [Glasgow] today . . . It is particularly requested that no account of that meeting should be published other than a general statement that the meeting was held.
> The reason for this request is that at the meeting many things may have been said the publication of which is not desirable in the national interest.
> Mr Lloyd George will address a meeting in Glasgow tomorrow and it is particularly requested that no report other than the authorised version of his speech should be published. Should any disturbance occur at or in the neighbourhood of the meeting the Press are earnestly requested to refrain from publishing any reference to it.[21]

The official report of the meeting was made by the Press Association reporter, and circulated to the papers which subscribed to that Association. This report stated:

> At the outset attempts to disturb the proceedings were made and there was a good deal of interruption and some singing of 'The Red Flag' by Syndicalists present and

a small section who were apparently opposed to the war. The interrupters were, however, in a distinct minority, and the meeting was on the whole good humoured.[22]

Forward was not a subscriber to the Press Association: and it did not receive Press Bureau circulars for reasons which become sufficiently obvious on reading the one just quoted. So it received neither the request nor the report, and it printed an account of the meeting taken down by its own shorthand reporter, who had been present. Introducing this report, Thomas Johnston, the editor wrote:

> We have no desire to touch the military or 'preparedness' side of the speech, but the purely political side must not go unrepresented. It is simply stupid to go about deluding people that only an insignificant minority, and not the vast overwhelming majority of the meeting, was angry and the journalist, whoever he was, who drew up the report and omitted the political references to Ramsay MacDonald and the efforts of the Socialists to secure a hearing for Mr. George, is really *not* playing a patriotic part.[23]

At a meeting at the Ministry of Munitions, held on 31st December 1915, and attended by Lloyd George, Addison, Llewellyn Smith, Rey[24] and Beveridge, it was decided 'provisionally' to suppress the *Forward*,[25] and the procedure was worked out after a meeting in Edinburgh between Paterson, the Lord Advocate, and General Sir Spencer Ewart (the G.O.C. Scotland).[26] Answering questions in the Commons on 4th January, H. J. Tennant, the Under-Secretary for War, said that the *Forward* had been suppressed under Regulation 27 of the Defence of the Realm Regulations: 'No person shall spread false reports or make false statements or reports or statements likely to cause disaffection to His Majesty'.[27]

Both Tennant and Lloyd George, who spoke later after a flurry of angry supplementaries had left Tennant non-plussed, stressed that the *Forward* had been deliberately encouraging restriction in the production of munitions.[28]

On a request from W. M. R. Pringle, Asquith, who averred that this was the first he had heard of the matter,[29] agreed to consider granting an adjournment debate. This took place on 10th January, and Lloyd George gave a vigorous defence of his action. He escaped from the debate not entirely unscathed by his Radical and Labour critics, but no Parliamentary action followed. In due course, after Johnston had given an undertaking to publish nothing which might cause 'disaffection with the Munitions of War Acts, or with the policy of dilution of labour',[30] he was allowed to resume publication. In the first issue after the suppression, he printed the above guarantee, and continued:

> It was that or nothing, and being Scots we took that. So all our readers and contributors — and especially contributors — will understand that our defence of the working class of this country must henceforth partake of the nature of rearguard action.[31]

Why was the *Forward* suppressed? Four sorts of explanation might be given. There was, firstly, the official case — or rather, the two official cases, for there was little in common between the case against the *Forward* prepared at the Ministry of Munitions and that expounded by Lloyd George at the adjournment debate on 10th January. Secondly, there is the argument which has often been put forward since the incident, that the whole business ought to be attributed to Lloyd George's pique at the blow to his self-esteem caused by such an unflattering report. In the third place, Terence Brotherstone has argued[32] that it was part of a Government plan to suppress the C.W.C. Finally, it might be argued that the affair was less a conspiracy than a succession of minor blunders. These views will be examined in turn.

Between 4th and 10th January, Beveridge was asked, and agreed 'not very enthusiastically',[33] to prepare a brief to justify Lloyd George's decision. This was supplemented by an unsigned memorandum detailing 'Points likely to be made against the Minister'.[34] Beveridge's notes recommended procedure under DOR Regulation 27. But the speech made by Lloyd George in defence of his action, for which rough notes survive in the Lloyd George papers,[35] relied very little on Beveridge's brief. It passed very briefly over Regulation 27, but dwelt instead upon the new Regulation 42.

The case against the *Forward* was weak under either of the two DOR Regulations. After citing the text of Regulation 27[36] Beveridge remarked, 'It will be seen that this Regulation clearly covers not only false reports but also true reports if they are "likely to cause disaffection etc." '[37] It was no doubt sensible of Lloyd George not to base his apologia on this argument, which would have made a catastrophically bad impression on the Commons and the public. But the grounds for making any reference to Regulation 42 were even weaker. The Solicitor-General had suggested making a case against the issue on the grounds that the 'tone of the Editorial on page 5', the 'implications' of the headline *Mr Lloyd George does not speak on Munitions Act*, and

> the tenor of the comments and reports of the Minister's proceedings in the Clyde

were calculated to impair the authority of the Minister of Munitions and to undermine the operation of the statute in a dangerous and insidious manner, contrary to article 42 of the Defence of the Realm Regulation.[38]

This was to clutch at straws, and feeble ones at that. Beveridge argued:

> I think, however, it is in fact very doubtful whether any such *attempt* to impede or delay can fairly be proved against *Forward*. There is no doubt of the thoroughly harmful effects of *Forward*. It is not so easy to show harmful *intention*.[39]

And in his brief describing the conduct of the paper in general he added:

> it must be said at once that there is practically nothing that can be described as deliberately seditious any more, indeed, than the article in the suppressed issue can fairly be described as deliberately seditious. The *Forward* apart from tendencies to describe all wars as capitalist conspiracies does not appear anywhere as an anti-war paper.[40]

This fact was perfectly well known to the Ministry and its local officials, and even to military intelligence, whom later evidence suggests to have been more prone to accepting revolutionaries at their own valuation than anyone else:

> The Chief Constable and Detective Superintendent confirmed the impression that Johnston the editor of *Forward* does not belong to the dangerous section of Glasgow socialists . . . this attitude has caused some of his former followers to desert him and support the 'Socialist' for the purpose of expressing more advanced views.[41] ·

Although Lloyd George stated that he had received information about the *Forward* early in November, but had been loth to prosecute,[42] there is no evidence that the information consisted of anything other than the letter from Williamson passed on by Macnamara which we have quoted.[43]

Lloyd George also pointed out that the military authorities had been collecting quotations from *Forward* but none of them[44] were used in his speech, for the adequate reason that they were perfectly innocuous. The Scottish Office also had dealings with the *Forward* on two occasions, both the result of complaints from members of the public.

In October 1914, a complaint was levied against the paper's 'sustained campaign against recruiting'. It was handed to the Advocate Depute, who pronounced the following opinion:

. . . Scurrilous and offensive as are many of the statements made, they cannot in the opinion of the Advocate Depute be regarded as treasonable or seditious, or as constituting an offence under the Defence of the Realm Act and Regulations or under the Army Act . . . There is no incitement to obstruct or defeat the policy of the Government . . . At most there is only offensive and bitter *criticism* . . . In contrast however the tone of most of the articles published, contributions from Mr Barnes MP and other articles of an entirely unobjectionable character appear in certain issues *in favour* of the prosecution of the war to an end.

In the whole circumstances the A.D. would suggest that there is no ground for the institution of criminal proceedings and that any action by criminal or other authorities would only serve to secure notoriety and advertisement for the newspaper without any corresponding public advantage.[45]

Another complaint in May 1915 was dealt with more briskly. Its recipient wrote: 'It doesn't seem worthwhile sending this to the L[ord] A[dvocate]. This isn't a bad number. Put up?', and this was endorsed: 'Yes, nothing v. bad here'.[46]

So far from deliberately impeding munitions production — the offence dealt with by the expanded Regulation 42 — the *Forward* had, by refusing even to report strikes until they were over, kept well clear of any serious risk of prosecution. This was well known to every department concerned, even if not to enraged middle-class individuals who wrote in to complain. It follows that the case for the suppression was weak. The case compiled in the Ministry was feeble enough, in all conscience, but it was discarded by Lloyd George in favour of a tissue of distortions, innuendoes and lies whose sheer enormity ought to be given due credit. Beveridge, who was called in from the pantomime to listen to it, called it 'a Parliamentary triumph exceeding in dexterity the trick cycling which I had just seen at Drury Lane'.[47] To prove that the *Forward* had committed an offence under Regulation 42 by deliberately trying to resist the production of munitions was quite a task, even for Lloyd George, and he used several stratagems. He included, in his case against *Forward*, a number of quotations from John MacLean's *Vanguard*, advance proofs of which had been found at the office of the *Forward's* printers. A note in Lloyd George's handwriting among the rough notes says 'same ground — same steps'.[48] But as Beveridge recalled, 'The impression he left on my memory was that of defending the suppression of one paper in the main by attacking another paper'.[49]

Lloyd George went on to note a 'very savage attack upon the British monarchy'[50] written in the *Forward* by Morrison Davidson. But the author was an elderly woollyminded apocalyptic Liberal Home Ruler whose occasional appearance in *Forward* represented a link with the paper's Home Rule origins[51] rather than its industrial readership, and in any case the article's 'main point had been to suggest that the Kaiser was mad'.[52] Next Lloyd George quoted 'one of the most insidious and dangerous appeals to the working classes not to recruit which I have ever read'.[53] This was a dialogue from the *Forward* of 25th December between a workman and an employer which Lloyd George totally distorted by turning the employer into a canvasser for the Derby recruiting scheme.[54] Finally, he pointed out that the *Forward* itself did not care for the freedom of the press, and quoted the following doctored extract to prove his point: 'We weep no tears for the fall of the "Globe". We laugh at the fiery "slosh" penned about the freedom of the Press . . .'[55] This was simply to turn the truth upside down. The *Forward* had actually said: 'We weep no tears for the fall of the "Globe"': *as the 'Globe'.* 'We laugh at the fiery "slosh" penned about the freedom of the Press.'[56] — the argument being that however despicable the *Globe* might be, and however hypocritical its friends, nevertheless the freedom of the Press was something too valuable to discard. Johnston pointed this out in an angry letter to the *Glasgow Herald*:

> Will it be believed that this [the quotation read out by Lloyd George] is the first half of a sentence carefully extracted from two paragraphs protesting *against* the seizure of the 'Globe'?[57]

Thus neither version of the official case against the *Forward* carries much conviction. It has therefore been traditionally assumed that, in spite of Lloyd George's strenuous denials, the suppression of the *Forward* was due to a fit of pique at its report of his speech. Indeed, one of the stronger exponents of this view was the *History of the Ministry of Munitions:*

> a more generous confidence in the good sense of the British public would have been a wiser policy and more consonant with the traditions of the British Government[58]

— and this criticism is the more striking, given the official nature of that publication. Most modern authorities have assumed straightforwardly that the suppression was purely and simply a reaction to the speech. Marwick writes for instance:

> The Minister of Munitions first addressed a mass meeting in the St. Andrew's Hall on Christmas Day, but in that chill un-Christian assembly Lloyd George's Welsh wizardry for once fell completely flat — so flat, indeed, that the press was prohibited from publishing any record of the meeting save a small official hand-

out. For printing a full and circumstantial account, the Glasgow socialist weekly, *Forward*, was suppressed.[59]

Brotherstone does not deny the importance of this, but he adds that there was an ulterior purpose:

> the facts which can be established do seem to point to an interpretation concerned to stress the tactical struggle between the government and the real 'troublemakers' on the Clyde — those who sought to defend the workers' interests against the imposition of the employers' version of dilution. In this struggle the *Forward* was no more than a pawn. Whatever their initial intentions, the men at the Ministry of Munitions, by giving Johnston's paper an aura of martyrdom, helped to divert attention from the serious business in hand, the defeat of the Clyde Workers' Committee.[60]

However, there are problems with this interpretation too. The Ministry of Munitions had already had one chance to attack the C.W.C. — over the leaflet 'To All Clyde Workers'.[61] Not only did it have a chance, but it was attacked from within Whitehall for not taking it up; nevertheless, for whatever reason, it took no action. It seems perverse, therefore, to suggest that the suppression of the *Forward*, which had no direct connection with the C.W.C., *was* aimed at that body. If the suppression of the *Forward* was part of a plot against the C.W.C., why did the Ministry suppress a paper the C.W.C. did not support,[62] and not suppress a paper the C.W.C. did support — its own journal, the *Worker*? The *Worker* of 8th January reprinted *Forward's* report of the Christmas Day meeting *in toto*, but it was not suppressed for this, although a copy is in the Ministry archives. As the official history notes, 'the first three numbers did not bring the paper within the grasp of the law'.[63] It is true that the authorities did suppress the *Vanguard* which *was* a militant paper. But they came upon the *Vanguard* purely by accident, as it was being printed by the Civic Press, the associate company of the *Forward* which printed it as well as doing commercial and trade union printing. The suppression of the *Forward* was decided on before it was raided;[64] that of the *Vanguard* not until afterwards:

> It is urged that this paper [*Vanguard*] should be forthwith suppressed as its advanced proofs were found on the premises of a paper already suppressed and indicate a more advanced attack on diluted labour etc. On grounds of consistency alone, it would be undesirable to leave 'Vanguard' alone as it weakens the justification of the suppression of the 'Forward'.[65]

The date of the military warrant suppressing the *Vanguard* was not until 8th January.[66]

Was the Press Bureau incident part of a campaign against the C.W.C?

[It was] the more remarkable that the *Forward* should not have received the Press Bureau's instructions about the St. Andrew's Hall meeting (which Johnston would presumably have obeyed) and that the incident of the suppression should have occurred at all . . . it is impossible to say definitely what was improvised, what planned; to say, for example, whether the Press Bureau's oversight was deliberate or not.[67]

Whatever it was, it was certainly not an oversight. Beveridge saw that

the only weak point in the case [for proceeding against *Forward* under Regulation 27] is that the Press Bureau Notice requesting that no account of the meeting be published other than the official report (apparently on principle) was not sent to the *Forward* so that they had no official warning against publication.[68]

The Press Bureau, he continued, 'feel that they cannot safely send their instructions to that paper', and a glance at the contents of the notice sent out on 24th December will show why they should have felt this way. The Press Bureau could not send documents of this sort to newspapers it did not trust; so, paradoxically, it was they who received no warning against publishing unauthorised reports. This was no conspiracy, but a blunder in the system of organising news censorship — a blunder brought about by the attempt to keep censorship voluntary. The Press Bureau neither had nor sought legal powers for its directives, and was reluctant to use the powers it did have to censor publications under Section 27 of D.O.R.A., because it was framed in terms so vague as to be virtually unworkable.[69]

On this matter Johnston's tone of injured innocence is misleading. Despite his denials, he did know about the circular, as he admitted many years later:

. . . when Mr Lloyd George's officers, upon a famous controversial occasion in which I was implicated, ordered the press to print only a bowdlerised and fictitious account of a St. Andrew Hall oration, it was from the *Herald* office that there was slipped out to me an original of the ukase, as evidence of deliberate misleading of the public through attempted news corruption.[70]

Brotherstone's surmise that Johnston would 'presumably have obeyed' the Press Bureau circular if only he had known about it is thus badly off the mark. He also argues, however, that the *Forward* was suppressed for as long as it was, until the issue dated 5th February 1916 ('It is curious that so deferential an offender should have been punished for so long'[71]), because the Government needed time to perfect their machinery for smashing the C.W.C. Unfortunately, there is no evidence that either the Ministry or its Dilution Commissioners were interested in smashing the C.W.C. until after 5th February. Up until then, they had more obdurate enemies on their hands, and the only initiative which had been taken against the C.W.C. — the suppression of the *Worker* — had no immediate sequel.

If the argument that the suppression of the *Forward* was part of a plot against the C.W.C. fails, it might seem that we are forced back on the traditional explanation — that the suppression was an unfortunate reaction to the blow Lloyd George's pride had suffered. But this is as unsatisfactory as the opposite extreme viewpoint. Among other things, it is not easy to reconcile with the fact that the Press Bureau circular was issued on 24th December — *before* the St. Andrew's Halls meeting, a point made by none of the modern authorities who discuss the incident.[72] Certainly it could be argued that Lloyd George was able to seize on the circular as an excuse for the suppression. But we have to decide why the circular should have been sent out in the first place.

In fact, the suppression was a blunder, but not an accident; the *Forward* case was inextricably tied up with the dilution campaign. We should remember that the suppression was specifically authorised by a meeting attended by all the political and administrative heads of the Ministry.[73] Beveridge, Llewellyn Smith and Addison were not Lloyd George's yes-men. They authorised the suppression because they felt that the report of Lloyd George's meeting was very damaging to the dilution campaign — as it surely was. As Beveridge commented in his notes on the suppression:

> . . . (2) The question of *Forward* is, of course, bound up with the general unrest on the Clyde.
>
> (3) That the action taken in the past by the Government in regard to the appointment of Lord Balfour's Committee of inquiry and in regard to the imprisoned shipwrights has been interpreted as concessions wrung by force from weakness, and the same interpretation will undoubtedly be placed upon many of the concessions of the Munitions of War Act.[74]

The Ministry, in other words, had so often been criticised for weakness and appeasement that it must put up a stance of resistance at some point. The only part of Lloyd George's speech on the suppression which can be justified by any reference to any *bona fide* quotation from the *Forward* is the section in which he condemned the paper for its editorial agreement with Kirkwood's stance on dilution:

> The dilution of labour without the workers controlling the workshops will speedily mean a permanent deterioration in the working class standard of life.[75]

For some months the *Forward* had been bringing to the attention of the Glasgow working class comments on dilution which were not intended to be read by them. For instance, it twice[76] reprinted these comments from the *Scottish Law Courts Record*:

> In regard to our workers, whatever the unions may do, and notwithstanding any paper guarantee given, employment can and will never be the same again. The inevitable operation of the law of supply and demand must bring more women and girls into the ranks of our workers. It is only by means of this freedom to hire cheaper labour that our manufacturers can hope either to capture or to keep some of the German markets in low-priced goods of large and widespread sale.

This was to raise the sort of bogey about the worthlessness of the Restoration of Pre-war Practices Act which Macassey was later to find one of the 'common-form objections' always raised by the 'Socialist element' against dilution.[77] That this sort of opinion should be canvassed by the 'papers read by the more thoughtful workmen'[78] was, of course, very inconvenient for the dilution campaign. But, as W. C. Anderson pointed out a moment after Lloyd George's speech in the debate on the suppression:

> That may be entirely foolish and entirely wrong, but it is not a matter for criminal proceedings or for the suppression of a newspaper.[79]

The Ministry had suppressed the paper for statements hurtful to the dilution campaign, but the only *bona fide* ground it had for doing so rested on Beveridge's interpretation of Regulation 27: that a report likely to cause disaffection to His Majesty rendered a paper liable to suppression even if true. What was left of the liberal conscience would have revolted so emphatically if this bold interpretation were laid before the Commons that some evasion would have to be made. Beveridge might regard the whole business with distaste; but he was implicated in the original decision which placed the Ministry in such an awkward dilemma. Perhaps it was ultimately to Lloyd George's credit that the smokescreen of lies and total irrelevancies about Regulation 42 which he threw up succeeded in obscuring the real issue.

6

The Progress of Dilution,
January-February 1916

In the new year, the pace quickened because the Ministry was at last determined to enforce dilution. Its counter-attack coincided with the Military Service Bill. Conscription was a potentially powerful new source of grievance: Glasgow Trades Council sonorously resolved that it was 'dangerous to the stability of the nation, and totally opposed to the principles of British Freedom, and . . . will lead to serious social and industrial trouble in this district'.[1] This prophecy was inaccurate, but the Military Service Bill did make many engineers, already worried about dilution, even more uneasy because they feared it would open the way to industrial conscription. For some people, dilution enforced by military discipline was an even worse prospect than death in Flanders.

The ground for the counter-attack had been laid by the Munitions of War (Amendment) Act and the new Defence of the Realm regulations. The attack itself was planned in the Ministry, influenced but not determined by advice coming in from Paterson and Weir. Paterson wrote Llewellyn Smith a 'Strictly Personal' letter on 17th January[2] which very candidly opened with the names of 'the gentlemen whose removal from the Clyde district for an indefinite period would go a long way towards helping production'. The list started with Kirkwood — the most important in Paterson's view — and ended with a misspelt John MacLean, who, Paterson thought, could be deported without provoking a strike. Paterson then continued, changing his mind as he wrote, by saying that any deportations should wait until there was a 'very much cleaner issue', namely 'a strike against the enforcement of the dilution of labour'.

Meanwhile, Weir was raring for just such a fight. He sent Lloyd

George a detailed scheme starting with a Prime Ministerial statement on the need for dilution (of which he thoughtfully provided a draft). Then a Commissioner would be appointed (Weir suggested C. F. Rey, one of the Ministry Under-Secretaries) who would visit each large plant in turn to lay down the law.

When he saw the shop stewards, for instance, he would tell them that they

> as Trade Union officials, are responsible for making the scheme a success . . . A shorthand writer will be in attendance and any expression of open resistance or obstruction on the part of any individual should be carefully noted with the name of the man concerned.[3]

If a strike started, Weir suggested a flurry of strong action: an immediate summons under the Act;[4] the arrest of any striking shop steward who attended the dilution meeting; and

> a careful watch by detectives on the actions of members of the Clyde Workers' Committee and the few others specified on a private list (Scotland Yard men).[5]

If this was ineffective and the strike spread, Weir suggested, among much else, the suspension of the Trades Disputes Act, military guards at works, and the proclamation of martial law whenever any rioting broke out.

Weir's biographer claimed admiringly that this scheme was the 'prime cause of the strike-breakers' success'.[6] Others[7] have accepted the claim but without the admiration. Both sides are wrong, however. The Ministry style was more urbane than Weir's; more the siege of Vicksburg, less the charge of the Light Brigade. Arguably a programme as draconian as Weir's would have been the only thing that *could* have produced revolution on Clydeside in January 1916. A great deal of resistance had to be broken down before confrontation could be risked, as advisers like Macassey and Paterson pointed out. Llewellyn Smith's own plan for the campaign, although firm, did not have the elaborate detail of Weir's scheme, which would certainly have provoked strikes:

1) Get out definite instructions as to dilution.
2) See that the Police and Military preparations are sufficient.
3) Prepare a statement to be made by the Prime Minister as soon as any stoppage is threatened.
4) In case of a strike, have no parleying or negotiation with the strikers, either directly or through the Labour Advisory Committee.
5) Report and bring to trial under the Defence of the Realm Regulations any person inciting to strike.[8]

In a minute (accompanying a memorandum which has not survived), Rey wrote to Lloyd George:

> Since this memorandum was prepared I have had some conversation on the subject with Mr. Weir and Mr. Paterson, and they are in full agreement with the principle suggested, namely that a selection of firms should be made and dilution insisted on in these Works. When taking any such action as suggested, plans must be laid very carefully as to the whole procedure in order that the thing may be carried out on well-thought-out lines quickly and firmly so as to give no time for opposition to be engineered.
>
> That there may be trouble whenever this is done is quite likely but I think that the extent and gravity of this trouble will be diminished in proportion as the measures taken are strong and comprehensive from the very start.[9]

On 19th January Addison recorded:

> We had a long conference this morning on the subject of Glasgow and provisionally arranged a scheme of operation with a good man, if we can find one, to act as chief advisor there to direct operations. I am sure we need one who is not dominated by Board of Trade traditions or by employers' prejudices.[10]

The final programme was based on Weir's memorandum 'with modifications'.[11] The modifications cut out Weir's excesses, which sprang from his undying hostility to craft unionism, but by and large the Ministry used the framework provided by Weir's memorandum, which ran along lines already[12] proposed at the Ministry. The Prime Minister's statement was eventually made on 21st January, in response to a prearranged Parliamentary question: as the employers and trade unions had agreed 'loyally' to support dilution,

> The Government accordingly propose to take steps to bring about this dilution of labour wherever needed in accordance with the necessities of the situation and on the conditions laid down after agreement with the representatives of the workmen in the Munitions of War Act, as amended, without further delay . . . (T)hey are sending special representatives to the most important districts to assist in giving effect to their policy.[13]

The Commissioners were appointed on the following day. Lloyd George had wanted Lynden Macassey appointed sole Commissioner, but after objections by Addison and Macnamara this number was changed at the last minute to three,[14] Macassey being joined by Isaac Mitchell and by Sir Thomas Munro, Clerk to the Lanarkshire County Council and later Sheriff of Lanarkshire.

An important difference between Weir's draft and the memorandum adopted was the line drawn in the Ministry between strikers and those who incited others to strike. The scheme suggested that measures under the Defence of the Realm Act should be taken against those who incited to strike, but that

> Prosecution of the strikers themselves under the Munitions of War Act would not be undertaken as a matter of course, but with regard to the circumstances of the case, and in particular to the size of the strike. If the strike is a general one, it may have to be left to take its own course.[15]

This shows the appreciation in the Ministry that the Commissioners would have to proceed with a mixture of firmness and tact: firmness, because of all the accusations of unwarrantable appeasement that had been thrown about; but also tact, because even the new provisions on imprisonment did not cover the case of the large strike. Furthermore, the Commissioners knew, or soon found out, that they had two quite different groups to deal with — the conservatives at Lang's covertly supported by the A.S.E. Executive and the militants at Parkhead, Weir's and elsewhere. The militants were, if anything, easier to beat than the conservatives, but we shall have to treat them separately.

The trouble at Lang's derived from Circular L2, which some Ministry officials had recognised as a potential troublemaker from the very beginning. It will be remembered that the L series of circulars were drafted by the Central Munitions Labour Supply Committee, and the first draft of the contentious section of L2 came from a sub-committee of that committee. It ran:

> 1) Where women are employed on time the minimum rate shall be £1 per week. . . . A. Except in the case of women employed in the place of skilled men, in which case women shall be paid the same rates as skilled men.[16]

Askwith immediately wrote to Beveridge:

> Note A is very objectionable. It goes beyond the guarantee in the Munitions of War Act. 'Skilled work' is not defined, and will give endless trouble . . . I might warn you that this general demand is the work of the A.S.E. who have worked in ['on'?] Miss Macarthur,[17] but the A.S.E.'s object is not to get women in, but to ensure getting them easily out as soon as possible, and probably keeping them out, as far as possible, and the Workers' Union view the plot with disfavour and may prove troublesome if not consulted . . . this letter is private.[18]

Beveridge wrote back:

> I agree with you in being a good deal frightened of Note A . . . I shall try and get the Committee to make some change . . . As regards the proposal generally I share your own apprehension lest it may be intended rather to keep women out than to bring them in. I believe that Miss Macarthur is not altogether satisfied with the proposal.[19]

However, the objectionable note A stayed in. The final form of the relevant section of L2 ran as follows:

> Women of 18 years of age and over employed on time, on work customarily done by men, shall be rated at £1 per week . . .
>
> This, however, shall not apply in the case of women employed on work customarily done by fully-skilled tradesmen, in which case the women shall be paid the time rates of the tradesmen whose work they undertake.[20]

This need not have been too serious if one of the A.S.E.'s 'blackmailing conditions'[21] had not been that L2 and L3 be made mandatory as a condition of their agreement to dilution. At the end of the stormy conference between the A.S.E. Executive, Asquith and Lloyd George on 31st December 1915, the Executive resolved:

> That we . . . having heard the statements and pledges of the Prime Minister and the Minister of Munitions, decide to accept on behalf of the Conference and membership of the Society the scheme of dilution, and to co-operate actively therein, provided that the Government pledge itself to incorporate in the [Munitions of War (Amendment)] Bill the power to enforce the rates of pay and conditions of labour as set out in document L3 as well as L2 in controlled establishments.[22]

Clause 6 of the Act empowered the Minister to give orders as to women's wages, and Clause 7 as to those of unskilled and semi-skilled men. And the men at Lang's who in 1915 had been able to fight dilution altogether and under any circumstances, retreated in 1916 to the narrower, but still effective, front of opposing it by a special interpretation of L2.

In pursuance of their policy of tackling plants one by one, starting with the important or controversial cases, the Commissioners invited Lang's to produce a dilution scheme. Immediately a dispute arose over the interpretation of L2, the men claiming that the words 'on work customarily done by fully-skilled tradesmen . . . the women shall be paid the time-rates of the tradesmen whose work they undertake' implied that women must be paid the full time rate whenever they undertook any part of what was previously tradesmen's work. It is perfectly clear that chivalry was not the motive power behind this interpretation; the idea was to make sure that management would save no money by employing women, and that therefore they would not bother. The dispute was referred to the Ministry, and Llewellyn Smith ruled that a woman was not as of right immediately entitled to a skilled man's wages,

inasmuch as she is not performing in its entirety the work customarily done by
skilled men.[23]

On 1st February the Organising District Delegate of the A.S.E.
informed the Ministry that the Paisley District Committee of the
A.S.E. refused to accept the Ministry's interpretation; whereat the
Lang's men struck. When the Ministry approached the A.S.E. Executive
asking them to attend an interview, they refused to do so immediately,
on the grounds that they themselves did not accept the Ministry's
interpretation of L2 and that they had not been consulted over the
setting up of the Clyde Dilution Commission.[24]

In the event the Lang's men went back to work on 7th February, but
the A.S.E. Executive's attitude produced an angry response from both
the Ministry and the employers. It also caused a split among the three
Commissioners.

The Ministry regarded the A.S.E.'s action as yet another betrayal. 'It
is regrettable in the extreme,' wrote Macassey on the 5th February, 'that
circumstances did not admit of holding the A.S.E. to their undoubted
bargain.'[25] The employers' response was similar; on the 8th they sent
the following telegram to Llewellyn Smith:

> At a largely attended meeting of the North-West Engineering Employers held
> today from a report submitted the meeting learned that Ministry of Munitions is
> discussing with A.S.E. interpretation of L2 in face of official interpretation already
> furnished to Dilution Commissioners in Lang's case. Meeting protests most
> strongly against such negotiations and points out that to resile in any degree from
> interpretation already given by Ministry will render further progress with Dilution
> absolutely impracticable.[26]

A meeting was already pending with the A.S.E. Executive, and
Llewellyn Smith noted, on receipt of this telegram, that it should take
place 'as soon as possible'.[27]

In fact, the negotiations over L2 with the A.S.E. Executive dragged
on for a full two months more. A first meeting appears to have been
held on, or shortly after, the 11th, when yet another issue had to be
settled immediately. Macassey had wired:

> With reference to Paterson's conversation with you last night as to Bunton,
> District Secretary Engineers seeing his Executive London, am just informed by
> Bunton that he cannot take any further part in accompanying commissioners to
> works on Dilution until matters are settled with the Executive in London . . .
> Think it imperative therefore you arrange immediately that Executive adjusts
> matters with Bunton.[28]

Beveridge added, reporting a supplementary telephone call from Macassey:

> It is clear that in view of the lack of support by the EC, Mr. Bunton, who is anxious to help the Commissioners, feels a difficulty in doing so, and it is probable (though there is no direct evidence of this) that Mr. Bunton has had something in the nature of an instruction not to continue his assistance.[29]

This matter was cleared up but the interpretation of L2 had to wait till a further 'long and at times stormy'[30] deputation of the A.S.E. Executive with Lloyd George on 24th February. At the outset of the proceedings Brownlie complained:

> Your interpretation strikes at the root of the whole of our existence as skilled craftsmen.

But Lloyd George countered this by pointing out that the Ministry's interpretation of L2 had been favoured by one of the A.S.E.'s own members, David Kirkwood at Beardmores.

> *The Minister.* He more or less represents the men down at Beardmores. He fought very hard.
> *Mr. Button.* It was his suggestion?
> *The Minister.* Yes. He argued it before the Commissioners and carried the Commissioners with him.

Lloyd George went on to paraphrase Kirkwood's proposal:

> 'If you are going to split this operation it means that the men who are still retained there would be working harder, and do more difficult work than they had done before': which was true . . . 'If the heavier part of the work falls upon the men, then the heavier part of the wages ought to come to them'.[31]

Button argued that the Parkhead dilution agreement[32] 'came from . . . our side . . . [but] we have not up to this stage endorsed it'. But eventually Brownlie stated that his Society 'could now go forward with greater confidence to fulfil the promise they had made to Mr. Lloyd George and the Prime Minister'.[33] Addison and Llewellyn Smith apparently believed him. Addison noted, 'They were pretty obstinate, but LG did not give way at all on his interpretation, which is certainly a right and fair one'.[34] Llewellyn Smith dismissed a long complaint from Macassey about the A.S.E.'s interpretation with a scribble on the cover sheet. 'This is all dead now. H. Ll S. 26-2.'[35] But it wasn't. Mitchell reported on 6th March that the A.S.E. was still blithely insisting on its interpretation as part of an 'insidious attempt to retard and prevent dilution altogether'. He recommended 'the necessity for a frank acceptance of the Ministry of Munitions' interpretation of L2'; Addison commented in the margin, 'All right if the politicians will leave us alone. But will they?'[36] (Does this mean that Addison suspected that Lloyd George was about to give in to the A.S.E?) In the end 'our old friend L2',[37] as Addison called it, was not settled in favour of the Ministry until after yet another conference with the A.S.E. Executive on 27th April.

The dispute at Lang's had caused a split among the Commissioners. Mitchell, who claimed that the strike was in fact aimed at any sort of dilution (although he allowed that his colleagues took it at its face value), thought it an excellent opportunity for firm measures because 'Bunton and Brodie were against the men [as were] the Clyde Workers' Committee, and the great majority of the men themselves were ashamed of the stoppage'. The grounds on which his colleagues disagreed can no longer be known for certain. Perhaps they were more wary than Michell (an ex-A.S.E. official!) of the power of the A.S.E. Executive; perhaps they were waiting for a C.W.C.-inspired, preferably political strike, as Mitchell commented that 'my colleagues would prefer the fight on that issue rather than on "dilution"'.[38]

The Commissioners were very ambivalent in their attitude to the C.W.C. Often they regarded it as an ally against the real enemy — viz. Lang's men and the A.S.E. Executive. Mitchell thought it 'may be used for good if properly directed',[39] while Macassey boasted to Addison that he was 'managing' the A.S.E. by playing the C.W.C. off against them:

> He has inspired them [the A.S.E. Executive] with a horrible fear of what may happen on the Clyde if we recognise the Clyde Workers' Committee. As a result they have asked him privately to meet some of their chief men tomorrow.[40]

But Macassey was subject to violent changes of mood. For him the C.W.C. was not worth mentioning on 5th February, the root of all evil on 9th February, an ally again on 15th March, and the tool of the Germans on 22nd March.[41] But although the Commissioners (especially Macassey) could not make up their minds how to handle the C.W.C., their negotiations with them were in two important regards easier than those with the conservatives: the militants were internally divided, and they had nobody as powerful as the A.S.E. Executive at their back. Mitchell noted that the C.W.C. supported the local officials as against the Executive, but 'they raise obstacles on all sorts of vague issues'.[42] The militants were also sharply divided from plant to plant in their readiness to accept dilution.

Immediately on their appointment the Commissioners tackled some of the key plants, which included Parkhead and Weir's as well as Lang's. In Parkhead the men, led by Kirkwood, were very co-operative. According to Kirkwood's own couthy account, when he heard that the Commissioners came without a plan already prepared he exclaimed, 'Ye couldnae rin a menage[43] that way, let alane a war'.[44] We have already noted the dependence of Kirkwood on Wheatley as his literary and political manager. On this occasion he went to see Wheatley and (according to Kirkwood's son) Rosslyn Mitchell. Wheatley wrote out a draft scheme:

> Together we thrashed out the problem, and John Wheatley began to write. In thirty minutes he had drafted the scheme. It was a perfect piece of work.[45]

Wheatley's scheme was accepted by the Commissioners without alteration on 26th January, twenty-four hours after their first visit to Parkhead, as the best way to 'blow the Germans over the Rhine'.[46] The most important clauses were numbers 1 and 2:

> 1. That the income of the new class of labour be fixed not on the sex, previous training, or experience of the worker, but upon the amount of work performed, every effort being made to secure the maximum output.
> 2. That a committee appointed by the skilled workers be accepted by the employers with power to see this arrangement is loyally carried out.[47]

One or two points arise from this agreement. According to the A.S.E.'s evidence given to the Labour Party committee which inquired into the Kirkwood case, the scheme was accepted by the A.S.E. on 29th January 1916, with the exception of Clause 1 which 'appears to have been modified or superseded later on'[48] when it was replaced by the standard terms of L2 and L3. Kirkwood's scheme made it quite clear that women were to be paid *pro rata* for the amount of the tradesman's job they did, and not the full tradesman's rate come what might. For this Kirkwood was to be commended (had he but known it) by Lloyd George in his interview with the A.S.E. on 24th February.[49] Clauses 1 and 2 of the Parkhead scheme, taken together, had virtually the same meaning as Llewellyn Smith's interpretation of L2:[50] women were to be paid *pro rata*, and the tradesmen were to have a say in the proportion of the skilled men's rate they were to get. The A.S.E. Executive, however, still did not accept this, as they continued to argue that it was a thin end of a wedge aimed at ousting the craftsman from his special status altogether. Accordingly, it was in their interest to restore L2, over which it was still possible to argue, in place of the unambiguous clarity of Wheatley's Clause 1.

Although the Parkhead scheme was drawn up on 26th January (a date for which we have the authority of the Labour Party report and a memorandum by Macassey),[51] it could not be put into force immediately. As an employer, Beardmore was as conservative as Weir was aggressive, and no preparations had been made for the change: as Macassey complained, nothing had happened at the time of his writing 'after the most difficult negotiations with the men' because 'no accommodation [is] available at the moment for women workers'.[52] The first women to come to Parkhead did not arrive until 29th February.[53]

This may help to explain a knotty problem of chronology: the delay in the public reaction to the Parkhead scheme. It was not reported in the Press until 12th February, and Gallacher quite clearly states that he and his C.W.C. colleagues did not hear of it until *after* his release from prison on bail.[54] This did not happen until 8th February. Certainly, the earliest known C.W.C. reaction — a rival dilution scheme — is dated 15th February,[55] so we must assume that news of the Parkhead scheme did not become public till then.

The Ministry had been expecting very rapid results from the dilution scheme. Weir's proposals had envisaged that each individual scheme would be settled within three days, and the whole Clyde district covered in a matter of a week or ten days.[56] Accordingly, the Ministry became concerned at the delay, and on 5th February Macassey wrote a long memorandum accounting for the slowness of proceedings. There were two difficulties, the employers and the men. His instructions, he wrote, 'assumed as indeed I myself inferred that the principal employers were both ready and able forthwith to accept dilution. It now appears that it is not so.'[57] The employers' attitude included elements of obstructiveness and elements of sheer incompetence. They were not prepared to help in introducing dilution, or they thought it could not be done, or if they were ready to help, then, like Beardmore, they had made no proper preparations.

On the men's side, Macassey wrote, the Commissioners at first encountered a rigid hostility to any sort of dilution. On Macassey's recommendation, the Commission deliberately avoided confrontation. Pressing dilution with schemes which were imperfect because of the employers' failings

> would have meant a more or less general strike on the Clyde against the principle of dilution, as distinct from a local strike against the details only of a particular

scheme, the principle being accepted. Having regard to the very lukewarm recommendation of dilution by the A.S.E. Executive to their local branches I have no hesitation whatever in saying that course would have wrecked dilution on the Clyde.

Instead, the Commissioners visited the works one by one, listening to the men's point of view. Although the men's opinion on the desired details of dilution 'varies amazingly', nevertheless 'the Socialist element have always two common-form and popular objections'. The first of these was that the Government might, before the end of the war, revoke its promise to pass a Restoration of Pre-War Practices Act; the second, that by the end of the war

women will . . . [have] become so proficient that the employers will after the Munitions Act has ceased to operate employ them at the lower wage than, and to the exclusion of, the skilled men.

Macassey outlined the arguments he used in combating these propositions, such as that post-war reconstruction would give work for everyone, and added somewhat plaintively:

If there is any better answer than the above it would be of the greatest service that I should be furnished with it.[58]

The memorandum met with broad approval in the Ministry. Llewellyn Smith minuted to Lloyd George:

Mr. Lynden Macassey defends . . . [the Commission] against the charge of slowness. I am bound to say that he makes out a good case in my opinion, and though evidently dilution will be slower on the Clyde than we originally expected, the first great difficulties have been surmounted . . . evidently the employers are a good deal to blame for the delay, due to their unreadiness.[59]

To Macassey, Llewellyn Smith wrote back in fairly strong terms:

I own that I am surprised that even the Clyde employers should have been so lethargic as to have made virtually no preparation for the introduction of women after the repeated warnings, exhortations and directions addressed to them. However, we must take both the workmen and the employers as they are.[60]

In the meantime, however, the Commissioners had taken the first step aimed directly at the militants. This was the suppression of the C.W.C.'s paper, *The Worker*, for an article entitled 'Should the Workers Arm?' in the fourth issue, on 29th January. The most cursory reading of the article shows that the answer the writer implied to his own question was 'No', but this did not for a moment deter the Commissioners:

It is undeniable that many of the more thoughtful among the toilers would consider their lives had not been spent in vain if they could organise their comrades to drilled and armed rebellion. Their minds turn pleasurably in the direction of rifles, bombs, and dynamite.

If the internal clash of armed forces can be avoided in this country it should be avoided. There is another method which, if conducted on a thorough scale, should prove completely successful. A worker's labour-power is his only wealth . . . [the article continues by advocating non-violent strike action].[61]

On 7th February, Gallacher, Muir, and Walter Bell, the printer of *The Worker*, were arrested and charged with attempting to cause sedition. The Commissioners had initially wanted to have them deported, but the Lord Advocate preferred a trial by jury.[62] A few days earlier John MacLean had also been arrested on sedition charges. On the 9th Macassey sent in another memorandum to the Ministry covering these events. It differs markedly in tone from the one sent only four days earlier; agitated where the other radiates quiet confidence, it makes mention for the first time of the C.W.C. as a serious threat to order:

It is ostensibly a Socialist Organisation if indeed it is not something worse . . .

I have been convinced for some days that the only effective way of handling the situation is to strike a sharp line of cleavage between the loyal workmen, who undoubtedly comprise the great majority of Munition Workers, and the disloyal Socialist minority who are pawns of the Clyde Workers Committee, and those, whoever they may be, behind the Committee. The means of effecting this was wanting until yesterday February 8th.[63]

This memorandum has been understandably, but wrongly, taken as evidence that the Commissioners aimed throughout at crushing the C.W.C.[64] But they had been relaxed about the C.W.C. earlier, and were to be so again later. Mitchell never shared Macassey's repressive vigour on the days when he was vigorous. On 31st January, Macassey had advised Addison against prosecuting MacLean, although he had favoured suppressing *The Worker*.[65] And the C.W.C. could be an ally, as the Parkhead dilution agreement showed.

As it happened, the 'sharp line of cleavage' was not really provided. The Glasgow Trades Council thought the Commissioners' action most provocative: in forwarding to the Government a resolution of protest about John MacLean,

the Secretary was instructed to draft a letter to be sent with this resolution, pointing out that discontent and dissatisfaction had been created among the workers by these arrests during the past week, and to refer to the arrest of Gallacher, Muir and Bell in connection with the 'Worker'.[66]

Discontent and dissatisfaction, however, proved to be very easily containable. The arrest provoked strikes in a number of C.W.C.-controlled factories: Weir's, Coventry Ordnance Works, Beardmores (Dalmuir), John Brown, Albion Motors, and Barr & Strouds — the last two being respectively Gallacher's and Muir's workplaces.[67] There was one notable absentee from this list. Parkhead did not strike:

> those who had struck returned to work, leaving a feeling, not very pronounced, but nevertheless there — that Parkhead under Kirkwood's leadership had not played its part.[68]

However, the strike did not last long enough for the Commissioners to take action; the accused men were released on bail, and the men returned to work. Macassey gives a perverse interpretation of the circumstances:

> During the day of February 8th, the men began to understand that they were out on strike in sympathy with men who advocated the policy of bombs and dynamite. Such a picture a quite considerable number of those on strike were not prepared to endorse.[69]

This interpretation is accepted, and reproduced almost verbatim, in the official history[70] in spite of its manifest variance with the facts. The writer in *The Worker* was precisely opposing the use of bombs and dynamite in the picture-book continental revolutionary fashion. Nevertheless, the incident foreshadowed the events of March 1916 insofar as it suggested difficulty in encouraging any strikes which went beyond the industrial aspects of dilution and conscription. (Gallacher, Muir and Bell were not brought to trial until 14th April, after the deluge. For the record, we may note here that Gallacher and Muir were then sentenced to twelve months' imprisonment each and Bell to three months.)

Parkhead had let the side down by not striking over *The Worker* arrests; but the recriminations did not really start to fly until news broke of the Parkhead dilution scheme. For the third and most serious time, it seemed, Kirkwood had broken the C.W.C.'s solidarity and had shown quite clearly that his attitudes were based not on revolutionary industrial unionism, nor yet on socialist pacifism, but simply on getting the most favourable terms attainable for his members in the dilution scheme, and securing for them the maximum control attainable over the introduction of unskilled labour.

Gallacher complained:

> In the course of our talk with Kirkwood he declared he was concerned with

Parkhead alone and as this agreement had safeguarded the Parkhead workers he was satisfied. This statement went circulating around the Clyde and caused incalculable harm.[71]

The solidarity of the Clyde Workers' Committee having been broken, and the chance of general strike action having been lost, each militant had to look after his constituency as Kirkwood had looked after his, and ensure that the system of dilution that was adopted gave the maximum achievable degree of control by the skilled engineers over the 'Diluting Units' — the phrase of the Shop Stewards' Convener at Barr and Strouds, who went on to explain:

> It was in the first months of 1916 that Dilution was first spoken of. The Firm approached the Shop Stewards, with a view to negotiate Dilution with them direct and thus avoid having the Commissioners interfering in the business. Recognising that the Unions had accepted the principle of Dilution, we had perforce to accept the situation, and make the best possible terms with the firm.[72]

Gallacher did the same in his own workplace, Albion Motors.[73]

Eventually the C.W.C. produced a scheme of its own for dilution, and gave it to the Commissioners. Macassey sent a copy to Beveridge, who circulated it in the Labour Department of the Ministry. Addressed to the Commissioners, it is preceded by a preamble, the conclusion of which is quoted followed by a number of the clauses:

> . . . Our suspicion that under the cloak of patriotism cheap labour will slip in arises from the fact that, naturally, cheap labour is welcomed by the employers. Now, if you are desirous of protecting us by keeping up the price of our labour, we submit the following as a reasonable working basis:
>
> *Conditions of the Dilution Scheme Recommended by the Clyde*
> *Workers' Committee*
>
> 1) That the income of the new class of labour be fixed, not on the sex, previous training, or experience of the workers, but on the amount of work performed, based on the rates presently obtaining for the particular operation, also that they obtain the district rate.
>
> 2) That a committee appointed by the workers be accepted by the employers with powers to see that this arrangement is loyally carried out . . .
>
> 9) Everyone who enters a shop as a result of dilution MUST be organised in some Union to be decided on by the Shop Committee . . .
>
> 10) It will be understood that the foregoing rules are only principles that can apply to all shops. The shops themselves decide on all detail arrangements . . .
>
> 12) . . . (c) That every second diluted Unit should be an apprentice of three years standing and to receive the district rate.[74]

This interesting document clearly borrows extensively from the Parkhead Dilution Agreement, which had brought such calumny down upon Kirkwood's head only a few days earlier. Clauses 1 to 4 are identical, apart from the last proviso of the C.W.C.'s clause 1; and, apart from that proviso, the document supports the Ministry interpretation of L2 and not the A.S.E. one.

But the C.W.C. was more ambivalent, and closer to Lang's and the A.S.E., than Kirkwood or Wheatley. 'Also that they obtain the district rate' in their clause 1 contradicts the rest of it; and clause 12c would have protected the skilled men almost as well as if dilution were not brought in at all.

Nothing, however, came of this scheme. The C.W.C. accompanied it by a request to meet the Commissioners, which they turned down on the grounds that members of the C.W.C. were all Trade Unionists and schemes were being duly discussed with the properly authorised officials of the Trade Unions.[75] They forbore to add that it was scarcely their job to 'protect' C.W.C. members by 'keeping up the price of their labour'. Nevertheless, the militants had been put in their place for the time being.

7

The Crisis, March 1916

For three or four weeks Clydeside was peaceful. The flurry of activity over the suppression of *The Worker* had subsided, and no further steps were taken to extirpate the C.W.C. as dilution proceeded steadily. The next (and as it turned out last) storm blew up in the middle of March, but the seeds of discontent were sown in Parkhead Forge at the beginning of the month.

Because of the unpreparedness of the management, the first women dilutees did not arrive at Parkhead until 29th February. When they did, Kirkwood appeared at the department they were working in to introduce himself ('Of course, you will know who I am, but if you don't you soon will'[1]) and the shop steward who was in charge of the department in which they were to work. The following day, the latter asked the girls to join the National Federation of Women Workers. The Women's Welfare Superintendent complained to the works manager, who immediately banned Kirkwood from the women's section of the forge, telling him that his behaviour was an 'intolerable interference'[2] with the women. Kirkwood was most hurt, as he thought he had only been doing as he always did, and immediately resigned as convener of shop stewards (although this appears to have made no difference to his behaviour during the next fortnight — he continued, as spokeman and chief negotiator, to act as if he was still chief shop steward. 'Mr. Kirkwood, whom [we] met on a number of times', wrote the Dilution Commissioners, 'was a man of somewhat dominating constitutional authority').[3] A still heavier blow fell when on 14th March Kirkwood was invited by the manager of another department to investigate a dispute there, but was refused permission by the works manager:

> Mr. Kirkwood was evidently very much surprised and annoyed by this, as he had never before been denied such permission under any similar circumstances.[4]

On his reporting the circumstances to the shop stewards they decided (in Kirkwood's absence) to call a strike which began on 17th March when Beardmore refused to budge on granting any of the privileges claimed for the convener of shop stewards.

Was the revocation of Kirkwood's rights the start of a plan by Beardmore and/or the Commissioners to crush the C.W.C?[5] An interview with an eye-witness, and some newly available documents, dispose me to reject this view.[6]

Parkhead Forge, at this stage, was adapting from a 'traditional' to a 'rational' structure of authority — from *Gemeinschaft* to *Gesellschaft*. The expansion of 1910 onwards, accelerated by the war, brought in its train the end of the old regime, picturesquely described by Bell in his account of the problems of moving large castings from the forge:

> To bring the load to the main road . . . there was a steep incline[7] from the gate up the New Road (now Duke Street) to Parkhead Cross. When, as often happened, the horses got stuck, I have seen Isaac Beardmore come up to the Parkhead Cross, and call upon the workers who were to be found at the street corner to come and give assistance to the horses and haul at a rope. Once on the straight road the men and Beardmore would adjourn to the corner public-house, and all engage in drinks at Isaac's expense.[8]

Within that sort of structure of authority there was no room for trades unionism, and as we noted in Chapter 1, Kirkwood had been excluded from Parkhead Forge for many years after the 1897 lock-out for his trade union activities. It was not until shortly after the beginning of the war, after a strenuous campaign in which Kirkwood had played a large part,[9] that trades unionism was recognised at the forge. As the Labour Party's Report on the Kirkwood case put it,

> Messrs William Beardmore & Co. Ltd. had strongly opposed the amalgamated Society some years previously, and had only made their place a 'Union Shop' about three months after the commencement of the war.[10]

The actual date of the agreement signed between Beardmore and the A.S.E. and Toolmakers was 29th October 1914. It ran:

> 1) that so far as the company find it possible trade-unionist men alone will be started in their machine shops in Parkhead.
> 2) that whenever the company is in want of workmen in the said shops, the shop stewards representing the said societies shall be offered an opportunity to assist in filling the vacancies.[11]

Thus at one stroke Parkhead had swung from being a non-union shop to being a closed-shop or at least an 'agency shop'. This may seem strange until account is taken of the continued paternalism involved in the arrangement. The attitude of Beardmore may be usefully contrasted with Glasgow's other great engineering employer, William Weir. While Beardmore, having once given in to the trade unionists, was prepared to co-operate with the craftsmen in regulating the supply of labour, Weir was opposed, root and branch, to all the traditions of craft unionism. We saw in Chapter 1 how one of the men's grievances in the February 1915 strike was the aggressive use by Weir of Taylorism: work-study, speeding-up, and bonus systems. And one of the written questions sent in to Lloyd George before the Christmas Day meeting was from a Weir's engineer alleging that Weir had been exceeding and abusing the Treasury Agreement:

> this is no new matter as the firm of G. and J. Weir have been moving for 12 years in this matter . . . note work taken from turners since then: [a list of 13 operations follows]. Then do you wonder at the opposition?[12]

The attitude of Beardmore was very much more conservative and encouraged co-operation with the craftsmen. But as the war progressed, with increasing division of labour and vast expansion in wartime conditions, it became more and more difficult to run Parkhead Forge in the paternalistic master-and-servant pattern in which Beardmore and Kirkwood had previously done so. This excluded not only the trade union officials (which gave Kirkwood the spurious appearance of being an advanced unofficial militant) but also most of management. The Works Manager, Admiral Adair (Coalition Unionist M.P. for Shettleston, 1918-1922) appears to have cordially disliked Kirkwood[13] — though Kirkwood thought 'A finer man never came into the works, but he knew nothing about the men',[14] and by 1916 the whole of the new middle management was actively resenting the usurpation of their functions by an artisan.

The crisis of March 1916 was sparked off, it will be remembered, by the complaint by the Women's Welfare Superintendent against Kirkwood's appearance before her girls; she regarded his manner as 'very impertinent'[15] and took her complaint to one of the managers, a Mr. Chisholm. He had no reason to love Kirkwood, if Kirkwood's own account is to be believed, since Beardmore had rounded on him while making a *volte face* on trade union recognition:

> 'If there is any trouble [said Beardmore to Kirkwood] you will come to me. Don't you allow manager or anybody else to come between you and me. Let me know, and we'll sort it out. None but Trade Unionists will be employed at Parkhead from this time on', and he shouted, 'Do you hear that, Chisholm?'[16]

So when Chisholm received the complaint, he was doubtless very happy to act. Ultimately, the harmony of the works depended for Beardmore on a proper management structure, rather than relations with one individual workman, so Kirkwood had to go.

When the strike broke out on 17th March the men had two complaints. One was that 'Soldiers, mostly Englishmen, were brought in, and these refused to join a Trade Union. An agreement existed to the effect that all men employed must be Trade Unionists.'[17] The fear of industrial conscription being used to break up trades unionism clearly sharpened the point of this complaint. But the main *casus belli* was the restriction placed upon Kirkwood when he tried to investigate this grievance:

> We feel that during the period when unskilled labour is engaged in our industry more than ordinary freedom is required by our shop-stewards to ensure that under the cloak of patriotism greedy employers are not allowed to ruin our trade.[18]

From 21st March the Parkhead men were joined by strikers at the North British Diesel Engine Works, Whiteinch, and men in gun departments at Dalmuir and Weir's. This was represented by Macassey and Addison at the time and by the official historians writing some six years afterwards as a C.W.C. plan to impede production of munitions:

> Whether or not from the outset a deliberate plot had been formed to strike at the most vital work of the Ministry of Munitions, the guns and howitzers required for the great offensive of 1916, it cannot be doubted that as soon as the men at Parkhead came out the occasion was exploited to the full with that end in view . . . But so skilful was the organisation of the strike leaders that no clear evidence of incitement could be found against any of them . . . such was their [the C.W.C.'s] ascendancy that the men threw down their tools without asking or receiving a reason.[19]

Addison made a statement to the Commons on 28th March in which he said:

> At different times strikes have been brought about, sometimes on the most trivial grounds, by a self-appointed body known as the Clyde Workers' Committee. This committee . . . decided about a fortnight ago to embark on a policy of holding up the production of the most important munitions of war in the Clyde district, with the object, I am informed, of compelling the Government to repeal the Military Service Act and the Munitions of War Act and to withdraw all limitations upon increases of wages and strikes, and all forms of Government control. The present series of strikes commenced on the 17th March . . . From that time the series of strikes appears to have proceeded upon a systematic and sinister plan.[20]

This was the Government's defence of its action when on March 24th it deported from the Glasgow area Kirkwood, James Haggerty, Samuel Shields, and Robert Wainwright from Parkhead, and James Messer and Arthur MacManus from Weir's; on 28th March they were joined by three more Weir's shop stewards, Bridges, Kennedy and Glass. The Ministry had been considering two courses: prosecution under an appropriate D.O.R. Regulation, especially the new Regulation 42, or the deportation procedure under D.O.R. Regulation 14. Sir Edward Carson had the gall to ask Addison:

> May I ask if it has been considered that these men are not guilty of assisting the King's enemies and thereby are guilty of high treason?

to which Addison replied:

> Yes. The whole matter is being considered, and I may say that the method of deporting these men was resorted to in the first instance because a criminal trial would require an interval of six weeks or two months before it could be held, and it was felt that immediate action was necessary.[21]

(He failed to add that the Procurator-Fiscal had decided that there was not enough evidence for a prosecution under Regulation 42.)[22] The men were duly deported by the Competent Military Authority under D.O.R. Regulation 14.

The Cabinet discussed the deportation on 30th March, and the discussion was summarised in Lord Crewe's report to the King:

> A long conversation followed on the Clyde strike and the unrest prevalent among some of the workers there. It was shown that the principal danger of the situation depends not so much on the proceedings of the small (by comparison) number of workmen holding syndicalist views and revolutionary aims, as on the fear that the vastly larger body of patriotic and loyal trade unionists may be deluded by misrepresentation of the facts into expressing sympathy with the violent minority, believing them to be unjustly treated. Mr. Henderson offered to use his best efforts to enlighten his friends as to the true state of affairs, both at an important meeting which is being held in London this afternoon, and by going to Glasgow to confer with the leaders there; and the Cabinet felt that the business could not be left in better hands, while any further necessary explanations should be given in Parliament without delay.[23]

On the same day, 30th March, the Commons debated Addison's statement of two days earlier, and Addison was introduced to two members of the C.W.C. by Ramsay MacDonald.[24] The two members were Gallacher and Muir,[25] and they told Addison that the conspiracy he mentioned was non-existent. Addison's response was to make a sharp diversionary attack on W. M. R. Pringle and Ramsay MacDonald for introducing them.[26]

In 1916, as later in 1919, the Government and the revolutionaries were united in seeing far more revolutionary potential in the strike movement than actually existed. Gallacher claims that he did indeed try to broaden the Parkhead strike into a general one, as Addison alleged in his statement to the Commons. If so, he failed totally. Attempts to bring out Barr and Strouds, the majority of men at Weir's, and Fairfields foundered on the men's resentment at Kirkwood's earlier behaviour:

> Parkhead had broken the front. Parkhead could take the consequences. Such was the situation we were facing.[27]

It is not even clear whether Gallacher's claim that he tried to start a strike is true. J. T. Murphy alleges, quoting the C.W.C. evidence to the Labour Party enquiry on the Kirkwood case, that Gallacher ruled out of order a motion for a strike in sympathy with Parkhead 'as it was against the accepted aims of the C.W.C.'.[28]

It was thus patently absurd to talk, as Addison had, about a 'series of strikes (which) appears to have proceeded upon a systematic and sinister plan' towards the restriction of munitions production. Kirkwood, after all, had so far abandoned his earlier pacifism as to have offered his co-operation with the Dilution Commissioners in producing a plan for shell production at Parkhead:

> You want shells to blow the Germans over the Rhine . . . Then we will do all in our power to meet your requirements. We will produce the guns, the shells, and all other munitions. In twenty-four hours we will submit a scheme that will satisfy both sides. We will give the production and keep the engineers safeguarded.[29]

Who, on the Government side, believed in the myth that there was a C.W.C. plot? Initially, it seems, everybody — perhaps even Mitchell. Addison developed doubts very soon, but Macassey never did, and his version of events even percolated to the *History of the Ministry of Munitions*. The real trouble was that Macassey had started to sniff German spies. He had set up an intelligence section, of which he was very proud (and later violently objected to the Ministry's taking it over).[30] This started producing reports of German sympathisers at work on the Clyde. He forwarded these to Addison who believed them: 'He has traced direct payments from Germany to three workers and also discovered that . . . the man who is financing the Clyde workers . . . has a daughter married in Germany, a son married to a German and his chief business is in Germany. He is evidently on the track of a very successful revelation.[31] This may all, now, seem very childish; but it was written just before the Easter Rising. The Germans did help the Irish rebels (after a fashion); but there is not a scintilla of evidence that they helped the Clydeside rebels.

Addison began to change his mind quite soon after the deportations. On 3rd April he got a message from Mitchell that Albion Motors 'were making transport wagons, and it is not possible to connect the work with the Beardmore strike — at any rate on the information before us',[32] and on 11th April he dictated a letter to Macassey which passed on with very evident lack of enthusiasm — 'for what it is worth' — a rumour that 'German Roman Catholic priests who live in or near Glasgow are sources of trouble'.[33] The Commissioners' very thorough report on the case does not even mention any allegation of German gold or sabotage; but even so Addison complained to Macassey that the report was biased against Kirkwood and in favour of Beardmore.[34] Addison came to share the view of every labour body that 'This fairy tale is assuredly the product of someone's excited imagination';[35] by late April he was already telling an A.S.E. deputation that 'I do not think myself that I have been associated with anything I hated more'[36] than the deportations. Crocodile tears, perhaps; but it is probably significant that Addison deleted every single reference to spies, agitators and Germans when he prepared his March 1916 diaries for publication. By 1924 he believed that 'There was never any evidence' of German involvement.[37]

Macassey, though, was unrepentant. In June he was still telling the Ministry that the C.W.C. 'organised the regrettable strikes lasting from 17th March to 7th April 1916[38] in defiance of the evidence contained in his own report. And when he went into print in 1922, he had not changed his mind:

> Finally, the direct actionists matured their plans. It was a principle of theirs always to use the sharpest weapons. There was one immediately to hand. The army in France was in dire need of heavy howitzers to smash the system of trenches which the Germans had commenced to consolidate, Mesopotamia urgently required flat-bottomed barges . . . The direct actionists therefore brought out, or tried to bring out, on strike, the employees in every shop or yard where the howitzers or any part of the howitzers or the flat-bottomed barges were in course of construction with almost complete success, and with disastrous national results.[39]

If there was a plot on Clydeside between 17th March and 24th March, it emanated not from the C.W.C. but from the Commissioners. The Labour Party Committee on the affair, after reading the Commissioners' own report and interviewing the Competent Military Authority, expressed surprise at the part played by the Commissioners.[40] Instead of deporting the men, the Commissioners ought to have intervened to arbitrate in the normal way, and all the uproar would have been avoided. This, after all, was precisely the sort of procedure Macassey had spoken of, rather complacently, in his memorandum of 5th February, as the way to keep the temperature down.

So perhaps there was a plot. But history tells of more balls-ups than conspiracies. The most parsimonious explanation is that Macassey panicked, and for two weeks or so carried all before him in an atmosphere fraught with the excitement of the Irish rebellion and the conscription crisis. At various dates Mitchell, Addison, and the Cabinet returned to earth, but Macassey never did. Plot or no plot, the strike did not long survive the deportation of its leaders. On 29th March, thirty of the strikers were fined £5 each before Sheriff Fyfe in a General Munitions Tribunal. On 31st March, on Glasgow Green, there was a large peaceful demonstration supported by the Trades Council against the deportations and the refusal of the Committee on Production to raise wages.

But the men were drifting back to work, until by 5th April only thirty-three remained on strike: whereupon the Commissioners ordered Thomas Clark, who had succeeded Kirkwood as Treasurer of the C.W.C., to be deported at once, and threatened the same to any of the strikers who did not return the following day.[41] Fines totalling £230 were levied on the men who had stayed out until 4th April. But these draconian measures produced no reaction. Without their leaders, the men were not prepared to venture a political strike, or even one in protest against the treatment which had been meted out to their leaders. Workers' control over the conditions of the implementation of dilution had been achieved, even if the Kirkwood incident showed that it was not as complete as the workers thought. To continue to agitate would bring only heavy fines, more deportations, or imprisonment. In this crisis, the men were not prepared to follow their leaders from industrial over to political issues, and belied the trust which had been put in them by MacLean to start off 'the Political Strike so often resorted to on the Continent in times past' (above, Ch. 2).

8

Aftermath

The diminution of revolutionary fervour is well traced in successive meetings of the Glasgow Trades Council after March 1916. A number of delegates to the Trades Council were district officials of their unions, who tended to look askance at the unofficial and anti-bureaucratic operations of bodies like the C.W.C. James Messer, the secretary of the C.W.C., explained:

> The relations between the Committee and the Official Side of the Trade Unions may be taken as *Nil*. The officials have always been very much opposed to us, owing I believe to the open and frank manner in which we have severely criticised their action since the beginning of the War.[1]

Nevertheless the initial response of the Trades Council to the deportations was sharp:

> This Council representing the organised workpeople in the West of Scotland, anent the action of the Government in deporting several men from this district demands the return of these men in order that a basis of industrial peace may be established, and further requests the affiliated Societies and the Trade Union movement generally to take direct action in support of this protest.[2]

The Trades Council's own part in the direct action was to take the form of a massive demonstration to be addressed by Robert Smillie.[3] But the magistrates banned the demonstration,[4] and George Shanks, chairman of the Council, said that he would not chair a banned meeting. The full Council wanted to proceed, but its executive insisted on 'postponing' the demonstration. No more was heard about direct action for the deportees.[5]

The deportees themselves had been banned from the Glasgow munitions district but were otherwise free to seek work. They went initially to Edinburgh, where the Competent Military Authority responsible for them, Colonel Levita, interceded with firms not to refuse to employ them just because they were deportees.[6] Having got them out of Parkhead and Weir's, Levita and the Ministry behaved quite leniently to the deportees. Levita stipulated that they had not committed any offence, and Addison (perhaps already feeling guilty?) wanted them to be allowed back to Glasgow, at public expense, for twenty-four hours to arrange their affairs.[7]

Later, Arthur McManus went off to Manchester. David Kirkwood stayed in Edinburgh. According to his (or Wheatley's) account, he refused to take a job until he could get back to Glasgow. On 10th June, Wheatley reported that all the deportees were at work except Haggerty, who was looking for work, and Kirkwood: 'Kirkwood refuses to work until set free. The authorities are said to have adopted a threatening attitude towards him, but Davie's mind is made up.'[8] It is impossible to say whether Kirkwood was really refusing to work as a matter of principle, or whether, since employers were refusing to consider taking him on, he was able to put a gloss of political principle on a position where in reality he had no choice.

Arthur Henderson had offered to mediate at the Cabinet meeting of 30th March. This offer had been enthusiastically taken up because the Cabinet was uncomfortably aware that the whole dilution crisis from its beginnings up to that point had been handled with hardly any reference to Henderson, who had nominal responsibility for labour matters.[9] Speaking at the 1917 Labour Party Conference debate on the deportations, Henderson made perfectly clear his differences with the Government of which he was still a member:

> He could only say that the deportation was an administrative act, for which he had no responsibility, and on which he was not consulted. He wished to make that perfectly clear. He was no more responsible for some things done by the Government than some delegates were responsible for what other delegates said in the Conference. The position was this, that if a decision was taken without his being consulted, his responsibility only began after the decision had been taken and when it became an actual part of the Government policy. Then he had two alternatives. If he disapproved of that piece of policy he had the choice of sending in his resignation or remaining in and doing everything possible to modify the operation of that policy.[10]

Later, speaking in some exasperation, he said:

> He had been asked why he did not resign. He had already told them. If he had to resign he would be resigning every day to please some of them. He was not sure that he would not resign if he were to please himself, but he was not there either to please himself or them, he was there to see the War through.[11]

Even when all due allowances have been made for the nature and temper of the body Henderson was addressing, these statements certainly show a remarkable lack of warmth for his Cabinet colleagues. It was in recognition of this feeling that his colleagues had sought to mollify him at the Cabinet meeting on 30th March by welcoming his offer to mediate between the deportees and their union. Crewe wrote to Lloyd George on 3rd April:

> Between ourselves, Henderson told me some time ago that he felt rather out of it with his Committee[12] at your office, and I advised him to go and talk to Asquith, as the Jupiter who rules over all Government Committees . . . What you said at the last Cabinet will, I think, have smoothed things down.[13]

In his role as mediator, Henderson proposed to all the deportees, through the Parliamentary Committee of the S.T.U.C., that they 'should give an undertaking that if they returned they would not advocate any "down-tools" policy, and any grievances would be submitted through their Trade Union for redress'.[14] He had secured the agreement of the Ministry's National Labour Advisory Committee that if they signed the agreement the deportees should be allowed to return to Glasgow.[15] The S.T.U.C. interviewed them, and found them mostly prepared to give the undertaking. But Kirkwood refused: 'when I get back to Glasgow it must be as a *freeman*. I will sign nothing.'[16] Hostile observers complained that Kirkwood's part was entirely stage-managed by Wheatley, with the object of building up Kirkwood at the expense of the other deportees.[17] This was not entirely fair, in so far as Kirkwood was clearly marked out as the ringleader. While the other deportees found work fairly easily, sometimes with Levita's help, nobody would employ Kirkwood. The Ministry of Munitions officials pointed out that they could not force private employers to take him on:

> Mr. Beveridge. Take the case of Kirkwood. It is extremely unlikely that a private employer would be willing to employ him again. You have to face that.
>
> Mr. Addison. We should have to see whether we could not find him a job in a National Factory or something of that kind. We cannot compel Beardmores to say that they will employ him.[18]

But there can be no doubt that Wheatley built up Kirkwood as a hero of the labour movement. The stage-management culminated in a debate on the deportations at the 1917 Labour Party Conference at Manchester at which Kirkwood himself appeared as an A.S.E. delegate. He read his speech 'slowly and impressively . . . from his notes'[19] (presumably they were Wheatley's notes). Kirkwood opened by rebutting, on the grounds that he was responsible for making Parkhead Forge a Union shop, the charge that he was a rebel against trade unionism. He went on to relate the history of the deportations, and concluded by saying that he was not prepared to sign the pledge which had been put in front of him:

> He was no criminal . . . Why should he sign this humiliating and degrading pledge? There was only one reason: in order to whitewash his persecutors. He refused, and his comrades refused. But he was determined to do more. That day, for the first time, he had an opportunity of placing their case before the representatives of British Labour . . . Great principles of constitutional liberty were challenged. They must defend them. When he left the conference he would not return to deportation. He went home to Glasgow, or he went to prison.[20]

The statement caused uproar, and a reply was demanded from Henderson. 'Speaking among some disorder',[21] he said that

> he had no desire whatever to burke the issue that had been raised in the statement by Mr. Kirkwood. He was not encouraged, however, to believe that the Conference was in a frame of mind to give the consideration to the case that the case deserved.[22]

To meet Conference's demands for action, he proposed the appointment of a special Commission to investigate the case:

> And without having consulted with the Prime Minister or any of his colleagues, he would take the responsibility of saying that every paper and every witness required would be placed at the disposal of the Committee in order that the investigation might be as full and complete as possible.[23]

The proposal was accepted and the Committee reported to the 1918 Conference. (We have already examined its findings in some detail in Chapter 7; it is worth noting that Henderson's promise of full facilities for the Committee was very generously carried out — another gesture by the Cabinet towards mollifying Henderson's feelings. The Ministry's 'Office Review of the Clyde Strike', which has survived in the Addison papers, was probably prepared for Henderson.) Kirkwood, for his part, did go to Glasgow, but stayed there for only three days before going to Crieff, where he was arrested by the military and imprisoned for a spell in Edinburgh. The deportation order against him was finally lifted in May 1917, but for some months longer he could not get a job. The Ministry of Munitions for some time took no action to find work for Kirkwood. In August 1917, however, Kirkwood and two members of the Glasgow Trades Council visited Churchill, who was now Minister of Munitions, to complain that Kirkwood could not get a job.

Churchill agreed that 'it amounted to victimisation', and promised that any unemployed ex-deportees in Glasgow 'would be offered employment by the end of another week in one or other of the National Projectile Factories in the district'.[24] Within a fortnight, Kirkwood had been given a foreman's job, which he at first (according to the *Forward* report) had wished to refuse, at the Mile-End Shell Factory run by Beardmore's:[25]

> Thus it came that in Mile-End Shell Factory, with David Kirkwood as foreman, worked David Hanton,[26] William Gallacher, and wee MacManus as shop stewards.
> What a team! There never was anything like it in Great Britain. We organised a bonus system in which everyone benefited by high production.[27]

Between the deportations and the return of all the deportees to work, Wheatley and the 'official' wing of the Labour movement took up the problem of maintaining them and their dependants — as also the dependants of Gallacher, Muir and Bell, and of John MacLean, James Maxton, and James MacDougall, who had all been imprisoned for sedition. A Financial Statement of the Clyde Workers' Defence and Maintenance Fund, of which Wheatley was treasurer, has survived: £1891:18:3 was raised, of which C.W.C. contributed £785:13:11. The expenditure included the following:

	£	s	d
Maintenance of Deportees & Dependants	1004	12	4
Maintenance of Prisoners & Dependants	543	17	8
Travelling expenses	59	10	11
Grants of C.W.C. for defence purposes	61	7	6
Legal expenses	170	0	0
Audit fee	4	4	0 [28]

These figures show that Clyde workers were prepared to contribute generously through what must have been an efficient and wide-ranging organisation. The militant movement itself might be restricted to a small unofficial section of the engineers, but the appeal against the treatment meted out to them drew wide sympathy.

After March 1916, however, industrial militancy on the Clyde was to be absent for three years. One contemporary observer, the Govanhill engineer Herbert Highton, saw events after March 1916 thus:

> Crisis — *Ideas stimulated* by war
> *Action repressed* by war

Effect of deportation and imprisonment on 1) C.W.C.

2) workers generally

. . . . .

Deportations (= dispersion of Jews) spread new gospel.
1917 May strike born on Clyde 1915-16.[29]

But the diaspora of the deportees was not directly responsible for the encouragement of militancy elsewhere. Some time before the deportations, Tom Bell, the leading theorist of the Socialist Labour Party on the Clyde, had gone to London and later to Liverpol, where he had been unsuccessful in getting under way a Merseyside Workers' Committee because 'the several local union committees were fairly militant, and seemed to the workers to be all-sufficient'.[30] Arthur McManus was more successful in Manchester in founding a national committee of shop stewards with himself as chairman — a committee which was to be of importance in the political history of the British Communist Party, but of very little importance industrially during the remainder of the war. For the militant movement continued along the same lines as before, with the same unsolved dilemma between revolutionary commitment and craft conservatism. In the first major incident after the Clyde deportations a Sheffield engineer named Hargreaves was enlisted although he was protected by the Trade Card scheme as an engineer employed on war work. The strike which followed in Sheffield was backed by the District Committee of the A.S.E., although the District Committee handed over the business of running the strike to the Shop Stewards' Committee in order to free the A.S.E. from any legal commitments.[31] It was a 'ridiculous and avoidable' strike, caused by the 'colossal stupidity' of the Manpower Board, in Addison's view,[32] and it ended in Hargreaves' reinstatement. Murphy, who had a much more realistic view than any Clydeside revolutionary of what was actually happening, described it as 'the revolt of the craftsmen and particularly the older craftsmen who saw their life's work being torn to pieces'.[33] Non-craftsmen, who were not exempt from conscription at all, cannot have had much sympathy with Hargreaves.

In spite of the National Committee of Shop Stewards, revolts of the craftsmen could not be transformed into national strike movements, especially when Press censorship made it very difficult for workers in one centre even to find out what was happening in others. Thus in March 1917, when the Barrow engineers struck, Murphy was in a 'most difficult position'[34] because the Sheffield engineers could not have been brought out on strike on the sympathy issue alone, and Murphy was 'relieved'[35] when Barrow went back before Sheffield had to be put to the test. Even the May 1917 strike, which did have its origin in a national issue, did not produce a uniform national response. The issues were the intentions of the Government to withdraw the Trade Cards scheme, which protected skilled men on war work from conscription, and to extend dilution to private work. It had been a condition of the A.S.E.'s initial agreement to dilution in 1915-16 that it would apply to war work only, and engineers felt understandably aggrieved when the Government, giving the manpower crisis as its reason, supported moves by employers in 1917 to have dilution extended to private work. Here, if anywhere, was the opportunity for a national strike, but it never developed. In spite of an increase in political revolutionary feeling, it produced no response on Clydeside. Gallacher correctly predicted 'that the strike would be over before we could get anything moving on the Clyde'.[36]

The unofficial strike of May 1917 was the largest in the engineering industry in the entire war; with the possible exception of the South Wales miners' strike of 1915, it was the largest wartime strike of any kind. But it has never received as much attention as events on the Clyde in 1915-16. Outside the Clyde, only one militant published his reminiscences — J. T. Murphy. Murphy was a disillusioned ex-Communist by the time his books were published, and his downbeat style does not have the self-glorifying heroics of Kirkwood, Gallacher, or Bell. But his books are much better history.

On Clydeside the C.W.C. 'had become small and sectarian after the arrests in 1916',[37] and neither it nor anybody else could bring engineers out on strike during 1917. But political unrest was increasing. The political climate had greatly changed since the beginning of the war, when the *Forward* had gloomily predicted,

> By Friday the working class will be out on the streets waving Union Jacks, and we may just as well face the fact that it is pure stupid cant to talk about a general strike by way of protest.[38]

The prediction proved right, even on Clydeside, which was to be the industrial area in Britain least hostile to anti-war speakers. Within a week of the outbreak of war the travelling propaganda carried out by Dollan each summer had been badly disrupted:

> The War Fever has hit the Van Propaganda, so that we are having lots of opposition, no collections (or meagre ones) and poor literature sales.[39]

But by 1916 and 1917 war fever was giving way to war weariness, and many sections of the labour movement besides the militants were delighted at the success of the first Russian Revolution. The Glasgow Trades Council agreed enthusiastically in May 1917 to affiliate to the Union of Democratic Control,[40] and two weeks later it was agreed to co-operate in a large demonstration to celebrate the Revolution, against only two members who voted 'not to co-operate until we were certain of the nature of the Revolution'.[41] The Trades Council agreed to send delegates to the Joint B.S.P. and I.L.P. Conference at Leeds in June 1917 at which MacDonald, Snowden, and W. C. Anderson spoke for the establishment of Workers' and Soldiers' Councils in Britain. The Trades Council delegates reported back that the Conference had been a 'splendid success and a triumph'[42] which showed that the workers were at last tired of the war, and it was agreed to nominate a 'conference in 13 districts . . . to appoint a delegate from each to act on the Central [Workers' and Soldiers'] Committee'.[43] A meeting of the Central Committee for the Glasgow area was fixed for 4th August,[44] and the Glasgow magistrates sent an anxious telegram to the Secretary for Scotland asking him to ban it, because

> there is apprehension of grave disorder arising because of disturbances at previous meetings of a similar character in other towns arising out of the Workers' and Soldiers' Councils . . . At a meeting held in Charing Cross Halls, Glasgow, on 12th April, addressed by Mr. Ramsay Macdonald, disorder actually occurred, and the presence of a large body of police was required to restore and maintain order.[45]

Robert Munro was no more venturesome as a Secretary for Scotland than his two predecessors, and he brought the Glasgow magistrates' request before the War Cabinet. He explained that he would have taken the initiative of banning the meeting under the Defence of the Realm Regulation 9A, but for his desire to ensure that any action he took was collated with what was being done in England, as 'there are, of course, further considerations of policy involved'.[46] The War Cabinet discussed Munro's paper on 8th August, and heard that the Home Secretary proposed to ban similar conferences in England. They decided

a) To confirm the proposed action of the Home Secretary.
b) To authorise the Secretary for Scotland to prohibit the Glasgow meeting, announcement of such prohibition not to be made until after 4 o'clock on Friday[47] next.
c) To call the attention of the Secretary of State for War to War Cabinet 200 Minute lc[48] and to the desirability of an announcement being made in Parliament, but not earlier than the Secretary for Scotland's announcement,

that the Cabinet regarded the objects of such meetings as illegal, and would not permit them to be held.[49]

On the announcement of the ban, the meeting was transferred into a demonstration of protest on Glasgow Green against the ban.[50] Later in August permission was still being sought for a meeting of the Provincial Court of the Workers' and Soldiers' Council,[51] and a month later, Miss Hughes, Treasurer of the Trades Council, and (surprisingly) David Kirkwood, who had not previously been a delegate to the Council, were chosen as Council delegates to the Central Workers' and Soldiers' Council.[52] The rest is silence; and Kirkwood describes it in his customary fashion:

> It died a natural death. It was choked by its own excesses. It was more Bolshevik than the Bolsheviks. The workers laughed and went on with their jobs.[53]

It would be a mistake to read too much into this outburst of support for Soviets in normally thoroughly bureaucratic bodies like the Glasgow Trades Council. As Johnston warned:

> The idea is good. It is more; it is dramatically good. But . . . we wish more of the speakers had given some indication of how it is proposed to fit in the Committee with existing working-class organisations.[54]

And the Conference had critics both on the left and on the right of the Glasgow labour movement. Wheatley remarked that

> while it was very inspiring to be in the midst of 1200 delegates whose hearts were throbbing with hatred of capitalism and all its crimes, the Conference lacked driving force . . . Everyone pointed to the Russian road, but none was ready to lead the way.[55]

And the right-wing columnist, 'Rob Roy', pinpointed the main weakness of the Leeds Convention when he said:

> One of the speakers or commentators referred to the voting as proof of the change that has swept over the public mind since the Manchester Labour Congress. The difference resides elsewhere. A Labour Congress rests on a carefully framed constitution so worked out as to give fair and proportionate representation to all sides and shades of opinion. Leeds was a scratch Convention of enthusiasts for one particular cause.[56]

But even if the whole Workers' and Soldiers' movement be dismissed as the product of a 'scratch Convention of enthusiasts', there is solid evidence of a shift of Labour opinion everywhere, not least in Glasgow. The 1916 Congress of the S.T.U.C., for instance, opened with a defiantly pro-war presidential address:

Personally I have held the view from the beginning, in common with the great majority of my colleagues of the Parliamentary Committee, that our country has been in no way to blame for the calamity that has overtaken the world.[57]

In 1917 the chairman of the S.T.U.C. was again pro-war, but his presidential address to the conference was introduced in a very different tone; he acknowledged that his views

will not command the undivided support of delegates to this Congress. The Labour Movement at present is like a river which has been divided by an island and flows in two branches.[58]

As if to underline this, the Congress voted to send a resolution of congratulations to the 'free peoples of Russia', 'to be sent to the Provisional Government and the Council of Workers' and Soldiers' Delegates'.[59]

Of the annual May Day marches through the streets of Glasgow, 1916's was rather a poor one. The *Forward* estimated that 10,000 had attended, and commented that 'Literature sales were lighter than usual'.[60] This compared with an estimated 25,000 marchers in 1915.[61] But by 1917 the May Day march had gained an enormous access of support. The *Glasgow Herald* estimated that 70,000 had attended the demonstration; so the *Forward*, applying a simple rule of thumb for the treatment of crowd figures given in the Capitalist Press, estimated that 100,000 demonstrators listened to the speeches on Glasgow Green.[62] In 1918 the same journal gave its own estimate of 110,000, or perhaps 100,000 omitting 'police spies, agents provocateurs, munitions spotters, [and] police (special, ordinary, and thinly disguised)'.[63] The *Glasgow Herald* again estimated a crowd of 70,000, which was all the more remarkable as the demonstration was for the first time held on a weekday in 1918.

The more formal bodies of Labour opinion were also changing their views on the war. In December 1916 the Conference of the Scottish Advisory Committee of the Labour Party came out in favour of peace by negotiation,[64] as had 'every federated Labour and Trade Union organisation in Glasgow',[65] namely the Trades Council, the I.L.P., the Glasgow Labour Party, and the Labour Group in the Town Council. Nationally, this movement was confirmed by the Labour Party's withdrawal from the Coalition after the resignation of Henderson from the Cabinet, and by the publication of its Memorandum on War Aims, calling for peace by negotiation, in December 1917.

Both the Liberal and the Labour Party were badly split by the war. In the end, it shattered the Liberals but strengthened the Labour Party because the first took their internal struggles to the electorate while the second did not. In the 1918 election Lloyd George Liberals (in coalition with the Conservatives) fought Asquith Liberals and the latter were crushed. The Labour Party, however, had succeeded in holding together a spectrum of opinion from the right of Henderson through MacDonald to outright pacifists, and went to the polls united. The majority of the Parliamentary Labour Party was pro-war when its supporters were, entered government in 1915 (to the immense advantage of the party and the unions), but pulled out at the right time. From August 1917 the whole party was associated with views which had previously been the preserve of a tiny, unpopular, minority. Reaction against the slaughter on the Western Front made popular opinion more receptive to these views; so the Labour Party as a whole was able to associate itself with feelings of malaise and war-weariness. The Labour Party's domestic and war policy became a focus for comment and analysis in the Press, including the hostile Press, such as the *Glasgow Herald*,[66] in a way it had never been before.

In 1917 and 1918 Clydeside reflected these national trends: left-wing and anti-war politics were much more popular than in the early years of the war. But industrial militancy was in decline, and never revived during the war after the crisis of 1915 and 1916.

9

Politicians, Revolutionaries and Engineers

The mainspring of wartime Red Clydeside was the revolt of the crafts-men — a revolt paralleled in some of the other munitions centres, especially Sheffield. But nowhere else was the revolutionary fervour so marked, nor did it become so celebrated. Did it, on Clydeside, have any life of its own independent of the engineers? In this chapter we shall consider four objections to the proposition that wartime Clyde-side was in a 'revolutionary situation'. These are: that the ideology inspiring many influential militants was not Marxist, except at the most superficial level, but if anything religious; that the most consistently revolutionary party was isolated by its sectarianism from the groups to which it might otherwise have appealed; that the most thoroughly revolutionary individual was cut off from his supporters; and that demands were couched in revolutionary language by individuals whose real purpose was merely the protection of craft interests.

Political revolutionaries and religious extremists have a great deal in common. Both believe that they possess the whole truth and nothing but the truth and that those who oppose them are not just wrong but evil. The analogy between Red Clydesiders of the 1920s and extreme Presbyterian schismatics of the seventeenth century has struck a number of writers.[1] It should not be pressed too far. But there is a real point here. The Clydesiders were socialised at home, at church and at school to venerate the heroes of Presbyterian secession — heroes the English have never heard of. They saw themselves as the heirs of the Covenanters, the Presbyterians of the seventeenth century who became more extreme (and more intolerant) as they were more ruthlessly per-secuted for their beliefs. The received version of Scottish history, which has been taught to many generations of non-Catholic Scottish school-children, has always emphasised the Covenanters' heroism, and never their intolerance. A fifth of the Scottish population is Catholic; but none of the Clydesiders was, except Harry McShane, who was not one of the leaders, and Wheatley, whom many of the others distrusted.[2] Most revolutionaries were engineers; all engineers had had to serve apprenticeships, few apprenticeships were open to Catholics. Small wonder, then, that the heroes invoked on Clydeside were not class heroes, nor yet nationalist heroes, but religious heroes. Ramsay Mac-Donald eulogised Keir Hardie at his death: 'In him the spirit of the Covenanter lived again — Airds Moss tempered with the lyrics of Burns'.[3] MacDonald praised the 'moral magnificence' of pacifists in the I.L.P. (while disagreeing with them) by calling them 'a body of political Cameronians'.[4] And when, in 1920, the Scottish Labour Housing Association urged a national campaign of resistance to the rent increases proposed in the Rent Act of that year, they adopted a 'Solemn League and Covenant'[5] to that effect.

The leaders of the C.W.C. were very respectable rebels:

> It wasn't easy to rouse up engineers; they were very respectable with their blue suits and bowler hats, and used to come to mass meetings with their umbrellas. Gallacher dressed like that as well.[6]

Kirkwood described himself and his fellow Clydesiders in 1922: 'We were all Puritans. We were all abstainers. Most of us did not smoke. We were the stuff of which reform is made.'[7] They gave themselves a thoroughly Presbyterian send-off after their General Election triumph in that year. After signing a Declaration which the Principal of Aberdeen University described as 'breathing the noble spirit of the Covenant',[8] they sang the 124th Psalm — 'Scotland's psalm of deliverance' — in the version used by the Covenanters to assure themselves and the world that the Lord was on their side:

> Now Israel
>   May say, and that truly,
> If that the Lord
>   Had not our cause maintain'd;
> If that the Lord
>   Had not our right sustain'd,
> When cruel men
>   Against us furiously
> Rose up in wrath,
>   To make us their prey,

Then certainly
They had devour'd us all . . .

But bless'd be God
Who doth us safely keep,
And hath not giv'n
Us for a living prey
Unto their teeth,
And bloody cruelty.[9]

The strength of the Scottish socialists' adherence to the principles of the Covenant was to be put to the test in 1927, when the revised Anglican Prayer Book was being discussed in the Commons. It was none of the Scots' business, and the Scottish Labour front-benchers had intended not to vote. But, according to Johnston,[10] they were swayed by the speech against the Bill by Rosslyn Mitchell, who objected that it would legitimate the Catholic doctrine of transubstantiation:

> Transubstantiation . . . is the dividing principle between the two Churches. If the Church of England wants that, then let her have it. Let her go on her journey, and God be with her; but if she does not want it then she cannot pass this Book . . . I myself can do nothing but vote against this Measure. I do not want to do it, but I can do no other, so help me God![11]

This led William Adamson to confess to Johnston that he 'couldna' look my forefolks in the face, if I didna' vote the nicht'.[12] The draft Prayer Book was thrown out by 230 votes to 205. Thirty-five Scottish M.P.s (nine of them Labour, including Adamson, James Barr, William Graham, Thomas Henderson, Johnston and Rosslyn Mitchell) voted against ratification, and only seven (none of them Labour) for. The Prayer Book, one of the very few measures before Parliament that was purely English, was thrown out on the Scots' votes.

This is not just picturesque anecdote. It has a political point. Adamson and Kirkwood represented the last generation of working-class Scots for whom nineteenth-century Presbyterian theological controversy still lived. Kirkwood's father had been a devout United Presbyterian.[13] But Presbyterianism, though it had many working-class adherents, was largely a middle-class affair which inhibited the growth of class politics. The language in which Kirkwood describes himself would seem more familiar and more palatable to a Scot who was not a radical than to a radical who was not a Scot. There is nothing new in the observation that the Labour Party owes more to Methodism than to Marxism. In Scotland it owed very little to either, but Free Churchmanship more than substituted for Methodism. If Kirkwood had ever led a revolution, it would not have been on behalf of class-based revolutionary ideology. His views were based on attitudes widely diffused among social classes. Perhaps he was the original of Andrew Amos in Buchan's *Mr. Standfast*.[14]

The Calvinists could not have started a revolution; could the sectarians have done so? The Socialist Labour Party, whose members included Muir, MacManus, Bell, and Kirkwood up to 1914, had the most consistently revolutionary outlook of any party operating on Clydeside during the war. It split from the Social Democratic Federation in 1903 because its adherents followed the 'impossibilist' doctrines of Daniel De Leon, who preached extreme doctrinal purity, abstention from capitalist politics altogether, and intensive education of the working class. (Another splinter from the S.D.F. took place in London, to form the Socialist Party of Great Britain. The S.P.G.B. also professed allegiance to the principles of De Leon, but the London and Scottish splinters detested each other.)[15]

So far, so sectarian; and in addition the position of the S.L.P. before the war was paradoxical. It was strenuously opposed to political action: Neil Maclean, its secretary and later Labour M.P. for Govan, was temporarily expelled in 1909 for leading a deputation on unemployment to Edinburgh Town Council. Instead, it preached industrial unionism — and this was the point at which it might break out of sectarianism into political importance. Industrial unionism might, in principle, be attractive to two different groups of workers. It might seem attractive to unskilled workers whose only strength lay in solidarity, among whom traditional unionism would fail in a strike but 'industrial unionism', in which they were supported by their craftsmen colleagues, might succeed. For different reasons 'industrial unionism' might secure the support of skilled men who were angered at the futility of having several small craft unions in an industry such as engineering. At different times the S.L.P. in Scotland had some success with each of these groups of workers, but it never brought them together, and never ran a successful strike on industrial unionist lines.

In the heyday of syndicalism between 1911 and 1914 the S.L.P. in Scotland ran only one large strike: at the Singer works in Clydebank in 1911, led by Neil Maclean, who was a maintenance engineer. Singer's was a plant which under largely American management had already extensively developed a process work production line. The strike arose in one department against a management attempt to cut piecework rates by speeding-up. This was the unskilled piece-workers' grievance, and it was the unskilled piece-workers who struck: '. . . every man in the Department but 20 came with us (about 400). Of these 20, 8 were under-foremen, and 10 were fitters'.[16]

The strike spread from department to department, and membership of the Singer's group of the Industrial Workers of Great Britain rose sharply. By April 1911, 37 of the 41 departments were out, and a total of 11,000 men and women were on strike. However, the management sent postcards to all their 'former employees' asking them to resume work: 6,527 voted to resume by sending their cards back to the management, and only 4,025 refused, sending the cards to the strike committee, which had to abandon the strike. 'This was not a collapse, as the capitalist Press had it, but an orderly return on a compromise'.[17]

The strike had been undermined by the skilled men, especially the engineers. The journal of the S.L.P. wrote:

> Next we come to the Engineers, the blue blood of the working-class, the aristocracy of labour, who added still further to their reputation which stinks in the nostrils of all honest men. After being virtually shamed out, they lived up to A.S.E. ethics, deciding at a meeting of A.S.E. members by a large majority to kow-tow to the firm by sending back their cards. Requiescat in pace.[18]

Two months later the journal was still analysing the strike. The strike committee had avoided the errors both of being craft-bound and of being an amorphous mass like the Gas Workers' Union ('the big ditch into which 'pure and simple' unions relegate all sections of Labour which do not fit into any recognised trades'),[19] although I.W.G.B. members had become a minority on their own strike Committee. However, the blame for the ending of the strike was again put fairly and squarely on the skilled men:

> In strong contrast with the fine spirit of loyalty displayed by the unorganised and 'unskilled' strikers is the pitiful part played by those aristocrats of labour, the 'skilled' trade unionists . . . The great majority of them stayed in altogether or only came out either because there was no work for them to do . . . or because they were shamed into it by the well merited stigma of 'scab' which was hurled at them by the indignant strikers. It was under these circumstances that the members of the A.S.E. came out . . . cursing the strikers as a mob, ignored the strike committee, and tearfully apologised to their officials for their actions, explaining that they did not come out on account of sympathy with the strikers but because their sentiment of self-respect was hurt by the odious monosyllable which greeted them as they entered the works gate.[20]

Many of the leaders of the strike were dismissed by the firm. One of them wrote:

> Socialism thrives best in adversity, and perchance this will be one of the best fillips it ever received.[21]

Bell claimed incorrectly that the dispersal of the leaders of the Singer's strike aided the setting up of the Clyde Workers' Committee in 'factory after factory'.[22] But the gulf between skilled and unskilled was never bridged, even though some tradesmen — such as those at Weir's — faced the same sort of American 'scientific management', with its intensified division of labour, as the process workers at Singer's. When trades unionism revived at the Singer plant after the war, it became a stronghold of the most successful of the 'new unions', the Workers' Union:

> In Glasgow itself, efforts at the major munitions firms yielded disappointing results, but Government and private works in the Clyde area were the source of many large branches, after 1916 composed of female 'dilutees' and giving a membership of 5,000. At the single firm of Singer's at Clydebank, employing 12,000 workers, several thousand more members were obtained by the end of the war.[23]

But in 1911, given the craftsmen's active hostility, the revolt of the unskilled men and women collapsed, and it was impossible to keep up any sort of trade unionism among them, let alone revolutionary industrial unionism. When the war came, the militant left was politically much less strong than the industrial upheavals of 1911 to 1914 might lead one to suppose. The S.L.P. had failed to organise the unskilled because of their sheer industrial powerlessness; during the war it had less power over the skilled men than it might because of its sectarianism.

On somewhat esoteric grounds, the S.L.P. was bitterly opposed to the best-known leader of unofficial unrest, Tom Mann (the only one to have a foot in both the skilled and the unskilled camps); his crime was to preach 'industrial syndicalism' instead of 'industrial unionism'.[24] It had no time at all for conventional trade union or political leads. So, although it condemned the 'liberal-labour opportunists' at the head of trades unions, yet because of its uncompromising refusal to involve itself in capitalist, including trade union, politics, it provided no means whereby the workers could choose a revolutionary leadership instead. At the same time it was hampered by its rigid intellectualism. No candidate could be admitted to membership without passing an entrance examination on the principles of Marxism, and Bell found out that in spite of constant heckling at labour meetings 'the workers wouldn't join. They thought we were terribly intellectual . . . Over 3 years we gained 350 members and lost 350'.[25] This pessimistic estimate seems to be confirmed by the reports of membership which appeared from time to time in *The Socialist*.[26] One survivor has related how he was admitted to the S.L.P. by one vote, opponents of his entry claiming that 'one so young as me wouldn't know enough to justify them letting me in the S.L.P.' He compounded his offence by being a shop steward, though 'I shouldnae have been', according to the S.L.P. rules.[27]

The S.L.P. was the only one of the three left-wing parties operating on the Clyde during the war which had a theory of revolution — industrial unionism. But its sectarianism prevented it from putting the theory into effect. As we shall see later in this chapter, it was only as it became heretical in its own terms that it gained any wider appeal.

Of the Clydesiders other than S.L.P. members, Kirkwood (after 1914) and James Messer were I.L.P. members, as was John Wheatley; Gallacher and John MacLean were members of the British Socialist Party, which was the name taken by the Social Democratic Federation after 1912. Neither the I.L.P. nor the B.S.P. was a revolutionary party in a Leninist sense. The I.L.P. was by far the larger, and the views of its Glasgow members ranged from Kirkwood's superficial Marxism to the Christian pacifism of William Regan, secretary of the Catholic Socialist Society.[28] Unlike the other two parties, it did not suffer severe internal dissension on the issue of support for the war, although the pacifism of some of its members was more determined than that of others. In 1914, when Kirkwood was still in the S.L.P., he moved that the Glasgow Branch should declare its opposition to the war. The motion was opposed by Muir, who, on its being carried, resigned his position as editor of *The Socialist*.[29] In Gallacher's version of the incident,

> Johnny Muir, who was editor of *The Socialist*, the S.L.P. organ, was trying to argue a case for a Socialist defending 'his own' country at a special meeting in their hall in Renfrew Street. In the midst of the discussion, and while Johnny was arguing a certain point, Davy [Kirkwood] jumped up and shouted, 'Naw, naw, Joanie, that'll no dae, the workers have nae country. Ah'm feenished wi' ye'. He shook the dust of Renfrew Street from his feet and found a new haven and ultimately an empire in the I.L.P.[30]

Kirkwood's real attitudes, however, seem only to have been covered by a patina of vulgar Marxism, which was polished off after he left the

S.L.P. In any case, his prime concern was industrial, not political. We have seen how anti-war themes were muted in his attitude to the dilution crisis, and at the end of the war, when Beardmore made him manager of the National Projectile Factory, Mile End, he won 'the best hat in Glasgow'[31] from Beardmore for breaking production records there. The wartime strikes, as Murphy saw,

> were frequently led by men such as myself who wanted to stop the war, but that was not the actual motive. Had the question of stopping the war been put before any strikers' meeting, it would have been overwhelmingly defeated.[32]

The I.L.P. could not be a revolutionary party because it did not want to be, not because it was split over the war. The British Socialist Party was the other way round. It was gravely weakened by the jingo patriotism of Hyndman, who controlled the party's organisation, its money, and its journal. In face of this, the powers of the anti-war majority of the party membership were severely circumscribed. On Clydeside, the worst internal row occurred when Hyndman issued what the C.W.C. militants regarded as a blatant invitation to the authorities to deport John MacLean's friend Peter Petroff:

> Who and what is Peter Petroff? Peter Petroff . . . has now been for some weeks on the Clyde. What he is doing there and what may be his object is best known to himself. It is for the representatives of the Glasgow workers to determine what is his status on the Clyde Workers' Committee, and to make whatever enquiries concerning him as (sic) they may deem necessary.[33]

Gallacher strongly disliked Petroff ('I had seen his type in many a popular melodrama — always as the suave and cunning villain')[34] and ascribed MacLean's wartime disagreements with himself to the sinister influence of Petroff. This is part of Gallacher's 'Party Line' on the history of Red Clydeside which recent writers,[35] often rightly, have refused to swallow. But over-reaction has led them to put an excessive stress on the role of MacLean. On one point they are right to point to his importance. His most famous activity was his economics class in which he instructed thousands of Clydeside workers in the principles of Marxist economics. In the 1917 season, for instance, 'a class of two or three thousand' was anticipated.[36] MacLean's printed 'Notes for lectures on Economics',[37] used later in his Scottish Labour College, are a lucid explanation of the theory of surplus value and the immiseration of the proletariat. Yet there is no evidence that, even here, his influence was particularly profound. His most distinguished pupil, in terms of later achievements, was William Gallacher; but Gallacher's knowledge of Marxist economics was superficial.[38] Most of the other ideologues of the C.W.C. were members of the S.L.P., which took a severe view of MacLean and his economics classes. The S.L.P. held classes of its own, whose alumni included Muir, MacManus, and Thomas Clark.[39] Bell, the tutor, commented thus on his rival:

> Maclean's method had the merit of popularising economic study amongst large numbers of the workers, but had the defect of becoming a propaganda lecture. The S.L.P. method was more intensive and produced a crop of competent class tutors, who led classes inside the factories. No such tutors came from MacLean's classes in this period or during the period of the war.[40]

MacLean's modern admirers see him as standing 'head and shoulders above' his contemporaries.[41] This may have merits as a moral judgment; it has none as a description of his effectiveness. To Paterson, the Ministry of Munitions' Labour Officer on the Clyde, it was Kirkwood, not any of the others named, who 'has a much greater influence over the workmen in the district than any half dozen trades union officials who could be named'; he thought the outsiders MacLean and Peter Petroff were less dangerous than the working class C.W.C. leaders:

> I am afraid that the removal of almost any one of these men (with the possible exception of MacLean and Petroff who are not working men or officials of societies here) would at once cause a big strike.[42]

And Walton Newbold, the ex-Quaker who became Communist M.P. for Motherwell between 1922 and 1923, wrote:

> . . . the fact that he [MacLean] was external to the life of the working-class by reason of his professional work as a school teacher of considerable academic distinction made him of less account in the day-to-day struggle than the Paisley engineer Willie Gallacher.[43]

The disjunction between the intellectual and the engineer, together with the parallel distinction between political and industrial ends, led to the row between MacLean and Gallacher which occurred in 1915. It took place at a meeting of the C.W.C. which had been addressed by Muir — a leading industrial militant but not opposed to the war. James MacDougall and Petroff, later joined by MacLean, protested that political issues should be discussed: they wanted a general strike against the war. The response of Gallacher was to ban them from attending C.W.C. meetings.[44]

The middle-class revolutionaries were far more concerned than the working-class ones about militant action against the war. Seven

Clydesiders were imprisoned for sedition during 1916. Of these, Muir, Gallacher, and Walter Bell were charged in respect of the article 'Should the Workers Arm?' which in fact said they shouldn't.[45] Of the other four, three were middle-class: MacLean, a teacher, Macdougall, a bank clerk, and Maxton, another teacher. Only one industrial worker was imprisoned for urging action against war.

MacLean was prosecuted under D.O.R.A. in November 1915 and again in April 1916. On the first occasion he was fined £5, and served five days in prison for refusing to pay. The second time, he was imprisoned for three years with penal servitude, of which he served rather over one year. A study of the indictments and witnesses' statements at his trials shows how far out of touch with the C.W.C. he was, and how little there was in common between middle-class and working-class views of revolution.

The 1915 trial arose from an alleged reply to a heckler at one of MacLean's open-air meetings who said, 'Away and 'list!'. MacLean replied, in his version of the words:

> I have been enlisted for 15 years in the Socialist army. It is the only army worth fighting for. God damn all other armies.[46]

No Clydeside engineer ever said anything like that in public.

In his 1916 trial MacLean was charged with advocating strike action, with seditiously saying that industrial conscription would be introduced, and on a number of other counts relating to six public meetings in January 1916. His defence statement refers thus to a meeting at Parkhead on January 19th:

> I merely spoke to the men telling them of the meeting [viz. a demonstration to be held the following day] only until such time as a man named Thomas Clark intervened and told the workers that they were not to listen to that man's blethers.[47]

One of the defence witnesses, Helen Crawford (a suffragist, at this time in the I.L.P., later in the C.P.G.B.) thus described MacLean's intervention in a demonstration on 20th January, at which he had not been invited by the C.W.C. to speak:

> [MacLean] dealt principally with the differences between himself and the C.W.C. He laboured this so much that a part of the audience seemed to think that he should stop this line of argument and go on with the business of the meeting which was to protest against conscription. I personally had very little sympathy with Mr. MacLean at the meeting in question . . . I was a member of this committee, and I did not think his criticism was justified.[48]

There is no evidence that any working-class organisation ever responded to MacLean's appeal for a general strike against the war.

MacLean's classes certainly helped, in a diffuse way, to create a vaguely revolutionary atmosphere (but nothing positive, as MacLean was no organiser of men or meetings).[49] He also suffered much in prison (he was allowed two letters out a year), and his imprisonment brought waves of protest from the whole labour movement.[50] Some people have seen him as the *éminence grise* of, for instance, the February 1915 strike at Weir's,[51] the Govan rent strike,[52] or the disorder at Lloyd George's meeting.[53] But establishing these claims would be like proving that Macavity the Mystery Cat really was the Napoleon of Crime. They rely on the fallacy of *post hoc, ergo propter hoc:* 'MacLean wished X to happen; X happened; therefore MacLean caused X to happen'. He was isolated in several ways. He had (to say the least) a suspicious and prickly personality;[54] he was not an industrial worker; he differed ideologically from the S.L.P; and his row with Gallacher had cut him off from working-class members of his own party, the B.S.P.

Over dilution, neither Muir nor Kirkwood was prepared to go as far as MacLean, whose paper was suppressed for making 'a more advanced attack on diluted labour'[55] than any other. Muir put the S.L.P.'s case to Lloyd George on December 24th 1915. After announcing that the dilution had come about under pressure from the inexorable forces of capitalism, he went on:

> we have no objection to that [viz. dilution] provided its application conforms to certain clearly defined conditions,

namely that

> all industries and industrial resources must be taken over by the Government and organised labour should be vested with the right to take part directly and equally with the present managers in the management and administration of every department of industry.[56]

Kirkwood's perspectives were more limited. In his speech to Lloyd George the previous day he had said:

> But this scheme of dilution must be carried under the control of the workers. We recognise that if we have not the control cheap labour will be introduced, and unless our demand is granted we will fight the scheme to the death.[57]

Some time later he wrote an article in *Forward* outlining his notions of workers' control:

The worker at present occupies a subjected position in the workshop — a position that is degrading to his manhood and makes him a poorer-spirited citizen than if he occupied in the workshop some degree of independence. The worker has no voice in fixing his starting hour, his meal hour, or his stopping time . . . [the] value of the product of his labour or the manner of its disposal, or with the sanitary conditions of his workshop, or anything associated with or arising from his labour. The workers must have a new status . . . I don't think the workers in any particular industry should absolutely own and control that industry as this might enable them to exploit the remainder of the community.[58]

Muir focuses on the national aspects of the demand for workers' control; Kirkwood's gaze is fixed firmly on the workplace, except at the end of his *Forward* article, where he uses the best radical argument against syndicalism. In 1916 Kirkwood had only one end in view: the protection of the rights of the craftsmen. When, as he thought, he had secured that, he broke the C.W.C. front by his part in securing the Parkhead dilution scheme. The S.L.P.'s aims were much more ambitious. But their only appeal to the unskilled workers at Singer's in 1911 had been a failure, and their sectarianism kept them at arm's length from the skilled men. It was only by breaking their own rules that they could appear at the head of the 1915-16 agitation — which surely counted as taking part in capitalist politics. The S.L.P. was most successful when most heretical.[59] In 1915-16 S.L.P. leaders were relying on the powerful forces of craft conservatism to promote a revolutionary programme. As Murphy realised,

We who were developing the organisation of the shop stewards won the whole-hearted support of craftsmen and the most conservative of the trade unionists, along with the advocates of industrial unionism, for a campaign to control the dilution process.[60]

This was a paradox which had been at the heart of engineering trade unionism since at least 1896. But while revolutionary agitation could not thrive without craft conservatism, the reverse is not true. A large part of Chapters 3 to 6 was devoted to showing that the revolutionaries were by no means the only opponents of the dilution campaign, nor were they the most formidable. The Ministry of Munitions had to spend far more energy fighting the pure craft conservatism represented by the A.S.E. Executive and the men at Lang's, Johnstone, than it ever devoted to the Clyde Workers' Committee. The first action it took against this body was the suppression of the *Worker*, which did not take place until February 7th, 1916.

On the other hand, it is reasonable to try to assess how well the

S.L.P. militants acted as a revolutionary vanguard. After all, the success of the October Revolution in 1917 did not depend on the majority of the Russian population being converted to Leninism. It depended on the Leninists' ability to channel popular grievances into bringing about a revolutionary seizure of power. In Britain, December 1915 on Clydeside was one of the few occasions on which men with professedly revolutionary aims had an important section of the industrial working class under their control. But there remained two gaps — between the political and the industrial, and between the skilled and the unskilled. Once conditions of dilution safeguarding the position of the skilled men had begun to be obtained, the Government removed by imprisonment or deportation all the militants; and protest vanished. Because the men were not prepared to follow their leaders from industrial to political action there was no effective protest from the engineers. *A fortiori*, none could be expected from other groups of workers, as dilution was exclusively an engineers' grievance. More precisely still, it was a grievance of craftsmen in *general* engineering. The railway workshops and (still more) the shipyards do not feature in the anti-dilution campaign because boilersmiths, shipwrights, platers, caulkers and so on had specialised skills that were not at risk.

Moreover, conscription drove another wedge between skilled and unskilled in engineering. Skilled men were protected from being drafted into the Forces if they were working on munitions. The official and unofficial engineers' agitations between 1916 and 1918 were almost all centred round disputes over the operation of this system, and this was not a fight in which the unskilled men could be expected to have any sympathy with the skilled. This is picturesquely illustrated in a newspaper account of the engineers' strike of May 1917 in Sheffield. Headed 'Sheffield Strike/Numbers of Men Already Resuming Work/An Unpopular Cause', the report continues:

A New Soldiers' Chorus.
The amateur poets and parodists are very busy spending 'ammunition' on the strike. Several of their efforts have caught on. One of the most popular, which is attributed to a soldier, parodies a music-hall song and goes to a catchy air, although [sic] its title is 'A Prayer to Lloyd George'. One verse, which a party of 'civvies' and soldiers joyously chorused, runs thus:

Don't send me in the Army, George — I am in the A.S.E.
Take all the . . . labourers, but for God's sake don't take me.
You want me for a soldier? Well, that can never be:
A man of my ability, and in the A.S.E.!

Other parodies, a number of which were chalked yesterday on doors and pavements, deal with heroes, shirkers, and badges — and nearly always the A.S.E.[61]

The Clyde dilution conflict hardly involved the issue of conscription at all, at least overtly. But from 1916 onwards conscription did help keep the skilled and the unskilled apart and prevent any chance of revolutionary agitation. The revolutionary unionism of the S.L.P., let alone the more thoroughgoing revolutionism of John MacLean, had been unable to spark off a revolution.

Part II

From George Square to St. Enoch Square

10

The Origins of the Forty Hours' Strike

Clydeside lost the initiative in industrial militancy after March 1916, and the national unofficial strike movements in engineering of 1917 and 1918 found no response on Clydeside at all. The strike movement of January 1919 represented the second (and, as it turned out, the last) in which the Clyde Workers' Committee played an important part. In this chapter we shall examine the origins of the strike, while in Chapter 11 we describe its somewhat unhappy progress, concluding with a more extended discussion of some of the problems of interpretation to which it gives rise.

After the defeat of 1916, revolutionary militancy on Clydeside lapsed for a spell into ineffective sectarian squabbling. When Gallacher returned in 1917 from his prison term, he found the C.W.C. in the hands of the Workers' International Industrial Union, who told him, 'You're finished, you and your policy of perpetual strikes. Now we'll leave you'.[1] By 1917, also, Muir had defected to the I.L.P., like Kirkwood before him, and 'never moved apart from Wheatley',[2] so that Gallacher was the only one of the 1916 strike leaders still actively trying to promote militant strike action. He succeeded in refounding the C.W.C. in September 1917, with himself and Messer again as chairman and secretary. By 1918 it had regained some of its old standing among the engineers, thanks largely to its role in organising opposition to Auckland Geddes (in a similar manner to the barracking received by Lloyd George in 1915) at a meeting of shop stewards called to discuss the Manpower Bill early in 1918.[3]

Besides the revived C.W.C., several other organisations were becoming involved in resolutions and actions which would commit them to strike action after the war. Most prominent among these were the Glasgow Trades Council and the Parliamentary Committee[4] of the Scottish Trades Union Congress, though political bodies such as the

I.L.P. were involved as well. At the end of the war, as at the beginning, labour organisations were seriously worried about the dislocation and unemployment which they expected would occur; and the grounds for anticipating widespread unemployment after 1918 were, because of demobilisation and the ending of munitions productions, much better than in August 1914. This was one of the sources of the widespread demand for a shortening of the working week. For instance, the Glasgow Trades Council invited the S.T.U.C. in December 1918 to resolve:

> That this Conference, for the purpose of reabsorbing Sailors and Soldiers into civil life, and giving greater leisure to the working classes, demands the reduction of hours by legislative enactment to a maximum of 40 hours per week, preferably 5 days a week of 8 hours each.[5]

It was a request with solid precedents. At the 1918 S.T.U.C. Congress, held in Ayr over Easter, the President (Hugh Lyon of the Scottish Horse and Motormen's Union) had said in his opening address that 'as Trade Unionists we have a right to demand that no man or woman should be allowed to work more than 8 hours per day and 5 days per week'.[6] But he was outflanked by his own Congress. A resolution submitted by the Parliamentary Committee (henceforth the P.C.) and by the Scottish Advisory Council of the Labour Party called for a 40-hour week, but it was defeated by 77 votes to 51 in favour of a resolution from the Glasgow Trades Council demanding a 30-hour week, 'the first act of reconstruction after the War'.[7] The views of the P.C. and Congress were thus 'to some extent in conflict'.[8] An *ad hoc* conference on 20th June 1918 supported 40 hours against 30 by the narrow majority of 40 votes to 37. No further action was taken at the time.[9] After the Armistice the question obviously became an active one again, and the Committee summoned a special Conference on Demobilisation Problems for 27th and 28th December.[10] When this Conference met, it settled for 40 hours, with the rider: 'Failing Government action in this direction the Parliamentary Committee be empowered to devise such methods of industrial action as will enforce this demand'.[11]

Others were moving towards a strike at the same time but for different reasons. Immediately after the Armistice, the A.S.E. and the federated engineering and shipbuilding craft unions (the 'Allied Trades') had negotiated for an immediate reduction of hours in the basic working week from 54 to 47 'on the "one break" system, to come into effect on 1st January 1919'.[12] The A.S.E. Executive, naturally, recommended acceptance of the 47-hour week to their members, and ballot papers to vote on it were distributed to the branches. In recommending its members to vote for the agreement, the Executive said proudly:

> The concession of a 47-hour week without reduction of wages will rank as one of the greatest triumphs of British Trade Unionism.[13]

But the proposal was regarded unfavourably in the Glasgow district for both long-term and immediate reasons. Since the dilution crisis, the local leadership of the A.S.E. had changed. At that time the local officials had been wholeheartedly on the side of the Dilution Commissioners and thus were caught in the crossfire between their own Executive and craft conservatism on one hand, and the militancy of the C.W.C. on the other. However, Sam Bunton, the full-time District Secretary of the union, had resigned in July 1917,[14] to be succeeded by Harry Hopkins of Govan,[15] who had already built up a reputation as a militant by the prominent part he had played in the Govan rent strikes of 1915.[16] In 1919 the District Committee set up a Sub-Committee on Reconstruction which 'reported, *inter alia*, in favour of a 5-day week of 40 hours'.[17] Later, a Joint Sub-Committee on Post-War Reconstruction Policy had been formed by the six District Committees of the union in the West of Scotland. This had reported in favour of a 40-hour week, whereupon 'the Executive Council disapproved of the sub-committee meeting further. Prior to this the Glasgow District Committee had changed its policy to one of a 5-day week of 30 hours'.[18] When the A.S.E. issued the ballot papers to its members, the revived C.W.C. took a hand:

> Immediately following the issue of the ballot papers on the 46-hour proposal, the 'unofficial element' convened a Scottish Conference of Shop Stewards and Workshop delegates from all industries as a result of which a 'Ways and Means Committee' was appointed to agitate for a 30-hour week as a solution to the unemployment problem, which the demobilisation of the Army and Navy was certain to create.[19]

This 'Ways and Means Committee' complained that 'a 47-hour week means increased productivity, increased productivity means increased unemployment, increased unemployment means lower wages'.[20] The newly militant A.S.E. District Committee agreed, and recommended the rejection of the 47-hour deal. By two to one, members in the area backed the District Committee against the National Executive.[21]

Nationally, the voting on the 47-hour proposal of all unions involved was 329,793 for acceptance of the offer and 157,375 against; the voting of the A.S.E. itself was 36,397 for and 27,684 against.[22] The West of Scotland area delegate explained that the 47-hour offer had been badly received in the area

> owing largely to the fact that it has been gained by constitutional methods. A certain section of our members, who are always affected by outside influences, have put up a strong opposition to the acceptance of the concession.[23]

The new militancy of the Glasgow District Committee would not on its own have been enough to provoke a strike, however. Unrest did not really begin to spread until after the adoption of the new working week on 1st January. Resentment was centred on the 'one break' question. Previously the men had worked for 54 hours, starting at 6 a.m., and breaking at 9.15 for breakfast and again at 1 p.m. for lunch. Finding under the new system that they were expected to work continuously from 7.30 until 12, the men protested vigorously:

> It is certain the men in the Clyde Area resented the manner in which the question was put . . . Very many contended that the longer spell of work between meals due to [only] one stop was most unsatisfactory.[24]

Accordingly, the men rallied round the 40-hour week demand as a means of restoring their $3\frac{1}{4}$-hour work periods. This very practical grievance was clearly more powerful in gaining massive support from the engineers for the 40-hour demand than any of the theoretical arguments which had moved the I.L.P. or the S.T.U.C. to endorse it.[25]

The industrial position in the first few days of January 1919 was thus complex, but it can be roughly summarised as follows. In the first place, the Labour Party (Scottish Advisory Council),[26] the Scottish Division of the I.L.P.,[27] the S.T.U.C., and the Glasgow Trades Council all officially supported the 40-hour demand. Secondly, the District Committee of the A.S.E., and the local membership of the skilled engineering unions, were in favour of (at least) a reduction to 40 hours, and hostile to their Executive's request to accept the 47 hours offer. Thirdly, the C.W.C. had been reactivated, and in the guise of the 'Ways and Means Committee' was calling stridently for a 30-hour week.

From about 9th January these bodies wrestled to take the initiative from one another. On that date the P.C. of the S.T.U.C. met the Executive Committee of the Scottish Labour Party. They resolved jointly

> to use every means to unify the forces of Labour to bring about a reduction of the
> working hours to a maximum of 40 hours per week of 8 hours each day

and to this end to co-operate with the local Trade Unions, the Glasgow
Trades Council, 'and other sections of the Labour Movements'. To
carry out its part, the S.T.U.C. summoned for 1st February a Conference of Trades Unions 'affiliated or unaffiliated to Congress'.[28] But
the Ways and Means Committee had already summoned a meeting for
14th January, to which both the Trades Council and the S.T.U.C. sent
representatives, with exactly the same end in view:

> He [Shinwell] had stated the position of the Trades Council who insisted [on] and
> supported the 40 hour per week movement, chiefly for the purpose of uniting the
> Labour movement in an effort to obtain a 40 hour week.[29]
>
> A meeting of the Shop Stewards' Unofficial Committee had been held on
> Tuesday 14th, at which the P.C. was represented. This Committee was working
> for a 30 hour week, but had summoned a conference . . . which was to meet on
> Saturday, 18th January in Glasgow and to decide the number of hours to be
> worked and the date when a strike would be called to enforce same. We were
> invited to be present. Resolved to accept such invitation and to endeavour to get
> 40 hours accepted by such conference.[30]

The meeting on 18th January, at which 'delegates of unofficial Shop
Stewards from all over Scotland'[31] were expected to appear, was in fact
attended mostly by Clydeside engineering and shipbuilding workers.[32]
It elected a Joint Committee to run the strike, to consist of

> representatives of the Shop Stewards movement known as the Ways and Means
> Committee with representatives from the Parliamentary Committee [of the
> S.T.U.C.], the Glasgow Trades Council, the Allied Trades Committee, and other
> individual unions.[33]

This committee met the same evening to consider the votes cast by the
delegates at the conference. In Glasgow 104 workshops or branches
had voted for 30 hours, 83 for 40, 13 for 47 and one neutral,[34] while
'reports from other parts of Scotland favoured 40 hours'.[35] The subsequent decisions of the committee posed acute problems for two of the
bodies represented: the S.T.U.C. and the A.S.E:

> The Joint Committee had by 27 votes to 18 adopted the 40 hours. This was con-
> sidered eminently satisfactory from the point of view of the P.C., but the Joint
> Committee proceeded to put in force the afternoon's resolution anent the date of
> the General Strike, which to us seemed premature and in opposition to our own
> dates for action . . . Thus far — and not as a deliberate action on the part of the
> P.C. — we seemed to be committed to a General Strike on 27th January 1919 . . .
> Prolonged discussion ensued. The opinion was freely expressed that we had

been rushed into precipitate action but on the whole members of the Committee felt it was difficult to avoid such a result, as undoubtedly if a movement for 30 hours had once been launched, it would seriously have jeopardised the function of the 40 hours movement and caused no end of dissension. On the other hand the co-operation of the P.C. with a non-official movement was seriously questioned by other members.[36]

The P.C. had been dragged by its desire to prevent a disastrous 30-hour strike into far hastier action than it wanted, and already members of it were trying to get out of the morass they had plunged themselves into. It was only by the casting vote of the chairman, William Shaw — who was also secretary of the Glasgow Trades Council — that the P.C. decided to keep its delegate, Hugh Lyon, on the Joint Committee. It summoned a conference of union officials for 25th January, and explained

> That while the P.C. considered the action of calling a General Strike on Monday, 27th January hasty and unwise, because of the lack of time for proper preparations, [it] recommend[s] the officials present who can do so to render all the support they can, and that those not yet ready to strike . . . speed up their preparations to fall into line at the earliest possible moment.[37]

Curiously enough, the officials adopted instead a somewhat stronger motion which deleted any reference to the strike being 'hasty and unwise' and endorsed the P.C.'s action, urging all affiliated organisations to support it.[38] But those who represented national unions faced a very acute dilemma, and for none was it worse than for the A.S.E. According to their *apologia*:

> The District Committee had then to decide what to do. It had taken a leading part in the agitation for a shorter working week, attended all the conferences on the matter and taken part in the discussions and the decisions arrived at . . . The decision to recommend our members to link up with our fellow-workers in the matter was a violation of the Rules of the Society; on the other hand to remain loyal to the constitution meant deserting our fellow-workers in the District and also meant leaving our members to fight under the direction of others.[39]

Thus the strike, which began on 27th January, was foredoomed, in spite of the involvement of bodies which were pillars of respectability in the labour world — especially the S.T.U.C. and the Trades Council. The few unions which did give official support were mostly local craft unions in engineering. Thomas Bell was, at the time, the President of the Scottish Iron Moulders' Union, which held a shop ballot on whether to strike:

There was a majority in favour of strike action, but only a majority of sixty: not sufficient to warrant the calling of a strike, according to pure and simple union standards. But our little group on the Executive Council, which was in close touch with the Clyde Workers' Committee, knew the feeling of the moulders in important factories, and understood they would strike. We therefore decided to go forward and the strike orders were issued.[40]

If even a local craft union could get a strike decision only by proceeding unconstitutionally, it will be readily understood that the national unions were unsympathetic. Only the Electricians gave the strike official backing,[41] possibly because a similar strike was about to start in London involving electricity supplies for the Underground. The A.S.E.'s reaction, on the other hand, was decisive:

The Executive Council strongly deprecate the continuance of unofficial action by their members, and whilst fully realising that during the deplorable period of the war, for a variety of reasons, it was necessary to deal leniently with those responsible for such unofficial action, they are conscious that, in the interests of the Trade Union movement, a firm stand has got to be taken.[42]

It then ordered all branches that no strike pay must be given, suspended the entire Glasgow District Committee for its support of the strike, and ordered Hopkins to quit his union-owned house.[43]

The unions involved in the Joint Strike Committee seem to have been those whose local officials happened to be prominent in the S.T.U.C. or Trades Council. Apart from the Engineers and the Allied Trades, the Strike Committee's manifesto named the following as being involved:

Scottish Union of Dock Labourers, Scottish Horse and Motormen's Association, Railwaymen, Municipal Employees' Association, the Building Trades, and Electricians.[44]

But, like the wartime strikes, it was mainly an engineers' affair. Admittedly, the 40-hour week appeal might attract workers from any industry, and the commitment of 'official' labour bodies to a 40-hour week was based on quite general arguments. But the fear of post-war unemployment obviously lay most heavily upon the engineers, with the abrupt rundown of munitions production. And the immediate *casus belli* — 'the cumulative effect of the difficulties caused by the practical working of the 47-hour agreement'[45] — was exclusively a question irritating the engineers. Of the unions listed as supporting the strike, only the Electricians eventually did so wholeheartedly. The Dockers initially supported the strike, but withdrew to negotiate separately for a 44-hour week. The carters (the Horse and Motormen) were brought in more or less by accident as their president, Hugh Lyon, happened to be the S.T.U.C. delegate to the Joint Strike Committee. They succumbed to a separate offer, 'faced with the fact that no other trade in the public service had stopped work'.[46] The Municipal Employees failed to strike at all, although Kerr, their local organiser, was a Trades Council delegate to the strike committee. There were angry recriminations within the Trades Council at this, George Buchanan moving successfully to eject Kerr from the chair at the meeting because

> Councillor Kerr, who was a member of the Joint Strike Committee in the 40 Hours movement had taken no part in the strike when it actually took place, and had given no lead to the members of the Union he represented.[47]

In his defence Kerr explained why the M.E.A. had not struck: they were in the midst of unity negotiations with the Workers' Union and the National Amalgamated Union of Labour, and when at a joint meeting he had proposed participation in the strike he had been overwhelmingly defeated, and had thereafter tried unsuccessfully to resign from the strike committee.[48] The hostility of these unions, the three largest 'unskilled' unions in the West of Scotland, was surely connected with the familiar vendettas between skilled and unskilled in engineering. The Forty Hours' Strike was regarded as another craftsmen's strike; its aims were largely restrictionist and designed to protect craftsmen from unemployment; why then should the unskilled men support it?

The 'Ways and Means Committee' had put forward its 30-hour demand by drawing a parallel with the miners — it had decided

> to go forward with the same demand as the Miners' Federation, viz. six hours per day, five days per week, £1 per day minimum for all adult workers in the Shipbuilding and Engineering industry.[49]

This was not enough to secure for the strike movement the sympathy of the miners' leaders. Although they were participating in their own 30-hour week negotiations, the executive of the National Union of Scottish Mine Workers stated that they 'entirely disassociate[d] themselves from the present erratic strike movement'.[50] On 1st February the *Forward* reported that

> In Fifeshire there are large numbers of miners out on the surfacemen question but the Union Executive is doing its utmost to get them back again.

John MacLean tried ineffectively,[51] and nobody else tried at all, to link the Glasgow engineers with any other workers of the world.

With support from workers outside engineering and shipbuilding so uncertain, the strike might have collapsed in ignominious failure distinguished only by the ridicule heaped on bodies like the S.T.U.C. for their involvement. That it has, instead, earned its place in the heroic annals of the labour movement can be attributed jointly to police misconduct on 31st January and to the Government's exaggerated and panicky reaction to the strike as it developed.

11

'Squalid Terrorism':
the Forty Hours' Strike and Bloody Friday

When it became clear that most of the union executives were not going to support the proposed strike, the local Press became more confident that no very serious unrest would ensue. The *Glasgow Herald*, reporting the drastic action taken by the Executive of the A.S.E., added that their stand 'makes the chance of a general stoppage of work more remote than it seemed a day or two ago'.[1] The principal Glasgow popular paper, the Northcliffe-owned *Daily Record and Mail*, was more exuberant. It assured its readers before the strike started that there would be no strike, and while it was in progress that it was on the point of collapse:

> It may be taken for granted that so far as the big Unions are concerned . . . the recommendations of their authorised representatives will be loyally accepted, and that there will be no stoppage of work.[2]
> Today the clang of hammers and the whirr of machinery . . . are expected to swell into robust chorus.[3]

In fact, the stoppage of work on Monday, 27th January was reasonably satisfactory to the strike organisers. The Joint Committee estimated that 40,000 Glasgow shipbuilding and engineering workers were idle on the Monday and 70,000 on the Tuesday, although 'other estimates', whose source was not specified, gave the latter figure as only 30 or 35,000.[4] For the strike leaders, however, the strike would stand or fall by whether they could involve non-engineers, and particularly public service workers. Here the first major rebuff was the failure of the Municipal Employees' Association (M.E.A.) to strike. This union organised the Glasgow tramwaymen, and also — a point of some importance — the power station workers at Pinkston, the station generating current for the tramways. In Belfast, all public utilities had been shut down a few days earlier in a general, unofficial, 44-hour strike. In Glasgow many feared, and the strike leaders hoped, that the same would happen. But it did not. The Electricians struck, and cut down industrial and domestic power supplies. But the M.E.A. did not:

> In the city of Glasgow the decision of the electricity workers to join in the strike movement seemed at first to make uncertain the extent to which the tramway and other Corporation undertakings might be affected, but an official assurance was given late last night that the decision of the meeting would not affect the Corporation power stations.[5]

Thus for the first two days of the strike, the various private electricity companies had to close down, and this in turn affected some industrial plants such as Parkhead.[6] But neither of the Corporation power stations — Port Dundas, supplying current for street lighting, and Pinkston for the tramways — was at first affected.

Mass picketing was a novel feature of the strike. The technique was later described by one of the secretaries of the Strike Committee:

> Pickets of five to ten thousand workers would march to a particular shop, then line up on either side of the roadway, and the workers still at work had to run the gauntlet. It was a most successful method, and entirely legal.[7]

On the second day of the strike, the *Glasgow Herald* noted that it had become 'more pronounced' in some shops, which had stopped work after lunch in many cases because of the 'massed picketing' methods of the strikers.[8] Opponents of the strike complained that the mass pickets were a form of intimidation. Shinwell rejected the charge, but not very convincingly. On the 27th he asked a strike meeting

> to place their confidence in the committee and carry out their instructions. One instruction was to preserve order (cheers), to indulge in no unseemly disturbance, to act in a perfectly legal and constitutional manner (laughter) . . . to indulge in picketing, but to adopt merely moral suasion (laughter), and to adopt these methods till the Joint Committee instructed them to act otherwise (loud cheers).[9]

Two days later he said:

> We have advocated constitutional action all along the line. The newspapers have now charged us with the crime of intimidation. Whether they charge us with that crime or any other, we are going to see to it that every class of worker in the city is out. (Applause). When we leave this hall we are going to take a walk — an orderly walk — (Laughter) with bands heading the procession, to the power stations (Applause) for the purpose of holding a meeting . . . If as a result of our meeting today there is no change in the situation other events will rapidly follow.[10]

This was the prelude to stepping up the strike. The power workers at

Port Dundas were called out[11] and the strikers then marched on Pinkston to try to bring out the workers there. Here they met their match in James Dalrymple, the pugnacious manager of the tramways, who 'gave assurances that he had made all arrangements for manning the power station — no matter what picketing may be attempted by the strikers'.[12] Dalrymple gave the workers board and lodging inside the power station, which was 'besieged' by strikers for at least five days.[13] The workers did not strike, and outside the gates of the power station Shinwell attacked the 'miserable attitude of the Municipal Employees' Association,' while Kirkwood added:

> he did not ask the strikers to rush the gates. The time had not yet arrived for that.[14]

The strike leaders sent a deputation to the Lord Provost the same day, Wednesday January 29th, to ask him to seek Government intervention. What happened at the meeting can be pieced together from the contents of the telegram sent by the Provost to Bonar Law,[15] and from the statements of the strike leaders, as later confirmed by themselves and others at the riot trial in April:

> The Lord Provost was reminded that unconstitutional tactics might develop if the workers' demands were ignored . . . Drastic action would have to be resorted to if the reply to the Lord Provost's message was unsatisfactory . . . The Deputation had given the Lord Provost till Friday to furnish an answer.[16]

So spoke Shinwell to the strikers after the meeting: while the deputation was inside Gallacher told those waiting outside:

> If the strike was not settled by the end of this week they would not hesitate to stop every tramcar, shut off every light, and generally paralyse the business of the city.[17]

According to a police witness who gave evidence at the riot trial, Shinwell told the crowd that the deputation had

> informed the Lord Provost that if they could not get what they wanted by constitutional methods, drastic action would be taken. Further, he said that they had told the Lord Provost that if he did not take the necessary steps to stop the tramcars interfering with the procession that (sic) the strikers would. Shinwell then advised them to assemble in their thousands on Friday 31st.[18]

The following day, the Town Clerk added that the strike leaders had spoken in the same terms inside the City Chambers as outside.[19] The Lord Provost said that, at Neil Maclean's request, no mention of stopping the tramcars was put in the telegram, but that otherwise 'Mr.

Maclean told him in a general way what they wanted to say, and he put it down'.[20] The strikers' requests formed the central passage of the telegram, to which the Lord Provost added some information of his own. The telegram, read out by Bonar Law to the War Cabinet, opened by explaining the demand for a 40-hour week

> so as to provide for those who are demobilised and are without employment. It was further stated that they had hitherto adopted constitutional methods in urging their demand, but that failing consideration being given to their request by the Government, they would adopt any other methods which they might consider to be likely to advance their cause. They have, however, agreed to delay taking any such action until Friday in order that I may be able to communicate your reply. I have just learnt from the manager of the electricity department that all men in generating stations have been compelled today to join the strike . . .[21]

The War Cabinet had already rejected the idea of intervening in the strike 'over the heads of the Union Executives'[22] — a line it took on all strikes at the time — so Law and Horne (the Minister of Labour) drafted a reply reiterating this decision. The Cabinet then turned to discussing how to deal with the unrest. Law first reported a telephone conversation with Lloyd George, and then went on to put forward his own views:

> the Prime Minister said that if it were necessary he would come to London, but he was of the opinion that his coming would have the appearance of interfering with Sir Robert Horne's authority . . .
> Mr. Bonar Law said he thought it vital for the War Cabinet to be satisfied that there was a sufficient force in Glasgow to prevent disorder and to protect those volunteers or others who could be made available to take over the operation of the generating stations and municipal services. It was certain that if the movement in Glasgow grew, it would spread all over the country.[23]

The Secretary for Scotland argued that 2,000 special constables be brought in to protect the public utilities, as they were 'more reliable' than soldiers. However, Sir William Robertson, who was in attendance, informed the Cabinet of the troop dispositions in Scotland. The troops available were all reserve units,

> and consisted of all sorts of men, old, young, convalescents, and men with wounds. As regards the officers, they were not very efficient. There were certain disadvantages in employing Scottish troops, but on the whole he thought it would be safer to use them than to import English battalions.[24]

The Cabinet eventually decided to take four steps. The military would be 'in readiness' to help keep up the public lighting; Mr. John Lamb of the Scottish Office would go to Glasgow 'in order to acquaint the Lord

Provost and the Sheriff[25] of the Government's policy and to keep the Government informed of any development in the situation'.[26] Next, an *ad hoc* committee should be formed 'for the purpose of consultation during the continuance of disorder',[27] and finally 'the Lord Advocate should examine the legal grounds for the arrest of the ringleaders of the strike, should it be found desirable to do so'.[28]

As promised two days earlier, a mass meeting of strikers assembled in George Square on Friday morning, the 31st, to hear Bonar Law's reply. While the leaders' deputation was in the City Chambers,

> an altercation occurred with the police through the stoppage of the tramcar service on the South side of the square. As a result the police drew their batons and made several charges. About 40 people were injured in the melee, including several who had been drawn to the scene, and who had no connection with the strike.[29]

The police made a second charge up the east side of the square, past the City Chambers, and a third one up North Frederick Street, a steep street leading up from the north-east corner of the square, where they were met by demonstrators who threw lemonade bottles taken from a passing lorry.[30] During the melee, the Sheriff of Lanarkshire, who was at the time in consultation with the Lord Provost and Lamb of the Scottish Office[31] (who had presumably just arrived with the Cabinet's instructions), read the Riot Act, though of course it was not heard by most of the demonstrators. Gallacher, Kirkwood, and a number of others were arrested. The same evening Shinwell was also arrested, having in the meantime destroyed all the documents relating to the strike in the Trades Council offices, which were being used by the Strike Committee.[32]

The War Cabinet met again on the afternoon of Bloody Friday, as the day was immediately labelled. After Horne had reported that he 'understood that foot and mounted police had charged the crowd in order to quell a riot, and casualties had resulted', the Cabinet fell to discussing the nature of the outbreak:

> The Secretary for Scotland said that, in his opinion, it was more clear than ever that it was a misnomer to call the situation in Glasgow a strike — it was a Bolshevist rising. It was, he thought, of limited dimensions in numbers, if not in effect.[33]

However, the Cabinet was not called upon to take any new decisions, since the moves to send troops to Scotland had already been put into effect. It heard that six tanks and 100 motor lorries were being sent north by rail that night, and after listening to the Lord Advocate describe various actions which might be taken against the leaders under D.O.R.A.,[34] decided to take no further action in the meantime. The following morning, the army was in occupation, and the six tanks were stationed in the Cattle Market.

The events of Wednesday to Friday had given rise to an acrimonious conflict between the Lord Provost and the leader-writers of the *Glasgow Herald*. The *Herald* thought the telegram was 'not pleasant reading for loyal citizens'[35] because it appeared to show that the Provost had some sympathy with the strikers' demands. He should, said the paper, have ignored them altogether. When, on Friday 6th, the Provost successfully defended himself in the Town Council, he made his motives in sending the telegram quite clear. Wheatley, after hearing him, expressed a view which was shared by other labour representatives: 'he believed until that day that the Lord Provost had acted out of a high sense of fair play'.[36] Instead, by the Provost's own admission, his purpose in passing on the strikers' demands had been to convince the Government of 'their necessity for immediately providing a sufficient force to aid the civilian force in any emergency which might arise'.[37] His action, in fact, had been designed to an end of which the *Herald* thoroughly approved; from its own political standpoint, its criticism was quite misconceived. The strikers, far from getting the Government to intervene on their behalf to end the strike, had simply put their heads into the noose by dictating to the Provost the intransigent terms of the central part of the telegram. The threats it contained spurred the Government to vigorous intervention — exactly what the Provost wanted.

As the strike progressed, and it became increasingly clear that it was not going to spread to other industrial centres, there was a slow drift back to work, starting with those trades other than the engineers who had joined the strike. The miners of Blantyre (just outside Glasgow) were among the few who had joined the strike, but on 2nd February their district president complained that they 'had now been out for a week and were being led nowhere, and he advised the men to return to work at once'.[38] The mass pickets did not continue beyond the 3rd,[39] and some engineering shops, including Weirs, reported that they had restarted on the 4th.[40] By the 5th, power supplies were being reported as being back to normal;[41] although the E.T.U. was on official strike, the Corporation's Port Dundas station and the works of the Clyde Valley Electric Power Company were being adequately manned by 'volunteers'.[42] Some plants, especially the shipyards, stayed out for a further five or six days. Eventually, on 10th February, the Strike Committee recommended

> a full resumption of work by all strikers on Wednesday, 12th February, until such time as we can perfect the organisation of our forces with a view to making our claim for 40 hours on a national basis and to enforce it by a national strike of all workers in the near future.[43]

Both the *Strike Bulletin* and the *Forward* insisted that the reason for the resumption was a bogus statement purporting to call off the strike printed in the *Evening Times* the previous day, which had led to a drift back to work.[44] But clearly the strike could not have lasted much longer in any case.

The sequel was a long-drawn out anticlimax of retreat from militancy, punctuated by the trial of twelve persons for riot or incitement to riot in the High Court in Edinburgh in April. The S.T.U.C., in particular, came to nothing but harm as a result of its involvement. While the strike was still under way it tried desperately, but unavailingly, to get the Government or the T.U.C. to intervene in any way at all. A deputation from the P.C. to London, sent on February 3rd, returned with its tail between its legs:

> The impression . . . conveyed to the deputation was that the General Secretaries in London were strongly opposed to any Government action, had used all their influence to prevent such intervention, and that the parties named[45] followed along that line. They persisted in regarding the Scottish movement as an unofficial strike, and apparently nothing could move them from this position.
> Prolonged consideration was given to the whole strike position, which was felt to be very unsatisfactory.[46]

After the end of strike, the P.C. unanimously resolved to withdraw from the Joint Committee,[47] which then faced the task of raising money for the strike trial defence. In this task co-operation was strained to the limit in wrangles over responsibility for looking after the money:

> The first meeting of the Joint Committee had been of very little use owing to the attitude of the Clyde Defence Committee who advised that all monies should be paid to their Treasurer[48]

— as Shaw reported to the Glasgow Trades Council. An enormous sum of money had to be raised for the defence. Although no papers have survived relating to the conduct of the strike — doubtless much was destroyed by Shinwell and Shaw on the afternoon of Bloody Friday — a little file does survive on the defence fund. It consists mostly of letters from lawyers to Shaw, alternately pleading and threatening in their requests for immediate payment. In the final audited account, dated May 1920, £2,562:19:11 had been collected, and almost all of it paid through a Glasgow solicitor to five solicitors' firms and three K.C.'s; and it was reported that £1,400 was still due to Glasgow solicitors.[49] In the months after the strike, and indeed for a full year after the trial, the raising of money on a scale far outside any previously required occupied the principal energies of many of the prominent local leaders.

On April 7th the trial started, before Lord Scott Dickson and a jury, of Shinwell, Gallacher, Kirkwood, Hopkins, George Ebury[50] and James Brennan on charges of incitement to riot and riot; and of six others,[51] who held no official position in labour organisations, on charges of rioting. The Crown case, which was led by Clyde, the Lord Advocate, was that from 27th to 30th January Shinwell and his colleagues had been inciting strikers to form a riotous assembly in George Square on the 31st in order to stop the tramcars. On that day, he dramatically concluded, 'every act of revolution was in progress, and could be traced to the previous incitement'.[52] The effect of this was somewhat marred by his withdrawal of the incitement charge against Kirkwood. After the chief defence counsel had argued that the Crown had quite failed to prove any 'preconceived arrangement and intention to do mischief'[53] on the part of the crowd on Bloody Friday, the Lord Advocate again restricted the number of incitement charges. The judge further ruled out all incitement charges relating to dates earlier than the 29th, on the grounds that he accepted the defence contention that 'there was then no idea of holding a meeting on the 31st, and consequently there could be no incitement'.[54] He pointed out that the evidence of the Town Clerk and of Neil Maclean conflicted as to whether the strikers' promise to 'stop the cars' was a threat of violence, or merely a promise that the tramwaymen would be brought out on strike. He further pointed out that it was a question of fact for the jury whether the stoppage of cars on the south side of the square was deliberate or merely the result of the pressure of the crowd. He concluded by dismissing all the charges against two of the accused.

The jury returned a 14-1 majority verdict that Gallacher and Shinwell were guilty of incitement to riot, and Gallacher, Murray and MacArtney were guilty of rioting. They acquitted all the other defendants. This verdict appears to have caused some confusion:

> Considerable delay took place in an endeavour to adjust the terms on which the verdict should be recorded, and eventually the Lord Justice Clerk,[55] the Clerk of the Justiciary, and his Depute returned for the purpose.[56]

The *Forward's* version of the same incident was that 'eye-witnesses in Court declared that they never saw a man so obviously nonplussed as was the Lord Justice Clerk at the jury's verdict'.[57] A later article purported to describe the jury's thought-processes:

> Brennan got off, not guilty, because in the opinion of some of the jurymen he had a 'nice open face' and because he had saved a policeman from being thrown into the Clyde. As a matter of fact, it was Kirkwood who had saved the policeman, but Davie was getting off anyhow and his surplus Kharma fell upon Brennan.[58]

The chief defence counsel immediately gave notice of appeal:

> The verdict was not only contrary to the evidence but was inconsistent with the Judge's charge. Particularly this is said to refer to Shinwell and Gallacher, who were convicted on charges of incitement which those accused maintained had not been legally proved.[59]

Eventually Shinwell was sentenced to five months' imprisonment and Gallacher to three. Even if the argument that the jury's verdict was inconsistent with the judge's charge be rejected, it is clear from the limited nature of the sentences that neither judge nor jury was in much sympathy with the Crown submission that Bloody Friday was the culmination of a violent and illegal conspiracy.

After the trial was over, labour organisations in the area settled down to money-raising and recrimination. The recriminations reached their peak at the 1919 congress of the S.T.U.C., held in early May, for which the P.C. produced a long statement justifying their action. Criticism centred on the P.C.'s role in backing a strike disowned by the union executives. Bailie Whitehead of the Brassfinishers pointed out that the majority of A.S.E. members had accepted the 47-hour offer, and 'Agreements were agreements, whether they liked them or not'.[60] In defence of the P.C. spoke not only the pugnacious men of the left ('Mr. Hugh Mulholland (Sheet Iron Workers) asked if a Revolution took place was it to be turned down because it was unconstitutional?')[61] but the right-wing members of the committee itself. Robert Allan of Edinburgh put the committee's view:

> He agreed the strike was the outcome of hasty and unwise action, but the P.C. could not ignore it. If they could not control the forces behind the strike, they at least attempted to guide them along proper lines.[62]

No resolution was put, so the P.C. was saved the embarrassment of a vote of censure. But outside Glasgow their involvement seems to have widely disturbed Scottish trade unionists. The Edinburgh Trades

Council, for instance, had throughout looked at the whole affair with a jaundiced eye. During the strike itself the chairman of that council had said:

> in the present strike all semblance of democracy had been thrown to the winds. The movement for a shorter week was sound, but the way in which the strike had been started was a disgrace to Trade Unionism.[63]

And in their report for 1919, the executive of the council returned vigorously to the theme:

> Many trades were, at this time [January 1919] negotiating for shorter hours, and they did not feel inclined to immediately drop bargaining and go out on strike without giving an opportunity for an amicable settlement . . . The lesson to be learned from the strike is that democracy must fully operate in Trades Unionism, that all workers who are to be called on to take action have a right to be consulted, and their opinions considered, that King Stork of the unofficial movement may be an even worse leader than King Log of the official movement, that the workers are not to be stampeded into a course of action that has been determined on without their express approval. The shortening of hours is of such importance to the working class that any bungling in efforts to secure it should be deprecated and condemned.[64]

Both the S.T.U.C. and the Glasgow Trades Council emerged from the 40-hour strike 'once bitten twice shy'. In August 1919, when a special conference of the S.T.U.C. was considering a suggestion that unions should be asked to ballot on a strike on housing conditions, Allan warned:

> It was not in the power of the Executive of Congress to call for a stoppage of work, and therefore they were bound to ask for an expression of opinion.[65]

But the Executive had done precisely what was 'not in their power' seven months earlier. During the national railway strike of September 1919, they took great care not to burn their fingers again:

> After full consideration it was resolved to convene a Conference of Trade Union officials in Glasgow . . . Secretary to send invitation to officials representing head offices of unions. Agreed not to invite branch representatives or trades councils.[66]

A year later, they were still warning the Scottish Labour Housing Association against a proposed strike in protest at rent increases.[67]

The Glasgow Trades Council reacted similarly. Shortly after the riot trial it heard with less than ecstasy a call from Jack Leckie of the C.W.C. for drastic action to secure the release of the prisoners:

> Mr. Leckie was asked by Mr. Shanks to explain what he meant by drastic action?

And if he meant a down tools policy had any hope of success? He answered that he had nothing of a concrete proposal to make . . . Mr. Kiddie seconded by Mr. Marchbanks moved that we do not send representatives [to a proposed joint meeting to decide on action to be taken] . . . and do not countenance the proposal to stop work. Mr. Marchbanks [said] such action would be sure to end in a farce.[68]

After several votes, it was agreed

that Council be represented but delegates to have only a watching brief.[69]

Where the official bodies retreated, the unofficial ones just faded away. The end of wartime conditions marked the end of their opportunity. One aspect of 'official' intervention in the 1919 strike was undoubtedly the desire of local officials to regain that control over their shop stewards and members which had been lost to them in wartime conditions. But they were caught out in a most embarrassing position, because exactly the same desire caused national organisations to set their face against the strike in the most determined way — as witness the reaction of the A.S.E. Executive or the Labour Party and T.U.C. officials to whom the S.T.U.C. deputation had spoken. With the Restoration of Pre-War Practices Act imminent,[70] the bargain struck in the Treasury Agreement was being fulfilled on the Government side, and the militants no longer had the opportunity of attacking their executives because of the latter's apparent tolerance of dilution and of the ban on strikes. But

. . . as it was, the District Committee was left to act as a buffer between the rank and file on the one hand and the central authority on the other, the members being right up against it, and the Executive Council remaining almost inactive, 400 miles away. The possibility of a local disruption in the Society was another consideration which was present to the minds of the Committee.[71]

Wartime militancy had a sting in its tail — or rather, like a bee, it left its sting and then died. The result of the 40 Hours' Strike was a fatal blow to the unofficial movement and a damaging one to the official labour organisations. By discrediting militant industrial action, it helped swing the pendulum towards political and electoral action of a reformist rather than a professedly revolutionary kind. This will be examined in the next three chapters. But before passing on, we must consider what sort of riot occurred on Bloody Friday and whether there was any sense in which the strike was revolutionary in intention, and in which the Government response was therefore justified.

The *Glasgow Herald* and the Lord Advocate were in no doubt that the trial showed up the revolutionary intentions of the strike leaders. On the day of the verdicts, the first leader in the *Herald* more than compensated for the disappointingly meagre sentences:

> The tiresome and confused nature of much of the evidence was in significant contrast to the sinister simplicity of the main purpose which the whole case revealed . . . For the lightness of their [Shinwell's and Gallacher's] sentences they had to thank, in the first place, the phlegm or hesitancy of the mass of those they led, and in the second place, and more especially, the admirable self-restraint displayed by the civic and legal authorities and by the police force.
> . . . The formation of the Joint Strike Committee was . . . the first step towards that squalid terrorism which the world now describes as Bolshevism.[72]

According to the Lord Advocate,

> The incidents on January 31 in George Square . . . constituted the greatest imaginable menace to public order and security. There were not, thank heaven, many incidents like them recorded in our time, and as incidents of that sort were not only in the highest degree criminal in themselves, but involved a menace to the foundation of public peace and security, he asked the jury by their verdict to express the guilt of those who instigated them.[73]

But, in fact, the Crown almost entirely failed to convince the judge and jury that any conspiracy, Bolshevist or otherwise, existed. The news columns of the *Glasgow Herald*, both after Bloody Friday and during the trial, carry conclusive evidence that the editorial opinions in adjacent columns were based on fantasy. Bloody Friday was a police riot; or, to speak less dramatically, was caused by the inexperience and incompetence of the police in handling a large crowd with no revolutionary ambitions. Not one of the accounts which will be drawn upon to justify this contention comes from a source friendly to the strike; most come from its arch-enemy, the *Glasgow Herald*.

The personal feelings of shock and disapproval on the part of the *Herald* reporter who witnessed the riot emerged from his account. After the arrest of Gallacher and Kirkwood, he wrote, the police proceeded to clear the Square

> with a vigour and determination that was a prelude to the extraordinary scenes the Square was afterwards to witness, and to which the city, with all its acquaintance with labour troubles, can happily offer no parallel. A strong body of police . . . swept the crowd in front of them, raining a hurricane of blows which fell indiscriminately on those actually participating in the strike and on those who had been drawn to the scene merely through curiosity.[74]

The Special Correspondent of the *Daily News* commented:

Even if one takes the least favourable view of the intentions of the strikers, it cannot be said that the authorities managed their business very happily on Friday. In the first place, if it was intended to maintain a service of tramcars through George Square during the demonstration, it was inexcusable to leave the square virtually unguarded by police until the whole of the roadway was blocked by a dense crowd, and then endeavour to force the tramcars through it . . .
I was within a few yards of the tramcars during the forcing through process, and I have no hesitation in saying that the baton charge, made with the object of clearing a way for the second tramcar, was the beginning of the trouble in the square. The temper of some hundreds of strikers was immediately fired.[75]

The official injury list was given as 19 police hurt and 34 civilians, which suggests that the police gave at least as good as they got.

During the trial several defence witnesses testified that the police had initiated the violence by their baton charges, and had batoned innocent bystanders. One of them added, 'it was the usual Glasgow crowd, always up against the police when there was any row on'.[76] An essential part of the Crown case was to prove that the holding up of the cars was a deliberate and violent act on the part of the strikers, in pursuance of threats made by Shinwell and Gallacher on the Wednesday. This case hardly survived the cross-examination of Chief Constable Stevenson:

He admitted, however, that there was no sign during the week on the part of the processionists of any intention to make a violent attack on the tramways.[77]

The Lord Advocate called the defence argument that it was the police who rioted

absurd when they remembered that there were 140 police and 25,000 persons in the Square, that the former were under the eye of the Chief Constable, and that there had been consultations among the authorities going on all week.[78]

Nevertheless, not all the police were directly 'under the eye of the Chief Constable', who specifically denied sole responsibility for the directions given to the police:

witness said he did not give orders for any particular charge. He left that to his officers.[79]

It was a subordinate officer, then, who presumably ordered the charges in front of the City Chambers and up North Frederick Street. This brings us to a curious point, which was surprisingly not raised by the defence at the trial. The purpose of the baton charges was supposedly to clear a way for the tramcars. But no tramlines ran along the east side of the square, in front of the City Chambers, in 1919.[80] Nor were there any in North Frederick Street, which was, and is, a steep minor road leading nowhere in particular. These charges can therefore only be regarded as unprovoked attacks by the police designed to intimidate or scatter the crowd — a fact which gives the lie to the Lord Advocate's curious argument that, since there were more strikers than police, the latter cannot have caused the rioting. There was no evidence, even in the incitement charges, that any leader was encouraging any striker to assail the City Chambers, and this was at no time adduced as a reason for the behaviour of the police. It was surely the conduct of the police, not the revolutionary intentions of any of the crowd, which brought about Bloody Friday.

This conclusion does not, however, entitle us to dismiss out of hand the idea that the strike involved a serious revolutionary threat. The problem here is to decide what to make of the role played by Shinwell. Before the strike began, he spoke in the Trades Council about its limited aims:

> The movement was not revolutionary in character, neither was it inspired by the legitimate desire of the workers for more leisure. It was attributable solely to the fear of unemployment in the near future, and the desire to make room for the man from the Army and Navy.[81]

Many years later, he recorded that he had made this statement because

> Still positive that the mass of workers had no aims beyond remedying the labour situation, I took the opportunity of reiterating my views . . . knowing that with the current anxieties of the country, my words would obtain national Press coverage and might bring a note of sanity into the hysteria being shown in London.[82]

The picture of Shinwell as a moderate presented by these statements accords with what we saw in Chapter 10 of his activities in trying to concentrate the strike demand on 40 hours rather than an impossible 30 hours. It accords much less well with the reports of his behaviour during the strike itself. We have already quoted his sometimes threatening-sounding speeches encouraging mass pickets. He was reported as saying outside Pinkston power station:

> When the workers in the power station knew that the strikers insisted on their participation, he believed they would not be at work in the morning. At the same time he recommended the police to take a holiday (Laughter).[83]

Kirkwood and Shinwell more than once threatened that 'other means' or 'drastic action' would have to be taken if the strikers' demands were not met, and both sides agreed that Shinwell and Neil Maclean had told the Lord Provost that they would stop the trams if Bonar Law did not send a satisfactory reply to the telegram. Further evidence comes from a most unexpected source: William Gallacher. On the 30th, he later wrote:

> I'd been reporting to the committee at the Trades Council offices in Bath Street, and Manny had made a suggestion of a pretty desperate nature. I had told him I would do whatever the committee agreed, but if his project was carried out I would insist on all members of the committee being right at the head of the demonstration. The subject had been dropped. But later, as I was walking down Bath Street with Messer and Davie [Kirkwood], Messer had said, 'You've got to watch that fellow Shinwell. He'll make trouble and leave you to face it'.[84]

The conspiratorial tone of Gallacher's accounts makes it impossible to guess what Shinwell's suggestion was — an assault on the City Chambers, or as Bell asserts, a proposal 'to lead the workers along the well-to-do streets and let them loose'?[85] We cannot tell, but Shinwell's speeches and actions during the strike were certainly not as 'moderate' and 'constitutional' as those he had made earlier. Did he really expect to promote a revolution? It seems scarcely credible. In the negotiations leading up to the strike he must have been uncomfortably aware of the difficulties which would flow from its lack of official backing. But no serious attempt was made to turn the 40 Hours' Strike into a national stoppage of work. Shinwell must have been well aware that without strike pay his supporters could not stay out indefinitely. Perhaps the key to his real feelings lies buried in the report of one of his many speeches during the strike:

> It was not the intention of the Joint Committee to have a long strike. If payment or non-payment of strike aliment was to stand between them and their objective then their objective would never be secured . . . he asked them to place their confidence in the committee and carry out their instructions.[86]

Perhaps Shinwell hoped to provoke some dramatic incident or other which would lead rapidly to intervention in the strikers' favour, in spite of their underlying financial and organisational weakness. If so, he got his incident, but not the sort of intervention he would have hoped for. In 1915, the rent strikes had apparently led straight to the Rent Restriction Act. In 1919, the war was over; Bloody Friday apparently led straight to the military occupation of Glasgow.[87] Gallacher, writing in 1936, complained that 'we were carrying on a strike, when we ought to have been making a revolution'.[88] If, instead of marching to George Square on Bloody Friday, the strikers had gone to Maryhill barracks to call on the soldiers there to support them, 'Glasgow would have been in our hands'.[89] It must be said, however, that Gallacher's reaction when he came out of the City Chambers on Bloody Friday and saw the melee before him was scarcely that of a dedicated revolutionary. He shouted frantically to the crowd to leave the square and to go to Glasgow Green:

> Now, keep order. Understand it has been a very unfortunate occurrence.[90] 'March, for God's sake. Are you going to do that much for us?' (Cries of 'Yes').[91]

Likewise, Kirkwood, for all his robust speeches earlier, was 'obvious[ly] . . . completely unstrung by the experience'[92] of Bloody Friday ('He was a very frightened man'[93] in Harry McShane's recollection). Compared to the storming of the Winter Palace or the First Battle of the Somme, Bloody Friday was not very bloody. But it frightened dedicated revolutionaries who had never seen blood spilt before. As pacific men, their first instincts were to get the crowd out of harm's way as soon as possible.

In the light of all this, the Government's reaction was unquestionably excessive. After the troops arrived, the *Daily News's* correspondent commented:

> In the course of a long experience of strikes and outbreaks of disorder in industrial disputes I have never seen such extensive preparations for repression.[94]

The Labour press was generally united in seeing the arrival of the tanks and motor lorries as an 'Absurd Parade of Military Forces',[95] and their view is echoed by modern commentators.[96]

It is certainly difficult to see what the tanks could have done if the rioting had become more serious, unless shell the City Chambers as if they were the Dublin G.P.O. But, however unrealistic the threats from Shinwell and Neil Maclean passed on by the Lord Provost, there was never a time when the Government would be more disposed to take them seriously than January 1919. A natural suspicion of Bolshevism had for some months been fanned by the so-called 'Fortnightly Reports on Revolutionary Organisations in the United Kingdom, and Morale in Foreign Countries' which were prepared for the War Cabinet by Basil Thomson, head of the Special Branch. These reports presented a great deal of miscellaneous alarmist information about the activities of 'pacifists' and other undesirables. Their tone is captured by the following four excerpts from the report for 2nd December 1918:

It is to be feared that, in the event of serious disturbances, the police in large cities cannot be depended upon . . .

The wirepullers behind [George Lansbury] have not yet been disclosed, but the plan is by holding a series of revolutionary meetings in what is regarded as a stronghold of the capitalist class, the Royal[97] Albert Hall, to test the strength of the revolutionary movement and fan the temper of the London workers with a view of preparing for action of a much more serious character . . .

A private letter from Sylvia Pankhurst to a friend in Glasgow which has come into my hands concludes with the words, 'I expect the Revolution soon, don't you?'

Mr. Will Thorne in conversation said a few days ago that Bolshevism or rather the state of dissatisfaction that might foster it, has never been so high in England as at the present moment. The industrial workers of Scotland are of a deeper red than the usual red-flaggers.[98]

Not only Russia, but the German and Austrian empires seemed to be collapsing into Bolshevism and anarchy. The Spartacist revolt in Berlin had just taken place, and self-proclaimed Communists were trying to take power in Bavaria and Hungary. It is hardly surprising, therefore, that members of the British Government saw the Glasgow strike as a 'Bolshevist rising' — and sent enough troops to quell a Bolshevik rebellion, or at the very least another Easter Rising. Thomson himself thought that

During the first three months of 1919 unrest touched its high-water mark. I do not think that at any time in history since the Bristol Riots we have been so near revolution . . . On the 27th of January there were extensive strikes on the Clyde of a revolutionary rather than an economic character.[99]

Furthermore, the War Cabinet was misinformed on one point, which made the strike seem more serious than it actually was. The Lord Provost's telegram, it will be recalled, had said that 'all men in generating stations have been compelled today to join the strike'. But this was not true. Pinkston was never affected, in spite of the strikers' most strenuous efforts. The power station supplying the tramways was organised by the tramwaymen's union, an 'unskilled' union, whereas other power workers were members of the 'skilled' E.T.U. The strike originated in a craftsmen's grievance, and relations between the skilled and unskilled were no better than they had been at any time since 1911 and the Singers strike. So Pinkston never came out, and the disruption to public utilities was far less than had been caused the previous week in Belfast — even though Port Dundas was on strike, the street lighting seems never to have suffered worse than a voltage reduction.[100] Once arrived in Glasgow, the troops were never used for their ostensible purpose — to protect the 'volunteers' manning municipal services —

although their presence may have been enough of a threat to make the strikers discontinue mass picketing.

January 1919 was almost a carbon copy of March 1916. Both times, the Government acted more severely than necessary on receipt of inaccurate and misleading alarmist information. Both times participants later remembered with advantage what feats they did that day, and have been applauded for them by admirers who have failed to check what actually happened. Both 'revolutionary' movements were actually protective reflexes on the part of the engineers, with whom unskilled workers had no common interests. It may be argued that the Government's firm stand in 1919 prevented any resurgence of revolutionary, anti-official militancy. But that is to forget the structural weakness of the strike. It would certainly have collapsed, and discredited unofficial action, without any help from the Government. Indeed, the net effect of the tanks in the Cattle Market was probably the same as that of the police misbehaviour in George Square: it gave the strike a romantic history which successfully concealed an otherwise ignominious failure.

12

The Lines Laid Down: the I.L.P., the Communists, and John MacLean

The debacle of 1919 broke the industrial power of the extreme left, but it remained for some time an open question how its political strength would develop. This chapter deals with the changing fortunes of the various sects and parties of the far left.

The Scottish Division of the I.L.P. had the reputation of being one of the most militant, as well as the largest,[1] of the divisions in which the party was organised; and here, initially, the omens seemed favourable for the Communists. The Scottish Division's 1920 Conference carried by 158 votes to 28 a resolution calling upon the I.L.P. to affiliate to the Third International.[2] The national conference, held in Glasgow in 1920, was less enthusiastic and listened to a condemnation of the Scottish I.L.P.'s decision by MacDonald. By a clear majority it voted to sever its links with the Second International, but by 472 votes to 206 it decided to try to form a new international rather than apply for membership of the Third.[3] (The confused story of the I.L.P. and the 'Two-and-a-Half International', which arose out of this decision, falls outside the scope of this work).

The pressure in favour of Communism on industrial organisations in the Glasgow area seems to have come somewhat later, at a time when reaction to the left wing was already setting in within the I.L.P. In December 1920 Glasgow Trades Council agreed to ask the Labour Party Executive to change the Party constitution in order to allow the Communist Party to become affiliated.[4] Three months later the Council, against the recommendation of one of its sub-committees, decided to ask the S.T.U.C. to join the Provisional International Council of Trade and Industrial Unions (later known as the Red International of Labour Unions), 'thereby allowing their members to par-

139

ticipate directly in framing the industrial policy of the workers of the world'.[5]

When this resolution was put before the S.T.U.C. meeting at Aberdeen in 1921, an opponent claimed that 'they would become automata controlled by an international bureaucracy centred in Moscow'[6] and it was declared defeated by 48 votes to 45; but on a recount the motion was then declared carried by 55 to 50.

The *Forward* reporter mentioned allegations that visitors had voted, and added:

> The proposal came on late in a thin house, or else it would have been lost. The narrow victory was pleasing to the young men of the Glasgow Trades Council, and was applauded loudly by many visitors who left after the result was announced.[7]

But the tide was already ebbing for the left. The I.L.P. reacted away from its early enthusiasm for the Third International when the terms of its acceptance were announced from Moscow.[8] Russian foreign policy in the early 1920s was still schizophrenically split between protecting Russian interests by conventional means and promoting world revolution by unconventional ones. Trying to do both at once — as when Grigori Zinoviev urged the Labour Party to accept Communists and simultaneously urged Communists to support the Labour Party 'as a rope supports a hanging man' — achieved neither. The I.L.P. was dismayed to learn that the '21 Conditions' for affiliating to the Third International included a promise to conduct simultaneous legal and illegal struggles for the revolution, and that two-thirds of its executive must in future be drawn from the members of a pro-Communist pressure group in its ranks consisting mostly of C. H. Norman, J. T. Walton Newbold, and Helen Crawfurd. Whatever the standing of these people in Moscow, they had none among the actual, living (though doubtless falsely conscious) members of the I.L.P. The Comintern's seal of approval in fact sealed their fate: they lost their platforms in journals like the *Forward* that ordinary people read and were forced back into talking to each other in periodicals read only by the already dedicated.

The attempt to make the I.L.P. revolutionary by correspondence course failed. Its Scottish conference of 1921 reversed the previous decision to join the Third International, and Tom Johnston expressed the hope that by another year, the current spasm of excitement about how many Soviet angels will sit comfortably on a Parliamentary needle, about the number of theses (good word) and conditions we must necessarily recite before a population that cares not one tinker's curse about any of them, will have spent itself.[9]

Its national conference, three months later, threw out the idea by more than five to one. Simply reading out the '21 points' 'caused a sensation',[10] and the Third International idea was laughed out of the I.L.P. British ethical socialists in blue serge suits with rolled-up umbrellas were sadly unwilling to struggle illegally for the revolution. This decision seems to have caused little dissension in the Glasgow I.L.P; *Forward* claimed that only two members defected to the new Communist Party.[11]

The reaction against the Communists in the 'industrial' organisations was tardier and less complete. As we have seen, the S.T.U.C. voted in 1921 to enquire about joining the Red International of Labour Unions. Left to itself, however, the Parliamentary Committee of the S.T.U.C. obviously shared the *Forward's* view that the vote was a freak result upon which no serious action was to be expected; it did nothing for several months, and then sent a circular to member unions to see whether they were in favour of the proposal. This drew an angry protest from the Glasgow Trades Council, on the grounds that the Committee was trying to reopen a question which the Congress had already decided in favour of the Third International.[12] But the manoeuvre had the desired effect. The Parliamentary Committee reported that 'the tendency of the replies was against affiliation to the Red Trades Union International', and subsequent desultory correspondence with George Peet, secretary of the Provisional British Bureau, was interrupted by Peet's imprisonment.[13] There is no record of protest at the 1922 Congress against the P.C.'s neglect of the instruction it had received from the previous congress, so one has to assume that enthusiasm for the R.I.L.U. had run its very brief course. The original proposers of affiliation, the Glasgow Trades Council, had also changed their minds, voting on 29th March 1922 to accept their Industrial Committee's recommendation that since 'affiliation to the Red International of Trades Unions would require an alteration in the Rules and Constitution of the Council', it be not proceeded with. Nonetheless, the Council, which since 1918 had combined the functions of Trades Council and city Labour Party, protested against the Labour Party's new rule (viz. that all delegates to a city Labour Party must accept the constitution and principles of the Party and must not be members of bodies running candidates in opposition to duly endorsed Labour candidates)[14] on the grounds that it excluded Communists. The question remained unresolved for the time being,[15] but was to cause trouble again in later years.

In Scotland in the early 1920s, 'Communists' meant revolutionaries recruited from the S.L.P. even more than those from the B.S.P. However, the S.L.P. itself had not sufficient resilience to adapt to post-war conditions. Its rigorous intellectualism and insistence on doctrinal purity kept its membership tiny, and only the near-coincidence of its industrial demands and the engineers' agitation, together with the temporary abandonment of its refusal to participate in capitalist politics, had given it prominence during the war. In 1919 a group of S.L.P. members headed by Arthur MacManus tried to enter the current Communist Unity negotiations. In due course they were expelled from the S.L.P. and joined the Communist Party. What was left of the S.L.P. returned to its pre-1914 position as a tiny sect. An attempt by John MacLean to use the S.L.P. as the basis for a new Communist Party to rival the C.P.G.B. failed, and by 1924, it has been suggested, 'it is not likely that S.L.P. membership exceeded 100'.[16] In the same year its journal, *The Socialist*, had to be closed down.[17]

So by 1922 the S.L.P. was dead, and the I.L.P. had become more exclusive; the only party which might act as any sort of revolutionary force in Scotland was the Communist Party of Great Britain. The disproportionately large number of Scots in the early leadership of the Communist Party has often been pointed out.[18] The recruits from the S.L.P.'s Communist Unity Group, numerically much smaller than the B.S.P., provided 'the dominant figures in the Communist Party during its first few years'.[19] These were Bell, MacManus, Murphy, and William Paul, of whom Bell and MacManus were Clydesiders. Thomas Clark, also became, a party functionary for the first two years of the party's existence.[20] Gallacher, the ex-B.S.P. member who was converted from heresy to orthodoxy after visiting Lenin in 1920, was somewhat apart from this group. He first came to real prominence in the Party after the adoption of the Organisation Report of 1922, which recommended a drastic pruning of the party apparatus. From this time on, the ex-S.L.P.'ers were somewhat eclipsed by the new leadership of Pollitt, Dutt, and Gallacher. The change was accentuated when the entire British party executive was summoned to Moscow and reprimanded by the Executive Committee of the Comintern. In the changes in leadership 'insisted on by the Presidium of the Comintern'[21] the

S.L.P.'ers lost more ground still, although the balance of power swung slightly back towards them in 1924.[22]

All these changes removed many prominent militants from the Scottish scene without increasing their political effectiveness. Because of the failure of the C.P.G.B. to grow in its early years, the abilities of Bell, MacManus and Murphy were dissipated in organisation and agitation with no visible results, and they would all have vanished from the political scene without trace but for the Zinoviev letter scare of 1924.[23] Gallacher was to be more important both within and outside the Party, but he had no further impact on Scottish politics until his election as M.P. for West Fife in 1935.

The local leadership of the Communist Party in Glasgow failed to make any notable impression up to 1922, except in organising the unemployed. John MacLean had been the first to do this in 1921, and after initial hostility the future local leaders of the Communist Party co-operated with him. But attempts to bring in the Glasgow Trades Council, which had an Unemployment Committee of its own, were very coldly received:

> Motion by Mr. Kerrigan that Council's Unemployment Committee should confer with the Unemployed Committee.[24]
> This found no seconder . . .
> Amendment moved by Mr. Kerrigan that Council's Unemployment Committee co-operate with the Communist Party. This did not find a seconder.[25]

The overt reason for this hostility was the behaviour of the Unemployed Committee and its supporters at public meetings:

> On Sunday they broke up another Trades Council demonstration for the unemployed on Glasgow Green — the first time a Labour meeting has ever been broken up there . . . the language used by some interrupters was obscene and filthy.[26]

Underlying this was the tension between employed and unemployed workers, which was to remain a prominent feature of inter-war labour politics. Those who were in work had a natural interest in preserving their own jobs. The careers of leading Communists of the inter-war period — Kerrigan, Aitken Ferguson and Harry McShane at the local level or Wal Hannington on the national stage — show that they had considerable success in controlling organisation of the unemployed, compared to their failure in almost every union activity of employed men, other than miners.[27] For a spell, this clash of interest and personalities crippled the Trades Council, whose every meeting broke up in violent arguments as soon as it assembled.[28]

The Communist Party in Glasgow, then, developed into nothing more than a rather noisy pressure group for the unemployed, whose main energies were spent attacking other labour organisations. Might it have become something more significant with John MacLean at its head? Undoubtedly the Party on Clydeside in its first few years was severely hampered by MacLean's failure to join it. But MacLean's attitude had, and has, more than local importance. Why did the sometime Bolshevik Consul in Glasgow, after whom one of the docks in Leningrad was named,[29] never join the Communist Party of Great Britain? A body of controversial literature has sprung up around this point, which we must assess.

Gallacher claimed, at the time of writing *Revolt on the Clyde* and later, that 'MacLean was . . . [in] a very sick condition . . . he was suffering from hallucinations'[30] after his release from prison in 1918; that his election speeches were 'marred by the sickness that had become firmly embedded in his mind'[31] because of his persecution mania and obsession with drugs and spies; that he was driven to political isolation by 'a bunch of toadies',[32] and that egged on by them he fought a hopeless fight until, on 30th November 1923, he died of pneumonia.

This view of MacLean's last years has been sharply criticised by a number of modern writers. For instance, Kendall claims of MacLean's writings:

> None of these documents present any evidence to suggest that the balance of Maclean's mind was disturbed, or that he was a sick, ageing old man, ruthlessly exploited by a band of sinister, but, significantly, unnamed socialist parasites. All on the other hand show clearly a defined political outlook at variance with that of the CPGB on a number of important issues.[33]

Others, while endorsing this view, have added that MacLean's real claim to fame should be as a Scottish Nationalist. Hugh Macdiarmid claimed that MacLean's doctrines were 'profoundly related to our hidden Gaelic traditions, . . . in logical accord with the entire evolution of his political thought, and did not betray but crowned his career'.[34] The available sources, including MacLean's own papers, give some credence to both the Gallacher and the Kendall version and none to the Macdiarmid one; they also show that all three versions err in their common overestimate of MacLean's importance.

There can be no doubt that MacLean's views and behaviour in his last years were distorted by a thoroughly developed persecution mania which 'coloured all his later years and rendered him gey ill to thole'.[35, 36] MacLean seems to have been a naturally suspicious person whose intemperance of language in personal disputes was, at least overtly, responsible for his dismissal as a teacher in 1915: he refused to withdraw a letter he had written to the Govan School Board attacking his former headmaster for the master's alleged affair with the infant mistress, and as a result was dismissed by the Board.[37]

Accounts of both MacLean's wartime terms of imprisonment show evidence of the growing paranoia which was to afflict him. A letter to his wife written during his first term of imprisonment betrays the first sign of the obsession that was to haunt the rest of his life:

> I again ask you to remember the detective incident the night I was arrested, and if you do you will think and act rightly just now. Not otherwise.[38]

Within a few months of his release on a ticket-of-leave in August 1917, the Government legal advisers claimed that he was again committing breaches of D.O.R.A. The matter was thought sufficiently important or delicate to take up at the level of the War Cabinet (partly because of the complications caused by MacLean's appointment as Bolshevik Consul in Glasgow). The Secretary for Scotland attended the War Cabinet to explain that MacLean 'had been liberated because of the state of his health . . . He was more or less a lunatic; imprisonment would lead to his ill health and to demands for his release'.[39] Nevertheless, the War Cabinet authorised 'proceedings to be taken in any case where the Lord Advocate was of opinion that a conviction would be probable'.[40] A study of MacLean's speech from the dock in 1918 shows that Munro's assessment of him as 'more or less a lunatic', while exaggerated, was nevertheless not merely a petulant reference to his political views. MacLean's first spell of imprisonment had given him a paranoid suspicion of prison doctors and prison food:

> (In December 1916) I protested that my food was being drugged. I said there was alcohol in the food lowering my temperature . . .
> From January to March [1917] . . . the doctor is busy getting the people into the hospital, there breaking up their organs and their systems . . .
> I call that period the eye-squinting period because the treatment then given puts the eyes out of view [sic]. Through numerous expedients I was able to hold my own.[41]

In the light of this, not only MacLean's friends but also the Government watched over his 1918 term of imprisonment with some anxiety. Trouble over his food began soon after he had been imprisoned, again in Peterhead. On 15th May 1918 he wrote to his wife to explain that he had been allowed to have food sent in instead of prison food, and asked her to contact William Stewart, Secretary of the Scottish I.L.P., William Shaw of the Glasgow Trades Council or William Gallacher of the Scottish Co-operative Wholesale Society[42] to make arrangements.[43] But when this food arrived, he refused that as well, and from July 1918 was forcibly fed.[44] This unquestionably further worsened his condition, as shown by his 'aged and haggard appearance'[45] which his wife discovered when she visited him. Rumours of his treatment excited great concern, and Ramsay Mac-Donald both protested to Munro that MacLean was being worse treated than Sinn Feiners[46] and wrote to Mrs. MacLean, after talking of a meeting with Barnes, 'I have private information that a strong labour protest is to be made shortly to the Cabinet'.[47] J. M. Hogge, the Edinburgh Independent Liberal, also wrote:

> I think . . . [his treatment] is abominable and I shall be quite glad to do anything in the House of Commons in conjunction with others to try and secure his release.[48]

The Scottish Office, meantime, was keeping a close watch on Mac-Lean's condition and kept elaborate records, including daily medical reports on the state of his health. Munro wrote after these investigations, in reply to Mrs. MacLean's complaint over her husband's treatment:

> Her first remark, before she knew he had been artificially fed, was to compliment him on his appearance. Food of good quality has always been placed before him at meal times, so that he might have an opportunity, in the first instance, of taking it in the ordinary way. The suggestion that his food was drugged is, of course, absurd, and is without a shadow of foundation.[49]

The labour protest of which Munro had warned and which Mac-Donald had promised culminated in a paper circulated by Barnes to the War Cabinet:

> Mr. Munro has been averse to releasing him, and I think has been very badly treated by those who have spread false reports about prison treatment. Mr. Munro, however, has said that he would be quite willing to release MacLean if it was a matter of a general amnesty.[50]

But, Barnes went on, there were only two political prisoners in Scotland — MacLean and a tramwayman called Milne; and so a 'general amnesty' implied only the release of these two, which he urged

on the grounds that 'the continued agitation about John MacLean con-
stitutes a serious danger for the Government'.[51] This paper was
presented to the Imperial War Cabinet, where Cave, the Home
Secretary, was the only objector to MacLean's release, on the grounds
that 'the revolutionaries would certainly regard it as a triumph, and
would probably send MacLean to make revolutionary speeches in
London and elsewhere'.[52] But the War Cabinet ratified MacLean's
release on 29th November.[53] He had served six months of his five years'
penal servitude.

After MacLean's release, his obsessions helped to create the final rift
between him and Gallacher which contributed to his failure to join the
Communist Party. For this we have the evidence both of Gallacher and
of those against whom no accusations of special pleading can be made.
In his old age Gallacher wrote an account which is much more specific
than his allegations in *Revolt on the Clyde*:

> After he had been speaking for three quarters of an hour about doped food the
> comrades coming from other meetings said he must be stopped as they were
> waiting for him at the next meeting. I passed him a note but he paid no attention.
> He showed no sign of stopping so, reluctantly, I interrupted him: I said, 'I'm sorry
> to interrupt you, John, but you must go to your other meetings'. He turned on me,
> with an angry scowl as he shouted, 'For Christ's sake, Gallacher, leave me alone. I
> know what I'm doing, my bowels are in perfect order [sic]. I never felt better', and
> on he went.[54]

This is corroborated by Harry McShane ('He was very erratic, and it
was obvious that he wasn't yet well'[55]) and by Tom Bell:

> Persecution obsessions and questions irrelevant to the Election made up the
> subject-matter of his speeches. The wild enthusiasm with which he was received at
> each of his meetings evaporated in murmurs of sympathetic concern, many people
> leaving the meetings while he was speaking, obviously disturbed by the state of
> their friend and comrade's mind.[56]

In his 'Fortnightly Report on Revolutionary Organisations . . .' Basil
Thomson assured the War Cabinet that MacLean was not too serious a
threat, as his supporters 'are beginning to realise that he is mentally
unsound'.[57] Nevertheless,

> there is sufficient method in his speeches to attract large audiences. He begins by
> telling them that he has been extraordinarily successful among soldiers and sailors.
> He then relates his sufferings in prison, and states that his food was drugged and
> poisoned, and that he would have died if he had eaten it; that CO's [conscientious
> objectors], Sinn Feiners and even convicts undergo such treatment; that many die,
> others become insane or commit suicide, and that the strongest have their con-

stitution undermined; that those of the CO's who died of pneumonia had a particular bacillus injected into them by the prison staff.[58]

A Scottish Office civil servant argued against official rebuttal of MacLean's claims on the grounds that

> Anyone who has dealt with lunatics' petitions would at once conclude from MacLean's remarks as to his food etc. in prison that he was insane and one would imagine that the remarks about eye-squinting etc. would convey the same impression to a normal individual, while anyone who swallowed MacLean's statements would probably not be moved by any answer from this office.[59]

MacLean explained that disturbances at his meetings were caused by the police, who

> rightly anticipated that I would dwell on my treatment by the doctor at Perth prison . . . When I was recently speaking in the great Albert Hall, London, I had perfect order until I began to attack the Government on the drugging of prisoners' food and then the hirelings of Scotland Yard began to create a disturbance . . .[60]

The Home Secretary's fears could not have been more absurdly misplaced. MacLean a martyr in jail was a considerable threat to public order; MacLean obsessional and free was none. His obsessions hastened the rift with Gallacher, blunted the edge of his propaganda speeches, and increased the instability of his political associations.

In 1920 Gallacher passed on an invitation from Lenin, whom he had met at the Second Congress of the Comintern, for MacLean to visit Moscow. Gallacher wrote to the S.L.P. Executive telling them to let him go to Russia, because he was suffering from 'hallucinations' and needed 'a rest and proper treatment'.[61] This letter was instead sent to MacLean, who used it in public, saying 'Gallacher wants to get rid of me, so he is circulating the story I am mad'.[62] No rapprochement was possible after this, and the row between MacLean and Gallacher reached its climax at a meeting on Christmas Day, 1920, which the *Daily Record* headlined 'Socialist Hatred/Leaders Kill Fusion/Angry Scenes/MacLean and Gallacher Duel'.[63]

The way in which MacLean's private obsessions, in his last five years, spilled over into his political convictions is aptly illustrated in this 1922 election leaflet:

> In 1919 I started a campaign for a united effort to overthrow British capitalism by a General Strike, and at my meetings I made public that I had been drugged in prison through my food like other convicts. The Government's reply was the break-up of my family, the blocking of my every move through traitors inside the Socialist movement, the attempted ruin of my reputation and loss of my tutorship

at the Scottish Labour College through the dirty work of the communist clown, William Gallacher.[64]

Writing in the *Socialist* in 1921, MacLean claimed that the Government had poisoned some soup in Cowdenbeath 'to check the tendency towards Communism implied in communal kitchens, laundries, etc'.[65]

When MacLean died, the sympathetic obituaries had one theme in common:

> There is no doubt that John's mind became unhinged during the past few stormy years. Many of his old co-operative friends felt that it was so from his speech and his behaviour, after his liberation from prison on the first occasion, and some of those who regretted the change in him were those whom he latterly reviled most.[66]
> [In his early years] the wrongs of the people, real and imaginary, did not then rouse him to the fits of frenzy which were later so marked a characteristic of his platform appearances . . . It is difficult to say what the cause of his later development was. It is probable that it was as much mental overwork as anything else.[67]
> *De mortuis nisi bonum* . . . none ever doubted his sincerity. His conviction that machiavellian attempts were made to poison him and that he was surrounded by cabals seeking his destruction coloured all his later years and rendered him gey ill to thole.[68]

MacLean unquestionably did suffer from paranoid delusions. But at the same time he had perfectly rational objections to joining the C.P.G.B. He was thoroughly suspicious of Gallacher for having gone to Russia an anti-Parliamentary anarchical socialist, and come back a devout Leninist bearing the message that a single Communist Party of Great Britain must be founded. In *Left-wing Communism*, Lenin devoted a special section to the heresy of anti-parliamentarism professed by Gallacher and Sylvia Pankhurst:

> Comrade Gallacher's letter undoubtedly betrays the embryos of *all* the mistakes committed by the German 'left' Communists and by the 'Left' Bolshevites in 1908 and 1918.
> [Gallacher] . . . is imbued with noble, proletarian . . . hatred for the bourgeois 'class politicians' . . But [he] apparently fails to take into account the fact that politics is a science and an art that does not drop from the skies, is not acquired for nothing, and that if it wants to conquer the bourgeoisie the proletariat must train *its own* proletarian 'class politicians', who will be as skilled as the bourgeois politicians.[69]

Before Gallacher left for home, Lenin catechised him as follows:

> 'Do you admit that you were wrong on the question of Parliament and the affiliations to the Labour Party? Will you join the Communist Party of Great

Britain when you return? . . . Will you do your best to persuade your Scottish comrades to join it?'
To each of these questions I answered 'yes'.[70]

MacLean had good reason to be suspicious of the abruptness of Gallacher's conversion. He objected both to being forced to join with the London leaders of the B.S.P. and to being told by Lenin what was best for the revolution in Scotland. He wrote:

> Gallacher and the 'Worker' have sneered openly at the idea of a Scottish Communist Party, as its object is the very same as that of the C.P.G.B. . . . I have no objections to the programme of the London gang, but to their honesty and to Col. Malone, who was on the E.C. of the Reconstruction Society . . . We refuse to be bluffed by Gallacher that Lenin says we must only have one Communist Party in Great Britain. Why does Gallacher help to start another Communist Party, if he is so anxious about Lenin? I for one will not follow a policy dictated by Lenin until Lenin knows the situation more clearly than he can possibly know it from an enemy to Marxian Economic Classes as Gallacher privately declared himself to be.[71]

MacLean had a special reason for wishing to see a separate Scottish Communist Party, and it was a strategic one. He was convinced that the inexorable forces of capitalism would dictate that the next war would be with the U.S.A. He not only wrote a pamphlet, 'The Coming War with America', to this effect, but even mentioned it in letters to his little daughters who were staying with their mother near Hawick:[72]

> Britain may soon be in a great war with the U.S.A. and it will be worse than the last. Your father is working day and night warning people so as to avert it. That is why the police are told to watch him day and night and put him in prison.[73]

Accordingly, MacLean thought Scotland needed a separate Communist Party to subvert the future imperialist war, in which Scotland, being closer to the U.S.A. than England, would be the jumping-off point for any offensive:

> The preparations to use the Scottish coast and Scottish lads in John Bull's fight with Uncle Sam forces on us the policy of complete political separation from England. Hence a Scottish Communist Party.[74]

It was this article in MacLean's paper, the *Vanguard*, which announced his intention of building a separate Scottish Communist Party based on the S.L.P. But the meeting to effect this degenerated into the unedifying brawl with Gallacher to which we have referred. Before long MacLean had resigned from the S.L.P., and he spent the rest of his life in increasing sectarian isolation. The 'Scottish Workers'

Republican Party', which he founded, was not a success; it fought no election, and did not long outlive him.[75] As a tireless propagandist, he did have some success as an organiser of demonstrations of the unemployed in 1921, and Kendall suggests, no doubt rightly,[76] that one reason for Gallacher's denigration was MacLean's success in this at the expense of the official Communist Party. But the violent conduct of MacLean's supporters towards the rest of the Labour movement soured relations between them. During his imprisonment in 1921, MacLean's remaining supporters deserted him,[77] and leadership of the unemployed slipped to the Communists — but the bad relations between employed and unemployed persisted to widen the rift between Communists and the rest.

We need not spend long on the 'celtic nationalist' version of the John MacLean myth. A marxist first, last, and always, he had no sympathy whatever with Scottish nationalism except as a means to world revolution. On being invited by the Scottish Home Rule Association and the Hon. Ruaraidh Erskine of Mar to sign a petition to President Wilson in favour of Home Rule, MacLean replied:

> Were I to thank anyone for actual services rendered to the cause of Home Rule, I would certainly thank my glorious comrades, Lenin etc. The only thanks they would appreciate would be the successful revolutionising of Scotland by its wage-slave class . . .[78]

It is just as well that MacLean was a Scot and not a Ukrainian.

Hence MacLean did have substantial reasons for differing with the Communists. Their denigration of him, however, is appropriate but for the wrong reasons. MacLean was a person of no real influence not because he was insane, but because he had neither common interests nor a common language with the Clydeside working class.

When MacLean went to jail in 1918, Johnston wrote:

> He is paying the price. He advocated a Social Revolution by Bolshevist methods, and, alas, the bulk of the workers do not want a Social Revolution by any method, but go on rivet-hammering competitions, and scrambling for overtime, and regard the John Macleans as 'decent enough, but a bit off'. The blood of the martyrs is said to have been the seed of the church, and John Maclean's dramatic sacrifice may do more to shake up the brains of the working class than did all John Maclean's years of educative propaganda for Socialism, but it is only upon such a presumption that the sacrifice can, in Socialist terms, be justified.[79]

It was a shrewd judgment. Although some Cabinet members thought militant action would be taken if MacLean was not released,[80] there seems to be little ground for their fears. If engineers were not prepared to stay out on strike for the return of their workmates, the deportees, in 1916, it seems hardly plausible that they would have taken militant action to release MacLean in 1918.

Even when MacLean was arguing about matters which were central to the concerns of industrial militancy, he was unable, as we saw in Chapters 7 and 9, to proceed from there to spark off a revolution. He was still more cut off after the war, when his political programmes appeared to be either hopelessly unrealistic or totally remote from the everyday world of working-class life. For example, he spent much of 1920 campaigning for his 'Fighting Programme', namely

1) A six-hour working day.
2) Rationing of work to absorb the unemployed, or payment of full wages to the unemployed.
3) A minimum wage of £1 a day.
4) Reduction of prices to half the present level.[81]

As Bell says, the Fighting Programme could make no impact on 'the mass of the trade union workers':

In 1919 they struck for a 40 hour week and were beaten. The call for a six hour day would hardly be likely to bring about immediate united action. Here, it would appear, Maclean's idealism outstripped his sense of reality.[82]

Two of MacLean's most off-beat campaigns were the visit to Lewis and the 'Burn Bradbury' pamphlet. We have already noted that MacLean thought the pressures of capitalism would imminently bring about a war between Britain and America. So, when the Lewis agitation of 1920 arose, MacLean immediately saw what he thought was the underlying cause. To a more superficial observer the conflict would appear to be between Lord Leverhulme, who was just starting his immense programme of totally unprofitable investment in the Western Isles, and crofters in the Stornoway area, who stubbornly refused to vacate their crofts to allow Leverhulme to create a dairy farm to serve Stornoway.[83] But MacLean visited Stornoway to speak on behalf of the crofters because 'I am convinced that my first impression is correct, that Leverhulme is preparing Lewis and Harris for the navy in case of war with America'.[84] Stornoway is, after all, the closest town in Britain to North America.

MacLean also had a bizarrely incongruous Friedmanite belief that the money supply determines the rate of inflation, and that therefore to reduce prices the working class should burn all their pound and ten shilling notes:

> Labour's cry then ought to be 'Burn Bradbury'; not the man, but his effigy composed of Treasury notes.
> If these notes were burned and gold payments resumed, supported as before by the usual bank notes, prices would at once fall to half their present level. Therefore, let the Labour campaign have as its slogan, 'Burn Bradbury'.[85]

Bell cannot escape the conclusion that

> the slogan, 'Burn Bradbury', found no response among serious and practical-minded trade unionists. This appears to have been a case in which Maclean's usually clear and sound judgment on economic questions was clouded by the impetuous zeal of an ardent agitator.[86]

It is not easy to draw a hard-and-fast line separating mere crankiness from paranoia, but it would probably be fair to say that the above quotations are different from the allegation that the Government was poisoning soup in Cowdenbeath — they indicate not mental imbalance so much as simply remoteness from the world inhabited by the working class to whom MacLean was appealing. This was MacLean's basic failure, which his paranoia merely aggravated. He was a True Believer, who had found all truth in one book. But a True Believer cannot convince others unless they have already had the same revelation, or at the very least read the same true book. MacLean was in a worse plight than a Christian fundamentalist: none of those he tried to rouse had read *Das Kapital*. To them he 'was a saint and a martyr, but too unpractical for everyday life'.[87] Even at the height of his influence, during the war, MacLean attracted no more than a diffuse sympathy for his revolutionary programmes, and that dwindled away during the last five years of his life.

MacLean died less than eight years after the great moment of revolutionary syndicalism on Christmas Day, 1915, less than five years after the revolution manquée — as some saw it — of Bloody Friday. Yet these incidents appeared already, by 1923, to belong to the remote past. Certainly, 'Red Clydeside' had made a new reputation, but it was a parliamentary reputation based on the non-revolutionary I.L.P. It had very little in common with the industrial militancy of earlier years. It is clear that neither the S.L.P. nor the C.P.G.B. nor John MacLean was capable of producing the Labour triumphs of 1922. So we must now see what did.

13

The Growth of the Labour Vote.
I: Unemployment and Housing

By December 1918, 'Red Clydeside' was an established journalistic cliché. Many, both socialists and others, imagined that Labour would make great advances in the General Election. The *Forward*, for instance, thought that five Labour gains were likely, and two (Shettleston and Govan) almost certain.[1] The Catholic *Glasgow Observer* tipped the same two certainties, and listed Springburn, St. Rollox, Bridgeton, Partick and even Cathcart as possibles.[2] For the *Glasgow Herald*, Govan, Shettleston and Bridgeton were certain, and Springburn and Partick likely, Labour gains. Outside Glasgow, it expected Labour to gain Hamilton and Linlithgow, while in Dumbarton Burghs the Coalition candidate 'will do well if he defeats Mr. David Kirkwood'.[3]

The result was a severe disappointment for Labour. The *Glasgow Herald* remarked that

> Expectations of winning at least 3 seats were generally entertained by the [Labour] party, and the claim was not regarded as extravagant by many of those who worked actively against Labour.[4]

Nevertheless, it could now conclude with relief that the city's 'honour is untarnished'.[5] Of all the Glasgow Labour candidates, only Neil Maclean in Govan was elected, with a majority of 815 (4%) over the Coalition candidate, while Wheatley lost in Shettleston by 74 (0.4%) to Admiral Adair, the works manager at Parkhead, who stood as a Coalition Unionist. In all, Labour took six Scottish seats (Govan, Hamilton, Edinburgh Central, South Ayrshire, West Fife, and one seat in Dundee); and in addition Barnes, now styled 'Coalition Labour', retained his seat in the Gorbals, where John MacLean was at the last moment disowned by the Labour Party N.E.C.

Two of the reasons for Labour's failure in Glasgow are local reflections of national situations, both foreseen by local observers: the failure of many servicemen (and others) to vote, and the effect of Labour's 'pacifist' appeal. Before the election, the only warning note amid the Labour euphoria had come from an organiser of the National Federation of Discharged Sailors and Soldiers, who

> puts it that not more than about 20% of absent voters will vote, and that not more than 20% of those who do will poll Labour.[6]

The first part, at least, of this prediction was borne out. According to the *Forward*, only a quarter of the soldiers on the register voted, except in safe Conservative Hillhead, where the proportion was much higher. Overall, the turnout in the city was only 57.3%. Since the previous election, the electorate had changed immensely; perhaps three out of every four voters were new.[7] However, the effects of the 1918 Reform Act were muffled in two ways: first, because of the failure of Hayes Fisher, President of the Local Government Board, to complete the electoral register efficiently, it was highly defective, and many servicemen and non-householders were disfranchised; and in the second place, the arrangements for those servicemen who were on the register to cast their votes were not adequately carried out.

Local observers also thought that Labour would suffer from its views on the war:

> The Glasgow electorate generally displayed a grip on the essentials. Domestic problems, especially housing, interested [them], but these assumed secondary importance to the question of peace terms and especially the question of indemnity. A Labour candidate frankly admitted on Saturday that his views on these subjects must have alienated support . . . Pacifism in its after the war, as in its prewar phase, was not in popular favour. The appeal of Labour rather waned in effect as the electoral battle developed.[8]

It has been pointed out that Clydeside, for all its wartime reputation, had a 'patriotic' majority like the rest of Britain. Taylor has remarked that

> South Wales and Clydeside, the two centres of industrial discontent, also provided the highest proportion in the country of recruits for the army.[9]

Nevertheless, however 'patriotic' the majority of workers may have been, the West of Scotland was the only industrial area in which the anti-war case could, throughout the war, be guaranteed a respectful hearing — a fact which, it has been suggested, gave MacDonald an

emotional dependence on the Clydesiders which was partly reciprocated, for instance when they helped to secure his election as leader of
the party in 1922.[10] The effect of Labour's views on its wartime
popularity was mixed. As we saw in Chapter 8, the resignation of
Henderson and the publication of the 'Memorandum on War Aims' had
helped Labour to profit from a widespread and growing war-
weariness. But it was a precarious position, because it was open to
challenge when the stalemate on the Western Front was broken in
either direction. In March 1918, for instance, Johnston had written in
the *Forward*:

> What is happening on the Western Front makes a peace propaganda impossible
> . . . One cannot indulge even in the customary amenities of criticism at a time like
> this.[11]

But the German collapse, and the swing of military fortunes abruptly
in the other direction, did not restore the popularity of pacifist sentiment. In the shadow of Lloyd George, the Labour Party wilted under
the burden of its 'pacifism'. Conducting a *post mortem* on his election
campaign, James Stewart, the defeated Labour candidate at St. Rollox,
freely admitted that his opposition to indemnities and to a policy of
expelling Germans from Britain had lost him votes to the Coalition 'in
the present state of public opinion'.[12] When the election came, the
whole Labour Party was tarred with the pacifist brush.

This, together with the later Parliamentary reputation of the Clydesiders, has possibly obscured the real stance of local socialists on the
war. By no means all Labour organisations had been pacifist, especially
early in the war; a number of Labour town councillors in Glasgow had
taken part in recruiting, and one Labour bailie 'said he would enlist
himself if they would take him'.[13] The only out-and-out pacifists on the
Town Council at the beginning of the war had been Wheatley and J. S.
Taylor,[14] though other socialists who were identifiably pacifist
included Maxton, who on refusing to enlist after the end of his prison
term was set to 'work of national importance', and spent two years as a
plater's helper;[15] Dollan, who was imprisoned in 1917 for failing to
remove more than fifty miles from Glasgow or cease encouraging
C.O.'s;[16] and William Regan, who was dismissed by the Post Office
from his employment as a telegraphist because he was a C.O.

This list is notable not so much for those it contains as for those it
omits. Shinwell, for all the vigour of his expression, and appearance of
greater militancy than Wheatley, never declared himself opposed to the

war. Kirkwood, as we observed in Part I, began the war with superficially held Marxist convictions which vanished in favour of a patriotic determination to blow the Germans over the Rhine with guns made at Parkhead. Campbell Stephen and George Buchanan, the other later stalwarts of the Glasgow I.L.P. group, make no appearance in wartime politics at all. Only Maxton and Wheatley (and, more dubiously, McGovern, who succeeded to Wheatley's seat in 1930) could legitimately claim that the pacifism they professed between the wars had been put into practice during the First World War.

This is but one instance of a spurious continuity which has often been implied or stated between wartime militancy and post-1922 Parliamentary radicalism. Some (not all) of the personnel were the same, but the policies were different, as were the political situations which brought the actors to prominence. The 1918 election result is the greatest obstacle in the way of those who over-emphasise the continuity between wartime and postwar radicalism. And the fundamental reason why the industrial upheaval led nowhere in 1918 is clear: the revolts of industrial Red Clydeside had been the work of a small section of the workers, namely those of the skilled engineers who worked in the munitions and shipbuilding industries. This was not a revolutionary mass movement: it was hardly even electorally significant. In 1919 it was wide open to the retort offered by Shackleton at the Ministry of Labour to the S.T.U.C. deputation:

> Why, for instance, if Glasgow wants the 40-hours' week, have they not sent to Parliament members to vote for it? You ask for legislation, and then it is supported by the argument of strike.[17]

At no subsequent General Election would such a remark have been appropriate, since the number of Labour M.P.'s returned by the city has never been less than the five mustered by the Labour Party and the I.L.P. between them even in the debacle of 1931. With the 1922 election Labour became the customary majority party in Glasgow, a position it has subsequently relinquished only for the election of 1931. We have to decide how this came about.

A large part of the answer depends on developments which were not peculiar to Glasgow. Labour was hampered in the 1918 election by the defective register, the low turn-out, and the jingo appeal of Lloyd George. But these were temporary factors, the disappearance of which added greatly to Labour strength even before the Coalition began patently to fail on the home front. Once the Coalition did falter, with the failure of postwar reconstruction and the slump of 1920-21, the dramatic collapse of the Asquith Liberals in 1918 left Labour as the only viable party which was not in government. In 1918 it was a feeble group of sixty, ineffectually led, with its most prominent figures out of Parliament; but after the 1922 election it was a large, though scarcely Government-orientated, opposition; and after the next election it was the Government.

These events were enacted on the national scale, and while we shall be looking at their manifestations in the West of Scotland, our chief interest is in Glasgow as a special case. For Glasgow undoubtedly did swing further to Labour in these years than other British cities, and retained its high degree of Labour loyalty through the inter-war years. An attempt to demonstrate this is made in Tables 13.1 and 13.2. Voting statistics in these years are notoriously difficult to handle: in particular, 'swing', as an analytical tool, is next to useless when movements between so many different, diffuse, and shifting political groups are involved. In Table 13.1 voting change in Glasgow is compared with that in the largest English provincial cities; the figures of those voting Labour in the General Elections of 1918, 1922, and 1935 are shown as a percentage of the registered electorate.[18] In each city, only those constituencies which had a Labour candidate at all three of these General Elections are included, in order that the figures should have some comparative value.

The table shows that Glasgow, from a middling position in 1918,

Table 13.1 *Proportion of the registered electorate voting Labour at the General Elections of 1918, 1922 and 1935: Glasgow compared with English provincial cities returning five or more M.P.'s*

	% of electors voting Labour		
	1918	1922	1935
Glasgow	18.9	41.6	37.7
Sheffield	14.7	42.5	41.0
Manchester	22.1	34.8	34.1
Bristol	19.1	32.3	37.6
Leeds	12.2	26.5	25.8
Birmingham	13.2	26.0	24.3
Liverpool	17.7	24.6	29.2

The figures are based on a comparison only of seats fought by Labour candidates at all three General Elections. For a more detailed note, see Appendix 1.

leapt up in 1922 to a lonely eminence shared only with Sheffield. For 1935, the position is less clear: Bristol has come up equal to Glasgow in votes (though not in seats), and Sheffield, Bristol, Manchester and Glasgow form a group of cities noticeably more pro-Labour than the other provincial British conurbations. Table 13.1, which actually puts Sheffield ahead of Glasgow, is possibly slightly misleading in that Sheffield had two unopposed Conservatives in the 1918 and 1922 General Elections, whereas Glasgow, with twice as many M.P.'s, had only one unopposed Conservative in 1918 and none in 1922; the Labour effort was therefore, presumably, spread into less winnable seats than in Sheffield, and the Sheffield Labour vote is therefore unduly high relative to the Glasgow figure. Table 13.2 shows the number of Labour M.P.'s returned in each large city outside London. On this crude index, Glasgow comes out ahead of Sheffield, but both again emerge as deviant in a pro-Labour direction.

Surprisingly little work has, to date, been done on the history of British city politics since 1918; Liverpool is, perhaps, the city which has received most attention. No study of Sheffield, however, fully explains why that city had so high a Labour vote from 1922 onwards.[19] Some of the explanations we shall tentatively advance for Glasgow may apply to Sheffield also; some, such as the role of the Irish, seem unlikely to. For the rest of this chapter, and the next, we shall examine Glasgow politics between 1918 and 1922 as a case-study in the growth of the Labour vote. In this chapter we shall look at the effects of unemploy-

Table 13.2   *Labour and I.L.P. M.P.'s returned in Glasgow, compared with other cities outside London returning five or more M.P.'s, at the General Elections of 1918, 1922 and 1935*

	No. of seats	Number of Labour M.P.'s returned		
		1918	1922	1935
Glasgow	15	1	10	9
Sheffield	7	0	3	4
Manchester	10	2	3	4
Leeds	6	1	2	2
Edinburgh	5	1	1	1
Bristol	5	0	0	2
Liverpool	11	0	0	3
Birmingham	12	0	0	0

ment and housing, while a number of topics centring on the Irish vote will be gathered into a separate discussion in Chapter 14.

The Glasgow Labour movement took some time to pick up the pieces from the debacles of December 1918 and January 1919. Regan (at the time Glasgow organiser for the I.L.P.) attributed municipal by-election defeats in June 1919 to lack of helpers:

> the Glasgow Labour and Socialist movement was under a cloud of depression as a result of the General Election, and also the failure of the 40-Hours' Strike.[20]

Considerable encouragement, however, came from the Bothwell by-election in late July 1919. In 1918 the Coalition candidate had won by only 300 votes over Labour. In mid-July local Labour supporters hoped that they would win by between 800 and 1500 votes, though Duncan Graham, the Labour M.P. for neighbouring Hamilton, expected Labour to win by as much as 3000.[21] In the event, it was a startling 7168, a majority of 37.6% over the Coalition candidate, and a swing of no less than 19.7% since 1918.[22]

The result of the Bothwell by-election was in fact a far better one for Labour than that of the Spen Valley election in December which prompts Cowling to say:

> 'Resistance to Socialism' first became a possible programme when Labour won the Spen Valley by-election in January 1920. In this story Spen Valley was crucial. From Spen Valley onwards, the Labour Party was the crucial problem.[23]

Labour won Bothwell (a mining district ten miles from Glasgow) because the war hysteria of 1918 had worn off, the Coalition was beginning to falter, and the Sankey Commission, sitting at the time, was making miners realise that radical reform of the mines might be within their grasp after all. None of these factors particularly affected Glasgow — the first two were entirely general and the last entirely specific. Working-class Glaswegians did not go to work in Bothwell, nor vice-versa. But of course the Bothwell result revived the spirits of Labour and I.L.P. activists in Glasgow.

Between the 1918 and 1922 elections, however, there was no by-election in Glasgow or Clydeside proper.[24] The only criterion for the growth of the Labour vote in these years, therefore, is the party's progress in the annual municipal elections held in November. There is a wealth of material from minutes and local newspapers on these elections; but we cannot be sure how good an indicator of Labour fortunes in national politics they form. Some factors which did not operate in national politics were at work in municipal elections; on balance, they probably worked against Labour. We shall deal with them as they arise.

The local elections held in November 1919 brought wide Labour gains throughout Scotland, although Labour did less well in Edinburgh than in the industrial west and in Fife. In a number of burghs Labour swept the board, all its candidates heading the polls at Cowdenbeath, Irvine, Lerwick, and Kilsyth. In Aberdeen, Labour made five gains, in Dundee no less than eight, and in Clydebank five: 119 gains were claimed in all.[25] In Glasgow the situation was complicated by the fact that ward redistribution and a municipal general election were known to be pending for 1920, so that the 1919 elections excited comparatively little interest, and there were a number of unopposed returns. Labour held four wards unopposed, held a further three in contests, and gained five.

Assessment of these results is hampered by the fact that the 1919 municipal elections were the first since 1914; the Labour gains, there-fore, represented changes not over one year, but over at least five. Nevertheless, they seem to show that a good deal of disillusion with the Coalition was making itself felt in local swings to Labour. The number of councillors in the burghs and cities of Scotland did not change sub-stantially between 1919 and 1974, and even in the previously un-precedented swings of the late 1960s and early 1970s very few parties gained (or lost) as many as 119 seats.[26]

The 1920 local elections were dominated by the results of Glasgow's municipal election. The spur of Labour organisation and the fact that all the seats were being fought encouraged the old 'non-political' councillors to organise a Good Government Committee to oppose Labour, and this sharpened the political contest. The I.L.P., under Regan and Dollan, was responsible for organising the Labour vote, Dollan criticising the tendency of some Labour supporters to assume that victory was a foregone conclusion:

> This tendency is most notable in places where comrades pretend that blowing theoretical trumpets is the most effective way of destroying the justifications of Capitalism.[27]

The result, claimed Regan, was 'almost a Red City', which 'stagger[ed] the Capitalist Press'.[28] Labour won 44 seats, sweeping the board in 11 wards, and making gains in others. The only inexplicable loss was in the Kinning Park ward, where the three Labour incumbents were defeated. It was pointed out that the municipal votes aggregated into Parliamentary constituencies would give Labour a majority in the Parliamentary divisions of Shettleston, Bridgeton, Springburn, Gorbals, Govan, St. Rollox, Maryhill, Tradeston, and Camlachie.[29]

In Scotland as a whole, 1920 seems to have more or less reproduced 1919. In Edinburgh, Labour suffered four losses when Leith councillors had to face re-election on their burgh being incorporated into the city. In Dundee, Labour made two net gains. Overall, gains and losses more or less balanced out.[30] Dollan later reckoned that 'only Glasgow and a few towns in Fife won an improvement on the position of 1919'.[31]

1921 represented if anything a slight setback. In Glasgow Labour suffered five losses, and in addition one councillor who had resigned from the Labour group and party retained his seat against Labour opposition. These results, however, are artificially depressed from Labour's point of view because in each ward the candidate with the fewest votes of the previous year's three successful candidates stood for re-election, so that in wards where Labour scraped in in third place in 1920 it would have had to improve its position to keep the seat. Elsewhere than Glasgow, Labour's position marginally worsened; there were two losses each in Edinburgh and Dundee, and such gains as were made were mostly in small burghs.[32]

The 1922 local elections were held only ten days before the General Election, and showed an improvement over 1921. Labour gained one seat each in Aberdeen, Dundee, and Edinburgh (where, however, the setbacks of 1920 and 1921 had been so severe that the gain gave Labour only three councillors out of 71). Labour made a number of net gains up and down the country, and in Glasgow had two losses and three gains. But the Labour vote showed a much higher rise over 1921 than these figures might seem to imply. For the 24 seats in the city fought by Labour in both 1921 and 1922, the *Glasgow Herald* compiled statistics which proved 'evidence of Labour's rally at the polls when the percentages are compared with those of a year ago'.[33] Between 1921 and 1922 the anti-Labour share of the electorate[34] had dropped from 31.06% to 30.04%, and the Labour share had risen from 31.49% to 38.46%.[35]

In summary, this series of annual figures seems to show that Labour made a large advance in 1919, stayed relatively stable (except in Glasgow) in 1920, fell back slightly in 1921, and revived substantially in 1922. Table 13.3 compares the municipal and General Election results of 1922 by grouping the wards together into the constituencies they made up.

Table 13.3   Glasgow: Municipal and General Election Results, 1922

Constituency	Municipal Election: Lab. % of votes cast	No. of wards in con- stituency	No. of wards returning Moderates without Lab. opposition	General Election: Lab. % of votes cast
1. Govan	63.3	2	0	62.3
2. Gorbals	62.6	2	0	54.5
3. Shettleston	61.8	2	0	59.1
4. Bridgeton	58.6	2	0	63.7
5. Springburn	57.4	3	0	60.5
6. St. Rollox	53.8	2	0	56.6
7. Tradeston	48.8	2	0	55.7
8. Camlachie	(60.8)	3	1	53.2
9. Maryhill	(48.2)	3	1	47.3
10. Kelvingrove	(61.9)	3	2	0
11. Central	(49.7)	3	2	41.9
12. Hillhead	(45.2)	2	1	0
13. Partick	(45.1)	2	1	0
14. Cathcart	0	3	3	34.0
15. Pollok	0	3	3	24.7

Sources: Municipal Results, *Forward* 18 November 1922.
General Results, F. W. S. Craig, *British Parliamentary Election Results 1918-1949*, Glasgow, 1969.
Boundaries: Contemporary maps in Mitchell Library, Glasgow.

The figures in the second column are in brackets where they represent a percentage Labour vote in fewer than the total number of wards in the constituency.

These figures are quite striking, considering that the municipal fran- chise was more restricted than the national, and presumably less favour- able to Labour. They suggest that all the Labour gains at the General Election except Maryhill and Cathcart (and possibly Camlachie) could have been predicted from a projection of the local election results — although no commentator seems to have done so at the time, perhaps simply because the General Election followed the municipal so closely that there was no time for detailed analysis of the results. The Labour Party had by 1922 constructed a machine which could get out Labour majorities for local elections in almost all the wards falling into working-class constituencies. In Gorbals, Govan, and Shettleston, Labour actually got a higher proportion of the vote in the municipal election than in the General Election which followed. Only one of Labour's ten successes in the General Election came out of the blue —

namely Cathcart; and that was a freak result depending on a split anti-Labour vote.[36] We must now look at the role of unemployment, housing and party organisation in laying the basis for the 1922 success.

Unemployment cut both ways. John Paton, a roving propagandist and Scottish Organiser of the I.L.P., commented that 1921 saw a deterioration of I.L.P. finances and a loss of activists, especially in the mining areas, where the lock-out of that year left many activists unemployed and all poverty-stricken.[37] In Scotland, as nationally, membership of the I.L.P. slumped during 1921.[38] In October, William Stewart appealed to middle-class supporters of the I.L.P. to help it out financially as so many unemployed members could not pay their subscriptions.[39] In November Dollan blamed the weakness of Labour organisation in the local elections partly on 'poverty and economic depression';[40] he returned to the theme after the General Election:

> The industrial slump of the past ten (sic) years had an adverse effect on the income for election purposes, and the money available had to be husbanded with unusual care. Considering the economic depression, the I.L.P. branches have exceeded all expectations in raising funds for 22 Municipal and 10 Parliamentary elections within three weeks.[41]

The conjunction of the two 1922 elections obviously put a heavy strain on the I.L.P.'s resources, especially since with the failure of trade unions to come forward sufficiently generously and the virtual non-existence of local Labour Parties the I.L.P. had to pay for almost every candidature. This doubtless accounts for the party's failure to fight seats such as Partick, where they might have had a reasonable chance of success, in the General Election, and likewise for the small number of Labour candidates in the 1922 municipal election, even though it was Labour's best year electorally up till then.

But in other ways unemployment boosted Labour support, even though it badly weakened the unions, as the collapse of the Triple Alliance (of miners, railwaymen, and transport workers) and the failure of the miners' strike of 1921 showed. On top of the fiasco of January 1919, this killed syndicalism.[42] Paton said that 'belief in the effectiveness of "industrial action" having been shattered for the time, all hopes were now centred on "political action".'[43] In the West of Scotland, massive unemployment in the shipbuilding industry in 1921 also led to pungent Labour criticism of the Coalition. The 1918 election, so the argument ran, had been won on the slogan 'Make Germany Pay', and what payment Germany had been able to make

Forging a marine engine shaft, Parkhead
(Glasgow University Archives & Business Records Centre)

Lloyd George at St Andrew's Halls, 25 December 1915
(Glasgow University Archives & Business Records Centre)

Women workers at Barr & Stroud, instrument makers Anniesland,
World War I *(Glasgow University Archives & Business Records Centre)*

4" naval guns, Parkhead; one week's output.
(Glasgow University Archives & Business Records Centre)

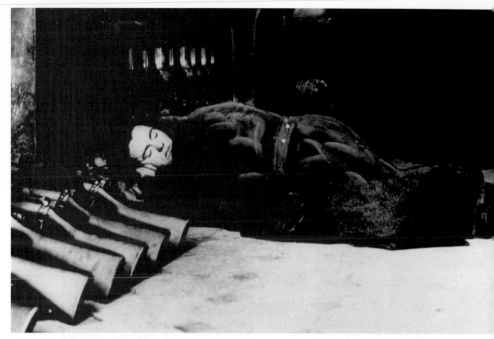

English soldier in City Chambers, ca 31 January 1919 *(Glasgow Museums: The People's Palace)*

'Bloody Friday 1919', Gallagher (2nd from right) and Kirkwood (3rd from right) held by police *(Glasgow Museums: The People's Palace)*

David Kirkwood 1872–1955 *(Glasgow museums: The People's Palace)*

...ent Strike 1915, Fighting the Prussians of Partick *(The Glasgow Museums: The People's Palace)*

...illie Gallacher 1881–1965 *(Glasgow Museums: ...e People's Palace)*

Tom Johnston 1881–1965 *(Glasgow Museums: The People's Palace)*

Back Court, workers' dwellings, Calton CA1900
(Glasgow Museums: The People's Palace)

Washing on Glasgow Green
(Glasgow Museums: The People's Palace)

John Maclean (centre, with Homburg hat), 1919 Strike *(Glasgow Museums: The People's Palace)*

Emanuel Shinwell (left) and Harry Hopkins(right), City Chambers, 31 January 1919
(Glasgow Museums: The People's Palace)

Jamaica Street CA1914 *(Glasgow Museums: The People's Palace)*

James Street from the south, Calton *(Glasgow Museums: The People's Palace)*

'"Silent Drama" at Westminster – Studies in Gesture'. Cartoon by David Low for *The Evening Standard*, 22 January 1929 *(Trevor York, Solo Syndication and Literary Agency)*.

'The Picture of the Year'. Cartoon by David Low for *The Evening Standard*, 3 May 1930. Foreground from left to right: Winston Churchill, Jimmy Maxton, David Kirkwood. *(Trevor York, Solo Syndication and Literary Agency)*

converted the thriving shipbuilding industry of 1919 into the desolation of 1921. As Dollan pointed out, 'two years ago . . . the orders indicated steady employment until the end of 1923. Then came indemnity ships; the cancellation of orders followed'.[44]

Housing was more unequivocally a 'labour issue' than unemployment. It had already produced a famous victory in the 1915 Rent Act, and it remained a very potent issue because Scottish working-class housing was dreadful beyond the imagination of most modern readers. On this, the Report of the Ballantyne Commission on Scottish working-class housing[45] provides facts of fundamental importance which have not been given the attention they deserve. The Royal Commission was appointed in 1912 at the instance of the Scottish Mineworkers; its working was suspended in February 1916, but restarted in January 1917, and its report was signed in September of that year.[46] The Commission expressed its amazement at the extent of overcrowding and insanitariness in Scotland:

> In brief, merely to relieve existing overcrowding, and replace houses that should be demolished, some 121,000 houses are required and, if an improved standard is adopted, as we recommend, the total number of new houses required would approach 236,000. For such gigantic figures our Report submits full justification. On this point the Commission is unanimous.
>
> If it be asked how this enormous accumulation has occurred, one answer is: that the conditions of Scottish housing have never been adequately investigated.[47]

Another reason for the magnitude of the problem was clearly shown by the Commission to be the chaos into which the financing of house-building had fallen. The Commission reproduced the 'careful account and classification' of different sorts of tenement housing given them by an Edinburgh witness, together with the average weekly rental for each class:

a) The lower class of subdivided house, viz. better houses that have come upon evil days . . . rented at from 1s to 3s 6d per week . . . and tenanted for the most part by the unskilled labouring class . . .

b) The better-class subdivided house . . . the rents here run from, say, £9 to £10 per annum . . . and the class of tenant is better.

c) The deliberately erected tenement — having four houses per floor, and 16 to 20 per common stair . . . Rents, £11 to £12 . . . Tenants of good artisan class.

d) The tenement having three houses per floor, and nine to twelve per common stair . . . Rents, say, £18 . . . Tenants superior artisan class.

e) The best class of tenement, having two houses per floor . . . rents varying from £27 to £29 . . . to as much as £37. These houses may hardly, however, be correctly described as working-class houses.[48]

These levels of rentals were incapable of giving private enterprise an adequate return for investment in housing:

> That it was impossible at these figures, as a commercial undertaking, to put up a house of three rooms and all ordinary accessories for the working classes of some years prior to the war cannot be gainsaid.[49]

According to the Commission's calculations, it seemed that although a builder had to sell the house he had built to finance further operations, nevertheless no rational buyer would pay him more than two-thirds of the cost in order to get a return to capital marginally higher than the current rate of interest. On this argument, no rational builder would have built any houses for many years before the war. Four members of the Commission produced a long Minority Report[50] in which they included a short section headed 'Difficulty of Securing Adequate Rents'. An agricultural witness told them that nobody

> would regard it as an ordinary commercial proposition to build a £300 cottage unless there were to be a rent of something like £12 . . . [but] a £12 rent is quite out of proportion to the earning and paying capacity of the farm-servant.[51]

The position was the same in the cities. In Glasgow the average weekly rent per room had risen from 1/8¼d in 1871 to 2/1¾d in 1911, 'decidedly less than the rise in building costs in the same period':[52]

> It seems probable that, owing to the rising cost of other necessaries of life, which tend to be given preference over house rent in a working-class budget, the expenditure on house rent has not risen as rapidly as that on many other articles; and it is certain that it had not risen sufficiently to recoup the house owner for additional expenditure forced on him even in the period before the war.[53]

In short, a sort of accidental Speenhamland system had already arisen in Scotland before the war: housebuilders and owners were providing, willy-nilly, below-cost housing for the working class, who were receiving wages inadequate to pay the economic cost of their housing. It was into this already unbalanced situation[54] that the rent agitation of 1915 and subsequent years was pitched. The 1915 Rent Act had been accepted reluctantly by Long and the Tory members of the Government only on the strict understanding that, unfair as it was, it would expire six months after the end of the war. But in 1919 the same pressures as in 1915 were at work; the Increase of Rent and Mortgage Interest (Restriction) Act[55] of that year prolonged the freeze on rent increases until 1921, because of the fear of labour agitation. The problem was put before the Home Affairs Committee of the Cabinet by a committee headed by Lord Hunter, the same judge who had been involved in the inquiry into the rent agitation in 1915. The report pointed out that, because of the housing shortage,

> the opportunity to exact scarcity rents will be present. Further, this increase of rents will take place at a time of extreme dislocation, when demobilisation is proceeding, when a certain amount of unemployment may be present, and when (if only because of the reduction in overtime) the income of wage earners may be lower . . .
> The problem upon which our advice is sought is an exceedingly difficult one. The policy adopted may determine whether housing is to continue on an economic basis, or whether it is to be permanently subsidised, and thus, in effect, to become a State enterprise.
> . . . The aim should be to return to economic conditions as soon as possible . . . During the abnormal conditions of the next few years subsidies will be required, but we would urge that so soon as possible housing should be again established on an economic footing. This cannot take place until restrictions on rent are finally removed.[56]

It seemed that it was politically intolerable to decontrol rents but economically intolerable not to. The political imperative overrode the economic, partly because the Government, though committed to 'homes for heroes', had not got the legislation ready (Addison's Housing and Town Planning Bill was enacted on 31st July 1919).[57] Another Rent Act was passed in 1920.[58] It permitted an increase of 15% of the net rent (to be imposed in 5% steps in some cases) and an additional 25% 'where the landlord is responsible for the whole of the repairs'[59] (a clause which covered almost every Glasgow working-class tenement).

It is clear that the Acts of 1915, 1919 and 1920 between them reduced the proportion of real income which Scottish working-class tenants were spending on rent. It is very difficult to qualify this, and such statistics as exist should be treated with great caution. Nevertheless, an attempt has been made in Tables 13.4 and 13.5 to show the reduction of rents in real terms. The first is based on such national indices as are available, the second on income statistics collected by the Glasgow Trades Council in 1923.

These tables show, insofar as we can trust them, that wages (both money and real) leapt far ahead of rents during the war; that the gap was at its greatest during the short post-war boom; and that, though the gap narrowed, rents were still relatively below wages, for those in employment, in 1923. But the political argument about rents from 1915 to 1923 was not couched in terms of real wages. Both the socialists and those in government such as Lloyd George who were sympathetic to

Table 13.4 Wages, Retail Prices, and Scottish Rents, 1914-23
(July 1914 = 100)

	1	2	3	4
Year	Industrial wage rates (Bowley 1921)	Industrial wage rates (Bowley 1937)	Retail prices (Min. of Labour)	House rents (houses subject to s.2 (1) d. of 1920 Act)
1914	100	100	100	100
1915	107.5	—	123	100
1916	117.5	—	146	100
1917	137.5	—	176	100
1918	177.5	—	203	100
1919	212.5	229	215	100
1920	260	276	249	140
1921	—	271	226	140
1922	—	212	183	140
1923	—	188	174	140

Sources and notes: see Appendix 2.

rent restriction argued about the money level of rentals; and the socialists would scarcely have cared if it had been pointed out to them that, according to the rules of the capitalist system, they were getting a very good bargain out of house rental. In the view of Wheatley, who was the socialists' mentor, capitalism had failed, and was bound to fail, in the provision of working-class houses. This emerges clearly from the analysis of the Royal Commission's findings which he made in a speech in Glasgow Corporation in 1919:

> Every increase of 1% [in the rate of interest] . . . meant an increase of 10% on the economic rental of each house. £65 would be the economic rental of these houses, but the rents charged would be something like £30, which meant a loss of £35 a year on each house. The whole capitalist system of finance would collapse, and until they had a new financial system they could make no progress.[60]

Though Wheatley drew a much more radical conclusion than that drawn by the members of the Ballantyne Commission or by Lord Hunter, they all started from the same observation: the traditional system of financing housing had broken down, probably irrevocably. Under Wheatley's leadership, the Scottish Labour movement enthusiastically supported the recommendation of the Ballantyne Commission Majority that

Table 13.5   Wages in selected occupations, and House Rents, Glasgow 1914-23
(1914 = 100)

Occupation	1914		Maximum between 1914 and 1923		1923	
	Wages	Rents	Wages	Rents	Wages	Rents
Engineers	100	100	227 (1)	100	170	140
Masons	100	100	267 (2)	100/140	190	140
Builders' Labourers	100	100	343 (2)	100/140	214	140

(1) May 1920.   (2) Date not given.   For further notes, see Appendix 2.

the State, in assuming full responsibility for housing, should operate through the Local Authorities and should place upon them the responsibility of seeing to the provision of housing.[61]

But, like many other reports proposing radical reform, the Ballantyne Commission's had led to absolutely no action. Addison's housing policy of 1919[62] was thrown, like Addison himself, to the Unionist wolves in 1921.[63] Effective local authority housing lay in the future, much of it to be built under Wheatley's own Act of 1924. In the meantime, nothing changed. Because of the structural factors analysed by the Ballantyne Commission, aggravated by a rise since 1914 of 240% in building costs (though wages, according to Wheatley, had gone up by only 120%),[64] no working-class houses were built in Scotland, in contrast to the short post-war boom south of the border.

Thus the appalling and unchanging quality of housing formed the basis of a very popular Labour appeal, and when the 1920 Act was on its way through the Commons, the militancy of 1915 revived in its full fervour. In April, Andrew McBride, who had been Wheatley's second-in-command in 1915, called for a 24-hour strike 'to be followed by a universal Rent Strike'[65] against any rent increases. In May, Wheatley urged the Scottish Labour Housing Association to wage a No Rent Campaign if rents were raised. Owners, he said, were no more entitled to a higher rent for pre-war houses than were the tradesmen who built them to come back for further payment.[66] According to Neil Maclean, speaking in the Commons on the Second Reading of the Bill, delegates to this conference 'are now signing 50,000 requisitions that no rent will be paid if this Act passes, and in the West of Scotland there is going to be a rent war if the Bill goes through'.[67] In July, the Bill became law, and initially McBride wanted a militant campaign to refuse rent altogether:

'No defence in Court will protect a tenant who refuses to pay rent in terms of the Rent Restriction Act, and the proper place to defend the tenant is the home'.[68] After this, opinion fluctuated between not paying the increase in rent and paying no rent at all. A special congress of the S.T.U.C. on 11th July did not commit itself to either line, but called

> on the E.C.'s of Trades Unions affiliated to take whatever steps are necessary to render the fullest possible support in the Rent agitation to a No-Rent Campaign until the threatened impositions are withdrawn.[69]

A meeting of the Scottish Labour Housing Association on 31st July agreed unanimously to a 24-hour strike on 23rd August against the increases — this being proposed by the chairman of the S.T.U.C., James Walker of the Steelworkers.[70] A motion to pay no rent at all until the increases were withdrawn was carried against an amendment from Dundee which wished the conference merely to refuse to pay the increases.[71] The rent strike, as in 1915, was most strongly supported in the 'skilled' districts. This may be deduced from the proportions in each district of the addresses of Authorised District Officials of the rent strike whose job it was to look after the rent money paid to them instead of to the factors. The largest discrepancy is that there are only two addresses from Hutchesontown and none from Gorbals, as against seven from the predominantly skilled districts of Kingston and Govan west of the Caledonian railway. After a fortnight McBride wrote, under the heading 'Has the Rent Strike Collapsed?',

> In South Govan, we have been putting in some real fighting, and Central Govan is all right. But the battle — the great fight — will be in the poorer localities: Bridgeton, Dalmarnock, and the Eastern districts generally; Garngad, Cowcaddens, Hutchesontown, and Kinning Park.[72]

In Chapter 14 I shall try to show that in 1920 the Labour organisation was very unequally spread throughout the city, that the party was primarily an artisan party with little hold over the unskilled workers. This may go towards explaining the unequal distribution of support for the rent strike.

The campaign faded away after the middle of September and tenants gradually accepted the higher rents. The rent strike had no significant Parliamentary support, and absolutely none in Government. The local militants again found themselves out of alignment with the National Labour Party. The *Forward* alleged that the Parliamentary Labour

Party, Neil Maclean and Duncan Graham dissenting, had agreed to support the 15% increase without strings proposed in the Bill.[73] This was denied by the Secretary of the parliamentary party.[74] But the strikers reserved most of their fire for the ultra-orthodox William Graham, who was the Labour front-bench spokesman on the Bill. McBride alleged that Graham had said in the Second Reading debate that he would sooner see an increase by 10% steps than by 5% steps proposed in the Bill.[75] None of the numerous speeches made by Graham during the progress of the Bill can, in fact, be construed in this way. But there is ample evidence of the coolness of his attitude. In his first speech he said:

> I think it is not merely fair to the movement which I represent, but also fair to myself, to say that this is a subject upon which there is a widespread division in the Labour ranks.[76]

Graham sat for Edinburgh Central, a seat in which the problem was not so acute or the agitation so militant, as in Glasgow; in any case, the extreme moderation of his views was well known. As the editor of his local evening paper wrote to him, 'the rumour strongly prevails that you will be Liberal candidate of Central Edinburgh at the next election. N.B. this is not a joke'.[77] So it is no surprise that, in the debate on the 1920 Rent Act, Graham showed himself to have Snowdenish economic views:

> Many of us indicated that we believed that in the long run houses would require to come to an economic rental and that, unless that was achieved, there could only be some form of subsidy or other economic disease to which we were opposed, but we also made it clear that in our view the cumulative burden which is imposed on tenants under this Bill is altogether too severe.[78]

The chilliness of Graham's approach made an embarrassing contrast to the fundamentalist oratory of Neil Maclean. McBride complained, 'the action of the Party in the present Rent Restriction Act is certainly calculated to embarrass us in our present struggle'.[79]

It may be queried whether an ephemeral and unsuccessful rent strike had any real or lasting effect on the growth of the Labour vote. To this there are two answers. First, the 1920 rents agitation was the first sign that the local Labour movement had recovered from the demoralisation of February 1919 and could organise a campaign which, while it lasted, had widespread success in the skilled working-class districts of Glasgow. Second, and more important, the rents issue produced an uncovenanted bonus for the Socialists on the very eve of the 1922 elections, a bonus from which they could not have profited but for the agitation of two years earlier. For much of 1922, the Clydebank branch of the Labour Housing Association, with the active help of Kirkwood and the solicitor W. G. Leechman, had been representing the tenants in the test case of *Kerr* v. *Bryde* as it made its way through the courts. The tenants' contention was that the drafting of the Act required that a factor must give a tenant notice of removal before any increase could be legally imposed. The judgment in an English case, *Newell* v. *Crayford Cottage Society Ltd.*, had supported a similar view: 'notice to quit is necessary before a landlord can enforce a claim to the increase in rental permitted by the act'.[80] Eventually, this view was sustained as applicable, *mutatis mutandis*, in Scots Law when the tenant's case was upheld in the Court of Session. The judgment of the Lord President (Clyde) was a reluctant one:

> I confess to have struggled . . . to avoid a result so technical and so liable to misunderstanding. But both the words and the general plan of the statute seem to me to leave no alternative open.[81]

The owner appealed to the House of Lords, who by a 3-2 majority upheld the view that increases in rent under the 1920 Act were invalid unless they had been preceded by a notice of removal.[82] One of the minority judges (Lord Wrenbury) pointed out that to get an increase he was entitled to under the Act, a landlord had first to give a notice of removal which he knew would be ineffective: 'This is reducing the Act to an absurdity'.[83]

The judgment of the Law Lords was given on 3rd November 1922 and immediately created a great stir. The *Glasgow Herald* stated that the decision had 'created a remarkable situation in Glasgow', and condemned it editorially as 'bizarre . . . [and] preposterous'.[84] The *Forward* concluded exultantly:

> By this decision every tenant of a working-class house in Scotland is entitled to have returned to him a sum equal to about 12 months' rent and rates combined. The tenant can deduct this sum from future rent.[85]

The decision was seen, rightly, as a triumph for the Labour Housing Association, which had taken up (and financed) the case of Bryde, the tenant. But Labour stood to gain votes not simply through gratitude for services rendered, but from the threat of an immediate reversal of the effects of *Kerr* v. *Bryde* by the other parties. The Labour Housing Association issued a manifesto which, after saying that it would advise tenants later on how to reclaim rents illegally collected, went on:

Meanwhile, we desire to warn them against a great danger. The owners have already asked the Government to pass legislation authorising them to retain money illegally collected. The Moderate Party on the Town Council supported the owners by a deputation from the Corporation[86]

— and so, the manifesto concluded, tenants must vote Labour to protect the gains they had just made. The *Herald* reported that 'the Rent Act decision . . . is being made an issue [by Labour] in both the municipal and the Parliamentary elections'.[87] This view was confirmed by reporters in constituencies who said that Labour was sure to gain votes from the decision, for instance in Tradeston[88] and Dumbarton, where

Mr. Kirkwood is a stronger man than he was at the last election . . . he comes forward with all the kudos from having won the case for the tenants in the Rents Act decision.[89]

In the *Forward* for 18th November, Johnston wrote in his 'Socialist War Points' that the decision was 'a gift from the gods'. Only Dollan, of all the commentators, seemed to think that 'the Rent Act was a helpful agency, but not a decisive one'[90] — but he was concerned to ensure that the Labour machine did not get overlooked in the general euphoria.

In summary, the housing question had both a long-run and a short-run effect on the Labour vote. On the one hand, the very real misery of working-class housing and the militancy of official Labour organisations in the area kept the issue in the public eye, and proved a vote-getter for Labour; on the other hand, the immediate circumstances of the 1922 elections gave Labour an added bonus. It could, indeed, be maintained that because of the long-term success of the local Labour Party as a housing crusade, the decision in *Kerr* v. *Bryde* would have benefited Labour whichever way it had gone. If it had gone against the tenant, then this would have mobilised a wave of protest at the poll, and Labour would again have benefited. Either way, housing was emerging as a particularly Glasgow issue, to which particularly Glasgow politicians were beginning to produce particularly Glasgow solutions. They were starting to make Glasgow what it is today.

Appendix 1. Note on the Compilation of Table 13.1

The figures in the table are derived from the following constituencies:

Glasgow	*Birmingham*	*Bristol*
Bridgeton	Aston	Central
Camlachie	Kings Norton	East
Cathcart	Ladywood	North
Central	Sparkbrook	South
Govan	Yardley	(4 out of 5)
Maryhill	(5 out of 12)	
St. Rollox		
Shettleston		
Springburn		
Tradeston		
(10 out of 15)		

Leeds	*Liverpool*	*Manchester*	*Sheffield*
Central	Edge Hill	Ardwick	Attercliffe
North	Everton	Blackley	Brightside
North-East	Fairfield	Clayton	Hillsborough
South	Wavertree	Gorton	Park
South-East	West Derby	Platting	(4 out of 7)
West	West Toxteth	Rusholme	
(6 out of 6)	(6 out of 11)	(6 out of 10)	

Compiling any such table for inter-war elections is always problematical, as it is often difficult to decide how to allocate candidates. For the purposes of this comparison, Independent Labour and (in Liverpool, Everton only) N.F.D.S.S. candidates have been counted as Labour, as have three I.L.P. victors in Glasgow in 1935; Coalition Labour and N.D.P. in 1918, and National Labour and other I.L.P. in 1935 have been excluded, as have the Nationalists in Liverpool, although it is clear that in the Exchange and Scotland divisions the Nationalist vote of the 1920s closely parallels the Labour vote in the 1930s.

The nature of the 1918 fight in the Gorbals division of Glasgow has made it impossible to include that constituency in the table.

Unopposed Labour returns in 1918 (Manchester Platting and Leeds South-East) have been allocated a notional proportion of the vote according to the following formula:

$$\frac{\text{City-wide Labour \%, 1918}}{\text{City-wide Labour \%, 1922}} \times \text{Constituency Labour \%, 1922.}$$

Because of the way in which it has been compiled, the table over-emphasises Labour strength in cities in which the party did not fight many seats (especially Birmingham) relative to cities in which it fought safe opposition seats (especially Bristol and Leeds). The city in which Labour was weakest of all, namely Edinburgh, is not represented in the table at all, because only one constituency (Central) is comparable. In 1918 Labour fought only Central and East; in 1922 only Central. This makes a sharper contrast to 'Red Clydeside' than does any other large city. Table 13.2, showing the number of

Labour M.P.'s (defined in the same way as in Table 13.1) elected for each city in the three elections, shows more explicitly the weakness of Labour in such cities — for instance, the party's failure to gain any seats in Birmingham at any election prior to 1945.

All the voting figures and percentages are taken from F. W. S. Craig, *British Parliamentary Election Results, 1918-49*, Glasgow, 1969.

Appendix 2.   Sources for Tables 13.4 and 13.5

Table 13.4

Column 1.   A. L. Bowley, *Prices and Wages in the United Kingdom, 1914-1920* (Oxford, 1921), p. 106.

Column 2.   A. L. Bowley, *Wages and Incomes in the United Kingdom since 1860* (Cambridge, 1937), as cited in *The British Economy: Key Statistics 1900-1966* (London, c. 1969), Table E.

Column 3.   Official figures from Board of Trade Labour Gazette, reproduced in *British Labour Statistics: Historical Abstract 1886-1968*, H.M.S.O., 1971, Table 89.

Table 13.5

Source: Report of the Glasgow Trades Council, 1923, pp. 20-21.

Engineers' rate in column 3 calculated by adding cumulatively 'Advances granted between 1914-20' on p. 20 assuming a 54-hour week to December 1918 inclusive and a 47-hour week thereafter. Rate per hour in 1923 (from which the top figure in column 5 is derived) calculated by dividing in bonus to weekly rate given, assuming 46-hour week. Masons' and Labourers' rates from table on p. 21.

It is to be noted that the wage columns show wage rates, not earnings. The apparent drop in real wages during the war years suggested by a comparison of columns 1 and 3 and Table 4 may or may not, therefore, be borne out when account is taken of the heavy overtime worked.

14

The Growth of the Labour Vote. II: The Irish and the Origins of a Labour Machine

In the Glasgow of 1918, Socialism was not the creed of the unskilled workers. Wartime militancy divided, not united, the working class; craftsmen joined the socialist parties, but labourers did not. Harry McShane recalled:

> You take my branch of the I.L.P. when I first joined it. I don't think there was a labourer in it: [they were] mostly engineers. The engineers were the most active people in the movement — and the moulders — they were pretty strong.[1]

According to McShane, the city was at the time rigidly stratified into 'skilled' and 'unskilled' working-class areas. 'Gorbals was almost entirely unskilled', but one had only to cross Eglinton Street into Tradeston, where McShane lived, to enter an area where the majority were skilled. In general, the unskilled areas corresponded with those which had no large-scale employment on the spot, but only small-scale domestic or sweated trades, while the more prosperous areas, at this time, were those close to heavy industry. Thus all the south-bank wards west of Eglinton Street and the Caledonian railway (Kingston, Kinning Park, Govan, and Fairfield) depended on shipbuilding and marine engineering. Govanhill, Cowlairs and Springburn had railway engineering, and the latter two wards had large settlements of railway fitters and footplatemen.[2] Townhead had general engineering; life in Parkhead and Shettleston revolved round Parkhead Forge, with a few miners on the fringe of the city, towards Baillieston. These were the artisan wards. Very different were Gorbals, Hutchesontown, Anderston, or Cowcaddens, with no industry employing skilled men. These were the unskilled wards; other working-class wards, such as Provan or Mile End, were more mixed.

The *Forward* from time to time voiced the scorn felt by socialist artisans for their inferiors, and the social stratification of the city by district adds political importance to suggestions such as this:

> The classes that read the *Forward* are not ignorant people,[3] but intelligent people, the well-read, thinking, reflecting, and clean-living decent people . . . Neither the bar-tender's pest nor the Sauchiehall Street dude ever spend a penny on the *Forward* . . . In the slum areas few socialist periodicals are purchased but many copies of *Red Welcome, Daily Record, Sporting Tit-bits, Weekly Mail,* and *John Bull* . . . Look at your slum wards — not a Socialist representative in the Town Council from Calton or the Cowcaddens or Gorbals or Broomielaw. Capitalism represents these wards. On the other hand, the better paid, and more comfortably circumstanced, and better read Govan, and Shettleston, and Cowlairs, and Townhead, look to them! Socialism represents these wards. And the reason is obvious. A man requires to reach a certain level of culture before he can under-stand Socialism, have a certain independence of position and character before he can break away from old traditions and mental prejudice and face the obloquy and criticism meted out always and everywhere to the pioneer.[4]

Johnston returned to the attack at least twice in the following six years. In 1917, in answer to a correspondent (whose letter had not been printed), he wrote,

> What you really hold is a variant of the old theory of increasing misery . . . We do not believe the theory to be true. We see no revolutionary ardour in the Cowcaddens slums, but we do see it among the better fed and more leisured working districts.[5]

In 1921 he attacked the same viewpoint, whose devotees had been condemning attempts by Kirkwood to alleviate distress in eviction cases in the Summary Ejectment Court:

> The crazy notion that the further the poor are impoverished, harassed, and starved, the more 'revolutionary' and 'class-conscious' they become, is scouted by all the facts of history. It is not in Anderston or Broomielaw or Cowcaddens that Socialist propaganda flourishes. The slum areas are represented by Capitalists on public bodies.[6]

But the charge was less true and more snobbish in 1921 than in 1915. Johnston was confusing receptivity to propaganda with propensity to vote Labour, a fallacy criticised by Maxton some weeks earlier in reviewing the local election results:

> There was no better propaganda district this summer than Maryhill, where we lost, and no worse than Gorbals, Hutchesontown, Cowlairs, and Springburn, where we won handsomely.[7]

The series of municipal election results from 1919 to 1922 shows how the Labour vote spread from 'labour-aristocratic' districts to 'unskilled' districts to produce a recognisable forerunner of modern voting patterns — a shift which surely goes some way towards explaining the differences between the 1918 and 1922 General Elections. An attempt to give these generalisations some numerical force, by relating the Labour vote to housing density, is made in Table 14.1. Housing density ought to be a good *prima facie* indicator of propensity to vote Labour: the more persons per hundred rooms are found in a ward, the poorer its inhabitants are likely to be. If poverty were the sole criterion of propensity to vote Labour, there would be something approaching a correlation of 1 between housing density and the Labour vote in the 1920 and 1922 local elections. The product-moment correlation r is, in fact, quite high: 0.813 in 1920 and 0.852 in 1922. Table 14.1 examines the results ward by ward in each year, and it depends on analysis of the 'residuals'. This is a method suitable for use when, as in our example, there is a strong linear correlation between the independent variable (housing density) and the dependent variable (Labour vote). It measures the deviance of any one ward from the established relationship between the two variables obtained from all the other wards in the observation. In other words, it puts the wards in a rank order depending on the extent to which their Labour vote was more or less than 'expected', given the city-wide relationship between housing density and Labour vote.[8]

It will be noted from Table 14.1 that the residuals are smaller in 1922 than in 1920: seven wards in 1920 have a higher residual than the most deviant in 1922. The wards were becoming more like one another, with fewer mavericks showing an outstandingly low (or high) Labour vote. The smaller number of wards appearing in the table for 1922 than for 1920 has a simple explanation: the poverty of the local Labour party, with two elections in quick succession to fight at a time when unemployment had seriously damaged the I.L.P.'s finances. Labour might have done still better than it did in 1922 if it had had enough money to fight more wards: pro-Labour deviants like Sandyford and North Kelvin were not fought at all in 1922. The deviance of Kinning Park in 1922 is probably because there was no Labour candidate, and John MacLean, standing as a Communist, has been counted as Labour for the purposes of this calculation. He got fewer votes than a Labour candidate would have done.

*Table 14.1   Glasgow Municipal Wards in 1920 and 1922: Analysis of Residuals:
Wards arranged in ascending order of deviance to Labour*

1920		1922	
Ward	Deviance, % (1)	Ward	Deviance, %
1 Cowcaddens	—22.99	1 Kinning Park	—10.40
2 Provan	—15.51	2 Maryhill	—9.60
3 Calton	—13.81	3 Cowcaddens	—8.28
4 Whitevale	—10.30	4 Provan	—7.35
5 Anderston	—8.28	5 Whitevale	—6.44
6 Dalmarnock	—7.59	6 Ruchill	—5.69
7 Camphill	—5.44	7 Calton	—4.50
8 Pollokshaws	—4.49	8 Partick West	—2.66
9 Whiteinch	—3.64	9 Dalmarnock	—2.64
10 Cathcart	—2.85	10 Townhead	—0.01
11 Govanhill	—2.76	11 Hutchesontown	1.23
12 Dennistoun	—2.16	12 Shettleston	1.78
13 Townhead	—1.79	13 Springburn	1.87
14 Kinning Park	—1.26	14 Partick East	2.32
15 Partick West	—0.36	15 Kingston	2.33
16 Maryhill	0.23	16 Parkhead	2.66
17 Partick East	0.83	17 Cowlairs	3.28
18 Shettleston	1.17	18 Woodside	5.57
19 Ruchill	1.97	19 Govan	5.70
20 Cowlairs	4.10	20 Anderston	6.85
21 Parkhead	5.47	21 Gorbals	7.03
22 Kingston	5.60	22 Mile-End	7.57
23 Fairfield	6.53	23 Fairfield	9.40
24 Woodside	6.68		
25 Gorbals	7.70		
26 Sandyford	7.73		
27 Govan	9.43		
28 Hutchesontown	9.66		
29 Mile-End	10.29		
30 Springburn	12.73		
31 North Kelvin	13.16		

Source: Election results, *Glasgow Herald.*
          Housing density: 1911 *Census of Scotland.*

(1) The figures are percentages of the vote cast. In Cowcaddens in 1920, for example,
Labour 'ought' to have had 53.49% of the votes cast; it actually had 30.5%, so the
deviance is 22.99%.

The principal value of Table 14.1, however, is in the information it can give us about a number or groups of wards. Not every ward can be easily categorised, and the classification has to be based on literary rather than statistical evidence. However, the groups of wards most worthy of comment are probably:

A. Seven 'artisan' wards	B. Four 'unskilled' wards	C. Two 'unskilled' and one mixed ward
Shettleston	Anderston	Gorbals
Cowlairs	Cowcaddens	Hutchesontown
Parkhead	Provan	Mile-End (mixed)
Kingston	Calton	
Fairfield		
Govan		
Springburn		

Group A. These wards cover three areas of the city: the further East End (Shettleston and Parkhead), the railway areas in the North-East (Springburn and Cowlairs), and the shipbuilding area south of the river west of Eglinton Street (the other three). They correspond quite closely to those named at one time or another by Johnston as containing the core of the Labour vote; Table 14.1 shows that Johnston was largely right. All seven wards, in both years sampled, showed a higher tendency to vote Labour than would have been inferred from their housing density. Townhead should perhaps be discussed along with this group. Though Labour were very distressed at losing it in 1922, and though the *Glasgow Herald* pointed out with some pride that 'Townhead has been a Labour stronghold for about a score of years',[9] it was not a particularly badly housed ward. Its failure to deviate in the same direction as the other seven studied may be attributable to the local influence of Councillor Turner, the Labour Councillor who defected to the Moderate group in 1921.

Group B. These wards 'came into line' at some point in the early 1920s. Though Cowcaddens, Provan, and Calton were still deviantly anti-Labour in 1922, they were far less so than in 1920, when they stand out clearly at the head of the list. And the Anderston ward is the only one to show a heavy swing from deviantly anti-Labour to pro-Labour between the two years. Serving the Anderston district was the largest Catholic Church in Glasgow — St. Patrick's, North Street, with 737 baptisms in 1920.[10] We shall shortly explore the connection between these facts.

Group C. These three wards contrast with Group B. Gorbals and

Hutchesontown were wholly unskilled, and Mile-End was a mixture, housing on its eastern side workers from Parkhead Forge and on its western side unskilled East-Enders. The three wards had at least as high a proportion of Catholics as those in Group B — Mile-End had two churches with a total of 876 baptisms in 1920[11] — but they were deviant, not in an anti-, but in a pro-Labour direction. Later in this chapter, we shall try to say why. However, we must start by examining the deviance shown by wards like those in our Group B.

There are three reasons why the mean residual was smaller in 1922 than in 1920: the recruitment of the unskilled to Labour as the divisive issues of wartime socialist politics faded into the background; the ending of the electorally damaging association between Labour and prohibition; and, far the most important, the swing of the Irish machine from Liberal to Labour in national elections, and its increasingly loyal commitment to Labour in local elections. Of course, the three overlap. Not all unskilled were Irish, but most of the Irish were unskilled. In many large plants, notably the Govan shipyards and the engineering shops where Harry McShane spent his apprenticeship, it was next to impossible for anyone of Irish descent to secure an apprenticeship, which alone opened the gate to craftsman status, because apprenticeships were in the gift of foremen, who were invariably Protestants and often Freemasons.[12] Again, much of Glasgow Irish community life revolved around the public house (though there were bitter disputes between the public-house mafiosi and their opponents); the Irish had none of the ideological convictions which drove socialists to advocate prohibition.

Not much more need be said about the first of our three explanations. After the 1919 fiasco, traditional wartime militancy was dead: it was bound to die anyhow, when the ending of wartime pressures for productivity and the passing of the Restoration of Prewar Practices Act removed the basis of the engineers' agitation. Since it had been an unofficial agitation, it had disdained to secure a foothold by way of places in union or Labour Party hierarchies: so it vanished like snow off a dyke. With militancy died the divisiveness which had accompanied it, and one (though not the only) obstacle to co-operation between skilled and unskilled in the same party was removed.

By 1920, Prohibition had become an albatross round the neck of the Labour leaders of Clydeside. There were several overlapping reasons why socialists should have been prohibitionist. Prohibition appealed to the Samuel Smiles in them; if only the working class would cease drinking, it would have not just more money but more opportunity to study political principles with a view to embracing socialism. Socialists also objected to subsidising the brewers, who were, and still are, notoriously generous contributors to Tory funds. Many of them shared Kirkwood's Free Church background which enabled him to think of non-smoking and temperance as 'the stuff of which reform is made'. One of Tom Johnston's proudest boasts was that there were no pubs in Kirkintilloch, where he was a councillor.[13] (There were none until 1969.) The Scottish Labour Party Conference voted 47 to 15 for Prohibition in September 1920,[14] while the S.T.U.C. carried Prohibition in 1920 by 110 votes to 74 'amid cheers and counter-cheers'[15] — the successful motion being an amendment from the Glasgow Trades Council.[16] The tide began to ebb in 1921, when the S.T.U.C. reversed its approval, in a thinly attended session, by 79 votes to 64[17] — the *Forward* thought that 'given a full attendance, Prohibition would have been carried'.[18] The I.L.P. carried prohibition as against municipalisation annually at its Scottish Conference.[19]

The conflict of ideals and realism on this issue was shown up at the confused debate on it at the 1921 Scottish Labour Party Conference, at which delegates successfully carried the 'previous question' against a prohibition resolution. The mover of the latter, a Glasgow Trades Council delegate, appears to have spent most of his time attacking what he was supposed to be supporting, describing Prohibition as 'inspired by all the claptrap of Puritanic repression . . . [aimed at] . . . attaching the Labour movement to the tail of the Liberal Party'.[20] Another delegate spoke more bluntly about the political consequences of the Labour attitude:

> Laurie Anderson (A.E.U.) . . . explained that the working class had not enough to drink . . . When he went to Dalmuir to address a workers' meeting . . . he had to wait until his audience came from the public house . . . The municipal elections of 1920 showed that Labour was out of touch with public opinion in advocating Prohibition.[21]

In the 1920 local elections a veto poll under the Temperance (Scotland) Act, 1913 was held simultaneously with the election of councillors in Glasgow (and some other burghs): that is to say, voters were asked to choose between 'No Change' in the number of licences in each ward, 'Restriction of Licences', or 'No Licence'. The ultimate vote was 4 wards for Dry, 9 for Limitation, and 24 for No Change.[22] But during the election it became obvious to local Labour leaders that their commitment to prohibition was an electoral hindrance rather than a help. The dual poll 'obscured the issue. Labour had succeeded in the early stages of the campaign in making Housing the issue . . .', but this became overlaid by the drink issue, which helped to produce the unprecedented poll of 78%. 'Every public-house became virtually a hostile committee-room, and in a ward like Calton with 82 such centres it meant a lot.'[23] All Labour candidates were pledged to support 'No Licence'. This brought them no support in middle-class areas of the city, where prohibitionists voted for middle-class prohibition candidates running in opposition to Labour. But it did hamper Labour in working-class areas, unless candidates and their helpers were prepared to bend closer to the view of their constituents:

> A letter . . . indicts some canvassers at Parkhead for shouting 'Vote Labour and No Change'. Regrettable, but in all the circumstances hardly surprising.[24]

Several working-class Catholic anti-prohibitionist candidates advertised their views in the principal local Catholic paper, the *Glasgow Observer*. One wrote:

> My policy and programme is Labour. I am opposed to Prohibition because Prohibition means Higher Taxes on your Tea, Sugar, Bread, and general Household Commodities, and because Prohibition is class legislation and undemocratic.[25]

Another, who was to be elected as what the *Forward* later described as the 'Irish Wet'[26] councillor for Cowcaddens, exhorted his supporters:

> Electors Awake! Remember that Every Prohibitionist will poll on 2nd November next, and that they are relying on your apathy not to Record your Vote. Make a Point of Recording your Vote, and support William T. Doherty, the only candidate who is opposed to Prohibition.[27]

Besides Doherty, the 1920 municipal general election saw returned to George Square two other councillors described by *Forward* as 'Irish and Publican':[28] one each in Provan and Calton. But in 1921 the profile of Labour candidatures had changed somewhat. Councillor Doherty was now described by the *Forward* as 'Unofficial Labour',[29] and the *Glasgow Herald's* potted biography drew its readers' attention to his undesirable characteristics:

> W. T. Doherty (Unofficial Labour). Wine and Spirit Merchant. A member of the Ancient Order of Hibernians.[30]

Altogether the *Herald* named six candidates — five Labour plus Doherty — as being members of the A.O.H; one of the others was also a publican, and others were shopkeepers. The Labour candidate of Provan was 'a member of the A.O.H. and late president of the Townhead branch of the United Irish League'.[31]

The *Glasgow Observer* commented:

> Notwithstanding the *Glasgow Herald's* assiduous care in rubbing it into the minds of its readers that a number of candidates standing at the recent Municipal Election in Glasgow were members of the Ancient Order of Hibernians, the electors in the greater number of cases seemed willing to take the risk, and ignored the *Herald's* bugaboo warning. The turnip lantern failed to frighten and five out of six A.O.H. men were elected. Of course, the printing of such a statement on the part of the *Herald* was the sheerest malice attempting to rouse race prejudice.[32]

The following year, the *Herald* repeated its potted biographies of candidates, doubtless with the same ulterior motive:

> *Calton.* J. Cruden (Lab.) Ex-publican. Member of the I.L.P. and A.O.H. Was formerly connected with the Home Government Branch of the U.I.L., now defunct . . .
> *Provan.* T. A. O'Hare (Lab.) Solicitor. Was a leading member of the now defunct Home Government Branch of the U.I.L. A member of the A.O.H. . . . Previously a member of the Glasgow School Board and the Glasgow Education Authority.[33]

Again, the *Observer* opined:

> The *Glasgow Herald* has tried to pump up some prejudice against Mr. Cruden by describing him as 'a member of the I.L.P. and the A.O.H.'. This bogey will frighten nobody.[34]

Cruden won:

> Mr. John Cruden, who won Calton, is a well-known Irish Nationalist, and his victory is the greatest achieved by Labour in the West of Scotland Town Council contests. He has a son who is a member of the Passionist Order.[35]

Thus an ex-publican, who had formerly run the Irish political organisation in his part of the city through the powerful Home Government Branch of the U.I.L., had become a Labour councillor. 'There was a time,' recalled a writer in the 1950s,

> when any man proposing to stand as candidate in the municipal elections in Govan had to appear before a committee headed by two Irish Catholic publicans, and answer their questions satisfactorily before they could expect the support of the Catholic vote.[36]

That time began between 1918 and 1922 as the radical socialist and prohibitionist Glasgow I.L.P. turned into something very different. We must now trace in detail how and why it did.

The leaders of the Irish Catholic community had far better propaganda tools at their disposal than had the socialists. The socialists had open-air meetings, sometimes workplace contacts, and one, initially struggling, paper — the *Forward* — whose circulation before the war was probably less than 10,000, although it benefited greatly from the row over its suppression and from Johnston's *History of the Working Classes in Scotland*, which it published in 1920.[37] By contrast the Catholics had all the advantages of a tightly knit community bound together by the bar, the pulpit, and an 'ethnic' press. The socialists were uncomfortably aware of the power of the public house as a hostile committee-room in 1920, and it was a power which could be turned to advantage only by having Irish community leaders, who were publicans or shopkeepers, as Labour candidates. The importance of the pulpit in political matters is witnessed by the unending debates before the war between Wheatley and various clerical opponents on the compatibility of socialism and Catholicism which were reprinted and discussed *in extenso* by the chain of thirty or so Catholic papers to which the *Glasgow Observer* and *Glasgow Star* belonged,[38] and which have obscured for some modern commentators[39] the real reasons for the transfer of Catholic votes to Labour.

Up to 1908 there were two rival Catholic weeklies in Glasgow: the *Observer* and the *Star*, whose often violent differences boiled down to the fact that the *Observer* and its editor and proprietor (respectively D. J. Mitchell Quin and Charles Diamond), who were temperance supporters, frequently quarrelled with the publicans who dominated many branches of the U.I.L., and whose organ was the *Star*. In 1908, however, Diamond bought the *Star* and added it to his chain, so that thereafter its views were identical with the *Observer's* (and sometimes expressed in the same words). The Catholic press was religiously orthodox and politically heterodox. But, unlike the *Forward*, the *Observer* and *Star* did not depend for their circulation on the intellectual appeal of their political views. The *Observer* called itself in the trade directory a 'Popular football medium',[40] not without justice. It profited by its close links with Celtic Football Club (which had been founded in 1887 by the local St. Vincent de Paul Society[41]) and carried a weekly column, 'In Celtic Inner Circles'. This was written in collaboration with the Celtic management, and as the best-informed football commentary in Glasgow it had a wide following.[42] Thus the Catholic press had a much higher circulation than the *Forward* (though no circulation figures exist, unfortunately), and, since it was preaching much less exclusively to the converted, its political views circulated to a larger number of uncommitted, marginal, and even hostile electors. A study of the changes over the years in the political advice it tendered may therefore be of some value.

Labour representation on Glasgow Town Council can be traced back to the 1890s, when a number of Lib-Labs, some of them union officials, banded together into the 'Stalwart Party' under the leadership of John Ferguson. This group 'could not be regarded as a party subject to very rigid discipline',[43] but was an amalgam of labour and Irish interests[44] which 'reached its high-water mark' around 1900 when it claimed about 12 of the 77 councillors. Its fate was disappointing:

> the old Stalwart party . . . elected on a democratic ticket, proceeded to scramble as quickly as possible to the Bailies' Bench, and there dissolved into gilded impotence.[45]

The policy of the *Glasgow Observer* before the war was broadly, though rather lukewarmly, pro-Labour:

> Generally speaking, where a Labour candidate of suitable calibre can be found, our readers ought to vote Labour, at least those of them who are themselves wage-earners.[46]

In 1910, Diamond described his papers' political stance by saying, 'They favour the Budget and the Progressist cause generally'.[47] (Up to 1908, the *Star* was less pro-Labour than the *Observer*, because it objected to prohibitionists like Joseph Burgess who became Labour candidates,[48] but after the amalgamation of the papers this difference vanished, of course.)

Diamond's use of the word 'Progressist' rather than 'Labour' gives a clue to the difficulties in the way of an Irish-Labour reconciliation. Up to 1906 there had been a Progressive coalition in Glasgow Corporation headed by the Irish and Labour members. It broke up in that year because of the death of Ferguson and the new militancy of the I.L.P., which broke with the tradition of the Stalwart Group and insisted that all Labour candidates must be members of the party. This infuriated the Irish, who thought that as part of the Progressive coalition they were entitled to a clear run for their candidates in wards containing a high proportion of Irish electors. The Labour Party was breaking the rules of the political game as the Irish ward bosses understood it: the Irish were being offered nothing in return for the marketable commodity, namely votes, which they were prepared to deliver. A good example of the feelings aroused is this piece of advice from the *Star* in the 1909 local elections:

> In Mile-End, whatever the Irish electors do, they should not vote for the Labour candidate, Mr. Gardner. Mile-End is a Ward where, in all fairness, a Progressive from the Nationalist wing might have been asked to bear the Stalwart colours. The action of the Labour people in ignoring the Irish electorate calls for emphatic resentment.[49]

The Catholic press was therefore quite happy to see every Labour candidate except James Stewart in Townhead defeated:

> The result of the municipal elections is effective proof of the strength and solidarity of the Irish vote. Those who are responsible for the leadership of Labour politics in Glasgow have been . . . so contemptuous as to the necessity of any alliance with other wings of the Progressive force in Glasgow that they indulged in an overweening and unwarranted certainty that Labour could carry its own men to triumph at the polls in wards where Labour candidates came forward. Well, now it knows different.[50]

In 1910, the *Observer*, presenting its annual ticket,[51] said:

> Where the Progressive forces have given the Irish electorate of Glasgow a fair opportunity of supporting the Progressive ticket, they will willingly do it . . . Where this has not been done, they will decline to be roped in, however plausible the pretext.[52]

Accordingly, it recommended the Irish to oppose some Labour incumbents, such as Hugh Lyon in Townhead and George Carson in Maryhill. After the election, when Lyon and Carson had both won, it returned to its favourite theme:

> If our friends, the Labour people, care to discuss a sound reciprocal scheme whereby the Irish electorate in Glasgow would be now and again the climber, and not always the ladder, they will find every disposition to a reasonable discussion awaiting them. But it is neither fair nor reasonable to expect that we shall always turn the wheel and they always grind their axe.[53]

In 1911 relations improved because two prominent Irishmen had been nominated, one of them a director of Celtic F.C., and the I.L.P. supported them.[54] 1912, however, marked the nadir. Instead of the annual headline 'The *Observer* Ticket', the paper ran a banner which read:

> Labour Candidates and Municipal Elections.
> Catholics, Be Gulled No Longer!
> Read This, Then Act Like Men!

Hitherto [the story began] our counsel to Irish electors has almost invariably been to support the candidates of the Labour Party in every constituency. That counsel we are no longer able to extend . . . [because] the Labour Party, while making the most profuse professions of sympathy with the Irish movement and with Irish sentiment, will not give the least help to any candidate standing who is an Irish Nationalist . . . Not even the absurd little Catholic Socialist Society can qualify its members for Socialist support. Mr. Wheatley is supported, not because he is the founder of the Socialist Society, but because he is a member of the Shettleston I.L.P. . . . Unless a Catholic is prepared to swallow the Socialist shibboleth, he may give his vote to a Labour man, but he must not expect to get one in return.[55]

When four out of the thirteen Labour nominees were returned, the paper claimed that 'with the Irish vote Labour could have won at least 10 seats', and went on:

The sensible men of the [Labour] Party . . . will recognise further that in municipal elections the Irish vote in Glasgow is still a disciplined and united vote . . . With the Irish vote in its favour, the Labour ticket should be the winning ticket. With the Irish vote against it, Labour is able to win less than 1/6th of what it seeks.[56]

The following year, the paper claimed to have detected a rift between the accommodating Labour leadership and their dogmatic followers:

If Labour candidates are to expect or receive Irish support hereafter, some provision had better be made to admit Nationalists by the front door . . . [Labour leaders are] universally in favour of such a course . . . Since the Labour Party had been wise enough not to advance any such aggressive secularists as, say, Mr. Shinwell . . . there is no new Labour candidate . . . whom . . . any Catholic or any Irish elector need have any scruple in supporting.[57]

In 1914 the usual message was repeated, after the paper had refused to endorse four Labour candidates, including Lyon.[58]

After the war, relations were noticeably warmer. In October 1919, Arthur Murphy, a leading U.I.L. politician, gave an address on '25 Years of Irish and Labour Municipal Politics in Glasgow'. Advertising this, the *Observer* said:

In view of the forthcoming municipal elections and of the [municipal] General Election next year the new relations between the Labour Party and the Irishmen in the city are a matter of supreme moment. The question of adequate representation of Irish Labour opinion on the City Council is an urgent matter that can no longer be delayed.[59]

The 'new relations' do not seem to have amounted to anything as definite as a pact, but certainly there was greater warmth in the *Observer's* reception:

[T]hough some who have received the Labour label are not quite the class of men with whom it would be safe to go tiger hunting, there is little doubt that the Irish vote in the main will go solid for the Labour candidates.[60]

The Irish were advised to vote Labour in every ward save two (Calton and Govan Central).

In 1920, relations were a little more strained again, almost certainly because of Labour's adherence to Prohibition. Dalmarnock, Calton and Cowcaddens were among wards in which the *Observer* ticket counselled voting for an Irish independent rather than one of the Labour candidates.[61] By 1921 the tone has changed again. If the pre-war advice was 'Support Labour *if* . . .', and the immediate post-war 'Support Labour *unless* . . .', by now it was 'Support Labour *notwith-standing* . . .':

. . . we unhesitatingly declare for principle before personality, and hope that the Irish vote in Townhead will go to the official Labour candidate.
The foregoing remark applies equally to other contests, in some of which the Labour nominees are individuals having but small claim (on personal grounds) either to the votes of Irish electors or to our support.
In politics, however, principle should be a paramount consideration, and on that ground we counsel our readers all round to cast their vote for the official Labour candidate.[62]

In 1922 this advice was repeated: 'Our counsel to our readers all over is to "Vote Labour"'.[63]

The immediate reason for this change of mood is not far to seek. In the years after the war, the Labour Party was at last returning to the notion of an Irish-Labour coalition, by letting the Irish have a say in the nomination of Labour candidates in Irish areas. No written record of a decision, or a pact, survives. This is partly because the archives become thinner after 1918 than they are for the war years, but more because this was either a pact made in private, or else a decision never formally taken but arrived at by the passive connivance of the local Labour leadership. The evidence cited earlier as to the appearance of Irish ex-ward bosses as Labour councillors is too clear to admit of any other interpretation. A more substantial question is *why*? Why did Labour feel more strongly that it needed Irish support, and why were the Irish readier to be embraced by the Labour organisation? A study of the political consequences of the 1918 Education Act may help answer both questions.

The education settlement of 1918 in Scotland differed from that in

England, among other things in the provision made for voluntary schools — which in Scotland meant, almost entirely, Catholic Schools. The Secretary for Scotland, in preparing a draft memorandum for the War Cabinet in 1917 on the first version of the Education Bill, explained why voluntary schools were a problem:

> There is no question that, because of the inadequate resources of the Managers, Roman Catholic children, who constitute upwards of 1/8th of the school population in Scotland, are being deprived of the opportunities of education which are afforded by the public schools. There are only two possible remedies for this state of matters.
> 1) that state-aid to denominational schools should be provided in much fuller measure than to public schools — to an extent in fact which would compensate them for what they lose in rate aid. This solution, having regard to the state of public opinion in Scotland, is clearly out of the question.
> 2) There remains the other solution, namely, that denominational schools providing elementary education should be compulsorily transferred to the local education authority and should be managed by them in all respects as public schools, but provision however being made for religious education according to the views of the former Managers, given by teachers who are acceptable to the representatives of these Managers, both as regards faith and character. This is the solution which I propose.[64]

This solution was accepted by the War Cabinet,[65] and it was embodied in successive versions of the Bill. The Catholic hierarchy provisionally accepted the Bill subject to the judgment of the Vatican,[66] and after a minor flurry caused by allegations that the Bill would not allow any new Catholic schools to be built,[67] word of the Bill's acceptance by the Vatican arrived in October 1918:

> Those of us who have had misgivings as to the safety of Catholic Education in Scotland for the future under the operation of the Bill may now shed our fears since the onus of acceptance lies on the responsible shoulders of the Vatican authorities . . .
> It would be uncandid to say that the Bill as now finally framed furnishes all the safeguards which all of us would desire. However, since the Catholics of the country will find their feet presently as a powerful political factor, we shall be able in future to demand and require any rectification which experience in working the measure may prove to be necessary.[68]

Section 18 of the Act provided that at any time the owners of a voluntary school might

> transfer the school . . . to the education authority, who shall be bound to accept such transfer, upon such terms as to price, rent, or other consideration as may be agreed . . .

> Any school so transferred shall be held, maintained, and managed as a public
> school by the education authority who shall be entitled to receive grants therefor
> as a public school, and shall have in respect thereto the sole power of regulating
> the curriculum and of appointing teachers . . .[69]

In Glasgow, the Roman Catholic schools were leased to the Education
Authority from May 1919, and sold outright, at the request of the
Catholic trustees, in 1928.[70] This gave Catholics an immediate vested
interest in the Education Authority and the Corporation much closer
than that of their co-religionists in England. The Catholics did indeed
'find their feet presently as a powerful political factor'. They had
organised their representation on the old School Board much more
successfully than the socialists, whose only representative was the
middle-class electrical contractor Martin Haddow,[71] and this pattern
was continued in the first Education Authority elections, which in
accordance with the provisions of s.23 of the Act were held under
proportional representation:

> The Catholics polled splendidly, and exhibited a magnificent organisation. In no
> Glasgow division did a Labour candidate get in on a first count, and James
> Maxton is the only candidate who is in without Catholic assistance. In the other
> cases where we have been successful, the success is due to the fact of Catholics
> giving Labour their 3rd, 4th, or 5th votes.[72]

Labour was not formally committed to supporting State provision of
denominational education, but it was not against it either. But Labour's
municipal opponents, banded together in the Good Government
League, were very suspicious of Catholic organisations:

> [Glasgow] had ceased to be purely a douce Scottish city. To a large extent it had
> become an Irish city. It had also a very large semi-alien population . . . they found
> working in their midst organisations which were alien in conception, alien at any
> rate, in operation to our Scottish ways of working, and it was intolerable that the
> administration of a Scottish city should be held up at the bidding of any class or
> party.[73]

The alleged iniquity of the 1918 Act was often discussed at the General
Assembly of the Church of Scotland, and in 1922 the *Glasgow Herald*
reported:

> 'The menace of Romanism' is not strictly an educational issue . . . But the question
> is very pertinent to education whether the Roman Catholic or other voluntary sect
> enjoys a privileged position in the schools. Many Presbyterian churchmen believe
> that this is the case, and, if they are right, the 1918 Act must be amended in the
> sense for which they contend.[74]

Because of the 1918 Act, the Catholic schools issue was politicised, and Catholics could no longer be content with returning representatives of Catholicism, *per se*, to education authorities and political bodies. They had to seek the support of one of the political parties. By elimination, that party had to be Labour, which was in any case the party to which the Catholics were closest. On its side, Labour welcomed the Catholics because the socialists came to realise how much they suffered from the lack of an efficient political machine. This was reinforced when Patrick Dollan began his long reign as city boss and I.L.P. organiser.[75] Dollan was a lapsed Catholic, although still claimed by the *Observer* and *Star*, in their annual lists of Catholic councillors, as one of the faithful;[76] and he certainly favoured the closer integration of Labour and Catholic forces. The movement was undoubtedly self-reinforcing: the mobilisation of a Labour municipal bloc led to the counter-mobilisation of an economy-minded and latently anti-Irish opposition party, which started as the Good Government League and became the Moderate (later the Progressive) Party, developing into a fully fledged political party whose main tenet was opposition to party politics in local government. This forced the Catholics all the more firmly into the Labour fold.

We must now turn from local to national politics. Though writers are beginning to appreciate the importance of the United Irish League in delivering and directing the Irish vote in Britain from about 1885 to 1918, little detailed research on the political behaviour of the Irish has yet been done.[77] The next few pages will be devoted to tracing the changes in the advice given to the Glasgow Irish through the local Catholic press.

For the 1906 election, the U.I.L. Executive issued a manifesto reasonably friendly to Labour:

> . . . we recommend our people in all cases where a Labour candidate, who is sound on Home Rule, is in the field to give their votes to that candidate, except in cases where he is standing against an old and tried friend of the Irish cause, or where the support of the Labour candidate would ensure the return of the Unionist candidate.[78]

In the Clydeside area, 'Mr. John Redmond has directed the disposition of the Irish vote'[79] to three Labour candidates: Joseph Burgess in Camlachie, George Barnes in Hutchesontown, and Joseph Sullivan in North-West Lanark. In Hutchesontown in 1900, the U.I.L. mandate had actually gone to the Unionist, Bonar Law, because the Liberal was regarded as a renegade on Home Rule. In 1906 this problem ought to have solved itself with the appearance of Barnes, but one or two local U.I.L. stalwarts wanted to continue supporting Law. They were later expelled from the U.I.L.[80]

In the 1910 elections, however, the U.I.L. mandate was withdrawn from Labour candidates other than Barnes, because Labour candidates were accused of vote-splitting and thus letting in the Conservatives:

> At the last election the Irish vote went Labour and the Labour candidate came in at the foot of the poll. Nationalists are always ready to vote Labour when there is a chance of winning but in a fight like this, and [with] the experience of the last election before them, the Executive could not possibly afford to waste the Irish vote.[81]

There was no doubting the *Observer's* loyalty to the U.I.L. at this time. It exhorted its readers:

> We call upon the Irish electorate in every constituency in Scotland to obey the mandate of Mr. Redmond and the Irish Party by taking their stand in the van of the onward forces which are irresistibly making for progress and liberty.[82]

After the result, it heralded the Executive's refusal to renew the mandate to Sullivan, who had fought and lost in North-East Lanark, under the heading 'T.P.'s Prescience':

> The North-East Lanark election shows anew the power of the Irish vote in the division and amply vindicates the wisdom of its disposition by Mr. T. P. O'Connor and the Irish leaders in the recent contest.[83]

In December 1910 also the mandate went to the Liberals and Barnes.[84]

The first serious note of dissension came in the January election, with a revolt of the Home Government Branch of the U.I.L., which according to Handley

> dominated for years Irish political life in the west of Scotland. It was easily the wealthiest and largest of the branches, with a membership at one time of nearly 1500. It was the parliament of the Irish people in Glasgow.[85]

It was out of favour with the *Observer* at this time because it was 'more a beer trade caucus than a National League centre',[86] and also, more unexpectedly, because its leaders were 'up to the neck in sympathy with the socialists'.[87] So the paper reported its revolt decidedly coolly:

> At the meeting of the Home Government Branch of the U.I.L. (Glasgow) on Sunday last, it was intimated that the office-bearers intended resigning consequent

upon the decision of the League Executive to direct the Irish vote in Camlachie in
favour of the Liberal candidate rather than of the Labour candidate there, in
whose direction the predilections of the Home Government Branch seem to lie.[88]

In answer to a correspondent who complained that the 'Archbishop
Walsh' branch had been revived purely in order to support the
mandate, it retorted:

> Better be spasmodically active than never active at all. A branch which revives
> itself to accept and sustain the Nationalist mandate had surely better do that than
> lie forever dormant.[89]

A great deal happened between 1910 and 1918, in both Irish and
British politics, to change this state of affairs. The Irish Party col-
lapsed; so did the Liberal Party; and the *Glasgow Observer* changed its
views. The Easter Rising of 1916 was not a severe blow to the Irish
Party, but the subsequent execution of the Sinn Fein leaders was. As
Dillon said in his passionate and despairing speech after the Rising:

> You are letting loose a river of blood . . . between two races who, after 300 years
> of hatred and of strife, we had nearly succeeded in bringing together . . .
> [In] this rebellion, for the first time in the history of Ireland, at least nine out of
> every ten of the population were on the side of the Government. Is this nothing?
> . . . It is the fruit of our life's work. We have risked our lives a hundred times to
> bring this about . . . and now you are washing out our whole life's work in a sea of
> blood.[90]

The doom of the Irish Party was sealed when Redmond and Dillon
accepted temporary exclusion of the six counties of Northern Ireland in
the negotiations with Lloyd George in 1916, only to find Lloyd George
selling the scheme to the Unionists as one for permanent exclusion.[91]
The constitutional nationalists appeared totally outflanked, and
seemed to be ceding ground they had already won. The threat to
impose conscription on Ireland in 1918 was a further blow to the Irish
Party. In the 1918 General Election it lost ground to Sinn Fein, and the
first-past-the-post electoral system turned defeat into rout. It got 28 per
cent of the Irish vote but only seven seats (one of them in Liverpool),
whereas Sinn Fein got 48 per cent of the vote and 73 seats, which
enabled it to claim a mandate for independence.

The independent Liberals were also routed. In some places they hung
on in opposition to couponed Coalition Liberals or Conservatives, but
not in Glasgow. There the Asquithian Liberals did not merely dis-
appear: they were annihilated. Among the retiring M.P.'s who actually
lost their deposits were W. M. R. Pringle, the consistent opponent of

wartime restrictions who had secured the adjournment debate on the suppression of the *Forward*, and McKinnon Wood, the ex-Secretary for Scotland whom the *Observer* had warmly supported in 1910. The Free Liberals were never again to have any success in Glasgow (or Lanarkshire); their strongholds in Paisley and Greenock became completely isolated in the industrial west of Scotland.

During the war the papers controlled by Charles Diamond had moved away from the implicit trust they had placed in the U.I.L. and the Irish Party in 1910. Diamond became increasingly sympathetic both to Labour and to Sinn Fein, and Mitchell Quin was the Labour candidate in Glasgow Central in 1918. Diamond wrote a number of articles in his papers urging their readers to vote Labour, of which the longest and most forthright was headed, 'The Irish in Great Britain/Their Political Future':

> . . . the policy of the Irish in Great Britain . . . has been confessedly modelled upon the policy of the Irish Party in Parliament. The Irish electors and non-electors of the country stood aloof from all political parties. They were friends of or foes of one or the other, as seemed best at the moment, in Ireland's interests . . . We advocate . . . the ending of the period of isolation and detachment of the Irish in Great Britain. We urge them to drop the policy of being, as it were, a foreign or floating factor in the body politic, giving their votes now on one side and now on another, moved thereto by the question of Ireland, and so trusted by no party in the State . . . The formation of a powerful democratic Labour Party gives us the opportunity. Formerly the weakness of Labour impelled us to give our support where we thought it would do most for Ireland . . . Toryism was an impossible thing. Liberalism, unhappily, embodied a great deal of anti-Catholic narrowness and bigotry . . .
> The new Labour Party is indeed and in truth the people's party, and as a vast majority of the Irish in Great Britain are toilers it is to that party they turn, drawn by bonds of affinity and common interests that make division or antagonism unthinkable.[92]

As for Sinn Fein, Diamond wrote:

> If Sinn Fein has Ireland at its back, it is the duty of those who have been discarded to make way for the new men and the new forces. Anything else is pure factionism.[93]

This change of attitude led the paper to regard the representatives of the old order sometimes contemptuously, sometimes merely dismissively. The U.I.L. and its whole system of mandates was rapidly disintegrating:

... T.P.'s 'mandates', he will find, no longer run. He may call his spirits from the vasty deep, but the Irish electorates in Great Britain will think and act for themselves. They will vote Labour.[94]

The first part of this prediction proved much more clearly true than the second, though exhortations to the Irish to vote Labour appeared stridently from almost every page of the *Glasgow Observer* and the *Glasgow Star* in the three weeks leading up to the election. The U.I.L. mandate, when it came, was much the same as before. In Scotland, it went to 26 Free Liberals (including Pringle and McKinnon Wood) and 15 Labour candidates. Eleven of the Liberals it supported faced both Labour and Coalition opposition. 'The selection,' said the *Glasgow Herald*, 'is too obviously capricious to merit the serious attention of electors.' Later, it added:

> The distribution of Irish 'coupons' among Liberal and Labour candidates in Scotland has given great dissatisfaction to local branches of the U.I.L., most of whom had already expressed a preference which does not harmonise with the 'dictation' from headquarters. Several branches have decided to disobey Mr. O'Connor's instructions and place the 'coupon' where the best result can be obtained. Local irritation at the ridiculous method adopted by the U.I.L. in selecting candidates will probably find an outlet in a 'split' Nationalist vote.[95]

The outcome of the election provoked the author of *Forward's* 'Catholic Socialist Notes'[96] to comment:

> Not the least remarkable feature of the recent election is the disappearance of Mr. T. P. O'Connor's Irish mandate as a factor in, at any rate, Scottish elections. In Glasgow Messrs. McKinnon Wood, Dundas White, Pringle and Watt, who had the Irish ticket, forfeited their deposits.[97]

The Irish did not vote Liberal in 1918. But they do not seem to have flocked to Labour in large numbers. Two out of the three Labour gains in the West of Scotland (Hamilton and South Ayrshire) were not areas particularly strong in Irish voters.[98] Why, in spite of the continued exhortation by Diamond and the Catholic press, and the desertion by many ward bosses of the mandate, do the Irish seem to have affected the vote in so few constituencies? Were their leaders at the head of only a stage army?

The Irish stood to gain, proportionately, more than other groups from the electoral reform of 1918; by the same token they doubtless suffered worse from the defective compilation of the register. Furthermore, we should beware of taking the claims of, say, the *Observer* too much at its own valuation. The Irish vote, obviously, could be effective only where there were a lot of Irish electors. This did not cover every constituency in Scotland, nor even every working-class constituency in Scotland. Nevertheless, it is difficult to accept that the Irish did in every constituency what the *Observer* told them to. Especially is this true in Gorbals, where Barnes had received the Irish ticket ever since 1906. After he had parted company with the Labour Party because of his refusal to resign from the War Cabinet in 1918, the *Observer* wrote, '. . . the Irish Nationalists of the Gorbals Division cannot change their politics when and because Mr. Barnes changes his'.[99] So it counselled its readers to vote for John MacLean.[100] But Barnes won by a majority of 31.4%, and after the result the paper recorded that 'notwithstanding official soothsaying to the contrary,[101] those on the spot declare that Mr. Barnes polled quite a substantial Irish vote'.[102]

It seems that there was a lag between the conversion of the Irish leaders to the Labour cause and the conversion of their followers. One reason can perhaps be seen in an implicit contradiction in Diamond's views. He advised his Irish-born readers to forget about Irish affairs and pull their weight as electors in Britain by rallying behind a British party. In the long run this was sound advice, and by 1922 many of the Irish in Britain were coming to take it.[103] But on the other hand he urged that his readers should support Sinn Fein, as the coming party in Ireland. This was to contradict his own advice to keep out of Irish politics — hard counsel to Irishmen between 1918 and 1921. And the British parties had little sympathy or understanding for Sinn Fein, especially before 1918. In particular, Diamond's and the *Glasgow Observer's* warmth towards Labour was not reciprocated when Sinn Fein was under discussion. From the Easter Rising to the 1918 election, Glasgow socialists regarded Sinn Fein with a jaundiced eye. To start with, the participation of James Connolly, who was well known in Scotland, in the Easter Rising had to be explained. What was a socialist doing in a nationalist rebellion?

Connolly's appearance in the Dublin outbreak is to Socialists on this side wholly inexplicable . . .
He can have been under no delusion either about the chances of insurrectionary success, or about the value of success if it were achieved.[104]

The authors of 'Catholic Socialist Notes' frequently returned to the theme that no movement of revolt which was backed by W. M. Murphy, the Dublin tramway-owner and newspaper proprietor who had broken Larkin's great strike in 1913, was worthy of socialist support:

> It is time the British Labour movement was warned against bestowing sympathy indiscriminately on every movement in Ireland that carries a banner bearing the device 'Revolt'. Our admiration for those who faced inevitable failure in the Irish rebellion to promote a cause in which they fervently believe, whether their action was wise or foolish, is apt to tempt us to accept without question policies that are now being offered by parasitical scoundrels in their name.
>
> Sinn Fein does nothing, and proposes to do nothing, to protect the Irish working-class from Capitalist parasites, provided they are Irish.[105]

The paper regarded the Sinn Fein attitude to conscription as purely selfish:

> Yet in this crisis the Irish patriots seem to have completely forgotten their exiles. Like the Jingoes of Britain, their objection to conscription is not one of principle, but only to its application to themselves.[106]

But after the 1918 election and the Black-and-Tan War, Labour opinion changed. The election revealed to socialists the strength of Sinn Fein; the Black-and-Tan War placed them strongly on Sinn Fein's side. A special trade union conference in July 1920 promised (though it failed to deliver) a general strike to stop the fighting in Ireland, and the Labour Party set up a Commission on Ireland, whose 1921 report fiercely condemned the British forces there. The Asquith Liberals also joined the attack; but they were compromised by their record and their electoral collapse in 1918. So Labour came to be seen as the most pro-Irish party. Not only this, but the Treaty of December 1921 really did remove the Irish Question from British politics until October 1968. From this point Irishmen could follow Diamond's first precept without any risk of its clashing with his second.

In September 1918 the writer of 'Catholic Socialist Notes' thought that

> there are many cross-currents in the local Irish movement at the moment. The Sinn Feiners have considerably strengthened their ranks . . . The U.I.L., which in previous contests was the unquestioned dictator, is now very weak. The divisional members of the central executive are mostly cordially pro-Labour, but T. P. O'Connor's influence . . . will be used in an effort to preserve the Irish vote for Liberal Capitalism.
>
> During recent years the Ancient Order of Hibernians . . . has to a large extent superseded the U.I.L. In this country at least, the leaders of the organisation are pro-Labour. The local Catholic paper, which until recently was anti-Labour, has under the direction of Mr. Diamond, its proprietor, become a warm advocate of the Labour Party.[107]

The ex-U.I.L. men sometimes went straight into the Labour Party, but more often went through a political twilight. For instance:

> A new political portent swims into our ken this week in the founding of an Irish Labour Party in Springburn . . . The new movement is officered by competent, experienced men formerly prominent in the U.I.L., but now sensible of the need of a more democratic and democratically governed organisation.[108]

The A.O.H. was a friendly society which had been banned by the Scottish hierarchy in 1899 because they regarded it as 'in part a secret society pursuing political ends'.[109] The ban was lifted in 1909, and the Order became increasingly popular as an alternative power-base to the U.I.L. In Ireland itself the Order was under the control of 'Wee Joe' Devlin, who used it to preserve the ascendancy of the old Irish Party among Belfast Catholics against the threat from Sinn Fein — no mean feat. In Glasgow it offered a home for those U.I.L. leaders who left the league to promote the Labour Party, especially those of the Home Government branch which, as we noted earlier, was both the largest in Glasgow and suspect among the orthodox for its pro-I.L.P. tendencies. Six A.O.H. members appeared among the 1921 Labour candidates, and two of the successful candidates in 1922 were specifically described as 'member[s] of the now defunct Home Government branch of the U.I.L. . . . member[s] of the A.O.H.'[110]

By the 1922 election the power of the U.I.L. had totally vanished. Commenting on a request by O'Connor for funds to pay off the U.I.L.'s debts, the *Observer* said:

> Nobody wishes any ill to T.P., and nobody wishes even to say one unnecessarily hard word to or of him. But his day is past . . .[111]

Earlier, Diamond had confidently dismissed 'T.P.':

> A very great number of the Irish in Great Britain, many of them former officials of T.P.'s League, are now members of the Labour Party. The great bulk of the Irish in Great Britain will vote Labour, and nothing T.P. can say or do will prevent their doing so.[112]

This claim seems to have much more force, at least as far as Glasgow is concerned, for 1922 than for 1918. Irish leaders were now without exception on the Labour side; the lag between their views and their followers' had been made up; the settlement of the Irish question, and the end of Labour's enthusiasm for prohibition, had removed the two policy issues which kept the Irish and Labour apart in 1918.

In one part of Glasgow, namely Gorbals and Hutchesontown, the integration of the Labour and Irish causes antedated 1922. Barnes had won the U.I.L. mandate in 1906 and was the only Labour candidate in Glasgow to keep it in 1910. Even the *Observer* admitted that its advice to the Irish in the Gorbals to oppose Barnes in 1918 had scarcely been heeded. Barnes had been at pains to keep on good terms with the Catholic community in his constituency, and for years was a regular contributor to the *Glasgow Observer*.[113] In local elections the Irish-Labour pact also came earlier than elsewhere in the Gorbals and Hutchesontown wards, which between them made up the Gorbals constituency as it was after 1918. In 1911, in Hutchesontown,

> The United League have already resolved to support Mr. John Stewart on account of the support given by the Labour Party to Nationalists in other contests

— although in Gorbals ward

> the Nationalists are under obligation to Bailie Archibald Campbell for services rendered . . . Otherwise it would have been a great pleasure to have supported Mr. Hardie,[114] who is an excellent Labour cadidate.[115]

In the 1920 municipal general election, Gorbals Ward was the only one to return two Catholics out of three[116] — both Labour councillors. Hutchesontown boasted one out of three, but the *Observer* supported his two Protestant colleagues (John Stewart and George Buchanan) with gusto.[117] It is therefore no surprise that Gorbals and Hutchesontown were deviant in a pro-Labour direction in 1920: the Labour-Irish coalition, which came into existence elsewhere around 1922, already throve in the Gorbals area by 1920.[118]

It would be wrong to conclude an account of the Irish and Labour without inquiring about the politics of the other group of Glasgow Irishmen — the Orange Protestants from the North of Ireland — and their Scots supporters. It is impossible to say how many Orangemen there might have been in Glasgow. The contemporary press was often prepared to guess at the size of the (Catholic) Irish vote,[119] but never the size of the Orange vote; there are no religious statistics to help us, of the sort which allow us to plot very roughly the distribution of the Catholic vote in Glasgow. At any rate, the Orange vote was certainly very much smaller than the Catholic vote, and it is not possible to trace its electoral effects. Orange organisations urged their supporters to oppose Labour:

We call upon every Orangeman and Orangewoman in Glasgow and throughout Scotland in all cases to vote for the moderate constitutional candidates, as opposed to the extreme Labour men.[120]

And, as we have seen, Orange anti-Catholicism was appealed to by the Moderate Party and lobby against the 1918 Education Act. But none of this amounts to very much, politically. We must conclude that the Orange vote was less coherent than the Catholic vote. It is not possible to point to any election result between 1918 and 1922 which was clearly influenced by the emergence of an anti-Labour Orange bloc of votes. In Glasgow, as in Liverpool, Labour eventually inherited the Irish machine; but in Glasgow, unlike Liverpool, it contrived to do so in a way which provoked no measurable Orange backlash.

It was the housing crusade and the Irish, and not anything connected with the wartime struggles, which led to Labour's triumphs in Glasgow in 1922. The housing crusade probably contributed more votes and the Irish more new leaders. They have left their mark on Glasgow in a way John MacLean and Willie Gallacher never could.

Part III

Consequences

15

Whatever Happened to Red Clydeside?
I: In Parliament

The carriage-load of M.P.'s who departed in triumph from St. Enoch
Station on 21st November 1922 with the 124th Psalm ringing in their
ears acquired instant fame. Maxton told the cheering crowds that they
'would see the atmosphere of the Clyde getting the better of the House
of Commons',[1] and several of the new M.P.'s stepped in immediately to
steep the (unfortunately empty) Government benches in it on the first
two days of debate. Kirkwood burst out with six years' bottled-up indignation at Lloyd George, who was not there to receive it, and
announced that he would 'smash' the atmosphere he found at Westminster. Other stirring speeches were made by Walton Newbold and
by Eddie Scrymgeour, the Socialist Prohibitionist from Dundee.[2]

It all made for colourful Press coverage. Red Clydeside had left the
streets and sat in Parliament. But the Press of 1919 had registered
genuine panic at the Bolsheviks of George Square; the Press from 1922
offered no more than condescending indulgence to Maxton and
Kirkwood. From the beginning the Scottish rebels were treated as
colourful curiosities and not as threats to public order. However much
it paid all sides to exaggerate, everybody knew — or soon found out —
that most of the new Labour M.P.'s from the West of Scotland were no
more rebellious than any others. Right from the beginning, the core of
the Clydeside revolt comprised only five men: Wheatley, Maxton,
Kirkwood, Stephen and Buchanan. So it remained (with the succession
of John McGovern to Wheatley's seat in 1930) until the group finally
disintegrated on Maxton's death in 1946. Newbold the Communist and
Scrymgeour the Prohibitionist shot brightly but briefly across the
parliamentary sky,[3] and the only other exotic was Gallacher, who
profited from the bitter divisions of the Fife miners to win West Fife as

a Communist in 1935 and hold it until 1950. Most of those elected in 1922 became worthy backbenchers. Two (James Stewart and John Muir) held junior office in 1924. Three became ministers. Emanuel Shinwell made a more statesmanlike impression than his colleagues in 1922,[4] becoming a thrusting junior minister in 1924 — creating a near autonomous Ministry of Mines under the benevolent but passive gaze of Sydney Webb, his nominal superior — and again in 1929-31. Staying with the Labour Party in 1931, he ousted MacDonald from his seat at Seaham Harbour in 1935, and was a Minister throughout the Attlee administration, in the Cabinet from 1945-7 and 1950-1. Outliving all the other Clydesiders by two decades, he resigned from the Labour Party in 1982 at the age of 97. Tom Johnston was junior minister at the Scottish Office for most of the second Labour Government, and in the Cabinet (as Lord Privy Seal) from March to August 1931. He was prouder to be remembered as Secretary of State for Scotland from 1941 to 1945, the creator of the North of Scotland Hydro-Electric Board in the territory of the lairds whom he had castigated for four decades. John Wheatley became Minister of Health in 1924, and was widely hailed, then and since, as the outstanding success of the first Labour Government. He was not offered a job in 1929 and died in 1930.

Shinwell and Johnston owed their election to Red Clydeside; the parts they played between 1914 and 1922 gave them enough prominence and popularity to win them Labour nominations and, later, seats. But they did not sit for Clydeside constituencies, and their subsequent actions owed nothing in particular to their Clydeside background, so they are not analysed here. Wheatley is another matter, and his career as a Minister must be studied carefully. Before doing so, howeve:, we should briefly look at the rest of the Clydesiders. They never wielded power in Whitehall, but not all power resides there; some lies at Westminster, some at party meetings and some (perhaps) in the country.

The Clydesiders are often described as the kingmakers of Ramsay MacDonald, who were responsible for making him Labour leader in 1922 and soon came to regret their choice. This story is neat and ironic. Unfortunately, it is also false. The election of a leader was a two-stage affair. M.P.'s who were members of the I.L.P. met first, and at that meeting Shinwell proposed MacDonald in place of Clynes, the incumbent. This was opposed by Snowden, and by Maxton 'with all the vehemence at his command',[5] but carried. Then at the full meeting of the P.L.P. Shinwell proposed MacDonald again, and this was carried by five votes. Beatrice Webb told her diary that 'the I.L.P. members, reinforced by the Scottish group of extremists, had determined to give . . . pride of place to their chief man', and this version of events is also propagated by Snowden, Kirkwood and Gilbert McAllister, the first biographer of Maxton.[6] But the only writer who directly identified the core Clyde group with MacDonald is Kirkwood, and his account (which was probably 'ghosted') is less reliable than Shinwell's. Webb and the others were not yet practised at telling the narrow and the broad Clydeside groups apart. They were all men with strange accents from the only city that had welcomed MacDonald during the war; they clustered round the *Forward*, which had carried his copious contributions for many years and still did so. MacDonald was the 'chief man' of John Muir and James Stewart and George Hardie far more than of Maxton or Wheatley. The Clyde did indeed make MacDonald the leader of the Labour Party, but it was the doing of the broad Clyde group — the only important time that it acted as a group. It represented an emotional identification with a persecuted fellow-Scot (as late as February 1921, after all, MacDonald had lost a by-election in Woolwich after being hounded as a traitor by Horatio Bottomley and other appalling super-patriots).[7] It could scarcely have represented an ideological identification, because it was quite hard to establish MacDonald's substantive views. He wanted socialism to arrive gradually and constitutionally; he wanted Labour to prove itself as a responsible party of power: these were themes he constantly repeated. But whether he intended to use that power more radically or more conservatively than Clynes was, or ought to have been, an impenetrable mystery.

MacDonald at first thought his differences with the core Clydeside group were of style, not substance. In the only entry for his diary during the 1923 parliament he wrote:

> My difficulty is to interpret myself to three or four good fellows who have no sense of Parliamentary methods and who expect Front Benchers to live in a perpetual state of fighting exaltation and be noisy. I go on exactly opposite lines . . .[8]

The 'three or four good fellows' were certainly the Maxton group, and after several Parliamentary scenes MacDonald became much more exasperated with them. Two of the scenes represented more than scene-making for the sake of it. On 27th June 1923 Maxton attacked those who had congratulated the Government for cutting the Scottish health estimates as 'murderers'. It was premeditated but also had great emotional force as Maxton's own wife had recently died after a difficult childbirth. Maxton referred to the case in his speech but not by name, so it is unclear how many M.P.'s realised that he was talking about his own bereavement. Spurning a conciliatory intervention by Mac-Donald, Maxton was suspended, whereupon Wheatley, Stephen and Buchanan committed copycat offences in order to get themselves suspended too.[9] MacDonald was reportedly 'white with anger at the folly of his own followers', but in September 1923 could still ruefully call Maxton 'such a good fellow' while deploring his speeches.[10] Another scene, in May 1924, was provoked by the behaviour of the Speaker, who reneged on a previous agreement to allow Buchanan to move the closure on (and thus keep alive) a Government of Scotland Bill which he had introduced. For once, the Clydesiders were entirely innocent,[11] but the Speaker's action killed the Bill, and MacDonald refused to provide Parliamentary time to revive it.[12]

The Government of Scotland Bill 1924 nevertheless merits more than a passing mention. Buchanan's thoughtful speech introducing it showed that he had a constructive side, and knew when it was necessary to go placidly in order to try to rally the 56 Scottish M.P.'s who he claimed supported it. He explained that he wanted to end the delays to purely Scottish business such as teachers' superannuation and the Lanarkshire electricity supply imposed by distance and the congested parliamentary timetable. In any case, some things, such as the proposed union of the Church of Scotland and the United Free (U.F.) Church, were no business of the English at all:

> On . . . a question of dealing with the religious feelings and aspirations of the Scottish people, members largely alien to our views should not be called upon in the main to decide a question of which they have no knowledge or thoughts.[13]

Buchanan proposed the devolution of most domestic Scottish functions to a unicameral assembly with powers to raise some taxation, and a relatively small subsidy, starting at £500,000 a year, from the 'Imperial' exchequer.[14] The Bill was modelled on an abortive one of 1914, which in turn closely followed the Irish Home Rule Bill of 1912 and thus had a direct lineage back to the first Home Rule Bill of 1886. It had two fatal flaws, one of which has bedevilled every attempt at devolution in the U.K. from 1886 to 1979. Buchanan had clearly thought about one of the problems, but not the other.

The first problem was: what happens to Scottish M.P.'s at Westminster after devolution? Gladstone had failed to find an answer in

1886 or in 1893 to this question for Ireland, and the Labour Government of 1976 repeated Buchanan's formula, in a cruder form, with fatal results. Buchanan proposed that neither the number nor the powers of Scottish M.P.'s at Westminster should be reviewed after Home Rule 'until separate provision is made for devolution in England and Wales'.[15] The Labour Government in 1924 (as in 1974) depended on Scotland for its majority; it would be suicidal for a socialist to propose cutting the number or the powers of Scottish M.P.'s. But this then made Scottish M.P.'s post-devolution as overprivileged vis-a-vis England as Buchanan complained that English M.P.'s were pre-devolution vis-a-vis Scotland. They would be able to interfere in internal English matters to their hearts' content. Indeed, we have already noted that a number of Clydesiders, broadly defined, did exactly that in 1927 on the very question which Buchanan had spotlighted, when they voted down the revised Prayer Book. But for Scottish votes, the Prayer Book, which was as purely an English matter as the U.F. union was purely Scottish, would have been carried. It is fair to add that none of the core Clydesiders voted against the Prayer Book, although Adamson, Johnston, Rosslyn Mitchell and the Rev. James Barr did: the last named egregiously introduced yet another Government of Scotland Bill in the same session, apparently blithely unaware of any inconsistency.

Thus Buchanan's solution, though it protected Labour, had no real chance of acceptance by the English, to judge by the fate of the 1976 Bill, destroyed by an English Labour backlash. At least Buchanan, unlike Barr or the draftsmen of the 1976 Bill, appears to have thought about the problem, as witness his ingenious clause deferring consideration of the position of Scottish Westminster M.P.'s until after devolution to Wales and England. Waiting for the Greek Kalends in this way was a formula that might just have reconciled the irreconcilable. The 1976 Bill had no such clause. Barr's 1928 Bill impaled itself on the other (1886) horn by removing Scottish M.P.'s from Westminster altogether. It was co-sponsored by all the core Clydeside group[16] and by seven other Scottish Labour M.P.'s, three of whom had voted against the Prayer Book. It is charitable to assume that most of these realised it had no chance of being enacted, as it would have been wildly inconsistent with their other preferences.

This points to the other weakness in Buchanan's Bill. As a socialist, he wanted redistribution from the rich to the poor. But if the rich are mostly in one place and the poor disproportionately in another, then giving Home Rule to the place where the poor live is no help. The land tax proposed in 1924 would have been a quite inadequate base for funding Scottish domestic services, and the proposed 'Imperial contribution' was ludicrously too small. In the nineteenth century, when politics was about Church privileges and land reform it made good sense for radicals to demand devolution to poor, oppressed areas. This is why the early socialists followed Gladstone in demanding Home Rule for Ireland and followed radical Liberals in extending the demand to Scotland and Wales. But in the twentieth century, when politics was about housing and welfare benefits, it no longer made sense for radicals from poor parts of the country to demand devolution for them. Essentially, Scottish Home Rule was a piece of old radical baggage which the Clydesiders and others carried through to an age in which it no longer held their clothes.[17]

The Government of Scotland Bill 1924 was the last constructive proposal from any of the Clydesiders (other than Wheatley) for many years. Maxton and Wheatley were elected to the Parliamentary Committee (that is, the front bench) of the P.L.P. in December 1924,[18] but lost their seats again a year later. Neither held any office in the Labour Party again, nor in the second Labour Government. In the same file as MacDonald's diary there survives a draft Cabinet list for 1929, not in MacDonald's handwriting, in which Wheatley appears as first choice for Minister of Labour and Maxton as second choice for Postmaster-General.[19] But MacDonald was strongly opposed to giving Wheatley a job, although (perhaps because) Snowden urged him to,[20] and the colourful spectacle of the Post Office run by Jimmy Maxton also failed to materialise. The Clydesiders concentrated not on office, but on propaganda; not on the P.L.P., but the extra-parliamentary movement. In one sense, they succeeded; but their success hides a great failure.

The success was to take control of the I.L.P. Maxton became chairman of the Party in 1926, and its policies moved noticeably to the left. He did not become the leader of the I.L.P. group of M.P.'s in the Commons but behaved as if he had, and constituted himself and his friends as the 'Parliamentary Group Executive' of the I.L.P. This gradually provoked many I.L.P.-sponsored M.P.'s to follow Snowden and MacDonald out of the I.L.P. Matters reached a head in November 1929, when the majority of P.L.P. members who were members of the I.L.P. (not necessarily sponsored by it) explicitly repudiated an I.L.P. amendment to the Government's Unemployment Insurance Bill. The Glasgow I.L.P. members not in Maxton's group lined up against him.[21] After Wheatley's death, Maxton pressed further, demanding an explicit pledge of loyalty to the N.A.C.'s programme from I.L.P.-sponsored M.P.'s and any others who were prepared to offer it. Only ten sponsored M.P.'s and eight others signed the pledge.[22] The I.L.P. clearly was on its way into the wilderness where Maxton led it in 1932 by dis-affiliating it from the Labour Party.

The Clydeside group were unable to spread their propaganda successes outside the shrinking ranks of I.L.P. activists. Like the rest of the parliamentary party, they were totally ignored by the T.U.C. during the General Strike, and almost totally ignored even by the miners. Nevertheless, Maxton found a kindred spirit in A. J. Cook, who as General Secretary of the Miners' Federation had led the miners into their disastrous isolation from May to November 1926. In 1928 they issued the Cook-Maxton Manifesto, a denunciation of the right-ward moves they perceived in the Labour Party:

> We propose to combine in carrying through a series of conferences and meetings in various parts of the country. At these conferences the rank-and-file will be given the opportunity to state whether they accept the new outlook or whether they wish to remain true to the spirit and ideals which animated the early pioneers.[23]

It was a disaster. It was conceived furtively — concealed even from the I.L.P. — launched half-heartedly, and followed up not at all. No organisation to press the views of 'the rank-and-file' ever came into existence, and Maxton failed to exploit those that already existed. In fact, he had scored a stylish own-goal. He had a respectable argument to hand which he destroyed by his own actions. That was the claim that the Labour Party (or at least the I.L.P.) in Parliament was there by virtue of the hard work of constituency activists; that they had a right to stipulate the policies they wished M.P.'s to follow; and that if M.P.'s did not like it, they should not have sought party endorsement, and need not seek it again. This is a perfectly coherent view of representation. It has been put forward by the left at various times and with varying success — by Ben Tillett in 1907-9, by the opponents of Hugh Gaitskell in 1960-1, and by the successful campaigners to change the Labour Party Constitution in 1979-81. But Maxton could not use it, because he himself defied the 'sovereign' I.L.P. conference when he issued the Cook-Maxton Manifesto. It was all so unnecessary, from his point of view — he could have got it through with ease.

Thus the Clydesiders other than Wheatley remained barren of achievement, in Parliament or outside (though Kirkwood did lead a successful lobby to have work restarted on the *Queen Mary*, left unfinished on John Brown's stocks in his constituency, and Buchanan eventually became the first chairman of the National Assistance Board in 1948). Wheatley was much respected, and Maxton and Kirkwood were much loved. After Maxton's suspension in June 1923, the Government spokesman (Walter Elliott) called him 'one of the most sincere, sympathetic and one of the finest characters in the House', and in his last illness Churchill wrote with genuine feeling, 'My dear James, I have been thinking a lot about you lately, . . . we all miss you vy much down here, and no one more than yr sincere friend Winston S. Churchill'.[24] Churchill also wrote a foreword to Kirkwood's autobiography — 'David Kirkwood has so many friends of all parties in the House of Commons and at large in the country that this engaging account of his career will receive a warm welcome'.[25] It is impossible not to feel warm towards a man who, when pompously told in the Scottish Grand Committee to pay attention to the maxim, *Qui facit per alium facit per se*, immediately replied:

> 'Is eenty-teenty halligolum, eenie meenie, manny moo, urky, purky tawry rope, ki mar ach an choo, pipe clay up the Lum, hickerty pickerty pease broose' — in the original Italian.[26]

In all this, however, we must not forget that the Tories and Liberals had the best of reasons for affection towards a colourful group of M.P.'s who often savaged the Labour leadership more effectively than they could themselves. 'From the Conservative point of view,' said the Glasgow *Evening Citizen* in 1929, 'nothing could be better than the triumph of the Clydeside group.'[27] From the Conservative point of view it was a pity that Maxton was such a disastrous tactician.

Thus the enduring achievement of Red Clydeside on the national stage begins and ends with Wheatley's performance at the Ministry of Health. Wheatley made his maiden speech on the same day as the other Clydesiders. Unlike them, he attracted no attention in the papers, but his close analysis of the housing shortage, which he attributed to 'trusts and combines',[28] obviously brought him to MacDonald's attention, and he was chosen in April 1923 to move the Labour amendment to Neville Chamberlain's Housing Bill.[29] When MacDonald started Cabinet-making in December 1923, he knew he had to consider Wheatley, as he was only too conscious that everybody with achievements or potential must be included, and he would still be left with 'some weak appointments'.[30] He asked Wheatley on 17th December 'if you would be disposed to consider coming into the team', but did not get round to offering him a specific job until 22nd January 1924, when he offered Wheatley the Under-Secretaryship of the Ministry of Health in charge of housing.[31] In last-minute negotiations Wheatley held out success-fully for the headship of the department, which was made possible because MacDonald's preferred choice, Arthur Greenwood, was willing to stand down 'in order to smooth things'[32] for MacDonald. At the end of the Cabinetmaking, which he detested, MacDonald wrote:

> Wheatley finally fixed. Necessary to bring Clyde in — will he play straight. Very anxious for office.[33]

In the nine months' life of the first Labour Government Wheatley was involved in three main departmental events: the rescission of the Mond Order against the Poplar Poor Law Guardians, the sponsorship (and eventual abandonment) of a Bill to prevent the evictions of un-employed tenants who fell into rent arrears, and the big Housing Bill, setting up an extensive system of subsidies to local authorities to build council houses. On all three issues, Wheatley scored parliamentary triumphs which were extravagantly praised by MacDonald to the King and by Beatrice Webb to her diary.[34] Whether he 'played straight', or made good, or original, administrative decisions are more complicated matters.

In 1924 there was no national network of Social Security benefits. Payments over and above the relatively meagre amounts available under Lloyd George's 1911 insurance scheme could only be made by local Boards of Guardians still operating under the Poor Law Amend-ment Act, 1834. They faced acutely the dilemma that the need for relief was greatest in exactly the areas where ratepayers could least afford to pay it. The dilemma was sharpened when the Boards of Guardians in a number of districts came under Labour control. Poplar, in east London, was one of those, and it decided in 1921 to pay more than the nationally approved scales to claimants. The Minister of Health, Sir Alfred Mond, issued an Order forbidding the Poplar Guardians to do so. They ignored the Order, incurring short spells in prison for doing so, but blithely continued to pay extra, and sent in hundreds of claims to the Ministry to be treated as 'special cases'. In February 1924 Wheatley abruptly rescinded the Order. This caused uproar in the Commons, with the Liberals threatening a no-confidence motion which would have ended the life of the Labour Government after a month. MacDonald was clearly furious at Wheatley for having acted without consultation:

> The Prime Minister made a strong appeal to his colleagues not to make public announcement or take administrative action on questions of great public interest, and particularly when they were of a controversial character, without previous consultation with the Prime Minister.[35]

However, Wheatley, and the Government, escaped unscathed. Wheatley was able to show that, once disobeyed, the Order was unenforceable; that neither Mond nor any of the three intervening Ministers of Health had seriously tried to enforce it; that it directed the Poplar Guardians to give relief according to scales that had anyway been superseded; that Poplar had in any case been mending its ways not because of the Mond Order but because of the burden their payments were imposing on the rates.[36] The problem was to be solved not by attacking an individual authority but by reforming local government. It would not be enough simply to abolish Poor Law Guardians and hand over their powers to borough councils, because these were run by similar, or the same, people; therefore Wheatley told the Cabinet it would be better

> to make the representation on the local Committees which are to administer outrelief proportionate to the respective financial contributions of the County Council and of the Borough Councils.[37]

In other words, Poplar's overspending should and would be stopped by bringing it under control of a London-wide organisation.

Having promised to deal with 'Poplarism' by means of local government reform, Wheatley had to confess to the Cabinet that his department was in 'an embarrassing situation'[38] because it had no detailed plans. He recommended an all-party conference on the matter, but the other parties did not take the idea up, so nothing happened before the fall of the Labour Government.

Nowhere in this saga did Wheatley express any sympathy with the Poplar Guardians. Of course, in public the Minister had to be seen to be upholding the rule of law, in order not to imperil the survival of a minority Government. But the tone of Wheatley's private statements to the Cabinet was no different. Some may see this as subtle, others as merely hypocritical. But it is certainly mildly surprising to compare Wheatley out of Government — protesting his 'great joy and pride in being associated with Poplarism . . . it was only as the policy of Poplar permeated the country that they would march towards a different order of society' — with Wheatley in Government assuring the Cabinet that 'Any expenditure on relief which is excessive or unlawful, whether incurred by Poplar or any other Board of Guardians, will continue to be liable to disallowance and surcharge'.[39]

At the same time as the Mond Order, Wheatley and his department were grappling with the problem of evictions. At the beginning of the session, a Labour member, Benjamin Gardner, introduced a Private Member's Bill to prevent all evictions except on the ground that the landlord both required the house for himself and had provided alternative accommodation. The Bill also reduced the maximum controlled rent from 140% of the August 1914 figure to 125%, and brought more houses under the scope of rent control. Wheatley asked the Cabinet for permission to take the Gardner Bill over as a Government measure. The Cabinet rejected his request, but authorised him to indicate the Government's general support of the Bill. This he did, and the Bill passed its second reading with Liberal support.[40] The Cabinet then asked Wheatley to 'take as a basis' the Gardner Bill and 'draft such amendments to it as would bring it into consonance with the policy of the Government on this subject'.[41] Wheatley, who was of course very busy with other things, seems to have done nothing about this request for some weeks; he told MacDonald that 'the lawyers advised that Gardner's Bill is quite well drafted, and the general view we took is that we should proceed with it'. MacDonald complained that 'We shall have to be ready with amendments however and opinions on such detail of importance or the Bill will not progress'.[42] No Government amendments came, and the Gardner Bill languished in committee, making no progress, while the Clydesiders bitterly complained that the Government was doing nothing to prevent evictions. Then when Wheatley acted, he acted fast. On 25h March he asked the Cabinet to approve a Government Bill in principle; on the 26th it agreed; on the 27th he presented a draft to the Home Affairs Committee; on the 28th it accepted it and referred it to the full Cabinet which, however, did not have the time to discuss it before Wheatley introduced it in the Commons on 2nd April.[43] Clause 1 of Wheatley's Bill made it unlawful to evict a tenant for rent arrears arising out of unemployment unless the landlord provided other accommodation or could prove that he would suffer greater hardship from a refusal to evict than the tenant would suffer from bring evicted. 'I do not think that an amendment [to the Gardner Bill] on these lines will meet with very much opposition,' he told the Cabinet.[44] He was wrong. The Bill was furiously assailed by both the Liberals and the Tories on the grounds that it discriminated arbitrarily between landlords whose tenants were unemployed and those whose tenants were not.[45] Asquith announced that the Liberals would oppose the clause. Clynes, who was in charge of Commons business, hastily convened a meeting of the few available ministers, including Wheatley, who agreed to substitute a clause 'which would throw upon public funds the cost of maintaining the distressed tenant in his home'.[46] This plunged the Government yet deeper into the mire. The Speaker immediately ruled that that would require a separate Bill and, probably, a Money Resolution. When the debate resumed, Clynes tried to evade that trap by producing a clause which threw the burden of relieving unemployed tenants with rent arrears on to the local authorities. The Opposition immediately demanded to know whether the Government would reimburse the local authorities for money spent. The Government was checkmated. If it answered 'Yes', it would have to introduce a Money Resolution. If it answered 'No', the clause was worthless, as the authorities with the biggest burden of unemployment would have the fewest resources with which to deal with it. After Poplar, Wheatley must have known this perfectly well. After some cloudy oratory by Ramsay MacDonald, the Commons rejected the Government Bill by 221 to 212. MacDonald salvaged what he could by announcing that the Government would, instead, support a Liberal Private Member's Bill on eviction which, however, made no special provision for unemployed tenants.[47]

How far was Wheatley responsible for this fiasco? The Secretary to the Cabinet's inquest on the affair concluded that 'Technically . . . the Minister of Health is almost completely covered', although it criticised him for circulating at 6.10 p.m. on 25th March a paper for discussion at Cabinet on the 26th.[48] Modern analysts tend to blame general Cabinet incompetence and lack of co-ordination, and let Wheatley off with a mild reproof for listening to the impracticable suggestions of his Clydeside colleagues.[49] They are too kind. The fiasco was almost entirely Wheatley's fault, because as soon as the Government Bill was introduced the Government was in a hopeless position from which the most talented leader of the House (which Clynes was not) could not have rescued it. Wheatley wanted to adopt the Gardner Bill, accepting advice that it was 'well drafted', and failed, despite pressure from MacDonald, to produce draft Government amendments until the night before the Cabinet was to discuss them. He never showed his Clause 1 to the Law Officers, or anticipated the objection of the Opposition — shared pungently by Beatrice Webb — that it was 'administrative folly' to lay the obligation of relieving the unemployed on those who happened to be their landlords.[50] To load the burden on to local authorities without Government compensation was to create more Poplars; but Philip Snowden at the Treasury would be bound to veto any proposal to offer compensation, and Wheatley himself was willing at other times to echo his officials' view that

> as a matter of general policy he was against special grants to particular areas such as was urged in connection with the relief of unemployment.[51]

Worst of all, the fiasco was unnecessary. It could have been avoided if Wheatley had listened to departmental advice that eviction on the grounds of rent arrears *due to unemployment* was very rare.[52] If he had directed some of his officials to spend the weeks following the introduction of Gardner's Bill on possible ways of minimising evictions without tying it to the question of unemployment, he could have yielded to the heavy pressure that Kirkwood, Maxton and Stephen were putting on him without checkmating the Government. In the end, the Clydesiders got nothing, nor did the tenants they were trying to protect. Beatrice Webb's jaundiced summary was, in fact, quite fair:

> Another example of Wheatley getting the Government into a deep hole, climbing out of it himself in a brilliantly successful speech, leaving the Government still deeper down in the hole which he had made![53]

Wheatley's enduring reputation, however, rests not on Poplar or on evictions, but on the 1924 Housing Act, which was easily the most important of the inter-war Acts offering subsidies to local authorities to build houses. In this area, Wheatley got off the mark quickly by appointing a committee of managers and trade unionists in the building industry to report on shortages of labour and materials. On receiving their unamimous report (Cd 2104), Wheatley promised to introduce a Bill to secure a steady and guaranteed supply of materials. This Bill fell with the Government, but more important than the Bill was the atmosphere of corporate co-operation that Wheatley had established. The 1924 Committee on the building industry was an early example of the now familiar technique of the 'incorporation' of the interested producer-groups in policy-making. It certainly helped the Housing Act to get off to a good start.

The Act itself was less novel. It contained the same structure of subsidies as Addison's Act of 1919 and Chamberlain's of 1923. Local authorities would receive a fixed payment per house per annum to offset the interest charges they incurred on the capital borrowed to build the houses. Wheatley followed his officials' advice in rejecting alterna-

tive patterns of subsidy on the grounds that local authorities must have
an incentive to build cost-effectively:

> The Minister in reply said that it was difficult for him to meet these hard cases
> because of (1) Treasury objections, (2) the nature of things.[54]

Until Wheatley's own scheme was ready, the Cabinet authorised him to
extend the time-limit for new starts under Chamberlain's Act to
October 1928: 'This will start the scheme with a straight run of $5\frac{1}{2}$ years
under known and generous subsidy conditions'.[55] As this shows,
Wheatley knew all along that the Chamberlain scheme, which he had
vigorously opposed as Labour spokesman in 1923, was actually quite
close to his own, and he successfully resisted Cabinet pressure to make
ad hoc grants in either England or Scotland: 'I cannot recommend my
colleagues to modify the policy of their predecessors'.[56]

However, this should not be held too strongly against Wheatley. He
belonged to a minority faction in a minority government. It was therefore excellent tactics to produce a scheme that relied on known and
trusted precedents, and merely offered increased subsidies. The
financial structure Wheatley inherited had one outstanding tactical
advantage. Most of the payments authorised in the Act would not take
place for a number of years, and virtually none in financial year 1924-
5. Local authorities would need time to plan and build their estates,
and they would get no reimbursement from the central Government
until they had paid their suppliers and their workmen. Thus a proposal
for massive public spending escaped unscathed from the Gladstonian
scrutiny of Philip Snowden. Furthermore, Wheatley insisted on more
generous space and density standards than his predecessors. James
Stewart[57] rejected a Glasgow Corporation scheme to build at 48 houses
an acre, insisting on the (then) unprecedentedly low density of 24 an
acre, and also ruled that the city must provide three 3-apartment
houses to every 2-apartment (the split under previous legislation was
reported to be 85 to 15 the other way).[58] This was a farsighted and
generous policy, even though, as we shall see in the next Chapter, it
was not quite farsighted enough.

Most commentators have always accepted the judgment of contemporaries that Wheatley was the outstanding player in the 1924 administration. There were always a few discordant notes — for instance
Haldane's reported comment, as late as June 1924, that 'Wheatley was
a brilliant Parliamentarian but his administrative capacity remained to
be tested'.[59] But the first sustained attack on Wheatley's reputation was

not made until 1980, when Dr. J. S. Rowett argued that it was mostly undeserved. Wheatley, according to Tom Jones, was 'from the Clyde, but "Pale Pink", rather than "Turkey Red"', and soon superseded Neville Chamberlain as the 'ideal Minister' in the eyes of Ministry of Health officials.[60] According to Rowett, Wheatley was 'ideal' because he not only accepted existing departmental policy, but usually pushed it through Cabinet, one exception being a proposal to restrict poor-law benefits to strikers' families, which was too *right-wing* for the 1924 Labour Government to accept.[61]

On the whole, Rowett's case is convincing, and he does not plumb the depths of Wheatley's disastrous handling of rent control and evictions. But on the Housing Act he perhaps goes too far. Admittedly Wheatley found a policy ready-made, admittedly he did not originate the idea of a joint labour and management committee.[62] But whoever may have been the mother, Wheatley was the wetnurse. The solid brick terraces which march across the inner suburbs of every British city could not have been built without John Wheatley. They will remain while newer houses are abandoned, vandalised, or blown up after becoming unlettable. They are the monument to the greatest of the Clydesiders.

16
Whatever Happened to Red Clydeside? II: In Glasgow

The Labour Party already controlled a number of local authorities by 1922, sufficient to alarm the Coalition Government as it made its cloak-and-dagger plans for strikebreaking:

> An instructional memorandum, called the Strike Book, has been prepared with the necessary maps . . . packets [are] ready addressed to send to all Local Authorities . . . [But] in view of the political complexion of certain Local Authorities it has been decided that the Local Authorities should not be given their instructions until the actual emergency.[1]

But Glasgow Corporation caused no trouble, then or later. The Labour gains of 1920-22 were not enough to give Labour control of the Corporation. Throughout the 1920s, Labour tantalisingly failed to improve its position, although the party was given some committee convenerships. (For instance, Dollan became sub-convener of the Tramways Committee in 1926. This is more momentous than it sounds. James Dalrymple had been getting more and more autocratic as Tramways Manager, and it seems that the Moderates decided to bring in Dollan, as somebody both tougher than themselves and a known opponent of Dalrymple, to control him. Successfully: Dalrymple departed angrily for Brazil in a blaze of publicity in January 1927.)[2]

Labour's breakthrough did not occur until 1933. After that, Labour controlled Glasgow Corporation until it ceased to exist in 1974, except for short breaks from 1949-52 and 1968-71. *Forward* claimed Glasgow as 'Almost a Red City' in 1920 and, confidently, that 'Glasgow Goes Red' in 1922.[3] But it didn't; not before 1933, nor (most people would say) after then either. This chapter will try to explore why not.

Up to 1933 Labour generally did worse in municipal than in Parliamentary elections. There were some local reasons for this. The Catholics were not completely integrated into the Labour machine until the Education Authority was abolished and its function taken over by the Corporation in 1929. Then, and perhaps in consequence, the Labour Party suffered from a 'flash party' called the Scottish Protestant League, which won two seats in 1931, one in 1932, and three in 1933, but thereafter faded rapidly. By 1933, indeed, it had become a blessing in disguise for Labour. It got votes from anti-Catholic working-class Orangemen and their sympathisers. In some wards, such as Dalmarnock, this cost Labour seats. But in 1933 the Protestant party seems to have siphoned off working-class *Moderate* votes, and no fewer than 11 of 12 Labour gains in that year were in formerly Moderate-held wards in which the Scottish Protestant League intervened. It was an idiosyncratic way for a city to 'go Red'.

Labour also suffered from the I.L.P. When Maxton took it out of the Labour Party in 1932, he naturally took some of his local supporters with him. Dollan had broken politically (though not, he said, personally) with Maxton in 1928, when the Cook-Maxton Manifesto was issued without consulting the I.L.P;[4] he was the only opponent of Maxton to be elected to the national committee of the I.L.P. in 1931; and when it disaffiliated from the Labour Party, Dollan formed the Scottish Socialist Party (note the title) for I.L.P. members who wished to stay with Labour. The split had consequences for local as well as national politics; from 1932 on, I.L.P. candidates often fought Labour ones in municipal elections, especially in the East End of Glasgow, and the *Forward* quite often recorded, in primly shocked tones, diabolical alliances among I.L.P., Protestant and Moderate councillors against the Labour Group as the 1930s wore on. The I.L.P. challenge did not reflect distinctive *policies*, though, and it petered out after 1936.[5] Labour control of the Corporation was next threatened by the anti-Government swing that affected the whole of the U.K. towards the end of the Attlee administration, and by the simultaneous, and connected, collapse of Labour and meteoric rise of the Scottish National Party in 1968-9.[6]

Glasgow was by no means the last big working-class city in the U.K. to come under Labour control (Birmingham did so for the first time in 1946; Liverpool in 1955; and Belfast never has). But it was not the first either, even though there are no aldermen in Scotland. (Aldermen, supposed to be repositories of experience and guarantees of consistency, were actually a device used by declining parties to hold on to power. In the 1920s that meant the anti-Labour parties; in the 1960s it meant Labour.) Sheffield, for instance, so similar to Glasgow in class and industrial composition, went Labour for the first time in 1926.[7]

Red Clydeside, then, left little impact on the party composition of Glasgow Corporation. It left little impact on its personnel either. Apart from Dollan, all the Clydesiders went off to Parliament in 1922 or subsequently and played no further part in Glasgow city politics once they had reached Westminster. Dollan unsuccessfully fought a parliamentary by-election in Ayr in 1925; but his heart was surely not in it. Ayr is usually a Tory seat, and Dollan could have had a safe Labour seat for the asking if he had wanted one. He presumably preferred running Glasgow to being a backbencher in London. The other leading Labour figures on Glasgow Corporation between the wars — Tom Kerr, William Leonard, Ernest Greenhill, J. M. Biggar, Adam McKinlay — had played no role in Red Clydeside. They had their quirks: for instance, Kerr was an enthusiastic musician who was conducting the Glasgow Socialist Choristers in a programme of Elizabethan madrigals in 1923, forty years before the general rediscovery of these immortal masterpieces.[8] But there is no evidence that he was an innovator in politics. He was often on poor terms with Dollan, as was McKinlay, whom Dollan once called a 'girner and bubbly-jock'.[9] But their disputes were more personal than ideological. In so far as they were ideological, they were wet-dry, rather than right-left.

A study of the class and religious backgrounds of Labour councillors in Glasgow shows up some interesting patterns. Table 16.1 actually shows that the Labour group was more working-class in modern times than it was in the days of Red Clydeside. The evidence must be handled carefully, though, because of the great problems of classification caused by what I have labelled as 'intermediate' occupations. These include: shopkeeper, publican, trade union official, and insurance agent. People who went into these jobs were overwhelmingly working-class in origin, but they are usually classed as 'non-manual'. Apart from union officials and party agents, most of them were self-employed. This was, of course, one reason why councillors and aspirant councillors were so keen on these jobs. Council work was not paid, and employers were under no obligation to give anybody time off to be a councillor. After the second world war, these conditions were relaxed a little, and this may account for the increase in proportion of working-class members of the Labour Group. None the less, it is interesting that the further it moved away from the heroic days (and heroic policies),

Table 16.1   Glasgow Labour councillors 1922-74. Occupation and religion

	Occupation			Religion	
Year of first service	middle class %	inter- mediate %	working class %	Roman Catholic %	Other or none %
Before 1931 (n=76)	32.9	52.1	15.1	21.1	78.9
1931-40 (n=70)	41.5	43.1	15.4	15.7	84.3
1941-50 (n=60)	28.1	36.8	35.1	21.7	78.4
1951-73 (n=145)	37.8	25.6	36.6	15.9	84.1

Source: Data collected by J. C. Gordon and analysed by author. See Appendix. The percentages under 'Occupation' exclude those for whom no information could be obtained, or who were not economically active — especially housewives. The figures in the column headed 'Roman Catholic' refer only to those for whom documentary evidence exists. The actual figures should probably be higher.

the closer it moved, socio-economically, to the people it represented.

Was the Glasgow Labour Group unusually working-class or unusually bourgeois, or neither? The comparative evidence in Table 16.2 is infuriatingly hard to handle, because writers differ in the way they assign people to social classes. But again, Glasgow appears to lie in the middle — not as bourgeois as Birmingham, nor as proletarian as Sheffield. Although the Glasgow councillors did not reflect the class make-up of their supporters, it seems that they did reflect the religious make-up, with Catholics accounting for about a fifth of both.

Did the class and religious differences among the councillors significantly affect their views on policy? It was a journalistic commonplace for many years that the latter did. The Group (and the Council) was divided from the 1920s to the 1970s on several issues related to drink. Should alcohol be served on Corporation premises? Should Labour councillors be disciplined if, contrary to the City Party's instructions, they signed documents to vouch for the character of applicants for liquor licences? Should pubs be allowed on Corporation housing estates? (They were not until the late 1960s.) All of these issues, though not overtly religious, were generally believed to reflect the division between wet Catholics and dry socialists on the Corporation. There were some more clear-cut religious disputes. Should the Corporation

Table 16.2   *Social background of Labour councillors*

	1 Glasgow 1922-31 (n=76) %	2 Glasgow 1951-73 (n=145) %	3 Sheffield 1967-8 (n=69) %	4 Birmingham 1945 (n=69) %	5 Birmingham 1966 (n=76) %	6 Tyne & Wear 1977 (n=71) %
Middle Class	32.9	37.8	17.2	53	37	36.2
Intermediate non-manual	52.1	25.6	39.4	47	53	17.4
Manual	15.1	36.6	43.4	0	9	46.4

Some columns do not add up to exactly 100 because of rounding.

Sources: (cols 1, 2) Author.
(cols 3, 4, 5) Reported in N. Collins, 'Social Background and Motivation of Councillors: a paper for the Robinson Committee', INLOGOV, University of Birmingham, 1977.
(col 6) Author. Data collected while author was a member of Tyne and Wear County Council for submission to Robinson Committee.

allow *Birth Control News* to be placed in the public libraries?[10] Should it keep Catholic schools separate, or integrate them into the non-denominational (but often called 'Protestant') system? In March 1970 the leader of the Labour Group said that school integration would be 'a politically retrograde step'.[11] Should the City continue to run selective and fee-charging (and largely Catholic) schools?[12] On a number of these issues, the position of individual councillors is known, either from roll-call votes in the City Chambers, or from lists published by journals like the *Forward* and the *Glasgow Observer*. None of these lists reveals a significant difference between councillors of different classes; but several of them reveal significant differences between councillors of different religions. Some examples follow in Table 16.3. Religion here is a genuine independent variable, not a surrogate for class. If councillors of one religion were predominantly of one class, it would be hard to say which factor underlay differences of attitude. But, as Table 16.4 shows, religion and class were hardly related at all to each other.

The class and religious profile of Glasgow's Labour councillors, then, shows both continuity and change from Red Clydeside. Is the same true of those who voted for them? In an attempt to answer this, each local election from 1922 to 1973 was looked at, and the results were com-

Table 16.3 Glasgow Labour councillors: religion and voting—some cross-tabulations

a) 'That alcohol be banned at Corporation functions', 20 October 1925

	For	Against	Abstained	Absent	
Catholic	1	3	1	7	12
Non-Catholic	18	4	2	8	32
	19	7	3	15	44

Asymmetric λ = 0.391

b) Whether reportedly in favour of *Birth Control News* being allowed into public libraries, October 1927

	Yes	No	
Catholic	0	10	10
Non-Catholic	24	18	42
	24	28	52

Asymmetric λ = 0.200

c) Whether for or against school integration, 1966

	Attitude to Integration:	Strongly for	For	Against	Strongly against	
	Catholic	1	3	0	6	10
Religion	Protestant	12	3	1	2	18
	Other or none	11	3	0	0	14
		24	9	1	8	42

Asymmetric λ = 0.154 (η^2 = 0.385)

Sources: (a and b) Author's data.
　　　　　(c) Reanalysis of Budge, Brand, Margolis and Smith data.
　　　　　See Appendix for details.

Asymmetric λ is a statistic for measuring the significance of nominal-level data and η^2 is an equivalent statistic for an interval-level dependent variable. They measure the proportionate improvement in the predictability of the dependent variable achieved with knowledge of the independent variable. For instance, knowing that a councillor was Catholic gives a 39.1% improvement in one's chances of successfully predicting his vote in the 1925 roll-call. For more on 'significance' see the Appendix. See also N. Nie, C. H. Hull, J. G. Jenkins, K. Steinbrenner and D. H. Bent, *SPSS Handbook*, 2nd ed. (McGraw-Hill, New York, 1975), pp. 222-230.

Table 16.4   Glasgow Labour councillors 1922-74: class and religion

	Class	Middle	Intermediate	Working	
Religion	Catholic	23	19	19	61
	Non-Catholic	75	89	52	216
		98	108	71	277

Asymmetric λ = 0.024

Source: Author's data.

pared with what could be measured of the class and religious profile of each ward — thus extending the technique of Chapter 14 and Table 14.1 (the Appendix contains a technical note on how it was done). The class profiles can be accurately drawn only for Census years, and the analysis therefore concentrated on the municipal elections of the Census years 1921, 1931, 1961, 1966, and 1971. For each of these years (but not, alas, in 1951) the Census gives usable data about the social composition of each ward. The number of Catholic births or marriages gave a measure of the 'Catholicity' of each ward. For 1921 the results were also known of the most recent referendum on drink — the veto poll of 1920. And for 1931 there was added in the 'Protestant' vote as measured by the Scottish Protestant League's best score in the ward. Table 16.5 is a matrix of the product-moment correlations among these factors. What does it show? First, that there was always a high correlation between the social class mix of a ward and its Labour vote.[13] There is nothing surprising about this, but it is an important first fact to establish. There are no signs here of the skilled-unskilled division that kept the Labour vote patchy and relatively weakly related to social class before 1920. In the second place, Catholicity seems to be a factor; it too has quite high positive correlations with the Labour vote. This could be spurious, resulting purely from the fact that Catholics tended to be working-class. In fact it is not, but the multiple regression of Table 16.6 will be required to show that. Thirdly, the dry vote correlates strongly negatively with housing density in 1920. This suggests (though it does not prove) that Labour was very wise to drop Prohibition after 1920. Finally, there is a rather low correlation between 'Protestant' vote and Catholicity ($r = -0.21830$). Hence the proportion of ardent Protestants in a ward probably bore little relation to the proportion of Catholics. The enemy did not have to live next door to be hated or feared. (Many studies in the 1960s and '70s found a

The Legend of Red Clydeside

Table 16.5 Municipal election results in Census years: correlation matrices

a) 1921	DENSITY	DRY VOTE	RC RATE 1
LABRANGE	0.89395	−0.76637	0.63268
DENSITY		−0.78987	0.57935
DRY VOTE			−0.60024

b) 1931	DENSITY	PROTRANG	RC RATE 1
LABRANGE	0.78975	−0.27340	0.56333
DENSITY		−0.10791	0.66273
PROTRANG			−0.21830

c) 1961	SEGMIX	RC RATE 2
LABVOTE	0.78564	0.57922
SEGMIX		0.48763

d) 1966	SEGMIX	RC RATE 2
LABVOTE	0.78619	0.66633
SEGMIX		0.55760

e) 1971	SEGMIX	RC RATE 2
LABVOTE	0.86830	0.51526
SEGMIX		0.44827

Source: Author's data.

Meaning of variables:

LABRANGE, LABVOTE: measures of the Labour share of votes cast.
RC RATE 1, RC RATE 2: measures of proportion RC in ward population.
DENSITY: housing density.
SEGMIX: proportion in lower socio-economic groups in ward population.
DRYVOTE: proportion voting Dry in 1920 veto poll.
PROTRANG: maximum proportion of votes going to Scottish Protestant League 1931-3.

similarly weak relationship between racism and proportion of coloured people in the neighbourhood.)

To some extent, all these factors are intercorrelated. In particular, the more working-class a ward, the more Catholic it is likely to be. To separate out these factors, statistical techniques such as multiple regression are required, and Table 16.6 shows the most important results of a stepwise multiple regression of the variables upon the dependent variable LAB RANGE or LAB VOTE. In plain language, Table 16.6 aims to show how much each factor contributed to the variance of the Labour vote in these Census years. The square of the product-moment correlation r is a measure of variance, and it is shown in the second and third columns of Table 16.6. For instance, the

Table 16.6   Municipal election results in Census years: Forward (stepwise) regression
results

a) 1921 Dependent Variable LABRANGE

	Multiple r	r²	r² change	simple r
DENSITY	0.89395	0.79914	0.79914	0.89395
RC RATE 1	0.90497	0.81897	0.01983	0.63268
DRY VOTE	0.90700	0.82265	0.00367	−0.76637

b) 1931 Dependent Variable LABRANGE

	Multiple r	r²	r² change	simple r
DENSITY	0.78975	0.62371	0.62371	0.78975
PROTRANG	0.81212	0.65954	0.03583	−0.27340
RC RATE 1	0.81228	0.65980	0.00027	0.56333

c) 1961 Dependent Variable LABVOTE

	Multiple r	r²	r² change	simple r
SEGMIX	0.78564	0.61723	0.61723	0.78564
RC RATE 2	0.81712	0.66769	0.05146	0.57922

d) 1966 Dependent Variable LABVOTE

	Multiple r	r²	r² change	simple r
SEGMIX	0.78619	0.61810	0.61810	0.78619
RC RATE	0.83277	0.69350	0.07540	0.66633

e) 1971 Dependent Variable LABVOTE

	Multiple r	r²	r² change	simple r
SEGMIX	0.86830	0.75394	0.75394	0.86830
RC RATE 2	0.87967	0.77382	0.01988	0.51526

Source: Author's data.

regression of DENSITY on LAB RANGE in 1921 gives $r^2 = 0.79914$. So 79.9% of the variance in the Labour vote is accounted for by housing density — an unusually high proportion for statistics of this sort. RC RATE 1 adds another 1.98% of variance explained, and DRY VOTE a pretty trivial 0.37%.

The figures in Table 16.6, first, confirm the overwhelming importance of class as a determinant of the Labour vote. But religion is not negligible. Catholicity accounts for 2% of the variance in 1921, 5% in 1961, 7.5% in 1966 and 2% in 1971. It is interesting that in the only year in which 'Protestantism' can be directly measured — 1931 — it accounts for more of the variance than Catholicity.[14] This could show that variance in the Labour vote is more sensitive to the number of

Protestants prepared to vote *against* Labour than to the number of Catholics ready to vote for the party.

It is a pity that the municipal elections of 1968 and 1969 did not take place in a Census year, because it would have been interesting to relate the Scottish Nationalist upsurge to class and religion. Casual and anecdotal evidence suggests[15] that the Catholic vote stayed with Labour in those years, whereas the non-Catholic vote defected to the S.N.P.

So far in this chapter, we have discussed the issues only in a sidelong way, mentioning only a selection of those that divided the Labour Group. We should look at others that divided them, and — just as important — at issues which did not divide them, either because everybody agreed or because nobody realised the importance of the question at stake. Then we ought to compare, as far as possible, the issues which seemed important to the local élites with those that mattered to the electorate. In doing this, we shall concentrate on peculiarly Glasgow issues, or issues which, although not unique to Glasgow, developed there in an unusual way. By studying two issues and a 'non-issue' (Catholic schools, housing policy and planning policy) we shall see that there was indeed a legacy of Red Clydeside. Not a legacy that anyone intended to leave, but one that is inescapably part of Glasgow.

We saw earlier that Catholic schools were eligible for 100% state support from 1918, and that the separate Education Authority, on which Catholics were always well represented by both elected and co-opted members, was absorbed into Glasgow Corporation in 1929. The *Glasgow Observer* starkly demanded of every candidate in the 1928 elections, 'Are you prepared to pledge yourself to support in all respects the status quo with regard to the administration of the Catholic Schools?'.[16] It printed a list of the twenty brave or foolhardy people who failed to say Yes promptly. Only six were Labour, and of these only one was elected. 'Beware of entrance to a quarrel', said the *Observer* with biblical solemnity, 'but being in, bear it that the opposed may beware of thee.' It was a lesson the Labour Group never forgot. 'The Catholic electorate of Glasgow has reason to plume itself on the remarkable effect of its solid and organised vote,' said the *Observer* smugly four years later.[17] Thirty-five years after that, with a world war come and gone, the Welfare State in existence, and the last tram in Glasgow only a memory, one thing had not changed. A Church of Scotland minister, campaigning for school integration, managed to lose Labour the normally safe Kingston ward on a swing of 10%, compared to only 4% in neighbouring wards.[18] Integration would certainly have been in the material interest of the Catholics: in 1970 as in 1918 their schools had poorer premises and fewer teachers than the 'Protestant' schools. But the hierarchy remained inflexible. The Very Rev. Canon John McGuckin explained in 1970:

> . . . people who want to have Christian schools are being told, in effect, that they must go into a system which is not Christian . . . If this [Integration] were general Labour policy it could be political suicide because Catholics in this part of the world are traditionally and historically Labour, and most of them vote that way.[19]

Accordingly, the leader of the Labour Group bluntly announced that school integration 'will not form one of the planks in our election platform' in spite of an overwhelming vote for it at a municipal policy-making conference.[20] School integration is an interesting case-study in political stratification. As Table 16.7 shows, Labour supporters at all levels favoured it, with party activists the keenest. So why did it not take place? Essentially, because an intense Catholic minority against — more intense although less numerous among ward activists than in the electorate as a whole — outweighed an apathetic non-Catholic majority in favour. Integration gained no votes among Protestants to offset those it lost among Catholics. In a sense, the Labour councillors' refusal to alter the 1918 settlement was an entirely fair reflection of their constituents' views. It may not have been socialist, but that is another matter.

As we have seen, the Clydesiders had a housing policy that was both distinctive and socialist, and it shaped national policy in the 1915 Rent Act and 1924 Housing Act. These two acts did more to shape Glasgow than any other city. Glasgow Corporation was quick off the mark, and built 4690 houses under Addison's 1919 Act, generally ineffectual though that was; and a further 7996 under the Act passed by the Conservatives in 1923. With the subsidies permitted by the Wheatley Act, 21,586 houses were built, and various further Housing Acts in the

Table 16.7   *School integration: preferences of Labour councillors, party workers and electors, 1966*

	For	Against
	%	%
Councillors	77	21
Party workers	83	17
Electors	60	36

Source: Budge *et al, Political Stratification*, p. 92.

1930s permitted another 17,822 houses to be completed.[21] The Corporation was financially responsible for six-sevenths of the new houses built in Glasgow between the wars.

None of this was controversial. Labour councillors of all shades wanted the Corporation to build as many houses as possible, and so did the people who voted for them. The 60,000-odd houses that the Corporation had built by 1947 were doubtless lamentably few by comparison with the horrendous scale of the problem: the magisterial Clyde Valley Regional Plan (completed 1946, published 1949) estimated that to achieve an acceptably low standard of density Glasgow would have to rehouse a quarter of a million people in the suburbs and a further 250,000 to 300,000 by 'overspill' into New Towns.[22] It may seem a sorry reflection on seventy years of municipal enterprise (the first City Improvement Act was in 1866) that half the population of the city should still need housing at the end of it. But the fault did not lie with the city housing programme, which was as big as the enabling acts and the city's land shortage between them allowed for. Quarrels broke out in the Labour Group, but only on fringe points. For instance, a few Labour councillors vigorously supported Weir and other industrialists who wanted to solve Glasgow's housing problem in the 1920s by massive production of steel-framed houses. Most equally vigorously opposed them.[23] For the wrong reasons, no doubt, among which the conservatism of building workers and trade-union hatred of Weir bulked large. But later experience shows that it was probably just as well that Weir got nowhere. 'Non-traditional' houses leak, they have intractable condensation problems, and they can only be built at very low density, unless they are prefabricated multi-storey flats — which is another tale of woe.

But the debate about Weir houses did not matter very much. Glasgow's housing stock was dreadful in 1918, dreadful in 1933 when Labour took over, and still dreadful, though in subtly different ways, when Glasgow Corporation ceased to exist forty years later. For this there were two main reasons: the level of rents, and the lack of land for building new houses.

As we saw in Chapter 13, the Ballantyne Commission found that by 1914 house rents in the Scottish cities were too low to allow an economic return to any entrepreneur. The Rent Acts of 1915, 1919 and 1920 imposed further heavy cuts in real returns. So no further houses for the working class were privately financed after 1918, and the existing stock deteriorated badly for lack of repairs. Exactly fifty years after Ballantyne, another official report (the Cullingworth Report) looked at the pre-1914 housing stock:

> We must underline our shock at the condition in which incredibly large numbers of Scottish families have to live . . .
>   We have seen conditions in Glasgow that can only be described as appalling . . .
>   Over a quarter of the tenants of privately rented unfurnished houses in Scotland pay less than £13 *a year* in rent. A further 37% pay between £13 and £26 a year. Only 9% pay £52 or more a year. With these rents . . . it is quite impossible to finance even the minimum amount of 'ordinary' repairs.[24]

Like their predecessors fifty years before, Cullingworth and his colleagues emerged from their own backyard amazed and horrified by the conditions they found there. Why had nobody in government looked behind the handsome sandstone fronts of Glasgow tenements to the squalor beyond? Essentially because nobody had asked them to — the electorate was seemingly satisfied with its 5/- (25p) a week rents — and very few politicians or administrators had the imagination to look for themselves. There were in principle a number of possible ways of making, and keeping, the pre-1914 housing stock in Glasgow habitable. One was to allow rents to rise to a market level; another was to make repair and improvement grants to owners. A third option was slum clearance and rehousing. But the Council was reluctant to do any of these. Rent decontrol was politically intolerable, and repair grants not much better. Cullingworth and his colleagues 'were appalled by the strong political line taken by some authorities' which refused to make grants because that would involve 'subsidising the private sector . . . If the situation were not so tragic we would regard it as Gilbertian'.[25]

Clearance and rehousing was thus the only viable option left. But Government was slow to give authorities the powers to do it and Glasgow was not very fast to use them. The 1924 Government, for instance, did not recognise slum clearance as a problem over and above the provision of new houses. Approving the draft of Wheatley's Housing Bill, the Cabinet resolved that

> If the Bill is criticised on the ground that it does not make special provision for dealing with slum areas, the Minister of Health should base his reply on the fact that Local Authorities have already ample powers for dealing with slum areas provided that alternative accommodation (which this Bill is intended to provide) is available.[26]

The second Labour Government, however, realised that this was too complacently optimistic, and passed the Housing (Scotland) Act 1930 which was the first to authorise slum clearance and the building of houses as replacements to the slums cleared.[27]

Glasgow used its powers under the 1930 and subsequent slum-clearance Acts in a way that echoed an ancient distinction between the deserving poor and the undeserving poor. The deserving were entitled to 'Ordinary' houses; the undeserving only to 'Rehousing' houses which were conceived, designed and built to lower standards throughout and at much higher density. This policy was bipartisan. Labour never changed it, and in the 1950s potential tenants were still being graded for cleanliness and formal inspections by Housing Department staff, and 'tenants who have been graded as only fit for a "Rehousing" type house'[28] were duly packed off to somewhere like South Pollok, jovially known as 'The White Man's Grave' because of the number of T.B. sufferers living there.[29] Is there an echo here of the puritanical socialist artisan's old contempt for the labourer? The *Forward's* 'bar-tender's pest and Sauchiehall Street dude' went to South Pollok or Blackhill; the 'better-paid, and more comfortably circumstanced, and better read' ended up in the rolling acres of Knightswood.

At all events there was very little slum clearance in Glasgow before 1957, when the first Comprehensive Development Area was designated in Gorbals-Hutchesontown.[30] By that time, people were living at a density of many hundreds to the acre in houses that had not been properly maintained since 1914. Even ten years later, as the Culling-worth Report shows, new housing and slum clearance between them had hardly even made a dent in the problem. Thirty-three per cent of households in the central Clydeside conurbation lacked exclusive use of a fixed bath in 1967.[31]

Apart from money, there was a second main reason why the Labour Group did nothing about the slums for all these decades: there was nowhere to put the people. This bald statement oversimplifies a long and complex argument. Politically, it was most striking for being like the dog that didn't bark. There is hardly a mention of it anywhere in the socialist press or the daily papers. And yet the unintended consequences of the decisions taken, and the non-decisions not taken, by the Corporation determined the shape of Glasgow for good and ill: mostly ill.

The story goes back to Wheatley's £8 cottages. Financially, the idea may have been utopian, but it had other good points. Wheatley had come to believe (so, many years later, did Dollan) that tenement living would always be overcrowded and squalid, and that new working-class housing should be in terraced or semi-detached houses with gardens, in low-density estates. Glasgow's inter-war 'Ordinary' estates were like that: Mosspark, Knightswood and Carntyne 'were laid out at net densities of no greater than twelve houses to the acre'.[32] This was fine for the tenants, but had the unintended consequence of making rehousing harder for everyone else. The problem hardly surfaced before the war, as Glasgow got a fairly substantial boundary extension in 1938. But the 1938 boundaries marked a limit, either physical, or political, or both. Physically, Glasgow was constrained on the north by the Campsie and Kilpatrick hills and on the south by the Renfrew moors; politically it was constrained on the east by Rutherglen and Coatbridge and on the west by Paisley and Clydebank. None of these burghs would let Glasgow expand to incorporate them, nor would they house decanted Glaswegians. And the tourniquet was given another turn by another wholly well-intentioned policy: the Green Belt.

Glasgow socialists, like many others, had long cherished the open country lying near the city. Every week in the summer, the *Forward* carried advertisements for socialist rambles from a suitable tram terminus. Milngavie, the gateway to the wilds, was the most popular: it had six times as many tramcars on Sundays as on weekdays.[33] Sir Patrick Abercrombie, the author of the Clyde Valley Plan, wrote, a little pompously but with genuine feeling, that

> Many a young unemployed shipyard worker from Clydebank or Glasgow retained his health and sanity in the evil days of the workless early '30s, by finding his way by one means or another to Loch Lomond . . . or to climb in the 'Arrochar Alps' area at the head of Loch Long. There is an epic quality in the adventures of these young people . . . who instinctively turned to the only defence they had against the insidious effects of civilisation gone wrong.[34]

For evangelistic planners, the Green Belt was no less than a moral crusade, marching down the 'spines of green wedges and corridors'[35] with the rivers Kelvin and White Cart, and the Pollok estate, to within a couple of miles of the centre of Glasgow. Ribbon development — that bête noire of early physical planners — was to be cut, and 'open space corridors' kept between separate communities.

All this was very good, humane and farsighted. But it tightened the noose still further. The Clyde Valley Regional Plan was broadly accepted by the Scottish Office, and by the constituent authorities including Glasgow.[36] Its new Green Belt went inside Glasgow's boundaries at several points, and thus made land in the belt unavailable for housing. This left the Corporation with a hard choice. Should it redevelop within the city boundary at (inevitably) extremely high density, or should it encourage people to move out to existing towns on the fringe, or should it help to set up completely new settlements beyond, or on the fringe of the Green Belt? Briefly, the council listened to very bad advice from one of its officers and wrongly decided to follow the first option; never seriously considered the second; and took up the third very grudgingly.

Robert Bruce was the City Engineer from some time before 1945 to his resignation in 1951. He was convinced that Glasgow should rehouse all those in need within the city boundaries. A few Labour councillors, notably Dollan and Jean Mann, opposed this on the grounds that it would retain unacceptably high density. Other city officers also disagreed, as did Abercrombie, whose bitter row with Bruce underlay a polite footnoted disagreement in the *Clyde Valley Plan*.[37] But the Corporation supported Bruce, and opposed the designation of East Kilbride New Town in 1947.[38] Their motives were mixed. Some people disliked losing population because it might lead to a loss of rates; others simply thought Glasgow ought not to dip below a population of a million and be forced to surrender the title of 'the Second City' to Birmingham; others disliked Abercrombie's idea that not only housing but industry should be moved out to New Towns.

For most councillors, however, the whole thing was almost certainly a remote dispute that didn't concern them. The main objective was to build as many houses as fast as possible. Few people saw that Glasgow was again restricting its own options as it continued its building programme at relatively low density. But by about 1950 the city was rapidly running out of land. The old city was still jam-packed at anything up to 700 people per acre. Then came the inter-war and early post-war estates, with the generous layout and low density. After that there was very little land within the city boundary, and much of what there was was Green Belt. However, there were a few odd corners a long way from the city centre. One of them was called Easterhouse, another Castlemilk, a third Drumchapel. So there the houses had to go, and they had to go in three- and four-storey tenement blocks as there was no other way of fitting the people in: 94.5% of the houses built at Castlemilk were flats in walk-up blocks, as were 99.4% of those at Easterhouse.[39] Glasgow gave itself a topsy-turvy pattern. The further one went from the city centre, from workplaces, from shops, from pubs, the *higher* the housing density became, reaching its peak on the vast publess and facility-less flatted estates on the edge of the city. It only required the comprehensive development of the inner city from 1957 on to give the pattern its final ironic twist. For by the time that most of the tenement blocks had finally been pulled down, in the 1970s, the population had voted with its feet and walked away from the jobless desolation of the inner city. Dalmarnock and Maryhill became empty wildernesses with only the ground floors of the tenements in the main roads — up to pub roof level — left standing.

Meanwhile the city had reluctantly abandoned Bruce's idea of rehousing within the boundary, and grudgingly accepted the new towns of East Kilbride and (later) Cumbernauld. The acceptance was all the more grudging because the few politicians who welcomed the New Towns were promptly shipped off to run them, and therefore were no longer available in the corridors of George Square to argue for overspill. Thus Dollan finally left Glasgow politics in 1947, when he became first chairman of East Kilbride New Town Development Corporation; thus also in the next generation William S. Taylor left the Corporation to lead the committee for Livingston New Town.[40] Only two of Dollan's contemporaries on Glasgow Corporation Labour Group showed any sign of understanding the argument about housing and planning policy — Jean Mann and Hugh McCalman. All three more or less agreed on matters of substance (though McCalman disliked Dollan and refused to record his obituary for the B.B.C.). They all believed that the working class must be got out of the tenements and into self-contained houses; that there was no space to do so in Glasgow; that substantial overspill and at least two New Towns would be required. Preaching this message took them all away from George Square. Jean Mann became M.P. for Coatbridge in 1945; Hugh McCalman became chairman of the inter-authority Clyde Valley planning committee and resigned from Glasgow Corporation in 1947 'in part because of his disagreement with the Labour Council over . . . planning'.[41] With no voices articulately proposing any alternative, the Corporation gradually blundered into Easterhouse, Drumchapel and the rest — the unintended consequences of half a century of socialist policy-making.

In all this, the electorate supplied little more than noises off. By 1969 Labour voters agreed, but not as strongly as Labour councillors, that the time had come to bury socialist prohibitionism and allow pubs on to council estates.[42] But the electorate was never consulted, and never gave an opinion, on the main chain of events we have just described. Probably, they actively favoured some components, such as low rents;

favoured, without giving much thought to the consequence, others such as the Green Belt; and had no view at all on others again, such as boundary extension or New Towns. But if the consequence was unintended by the politicians, it was all the more unintended by those who voted for them. For many years now, writers on community power have urged us to study not only decisions but non-decisions, in the hope that the latter would point to those who exercise their power by keeping options off the agenda.[43] The non-decision to build Easterhouse is different. Not only did nobody decide to do it, nobody kept the alternatives off the agenda. No powerful but shadowy group prevented the councillors or the voters of Glasgow from thinking how else the housing crisis might be solved. They just didn't. Easterhouse is the last, unintentional, legacy of Red Clydeside.[44]

Appendix   Technical note on the data presented in Tables 16.1 to 16.6

Three files of data were gathered, as follows:

1. GLASRESULTS

A list of the municipal election results for every year from 1920 to 1973.

Source: *Glasgow Herald.* Cross-checked against *Daily Record* and/or *Scotsman.*

2. GLASBIOGS

Biographical information about all Labour councillors in Glasgow 1922-73.

Sources: *Forward, Glasgow Observer, Daily Record, Glasgow Herald, Citizens' Union Yearbook.* Roll-call votes derived from Glasgow Corporation, *Official Minutes.* Votes on *Birth Control News: Glasgow Observer* 22 and 29 Oct. 1927.

3. GLASCENSUS

Demographic, socio-economic, and political data for each ward in Census years 1921, 1931, 1961, 1966 and 1971. There was no Census in 1941. Exhaustive enquiries about 1951 with the Census Branch, General Register Office for Scotland and with users, both academic and in local government, forced us to conclude that no useful *ward-level* socio-economic data for that Census will be available until enumerators' records are released in 2052. The main variables recorded, and their sources, are:

Population	Census, published tables
Electorate Labour vote	} *Glasgow Herald* on day after election day
Population density (collected for 1921, 1931 only)	Census, published tables

SEG (Socio-economic group) statistics	(1961) Census of Scotland: Unpublished Schedule: Scale D (1966) Census of Scotland: Unpublished Schedules: Ward Library (1971) Census of Scotland: Unpublished Schedules: Small Area Statistics — Ward Library
Social Class Statistics	(1966) Census of Scotland: Unpublished Schedules: Ward Library
N of RC Baptisms Priests' estimates of RC population	*Catholic Directory for the Clergy and Laity in Scotland* 1921, 1931, 1961, 1966, 1971
Veto poll votes	*Glasgow Herald* 4 November 1920
Protestant vote	*Glasgow Herald* on day following each of 1931, 1932, 1933 municipal elections

The computed variables in Tables 16.5 and 16.6 were derived as follows:

LABVOTE: $\dfrac{\text{Labour vote}}{\text{Electorate}}$

LABRANGE: LABVOTE grouped into 10 percentile bands

DENSITY: (Not a computed variable; derived direct from Census)
(1921) Population per 100 windowed rooms
(1931) Percent of population in two rooms or fewer

DRYVOTE: $\dfrac{\text{Vote for No Licence and Limitation}}{\text{Electorate}}$

PROTRANG: $\dfrac{\text{Maximum vote for Scottish Protestant League}}{\text{Electorate}}$ in 10 percentile bands

RC RATE 1: $\dfrac{\text{RC baptisms}}{\text{Population}}$

RC RATE 2: $\dfrac{\text{Priests' estimates of RC population}}{\text{Population}}$

SEGMIX: $\dfrac{\text{N. in SEGs 7, 8, 9, 10, 11, 12, 14, 15 (1961: and 16, 17)}}{\text{Population}}$

The above gives some hint of the huge volume of work that lies behind these tables. My grateful thanks to Colin Gordon, to the staff of the Census Branch, General Register Office for Scotland, and to everyone else who dealt with queries.

The data have been presented to the SSRC Survey Archive, Essex University, and are available for re-analysis.

A note on *'significance'*:

None of the above are sample survey data. All represent a 100% sample of the populations concerned (wards and councillors).* Therefore the usual statistical tests of significance, which test the likelihood that the sample distribution is a true microcosm

---

*So do Budge *et al's* data re-analysed in Table 16.3(c).

of the population distribution, do not apply and none are presented in Tables 16.5 and 16.6. In Tables 16.3 and 16.4, however, the cross-tabulations are hard to interpret without some measure of the 'significance' of the variations. The commonest test of significance with cross-tabulated nominal-level data, namely χ^2 (chi-square), is quite inappropriate here and is not given. However, asymmetric λ (lambda) and η^2 (eta squared), which are given, should enable the reader to judge which differences are 'significant' — in the ordinary, not the statistical, meaning of that word.

Conclusion

The Red Clydeside constructed by the excitable minds of John MacLean and Sir Basil Thomson never existed:

> The most revolutionary thing that ever happened in Scotland at that time was when J. S. Clarke's wife made Davy Kirkwood wash the dishes — which he'd never done before.[1]

But in political history (though perhaps not in analytical philosophy) a non-existent object can have tangible attributes. The most enduring consequence of the first Red Clydeside was rent control. As we have seen, the rent strikes of autumn 1915 were not the work of the Clyde Workers' Committee. But Glasgow's image at Westminster was already unruly and rebellious, and this persuaded the Coalition Government to pass legislation which 'violated all the principles of political economy'. Having passed it, they and all their successors found it politically impossible to revoke. Political economists complained, and have continued to complain to this day, that low rents were not part of the solution but part of the problem. The Ballantyne and Cullingworth Reports, half a century apart, alike bear witness to this. The Rent Act 1915 and its successors were, of course, nationwide legislation, not confined to Scotland or to Glasgow. But in Glasgow they bore heavily on a market which, as the Ballantyne Commission proved, was already unbalanced. No rational entrepreneur would have provided working-class housing in Glasgow in 1914; far less, therefore, in 1915 or 1919 or 1920. Thus there was no plausible alternative to state-subsidised housing. The form which that took was sketched by Addison and confirmed by Wheatley. In Glasgow the detail was filled in, not by the Clydesiders, but as a consequence of them.

If the political consequence of the first Red Clydeside was rent control, what about the industrial consequences? In the wake of the collapse of February 1919 and of the Restoration of Pre-war Practices Act, they probably seemed meagre indeed. Precisely because the shop stewards' movement was unofficial and anti-bureaucratic, it left no permanent structures. And yet in another way it did. It confronted the major unions with both new opportunities and new problems. New opportunities of incorporation in government because of governments' urgent need to control production; but new problems of relations with an increasingly independent membership which government and union executives both wanted to 'control'. After 1919 the emphasis remained firmly on control. But gradually unions swung back to allowing considerable independence to their shop stewards, especially in times of good trade. Of Britain's two biggest unions, the Engineers took this path in and after the Second World War; the Transport Workers were dominated for longer by the authoritarian structures built by Ernest Bevin, but gave much more autonomy to their shop stewards under the general secretaryships of Frank Cousins and Jack Jones in the 1960s and 1970s. The first shop stewards' movement showed the way towards one of the modern patterns of industrial relations.

The first Red Clydeside had little in common with the second, but it shaped it in one or two ways. For instance, it polarised Glasgow politics. Coalition politicians, both Conservative and Lloyd George Liberal, struggled to preserve Glasgow from the 'menace of socialism' in 1918. By their lights they largely succeeded, in the process crushing the Asquith Liberals out of existence inside the city. The 1922 election was brought about by a backbench Conservative revolt against Lloyd George and the Coalition. But in Glasgow (and, significantly, in Sheffield also) the Coalition went united into an election caused by its collapse everywhere else. The Unionist and National Liberal candidates issued a joint manifesto.[2] The Coalition failed to survive in only one constituency, namely Cathcart, which Labour proceeded to win on an even split off the opposition vote. In local government the 'menace of socialism' also generated an anti-socialist coalition in the Good Government League, later the Moderate (later still the Progressive) Party; this development too was paralleled in Sheffield. The image of Red Clydeside clearly had a large influence on all this: probably more than the reality.

The first Red Clydeside also produced some of the personnel of the second. The clearest case is Kirkwood, who would never have come into politics but for the events of 1915-16. A shrewd, though condescending, colleague later described him as

> the voice of the quintessential Glasgow of the working classes . . . He is simply the average man of the working classes of Glasgow endowed with a slightly greater power of expressing his sentiments than the average man possesses.[3]

Kirkwood and Neil Maclean were probably the first two Labour M.P.'s whose pathways to Parliament were never smoothed by trade-union office. Likewise, Shinwell, Johnston, and to some extent Wheatley depended on the first Red Clydeside, in the sense that it was the springboard for their later careers; but not in any significant ideological sense.

The second Red Clydeside entailed a broadening of Labour's social base. Labour had to get rid of issues like dilution, conscription and prohibition which split the working class; and it had to rebuild the alliance with the Irish that had tentatively begun before the war. The end of the war killed off the first Red Clydeside, but at the same time it killed the first two divisive issues; the last was much weakened when Prohibition disappeared from official Labour platforms after 1921. It did not vanish entirely until the resolution banning pubs on Council estates was finally rescinded in 1969. But long before that the Catholics were fully integrated into the Labour machine; as the statistics of Chapter 16 show, they have actually been *more* loyal to Labour than non-Catholics since 1922. Tensions between the components of the second Red Clydeside persisted for fifty years: for instance between 'dry' socialists and 'wet' Catholics on the Labour Group in Glasgow Corporation. But the Clydesiders' main legacy lies not where they were divided but where they were united: in housing and planning policy. The consequences of this policy were disastrous, but the intentions were not; and the policy, if not the consequences, probably had the warm support of the Glasgow working-class electorate.

At Westminster, Red Clydeside made the House of Commons a more colourful and livelier place. It had little impact on party fortunes and what it had was counter-productive. However, it did help to shape the 1924 Housing Act. That is no mean achievement; it should stand as the Clydesiders' monument.

Biographical Notes

Addison, Christopher (1st Viscount Addison). B. Hogsthorpe, Lincs, 1869. Qualified as doctor, St. Bartholomew's Hospital, 1892. Professor of anatomy, Sheffield University, 1897; gave name to 'Addison's plane' in human anatomy. M.P. (Lib.) Hoxton Jan. 1910-18; Shoreditch 1918-22; (Lab.) Swindon 1929-31, 1934-5. Created Baron Addison, 1937; Viscount 1946. Parliamentary Secretary, Board of Education 1914-15; to Ministry of Munitions 1915-16. Minister of Munitions 1916-17, of Reconstruction 1917-19, of Health 1919-21. Dismissed by Lloyd George to appease 'anti-waste' crusaders 1921. Parliamentary secretary, Ministry of Agriculture 1929-30; Minister of Agriculture 1930-1. Leader of House of Lords 1945-51, in Cabinet throughout, holding various ministerial posts. D. Bucks. 1951. 'How can we oppose this man? He is so decent' — a Conservative whip, 1931. A remarkable and still underrated politician.

Barnes, George N. B. Lochee, Dundee, 1859. Engineering apprentice, London, 1872-7; thereafter engineer. Assistant secretary A.S.E. 1892; general secretary 1896-1908. M.P. (Lab.) Glasgow Blackfriars 1906-18; (Co. Lab.) Glasgow Gorbals 1918-22. Minister of Pensions 1916; Minister without Portfolio, War Cabinet, 1917. One of the founders of the International Labour Organisation. D. London 1940.

Beardmore, William (Lord Invernairn). B. Greenwich 1856. Educ. Glasgow Royal Technical College. Partner, Parkhead Forge, 1879, with his uncle Isaac Beardmore; later founder of Wm. Beardmore & Co. Firm had massive share of munitions and ship production. Beardmore Glacier, Antarctic, named after him (appropriately). Bart. 1914; 1st (and only) Baron Invernairn 1921; d. Inverness-shire 1936.

Beveridge, William B. India 1879. M.A., B.C.L. (Oxford), 1902. Joined Board of Trade 1908. Director of Labour Exchanges 1909-16. Assistant Secretary, Ministry of Munitions 1915-16. Permanent Secretary, Ministry of Food 1919. Director, London School of Economics 1919-37; Master, University College, Oxford 1937-45. Chairman, inter-departmental Committee on Social Insurance and Allied Services, 1941-2. D. Oxford 1963. A progressive autocrat.

Buchanan, George B. Gorbals, Glasgow, 1890. Member (Lab.) Glasgow Corporation 1918-23. M.P. (Lab.-I.L.P.-Lab.) Glasgow Gorbals 1922-48. First Chairman, National Assistance Board, 1948-53. D. London 1955.

Dollan, (Sir) Patrick J. B. Baillieston, Lanarkshire, 1881. Miner, later journalist ('Myner Collier'). Member (Lab.) Glasgow Corporation 1913-46. I.L.P. organiser in Glasgow throughout 1920s; founded Scottish Socialist Party when I.L.P. left Labour Party 1932. Secretary, Chairman, Leader, Labour Group in Glasgow Corporation for most of period 1922-38. Lord Provost 1938-41. Knighted 1941. First chairman, East Kilbride New Town Development Corporation, 1946. D. Glasgow 1963. C.O. 1914-18; ardent supporter of war effort 1939-45 (gave servicemen free rides on tramcars and closed the pubs at 8 p.m.); the most astute politician on Red Clydeside.

Gallacher, William   B. Paisley 1881. Seaman, later brassfounder. Executive member, United Brassfounders' Association 1914. Joined S.D.F. 1906. Chairman Central Labour-withholding Committee 1915; Clyde Workers' Committee 1915-16. Imprisoned for 12 months 1916-17; for 3 months 1919. Organiser 40 Hours' Strike. Joined C.P.G.B. 1920 at Lenin's request; Vice-President 1921. M.P. (Comm.) West Fife 1935-50. D. 1965. Not as heroic as his autobiography.

Graham, William   B. Peebles 1887; journalist. M.A. (Edinburgh) 1915. Member (Lab.) Edinburgh Corporation. M.P. (Lab.) Edinburgh Central 1918-31. Financial Secretary to the Treasury 1924; President Board of Trade 1929-31. D. London 1932.

Henderson, Arthur   B. Glasgow 1863, but moved to Newcastle-upon-Tyne in childhood. Ironfounder; district delegate, Ironfounders' Union 1892. Election agent to Liberal M.P. for Barnard Castle 1895-1903. M.P. (Lab.) Barnard Castle 1903-18; Widnes 1919-22; Newcastle East 1923; Burnley 1924-31; Clay Cross 1933-5. Secretary, Labour Party 1906-34. Cabinet minister responsible for labour affairs 1915-17; member, War Cabinet, Dec. 1916-Aug. 1917; defender of manpower and munitions policies on which he was often not consulted. Home Secretary 1924; Foreign Secretary 1929-31; passionate campaigner for international disarmament. Leader, Labour Party, 1931-3. D. London 1935.

Johnston, Tom   B. Kirkintilloch 1881. Graduate of Glasgow University. Founder (1906) and editor for 27 years of *Forward*. M.P. (Lab.) West Stirlingshire 1922-4, 1929-31, 1935-45; Dundee 1924-9. Parliamentary Under-secretary of State for Scotland, 1929-31; Lord Privy Seal 1931; Secretary of State for Scotland 1941-5. First Chairman, North of Scotland Hydro-electric Board. D. Milngavie 1965. An inspired journalist, prohibitionist and scourge of landowners.

Kirkwood, David   B. Parkhead 1872. Engineer; member of A.S.E. Employed at Parkhead Forge 1895-7, 1910-16. Foreman, Mount Vernon Steel Works 1899. Member S.L.P., c.1910-14; of I.L.P. 1914 onwards. Chief Shop Steward Parkhead Forge 1914-16. Deported to Edinburgh 1916. Returned to 'blow the Germans across the Rhine' as foreman at Mile-End Shell Factory 1917. Tried for incitement to riot 1919; acquitted. M.P. (Lab.-I.L.P.-Lab.) Dumbarton Burghs 1922-50, Dunbartonshire East 1950-1. 1st Baron Kirkwood of Bearsden 1951. D. 1955. 'A man of somewhat dominating constitutional authority' — Clyde Dilution Commissioners, 1916.

Llewellyn Smith, Sir Hubert   B. Bristol 1864. Oxford and London graduate. Worked at Toynbee Hall 1887; helped strikers in London dock strike 1889. Joined Board of Trade 1893; Permanent Secretary 1907. K.C.B. 1908. General Secretary, Ministry of Munitions 1915. Chief Government economic adviser 1919-27. President, etc., of many public bodies in 1920s and 1930s. D. Wiltshire 1945.

Macassey, (Sir) Lynden   B. Carrickfergus 1876. Engineering apprentice on Clyde. Trained as graduate engineer (Dublin and London); then as lawyer (Middle Temple

1899; K.C. 1912). Board of Trade arbitrator in shipbuilding and engineering disputes 1914-16. Joint member (with Lord Balfour of Burleigh) of inquiry into grievances on Clydeside against Munitions of War Act, Aug.-Oct. 1915. Chairman, Clyde Dilution Commissioners 1916. K.B.E. 1917. Director of shipyard labour for Admiralty 1917-18. Various honorific offices 1922 onwards. D. London 1963.

McGovern, John   B. Glasgow 1887. Apprenticed as plumber; master plumber 1909. I.L.P. member from c.1914; said to be pacifist during war. In Australia during 1920s. Member (Lab.) Glasgow Corporation 1929. M.P. (Lab.-I.L.P.-Lab.) Glasgow Shettleston 1930-59. Suspended from Commons four times. Congratulated Neville Chamberlain on Munich agreement, 1938. Active in Moral Rearmament 1954 on; denounced 96 Labour M.P.s as fellow-travellers 1959. D. Glasgow 1968.

McKinnon Wood: see Wood.

MacLean, John   B. Pollokshaws 1879 of Highland parents. Father d. 1887 but mother worked to get children through university. Qualified as teacher 1900; M.A. (Glasgow) by evening study 1904, delayed by failing compulsory Latin at earlier attempts. Joined S.D.F. 1903. Active lecturer and speaker on Marxism. Dismissed as teacher 1915 for making allegations about his headmaster. Imprisoned for sedition and similar offences 1915, 1916, 1918, 1921. Soviet Consul, Glasgow, 1918. Broke with Gallacher (q.v.) 1920; never joined the C.P.G.B. D. Glasgow, Nov. 1923, of pneumonia; had given his only overcoat to a destitute West Indian who wrote to his widow to say 'He was the greatest Man in Scotland one great lump of kindness and sincerity'. Tragic but ineffectual.

Maclean, Neil   B. 1875 of Highland parents. Engineer to 1912; M.P. (Lab.) Glasgow Govan 1918-50; many rows with constituency party; sailed through them all except the last. C.B.E. 1946. D. 1953.

MacManus, Arthur   B. Glasgow, 1889. Engineer; member S.L.P. Deported from Glasgow munitions area 1916. First chairman C.P.G.B., 1920. Alleged recipient of Zinoviev letter 1924, in which he was instructed to improve his 'agitation-propaganda work in the army'. D. 1927.

Maxton, James   B. Pollokshaws 1885. M.A. Glasgow University 1909. Teacher from c.1905. Member I.L.P., 1904 on. Pacifist 1914-18. Imprisoned 1916-17. 'His dog was stoned to death for his master's opinions' — *D.N.B.* M.P. (Lab.-I.L.P.) Glasgow Bridgeton 1922-46. Chairman I.L.P. 1926-31, 1934-9; disaffiliated it from Labour Party 1932. D. Largs 1946. A Parliamentary institution, ineffective and universally loved.

Mitchell, E. Rosslyn   B. Glasgow 1879. Ll.B. Glasgow University 1904. Member (Lib., later Lab.) Glasgow Corporation 1909-25. Liberal candidate Bute, Dec. 1910. Labour candidate Glasgow Central 1922, 1923. M.P. (Lab.) Paisley 1924-9. Made Lutheran speech ('Here I stand. I can no other, so help me God!') opposing revised Church of England Prayer Book 1927. Believed to have 'ghosted' Kirkwood's (q.v.) autobiography. D. 1965.

Muir, John   B. Glasgow 1879. Engineer. Member, S.L.P. and editor, *The Socialist*, 1914. C.W.C. spokesman at Lloyd George meeting, Christmas Day 1915. Imprisoned

1916; health permanently damaged. M.P. (Lab.) Glasgow Maryhill 1922-4. Parliamentary Secretary, Ministry of Pensions 1924. D. 1931.

Munro, Robert (Lord Alness) B. 1868, Alness, Ross-shire. Educ. Edinburgh University. Advocate 1893. K.C. 1910. M.P. (Lib.) Wick Burghs Jan. 1910-18; Roxburgh 1918-22. Lord Advocate 1913-16; Secretary for Scotland 1916-22. Lord Justice-Clerk 1922-33. D.1955.

Shinwell, Emanuel B. London 1884, soon moved to Tyneside. Seamen's union organiser, South Shields, 1906; frequent waterfront battles with members of rival union led by Havelock Wilson. Moved to Glasgow just before 1914-18 war. Delegate, later chairman, Glasgow Trades Council till 1922. Member, I.L.P. and Labour Party, 1906 to 1982, when he resigned Labour Whip in Lords on account of leftward trends in Labour Party. M.P. (Lab.) West Lothian 1922-4, 1928-31; Seaham Harbour (later Easington) 1935 (defeating Ramsay MacDonald) to 1970. Baron Shinwell 1970. Parliamentary secretary, Board of Trade (Mines Dept), 1924. Parliamentary secretary War Office 1929-30. Secretary for Mines 1930-1. Minister of Fuel and Power 1945-7. Secretary of State for War 1947–50. Minister of Defence 1950–1. D. London 1986.

Stephen, Rev. Campbell B. 1884. Educ. Glasgow University and Glasgow U.F. Theological College. Minister, Ardrossan U.F. Church 1911-18. Qualified as barrister. M.P. (Lab.-I.L.P-Lab.) Glasgow Camlachie 1922-31, 1935-47. D. October 1947, four days after rejoining Labour Party. A man of impressive paper qualifications.

Weir, William (1st Viscount Weir) B. Glasgow 1877. Joined family firm of G. & J. Weir 1893; managing director 1902, chairman, 1912. (Self-) Appointed Director of Munitions for Scotland 1915. Aggressive dilutionist 'against every instinct of the industry' *(D.N.B.)*. Knighted 1917; Baron 1918; Viscount 1938. Controller of aeronautical supplies, later director-general of aircraft production 1917; Air Minister 1918. Various official committees after war. Adviser of Air Minister 1935-8. Relatively minor offices, 1939-42. D. Giffnock 1959.

Wheatley, John B. Co. Waterford 1869. Family emigrated to Bargeddie, Lanarkshire, 1878. Miner 1880-93, later grocer, reporter, advertisement canvasser, printer and publisher (from 1912). Supporter of U.I.L. Joined I.L.P. 1908; founded Catholic Socialist Society. Member (Lab.) Glasgow Corporation 1910-22; leader of Labour group. M.P. (Lab.) Glasgow Shettleston 1922-30. Minister of Health 1924, responsible for housing legislation. Associated with I.L.P. left wing after 1924; not offered office 1929. D. Shettleston 1930. A shrewd socialist entrepreneur.

Wood, Thomas McKinnon B. 1855, Stepney, of Scottish parentage. Educ. Mill Hill School and University College, London. Member (Progressive), London County Council 1892-1909; leader of Progressive group on council for some years. M.P. (Lib.) Glasgow St. Rollox 1906-18. Parliamentary secretary, Board of Education 1908; undersecretary of state, Foreign Office 1908-11; Financial Secretary to Treasury 1911-12; Secretary for Scotland 1912-16. Lost seat (and deposit) in rout of Asquith Liberals, 1918. D. London, 1927.

Notes

Introduction

1. *Glasgow Herald*, 20 November 1922, p.12.
2. C. Harvie, *No Gods and Precious Few Heroes: Scotland 1914-80* (London, Edward Arnold, 1981).

Chapter 1

1. H. Clegg, A. Fox and A. F. Thompson, *A History of British Trade Unions since 1889*, vol. 1 (Oxford, Clarendon Press, 1964), p.297.
2. J. B. Jefferys, *The Story of the Engineers* (London, Lawrence & Wishart, 1945), p.141.
3. F. W. Hirst, 'The Policy of the Engineers', *Economic Journal*, VIII, 29, 1898, p.124.
4. Ibid., pp.125-7.
5. Clegg *et al*, *British Trade Unions*, p.161.
6. Jefferys, *Engineers*, p.145.
7. Jefferys, *Engineers*, p.171.
8. W. Thomson, 'Some Factors Affecting the Economical Manufacture of Marine-Engines', *Proceedings of the Institution of Mechanical Engineers*, 1901, pp.883-4.
9. Lt-Col. R. E. Crompton, discussing paper on 'Modern Machine Methods', *Proc. Inst. Mech. Eng.*, 1902, pp.65-6.
10. *Proc. Inst. Mech. Eng.*, 1910, p.929.
11. Jefferys, *Engineers*, Introduction to Part Three, *passim*; J. Hinton, 'Rank and File Militancy in the British Engineering Industry', London University Ph.D thesis 1969, pp.32-40.
12. Clegg *et al*, *British Trade Unions*, p.129.
13. Amalgamated Society of Engineers, *Monthly Journal and Report*, January 1901, p.52.
14. A.S.E. *Monthly Record*, November 1906.
15. Hinton thesis, Ch. 4.
16. Lower case letters in original. But the workers' union was indeed the Workers' Union.
17. A.S.E. *Monthly Record*, June 1913, p.43. Quoted in part by R. Hyman, 'The Workers' Union 1898-1929', Oxford University D.Phil thesis 1968, Ch. 3.
18. Jefferys, *Engineers*, 166; cf.also Clegg *et al*, *British Trade Unions*, pp.342-3.
19. Jefferys, *Engineers*, p.166.

20. *The Treasury Agreement*. Published as pamphlet by the A.S.E., 1915. Copy in Cole Collection, Nuffield College Library, Oxford.

21. J. T. Murphy, *New Horizons* (London, John Lane, 1941), p.46.

22. Quoted in Hinton, thesis, p.222. This point was appreciated by Christopher Addison, who became Parliamentary Under-secretary at the Ministry of Munitions: see Addison Papers, Bodleian Library, Oxford, Box 55: 'Memo. on the difficulties of dilution', August 1916, and C. Addison, *Politics from Within* (2 vols., London, Herbert Jenkins, 1924), I, pp.187, 192. But the Ministry could never do anything about it.

23. Especially W. Gallacher, *Revolt on the Clyde* (London, Lawrence & Wishart, 1936); W. Gallacher, *Last Memoirs* (London, Lawrence & Wishart, 1966); D. Kirkwood, *My Life of Revolt* (London, Harrap, 1935); T. Bell, *Pioneering Days* (London, Lawrence & Wishart, 1941); E. Shinwell, *Conflict without Malice* (London, Odhams, 1955); H. McShane and J. Smith, *Harry McShane: No Mean Fighter* (London, Pluto Press, 1978).

24. *Forward*, 12 December 1914, p.1.

25. *Forward*, 6 March 1915, p.5.

26. *History of the Ministry of Munitions* (London, H.M.S.O., 12 vols. in parts, n.d.) vol. IV, part ii, pp.36-7. Hereafter cited as *HMM* followed by volume no., part no., and page.

27. W. Weir and J. R. Richmond, 'Workshop Methods: Some Efficiency Factors in an Engineering Business', *Proc. Inst. Mech. Eng.* 1901, p.895; C. Addison, *Four and a Half Years* (London, Hutchinson 1934, 2 vols.), I, p.135; Bell, *Pioneering Days*, p.109.

28. From question signed 'J. Hislop', submitted to Lloyd George before his meeting with shop stewards on Christmas Day 1915 (see Ch. 5). In file marked 'Questions and Answers for Meeting of A.S.E. [sic] concerning Munitions of War Act', Beveridge Collection on Munitions, British Library of Political and Economic Science, Vol. III, no. 9, folio 59. Hereafter cited as *BCM* followed by volume no., piece no., and folio.

29. A.S.E. *Monthly Record*, January 1913, p.59.

30. *HMM*, IV, ii, 38; *Daily Record* 19 February 1915, p.3.

31. *Glasgow Herald*, 26 February 1915, p.11.

32. *Glasgow Herald*, 18 February 1915, p.15.

33. Gallacher, *Revolt*, p.42.

34. Clegg *et al*, *British Trade Unions*, pp.342-3.

35. Gallacher, *Revolt*, pp.37 and 81-3.

36. A.S.E. *Monthly Journal and Report*, December 1917, p.4 and January 1918, p.4.

37. See below, Ch. 10.

38. Bell, *Pioneering Days*, p.162.

39. *HMM*, IV, ii, p.40.

40. *Daily Record*, 1 March 1915, p.4.

41. *HMM*, IV, ii, p.43.

42. *HMM*, IV, ii, p.41.

43. Gallacher, *Revolt*, p.51.

44. J. Melling, 'The Glasgow Rent Strike and Clydeside Labour — some problems of interpretation', *Scottish Labour History Society Journal*, 13, 1979, pp.39-44, quoted at p.41.

45. Information derived from a summary of the returns from the A.S.E. questionnaire made by Herbert Highton. Highton Collection, Glasgow University Archives.

46. Interview, ISMcL with the late (2nd) Lord Kirkwood, March 1970.
47. Kirkwood, *My Life of Revolt*, pp.68, 78-80.
48. Interview, Lord Kirkwood; J. Hume and M. Moss, *Beardmore: the history of a Scottish industrial giant* (London, Heinemann, 1979), Ch. 4.
49. Kirkwood, *My Life of Revolt*, pp.92-100.

Chapter 2

1. Addison's diary for 1 August 1916. Addison Papers, Box 89. Quoted in part in Addison, *Politics from Within*, I, 194, and in part in Addison, 4½ *Years*, I, 236. The draft Ministerial statements with references to the Scottish Office typed in and then deleted again are in the Lloyd George Papers (formerly at the Beaverbrook Library, now at the House of Lords Record Office), D/11/3/9.
2. Memorandum to the Cabinet by T. McKinnon Wood, 17 November 1915. Public Record Office: CAB 37/137, no.29.
3. D. Englander, 'Landlord and Tenant in Urban Scotland: the background to the Clyde rent strikes, 1915', *Scottish Labour History Society Journal*, no.15, 1981, pp.4-14.
4. R. Baird, 'Housing', in J. Cunnison and J. Gilfillan, eds., *The Third Statistical Account of Scotland: Glasgow* (Glasgow, Collins, 1958), pp. 448-74; R. Smith, 'Multi-dwelling Building in Scotland 1750-1970', in A. Sutcliffe, ed., *Multi-storey living: the British working-class experience* (London, Croom Helm, 1974), pp.207-43.
5. *HMM*, IV, iv, 29. Cf. also this discussion between Addison, his officials, and a deputation from the A.S.E. in 1917:
Sir Stephenson Kent: We have a great number of complaints from Englishmen working in Scotland saying that they do not like the climate and would very much like to come south.
Mr. Gorman: They object to the climate?
Sir Stephenson Kent: Yes, and the food.
Mr. Gorman, I do not wonder at that.
(Addison Papers, Box 70).
6. *HMM*, IV, ii, 43-4.
7. Cd 2669, 1917, para.8.
8. Minutes of the Glasgow Trades Council (hereafter cited as *TCM*), Mitchell Library, Glasgow, 16 September 1914.
9. *TCM*, 21 April 1915.
10. *Forward*, 25 July, 1 August and 8 August 1914.
11. C. A. Oakley, *The Last Tram* (Glasgow, Glasgow Corporation Transport Department, 1962), p.55.
12. *Forward*, 26 December 1914.
13. *Forward*, 27 February 1915, letter from McBride, p.3.
14. Objects of Glasgow Labour Party Housing Association (1915). Pasted into minute book of Glasgow Central Labour Party. Mitchell Library, Glasgow.
15. *Forward*, 5 June 1915, p.1.
16. *Forward*, 12 June 1915, p.1.
17. *HMM*, IV, ii, 103.
18. Quoted in letter from McBride to *Forward*, 5 June 1915.

19. *HMM*, IV, ii, 103-4.

20. *Forward*, 30 October and 13 November 1915.

21. CAB 37/137, no.29.

22. Ibid.

23. Ibid.

24. Chamberlain to L.G., 5 July 1915. L.G. Papers, D/16/7/1.

25. L.G. to Chamberlain, 8 July 1915. L.G. Papers, D/16/7/2.

26. Chamberlain to L.G., 9 July 1915. L.G. Papers, D/16/7/3.

27. St. Davids to L.G., 9 October 1915. L.G. Papers, D/18/12/3.

28. L.G. to St. Davids, 11 October 1915. L.G. Papers, D/18/12/4.

29. I.e., presumably, England.

30. Increase of Rent and Mortgage Interest: draft bill and memorandum by Walter Long. CAB 37/138 No.3.

31. *Parliamentary Debates (Commons), Fifth Series*, vol. 76, col.433. Hereafter cited as *H.C. Debs.* followed by vol. no. and column no.

32. *H.C. Debs.*, 76, 441.

33. *HMM*, IV, ii, 105; Gallacher, *Revolt*, 53-4.

34. *Forward*, 27 November 1915, p.1.

35. *H.C. Debs.*, 76, 447.

36. *HMM*, IV, ii, 105; T. Bell, *John Maclean: a fighter for freedom* (Glasgow, Communist Party, Scottish Committee, 1944), p.50.

37. Gallacher, *Revolt*, p.55.

38. *HMM*, IV, ii, 105; *Forward*, 27 November 1915, p.1.

39. *H. C. Debs.*, 76, 442.

40. MacLean Papers (National Library of Scotland), File 1, *passim*.

41. 'Saturday first' is a Scottish way of saying 'next Saturday'.

42. Quoted in *HMM*, IV, ii, 105.

43. There is nothing in the series of letters to the King reporting Cabinet proceedings (CAB 41). A search through the papers of relevant Ministers also drew a blank.

44. *HMM*, IV, ii, 103.

45. *H.C. Debs.*, 76, 749.

46. *Vanguard*, December 1915. Copy in MacLean Papers.

47. Gallacher, *Revolt*, p.52.

48. *HMM*, IV, ii, 43.

Chapter 3

1. See p.13 above.

2. G. M. Booth, a member of a shipping dynasty, and Sir Percy Girouard, a former colonial governor and railway administrator, were at the centre of Lloyd George's move to take control of munitions out of the hands of Kitchener and the War Office, being appointed in March 1915 as members of a committee to increase the supply of armaments, responsible not to the War Office but to the Treasury. *HMM*, I, iii, 61; D. Crow, *A Man of Push and Go: the life of George Macaulay Booth* (London, Hart-Davis, 1965), pp.90-120.

3. Llewellyn Smith's punctuation.

4. Llewellyn Smith to Lloyd George, 31 May 1915. L.G. Papers, D1/2/3.

5. Robert Wallace, K.C., to Lloyd George, 17 July 1915. L.G. Papers, D/11/1/6.

6. Lord Askwith, *Industrial Problems and Disputes* (London, John Murray, 1920), pp.395, 412.

7. My view concurs with that of José Harris in her *William Beveridge: a biography* (Oxford, Clarendon Press, 1977), pp.214-5. For an example of Lloyd George's inconsistency, see his claim to Frances Stevenson that the suppression of the *Forward* in January 1916 was a mistake into which he was dragged by blunders in the Labour Department. F. Stevenson, *Lloyd George — a Diary* (ed. Taylor) (London, Hutchinson, 1971), p.88.

8. Addison Papers, Box 15, *passim;* 'Investigation into Shortage of Output at Projectile Factories', Box 16.

9. A. J. Balfour was First Lord of the Admiralty throughout the First Coalition.

10. Addison's diary for 8 March 1916, Addison Papers, Box 97. Cf. Addison, *Politics from Within*, I, p.191; 4½ *Years*, I, pp.180-1.

11. See, for instance, his article in *Proc. Inst. Mech. Eng.* 1901, pp.895-907.

12. Dunlop, Brenner & Co. Ltd. to Secretary, Munitions Parliamentary Committee, 23 October 1915. Addison Papers, Box 55.

13. *HMM*, IV, i, 1.

14. Addison, diary for 6 July 1915. Addison, 4½ *Years*, I, p.103.

15. Addison diary for 16 August 1915. Addison, 4½ *Years*, I, pp.117-8.

16. Addison, 4½ *Years*, I, p.126; Addison, *Politics from Within*, I, pp.178-80.

17. *HMM*, IV, i, 2 and 16.

18. *HMM*, IV, i, 15; cf. also paper by C. F. Rey on W.M.V. scheme, Addison Papers, Box 16.

19. Askwith, *Industrial Problems*, p.371.

20. 'Labour Policy — Preliminary Note'. Initialled H. Ll. S. *BCM* I, 15, 365.

21. Addison, 4½ *Years*, I, pp.120-1.

22. A. Duckham to Lloyd George, 2 September 1915. L.G. Papers, D/11/3/4.

23. Addison, 4½ *Years*, I, pp.126-7. 19 September 1915.

24. *HMM*, IV, i, 2, fn.1.

25. Addison to Henderson, 14 October 1915. *BCM*, IV, 24, 137.

26. Ministry of Munitions Circular L6. Reproduced in *HMM*, IV, i, 108-9.

27. Addison, 4½ *Years*, I, p.85. 28 May 1915.

28. Addison, 4½ *Years*, I, p.135. 11 October 1915.

29. Ministry of Munitions, Report of the Labour Department September 1915. *BCM*, II, 8, 130.

30. Minutes of Proceedings of a Deputation from the Amalgamated Society of Engineers, 17 September 1915. Ministry of Munitions Records (Public Record Office), MUN 5/57. Hist. Rec. 320/4.

31. *BCM*, III, 8, 39-41.

32. Addison, 4½ *Years*, I, pp.126-7.

33. MUN 5/70. 324/2.

34. MUN 5/73. Notes by Mr. Beveridge for Minister's Meeting with A.S.E. Executive Committee, 11 February 1916. 324/15/8.

35. Clyde Workers' Committee, 'To All Clyde Workers' [November 1915]. *BCM*, III, 15, 95. Another copy in Highton Papers, Glasgow University Archives.

36. See below, p.41.

37. T. Wilson, ed., *The Political Diaries of C. P. Scott* (London, Collins, 1970), p.150; entry for 26 October 1915. Stress in original; the context makes it clear that industrial conscription is meant. Cf. also Scott's note of a discussion with Lord Derby on 15 October — p.145.

38. *HMM*, IV, ii, 48.

39. See below, p.62.

40. *Times*, 31 May 1915, quoted by *Forward*, 5 June 1915.

41. All quotations in this paragraph are from Mitchell to Llewellyn Smith, 21 February 1916: *BCM*, III, 44, 356-7. The relevant paragraphs are reproduced in full in my D.Phil thesis 'The Labour Movement in Clydeside Politics 1914-22', Oxford 1971, pp.116-7.

Chapter 4

1. *HMM*, IV, i, 36.

2. Both quotations from A. S. E. *Monthly Journal and Report*, October 1915, p.13.

3. *HMM*, IV, 37-41.

4. *HMM*, IV, i, 37.

5. Central Munitions Labour Supply Committee, Memo. no. 39. 3 November 1915. *BCM*, IV, 39, 224.

6. Ibid.

7. Report by J. Paterson in folder marked 'Material supplied to the Minister before Tyne and Clyde visits', December 1915. MUN 5/73.

8. Underlined in original.

9. Report by J. Paterson, as above. MUN 5/73.

10. Ibid.

11. E.g. R. K. Middlemas, *The Clydesiders: a left-wing struggle for parliamentary power* (London, Hutchinson, 1965), Ch. 3; W. Kendall, *The Revolutionary Movement in Britain 1900-21* (London, Weidenfeld & Nicolson, 1969), Ch. 7. The first scholar to study these events from primary sources, Dr. James Hinton, initially leant towards the version of events propounded by the C.W.C., but in more recent work has taken a view closer to the present version of the relative importance of Lang's and the C.W.C. See Hinton thesis; J. Hinton, 'The Clyde Workers' Committee and the Dilution Struggle', in A. Briggs and J. Saville, eds., *Essays in Labour History 1886-1923* (London, Macmillan, 1971), pp.152-184; I. S. McLean, 'The Ministry of Munitions, the Clyde Workers' Committee, and the suppression of the "Forward": an alternative view', *Scottish Labour History Society Journal*, 6, 1972, pp.3-25; J. Hinton, 'The Suppression of the *Forward* — a Note', *Scottish Labour History Society Journal*, 7, 1973, pp.24-9; J. Hinton, *The First Shop Stewards' Movement* (London, Allen & Unwin, 1973), Chs. 2-4.

12. Report on the Working of the Munitions Act. Fortnight ended 11 September 1915. Captain Superintendent's Remarks. *BCM*, III, 1, 1.

13. Addison, 4½ *Years*, I, p.142.

14. *HMM*, IV, ii, 52-3.

15. A copy of the Govan Trades Council circular in MUN 5/79 in a file dealing with the negotiations to release the prisoners.

16. Quoted in *HMM*, IV, ii, 55. The original letters seem not to have survived as

they were not collected into the files from which the *History* was written (now MUN 5).

17. *HMM*, IV, ii, 56.

18. *HMM*, IV, ii, 58.

19. *Forward*, 18 September 1915; 9 October 1915.

20. *HMM*, IV, ii, 55.

21. *HMM*, IV, ii, 60.

22. *Forward*, 6 November 1915, p.8; Bell, *John Maclean*, p.36.

23. The Minister of Munitions.

24. Cd 8136, paras 17-18. Printed as appendix to *HMM*, IV, ii, pp.110-1. Another copy, with Ministry notes on action to be taken, is in MUN 5/73.

25. Memorandum on the Progress of Dilution on the Clyde, 5 February 1916, by Lynden Macassey. MUN 5/73.

26. Notes relating Cd 8136 to proposals in the Amending Bill, December 1915. MUN 5/73.

27. Quoted in document headed 'Criticism of methods of dilution: notes for Mr. Lloyd George by Mr. Weir, December 1915'. MUN 5/73. This is quite likely the letter referred to sceptically by Addison in his diary entry of 11 October — see note 28 to Ch. 3 above.

28. Ibid.

29. All quotations in this paragraph are from J. Paterson, Report in file marked 'Material supplied to the Minister before Tyne and Clyde visits', December 1915. MUN 5/73.

30. R. Williamson to T. J. Macnamara, 27 October 1915. L.G. Papers, D/17/13/2.

31. Macnamara to Lloyd George, October 1915. L.G. Papers, D/17/13/3.

32. Above, Ch. 3 note 35.

33. *BCM*, III, 15, 94.

34. William Gallacher and James Messer.

35. *BCM*, III, 15, 98-9.

36. *BCM*, III, 15, 102. L.G. may have meant the Lord Advocate; there is no trace of an Attorney-General's opinion in this voluminous file.

37. Macnamara to Addison, 1 December 1915. *BCM*, III, 15, 101.

38. Note by Robert Munro, Lord Advocate, 16 December 1915. *BCM*, III, 15, 106.

39. *BCM*, III, 15, 104.

40. *HMM*, IV, ii, 81.

41. Addison, $4\frac{1}{2}$ *Years*, I, p.135.

42. *HMM* IV, ii, 81.

43. Notes on proposed amendments to Munitions of War (Amendment) Bill, n.d., unsigned and fragmentary. *B.C.M.*, III, 5, 20.

44. *H.C. Debs.*, 77, 878-81.

45. *H.C. Debs.*, 77, 1404.

Chapter 5

1. Central Munitions Labour Supply Committee, Memo. no. 22, n.d. [Oct. 1915]. *BCM*, IV, 22, 130.

2. Henderson to Lloyd George, 22 October 1915. *BCM*, IV, 32, 173.

3. MUN 5/73.

4. MUN 5/73. 324/15/2.

5. *HMM,* IV, iv, 103; *Forward,* 1 January 1916, p.5.

6. *TCM,* 22 December 1915.

7. Kirkwood, *My Life of Revolt,* pp.104-9; *Forward,* 1 January 1916, p.5; *Worker,* 8 January 1916.

8. *Worker,* 8 January 1916; *HMM,* IV, iv, 103-5.

9. Gallacher, *Revolt,* pp. 81-2.

10. *Forward,* 1 January 1916, p.5.

11. Gallacher, *Revolt,* p.88.

12. *Forward,* 1 January 1916, p.5.

13. Kirkwood, *My Life of Revolt,* p.94.

14. Kirkwood, *My Life of Revolt,* p.109; *Forward,* 1 January 1916, p.5.

15. *Forward,* 1 January 1916.

16. Kirkwood, *My Life of Revolt,* p.111.

17. Ibid.

18. T. Bell, *Pioneering Days* (London, Lawrence & Wishart, 1941), p.98.

19. J. McGovern, *Neither Fear nor Favour* (London, Blandford Press, 1960), p.43.

20. All comments in brackets are reported interruptions taken from the account in the suppressed issue of the *Forward,* 1 January 1916, p.5. After the suppression, Army officers solemnly went round confiscating every copy they could find. Fortunately, they did not confiscate the copy lodged in the National Library of Scotland under the Copyright Act.

21. Press Bureau Notice, 7.25 p.m. 24 December 1915. MUN 5/70.

22. *Glasgow Herald,* 27 December 1915.

23. *Forward,* 1 January 1916, p.5.

24. C. F. Rey, an assistant secretary in the Labour Department of the Ministry.

25. *HMM,* IV, iv, 111.

26. Ibid.

27. *H.C. Debs.,* 77, 801; 'Notes on the suppression of Forward', initialled W. H. B. MUN 5/70.

28. *H.C. Debs.,* 77, 801-4.

29. Ibid, 804.

30. *Forward,* 5 February 1916, p.5.

31. Ibid.

32. T. Brotherstone, 'The Suppression of the Forward', *Scottish Labour History Society Journal,* 1, 1969; McLean, 'Ministry of Munitions ...' (for full reference see Ch. 4, n.11).

33. W. H. Beveridge, *Power and Influence* (London, Hodder & Stoughton, 1953), p.133. Dr. Harris *(William Beveridge,* 222-3), on the other hand, describes Beveridge's 'Notes on the Suppression' as 'written in a tone, not of cold political calculation, but of highly emotional indignation' (p.222). However, this is not incompatible with Beveridge's claimed lack of enthusiasm *for preparing a brief for Lloyd George.* Beveridge genuinely detested the *Forward* but clearly also realised that Lloyd George's defence of his actions rested on a shaky interpretation of the Defence of the Realm Regulations.

34. The principal memoranda, all in MUN 5/70, are 'Notes on the Suppression',

initialled W. H. B; 'Regulations under which the *Forward* was suppressed', also initialled W. H. B; and the 'Points likely to be made against the Minister', unsigned.

35. D/27/1.
36. See n.27 above.
37. 'Notes on the Suppression'. MUN 5/70.
38. 'Note by T. B. Morison [Solicitor-General for Scotland] on the suppression forwarded by Mr. Munro [Lord Advocate]', 9 January 1916. MUN 5/70.
39. 'Regulations under which Forward was suppressed', MUN 5/70.
40. 'Notes on the Suppression', MUN 5/70.
41. Notes from Intelligence Officer, Glasgow, to Lt.Col. Levita, General Staff, Scottish Command. MUN 5/70.
42. *H.C. Debs.*, 77, 1417.
43. See Ch. 4. n.30 above.
44. From the large collection (presumably the fruit of the military labour) in MUN 5/70.
45. Advocate Depute's opinion on 'Forward', socialist newspaper. 8 October 1914. Scottish Record Office: HH 31/5. File 25478/250.
46. HH 31/5 No. 25478/3791. May 1915. The notes may be from one civil servant to another, or from a civil servant to a Scottish Office minister — I cannot identify either writer's handwriting. 'Put up' means 'File and take no action'.
47. Beveridge, *Power and Influence*, p.133.
48. L.G. Papers D/27/1.
49. Beveridge, *Power and Influence*, p.133.
50. *H.C. Debs.*, 77, 1404.
51. See T. Johnston, *Memories* (London, Collins, 1952), pp.32-3.
52. Brotherstone, 'Suppression of the Forward', p.15.
53. *H.C. Debs.*, 77, 1404-5.
54. See Johnston's mightily aggrieved defence of himself in *Forward*, 5 February 1916.
55. As quoted in *H.C. Debs.*, 77, 1413.
56. Copied out in 'Notes on the Suppression', MUN 5/70.
57. *Glasgow Herald*, 12 January 1916.
58. *HMM*, IV, iv, 114.
59. A. Marwick, *The Deluge* (London, Bodley Head, 1965), p.73.
60. Brotherstone, 'Suppression of the Forward', p.18.
61. See above, Ch. 4, n.37.
62. *Worker*, 8 January 1916.
63. *HMM*, IV, iv, 123. Of course, Lloyd George argued that it was not only for this report that the *Forward* was suppressed. But the bulk of the case made out in the Ministry against the paper was based on this report; it was because of this report that action was originally taken; the other offences mentioned by Lloyd George mostly originated from his fertile imagination. If the authorities had really wanted to suppress the *Worker*, they would have thrown the same Defence of the Realm Regulations at it as they did at the *Forward*.
64. *HMM*, IV, iv, 111.
65. Notes from Intelligence Officer . . . Particulars of *Vanguard*, n.d. MUN 5/70. The raid took place on 3rd January.

66. Copy in MacLean Papers.
67. Brotherstone, 'Suppression of the Forward', pp.12, 18.
68. 'Notes on the Suppression', MUN 5/70.
69. See E. T. Cook, *The Press in Wartime* (London, Macmillan, 1920), pp. 57-117, esp. pp. 79, 91. Cook was Press Censor for most of the war.
70. T. Johnston, 'An Appraisal from the Left', in *The Glasgow Herald 1783-1958* (Glasgow, *Glasgow Herald*, 1958), p.20.
71. Brotherstone, 'Suppression of the Forward', p.17.
72. E.g. Marwick, *Deluge*, p.73; A. J. P. Taylor, *English History 1914-45* (Oxford, Clarendon Press, 1965), p.39; Kendall, *Revolutionary Movement*, p.123. The correct sequence, however, is in Anon [T. Henderson], *The Scottish Socialists: a gallery of contemporary portraits* (London, Faber & Faber, 1931), p.125.
73. *HMM*, IV, iv, 111. In my article 'The Ministry of Munitions, the Clyde Workers' Committee and the Suppression of the Forward . . .', published in 1972, I wrongly stated that Lloyd George was not present, quoting Frances Stevenson, to whom Lloyd George complained that the suppression was all the fault of the Labour Department of the Ministry of Munitions, who 'are continually letting him down'. This was blatant buck-passing, which I failed to spot. Stevenson, *Lloyd George — a Diary*, p.88: entry for 21 January 1916.
74. 'Notes on the Suppression', MUN 5/70.
75. *Forward*, 1 January 1916, p.5; *H.C. Debs.*, 77, 1411.
76. 24 April 1915 and 1 January 1916.
77. See below, Ch. 6.
78. *HMM*, IV, ii, 48.
79. *H.C. Debs.*, 77, 1416.

Chapter 6

1. *TCM*, 5 January 1916.
2. Reproduced in full in my D.Phil. thesis, pp.114-5. As it is in the Beveridge papers (*BCM*, III, 16, 109-11), Llewellyn Smith obviously failed to treat it as strictly personal.
3. *BCM*, III, 36, 231.
4. He does not say which Act: probably the Defence of the Realm Act.
5. *BCM*, III, 36, 231.
6. W. J. Reader, *Architect of Air Power* (London, Collins, 1968), p.54.
7. Hinton, *Shop Stewards' Movement*, p.143.
8. 'List of points relating to dilution policy', n.d. Unsigned but in Llewellyn Smith's handwriting. *BCM*, III, 34, 218.
9. 'Dilution on the Tyne and Clyde', minute by Rey to the Minister, 18 January 1916. *BCM*, III, 35, 222.
10. Addison's diary, Addison Papers, Box 97. The last sentence was deleted from the version of the diary prepared for publication.
11. 'Summary of Dilution Programmes based (with modifications) on Mr. Weir's Memo.' MUN 5/70, 324/5.
12. Llewellyn Smith's undated memorandum comes before Rey's note dated 18 January in the Beveridge collection. More conclusively, Rey's note, although dated on

the same day as Weir's memorandum, was clearly prepared before the latter reached the Ministry.

13. *H.C. Debs.*, 78, 766. A draft of the statement is in MUN 5/70.

14. Addison, 4½ *Years*, I, 162.

15. Draft in MUN 5/70; final version printed as Appendix XVII to *HMM* IV, iv, at pp.173-4.

16. Central Munitions Labour Supply Committee, Sub-committee on wages, draft statement, n.d. [September 1915]. *BCM*, III, 10, 71-2.

17. Mary Macarthur, secretary of the Women's Trade Union League.

18. Askwith to Beveridge, 29 September 1915. *BCM*, III, 10, 66.

19. Beveridge to Askwith, 4 October 1915. *BCM*, III, 10, 63-4.

20. Circular L2, as reproduced in *HMM*, IV, i, 103.

21. Notes by Llewellyn Smith for the Prime Minister concerning A.S.E. deputation on dilution, 31 December 1915. MUN 5/70, 324/2.

22. Transcript of the proceedings in MUN 5/70, 324/3; text of resolution in *HMM*, IV, i, 87-8.

23. Quoted in *HMM*, IV, iv, 120. 29 January 1916.

24. *HMM*, IV, iv, 122.

25. MUN 5/73, 324/15/6.

26. *BCM*, V, 4, 28.

27. Ibid.

28. Quoted in Notes by Mr. Beveridge for Minister's Meeting with A.S.E. Executive Council 11 February 1916. MUN 5/73.

29. Ibid.

30. *HMM*, IV, iv, 123.

31. Minutes of a Conference with the Amalgamated Society of Engineers on Dilution, 24 February 1916. MUN 5/70.

32. See below, pp.71-2.

33. *HMM*, IV, iv, 123.

34. Addison's diary, 24 February 1916. Addison Papers, Box 89.

35. *BCM*, V, 15, 86-95.

36. Mitchell to (?) Llewellyn Smith, n.d. but received 6 March 1916, 'The Difficulties Still to be Overcome'. Marginal note in Addison's handwriting. Addison Papers, Box 56.

37. Minutes of the Proceedings at a Conference with a Deputation from the A.S.E., 27 April 1916. MUN 5/57.

38. Both quotations from Mitchell to Llewellyn Smith, 21 February 1916. *BCM*, III, 44, 356-7.

39. Mitchell to (?) Llewellyn Smith, received 6 March 1916. Addison Papers Box 56.

40. Addison's diary for 15 March 1916. Addison Papers, Box 89.

41. See, respectively, 1) Memo on the Progress of Dilution, 5 February, MUN 5/73; 2) The Industrial Situation on the Clyde, 9 February MUN 5/73; 3) Addison diary 15 March, Addison Papers Box 89; 4) Addison diary 23 March, Addison Papers Box 89.

42. Mitchell to Llewellyn Smith, 21 February 1916. *BCM*, III, 44, 356-7.

43. Clothing club.

44. Kirkwood, *My Life of Revolt*, p.116.

45. Ibid., pp.117-8.

46. Ibid., p.118.
47. Labour Party, *Report of a special committee appointed by the Annual Conference of the Party held at Manchester in January 1917 to inquire into and Report upon the circumstances which resulted in the Deportation in March 1916 of David Kirkwood and other workmen employed in Munition Factories in the Clyde District* (1918), para. 17. Hereafter cited as *Kirkwood Report*. Other versions of the Parkhead Agreement, with minor differences of wording, are in: HMM, IV iv, 129; Gallacher, *Revolt*, pp.103-4; *Forward*, 12 February 1916, p.1.
48. *Kirkwood Report*, para.18. This contradicts Button's statement at the conference with Lloyd George on February 24.
49. See above, n.31. Somebody must have told Lloyd George about the Parkhead agreement: very likely one of the Commissioners, in accordance with their policy of using the C.W.C. to threaten the A.S.E. Executive.
50. For Llewellyn Smith's interpretation in full, see *HMM*, IV, iv, 120.
51. Memo on Progress of Dilution by Lynden Macassey. 5 February 1916. MUN 5/73.
52. Ibid.
53. *Kirkwood Report*, para. 61.
54. Gallacher, *Revolt*, p.103.
55. *BCM*, V, 6, 37.
56. *BCM*, III, 36.
57. Macassey, memo of 5 February (as before). MUN 5/73.
58. Ibid.
59. Minute by Llewellyn Smith, 7 February 1916, attached to Macassey memo of 5 February. MUN 5/73.
60. Llewellyn Smith to Macassey, n.d., but on same file as preceding. MUN 5/73.
61. *Worker*, 29 January 1916.
62. *HMM*, IV, iv, 125.
63. 'The Industrial Situation on the Clyde', memo by Lynden Macassey, 9 February 1916. Incomplete. MUN 5/73.
64. See, e.g., Hinton thesis, Ch. 7 *passim*, esp. p.190; C. J. Wrigley, *David Lloyd George and the British Labour Movement* (Hassocks, Sussex, Harvester, 1976), p.161. Harris's review of the whole controversy (*William Beveridge*, 215-227, esp. at p.226) concludes that while Hinton seriously overestimates the Ministry's repressiveness, my earlier work rather underestimates it.
65. Macassey to Addison, 31 January 1916. Addison Papers, Box 56.
66. *TCM*, 9 February 1916.
67. *HMM*, IV, iv, 125.
68. Gallacher, *Revolt*, p.102.
69. Macassey, memo of 9 February (as before). MUN 5/73.
70. *HMM*, IV, iv, 125.
71. Gallacher, *Revolt*, p.105.
72. Letter from Shop Stewards' Convener (name indecipherable because bottom of sheet is torn) to Herbert Highton, 20 October 1917. Highton Collection, Glasgow University Archives.
73. Gallacher, *Revolt*, 105.
74. *BCM*, V, 6, 37-8. Circulated by Beveridge, 15 February 1916.

75. *Kirkwood Report*, paras. 36-7.

Chapter 7

1. *Kirkwood Report*, para 61.
2. Ibid., para. 65.
3. *Report of the Findings of the [Clyde Dilution] Commission in regard to the alleged differences arising out of the dilution of labour between the Management and the Engineers at the Parkhead Forge Works of Wm. Beardmore & Co. Ltd.*, para.59. The report is dated July 1916 and marked *Proof*. It was never circulated or published, but a copy is in the Addison Papers, Box 56. It was made available to Arthur Henderson for the Labour Party enquiry, but he had to return his copy and its existence was never publicly acknowledged.
4. *Kirkwood Report*, para.74.
5. J. Hinton thesis, p.205; Hinton, 'The Suppression of the *Forward*', p.4
6. The eyewitness was the late (2nd) Lord Kirkwood. The newly available documents are in the Addison Papers, Box 56; especially the Commissioners' Report on Parkhead (see note 3 above; cited as *Commissioners' Report)* and a file marked 'Office Review of the Clyde Strike, Beardmore's'.
7. About 1 in 25 or 30, in fact.
8. Bell, *Pioneering Days*, p.29. See also Hume and Moss, *Beardmore*, Chs. 4 and 5 *passim*.
9. See Kirkwood's speech to the Labour Party Conference, 1917. *Report of the Sixteenth Annual Conference of the Labour Party, Manchester, 1917*, p.105. Hereafter cited as *L.P. Conference Report.*
10. *Kirkwood Report*, para.44.
11. Ibid., para.11.
12. 'Questions and Answers for meeting of A.S.E. concerning Munitions of War Act', *BCM*, III, 9, 59.
13. Kirkwood, *My Life of Revolt*, pp.96 and 123.
14. Ibid., p.96.
15. *Kirkwood Report*, para.61.
16. Kirkwood, *My Life of Revolt*, p.94.
17. Manifesto from the Parkhead Forge Engineers to their Fellow Workers. Highton Papers.
18. Ibid.
19. *HMM*, IV, iv, 130.
20. *H.C. Debs.*, 81, 564-5.
21. Ibid., 566-7.
22. Communication from Mitchell, 24 March 1916. 'Office Review of the Clyde Strike', Addison Papers Box 56.
23. Lord Crewe to George V, 30 March 1916. CAB 37/144. Reproduced from original in Royal Archives.
24. *H.C. Debs.*, 81, 990-2.
25. Gallacher, *Revolt*, p.107.
26. *H.C. Debs.*, 81, 992. Cf. also Addison, *Politics from Within* I, p.193: 'I am afraid I got across Pringle very badly . . . and he will not forgive me'.

27. Gallacher, *Revolt*, p.107.

28. J. T. Murphy, *Preparing for Power* (London, Jonathan Cape, 134), p.123.

29. Kirkwood, *My Life of Revolt*, p.117.

30. Macassey to Llewellyn Smith, 20 February 1916; Macassey to Addison, 4 June 1916. Both in Addison Papers, Box 56.

31. Addison's diary (original version), 15 March 1916. See also entries for 23 and 27 March. Addison Papers, Box 97. All these references are deleted from later versions (e.g. Box 89 and the two books).

32. H. Wolff to Addison, 3 April 1916. Addison Papers, Box 56.

33. J. A. Barlow (Addison's private secretary) to Macassey, 11 April 1916. Addison Papers, Box 56.

34. Barlow to Macassey, 12 June 1916. Addison Papers, Box 56.

35. 'Rob Roy' in *Forward*, 8 April 1916, p.2. Cf. also Johnston in *Forward*, 8 April 1916, p.1; STUC *Annual Report* 1917; *Kirkwood Report*, paras. 47 and 50.

36. Minutes of the Proceedings at a Conference with a Deputation from the A.S.E., 27 April 1916. MUN 5/57.

37. Addison, *Politics from Within*, I, p.193.

38. Macassey's six-monthly report, July 1916, p.7. In 'Office Review of the Clyde Strikes', Addison Papers, Box 56.

39. (Sir) Lynden Macassey, *Labour Policy, False and True* (London, Thornton Butterworth Ltd, 1922), p.79.

40. *Kirkwood Report*, para. 155.

41. HMM, IV, iv, 134. In the light of this, the lavish praise of Clark in the closing paragraphs of the *Commissioners' Report* seems rather hypocritical.

Chapter 8

1. Messer to Highton, 15 October 1917. Highton Papers.

2. *TCM* 29 March 1916. Original punctuation.

3. *TCM*: Executive Committee, 4 April 1916; full Council 5 April.

4. *Forward*, 15 April 1916, p.4.

5. *TCM*: full Council 12 April 1916; Executive Committee 15 April; 'Catholic Socialist Notes', *Forward*, 22 April 1916.

6. *Kirkwood Report*, para.155.

7. Levita to Addison, 20 May 1916; Addison memo 17 May 1916. Both in Box 56, Addison Papers.

8. *Forward*, 10 June 1916, p.2.

9. See, e.g. Addison, 4½ *Years*, I, p.188.

10. *L.P. Conference Report, 1917*, p.107.

11. Ibid., p.110.

12. The Central Munitions Labour Supply Committee.

13. Crewe to Lloyd George, 3 April 1916. L.G. Papers D/16/9/8.

14. STUC *Annual Report*, 1917, p.41.

15. *Kirkwood Report*, para.175.

16. Kirkwood to James Allan (secretary of the STUC), 24 November 1916. Quoted in STUC Annual Report 1917, p.41.

17. E.g. Bell, *Pioneering Days*, p.118.

---

18. Conference with Deputation from A.S.E., 27 April 1916. MUN 5/57.
19. *Forward*, 3 February 1917, p.2.
20. *L.P. Conference Report 1917*, p.106.
21. Ibid.
22. Ibid.
23. Ibid., pp.107-8.
24. *Forward*, 18 August 1917, p.2.
25. *Forward*, 1 September 1917; Kirkwood, *My Life of Revolt*, pp.164-7.
26. Not a deportee, but the shop steward to whose department the first women at Parkhead had come in February 1916, thus sparking off the crisis. *Kirkwood Report*, paras.61-70.
27. Kirkwood, *My Life of Revolt*, p.168.
28. Clyde Workers' Defence and Maintenance Fund, Financial Statement 1918. Highton Papers.
29. Notes for lecture on 'Labour on the Clyde and the Control of Industry', October 1917. Highton Papers.
30. Bell, *Pioneering Days*, p.56.
31. Murphy, *New Horizons*, pp.50-1.
32. Addison, 4½ *Years*, I, p.262.
33. Murphy, *New Horizons*, p.50.
34. Ibid., p.54.
35. Ibid., p.55.
36. Gallacher, *Revolt*, p.147; *Last Memoirs*, pp.97-8.
37. According to Harry McShane. McShane and Smith, *No Mean Fighter*, p.90.
38. *Forward*, 8 August 1914, p.1.
39. *Forward*, 15 August 1914, p.8; interview, ISMcL with Mr. J. H. Dollan, March 1970.
40. *TCM*, 18 April 1917, 2 May 1917.
41. *TCM*, 2 May 1917.
42. *TCM*, 6 June 1917.
43. Ibid.
44. *TCM*, Executive Committee, 3 July 1917.
45. Quoted by R. Munro in Memorandum to War Cabinet: 'Proposed prohibition of meeting at Glasgow', GT 1625, 6 August 1917. CAB 24/22.
46. Ibid.
47. 10 August.
48. This recorded a decision of the War Cabinet on 31 July to forbid soldiers from joining Soldiers' and Workmen's Councils, and to announce the Government's intention to enforce civil and military law at public meetings. 'In reaching these decisions the War Cabinet did not overlook the fact that they would have to enforce their policy in all circumstances.' W.C. 200, 31 July 1917. CAB 23/3.
49. War Cabinet 207, minute 6. CAB 23/3.
50. *TCM: EC*, 6 August 1917.
51. *TCM*, 28 August 1917.
52. *TCM, EC*, 26 September 1917.
53. Kirkwood, *My Life of Revolt*, p.171 (mistakenly dating the Council to 1918); Murphy, *New Horizons*, p.63.

54. *Forward*, 19 May 1917, p.2.
55. *Forward*, 16 June 1917, p.4.
56. Ibid., p.2.
57. STUC *Annual Report* 1916, p.56.
58. STUC *Annual Report* 1917, p.50.
59. Ibid., p.49.
60. *Forward*, 13 May 1916, p.2.
61. *Forward*, 8 May 1915, p.3.
62. *Forward*, 12 May 1917, p.4.
63. *Forward*, 11 May 1918, p.1.
64. *Forward*, 30 December 1916.
65. Ibid.
66. See, for instance, the not unsympathetic articles on 'Clyde Labour' by 'A Special Correspondent', 9 to 12 October 1917.

Chapter 9

1. E.g. Kendall, *Revolutionary Movement*, pp.13-14; Middlemas, *Clydesiders*, p.111.
2. For instance John MacLean: 'He was opposed to the Catholic Church in a calvinist way as well as a marxist way, and he never got on with Wheatley' — McShane, *No Mean Fighter*, p.56.
3. *Forward*, 9 October 1915.
4. *Forward*, 21 April 1917. The Cameronians were followers of Richard Cameron, who fought on in south-west Scotland for the Covenant in the 1680s when it was a totally lost cause. They refused to swear allegiance to an uncovenanted state. Incongruously, they gave their name to a regiment of the British Army.
5. *Forward*, 5 June 1920. Not only socialist organisations used the symbols of the 1630s: the Ulster Covenant of 1912 and the nationalist Scottish Covenant of 1950 both likewise drew their inspiration from the original National Covenant of 1638 and Solemn League and Covenant of 1643.
6. McShane, *No Mean Fighter*, p.74.
7. Kirkwood, *My Life of Revolt*, p.192.
8. Ibid. The meeting may have been religious in tone, but it made a profit of £30:0:9½d. *TCM: EC* 28 November 1922.
9. Psalm 124, Second Version, Scottish Metrical Psalter 1929. (The version was composed in the early 17th century.)
10. Johnston, *Memories*, p.102.
11. *H.C. Debs.*, 211, 2566-7.
12. Johnston, *Memories*, p.102.
13. Kirkwood, *My Life of Revolt*, p.20.
14. 'I'm a shop steward. We represent the rank and file against office-bearers that have lost the confidence o' the workin'-man. But I'm no socialist, and I would have ye keep mind of that. I'm yin o' the old Border radicals, and I'm not like to change.' J. Buchan, *The Four Adventures of Richard Hannay* (London, Hodder & Stoughton, 1930), p.506. Readers may enjoy putting names to the Clydesiders who appear in Ch. 4 of *Mr. Standfast* (Ch. 36 of the omnibus edition).

15. Their disagreements are paraded at enormous length in *The Socialist* (organ of the S.L.P.), December 1911.

16. *The Socialist*, April 1911, p.60.

17. Ibid., May 1911, p.65.

18. Ibid.

19. Ibid., July 1911.

20. Ibid., quoted in part in Hinton thesis.

21. W. J. Douglas, *The Socialist*, June 1911.

22. Bell, *Pioneering Days*, p.75.

23. Workers' Union, *Record*, February 1919. Quoted in Hyman thesis, p.115.

24. *The Socialist*, January 1911, p.1.

25. Bell, *Pioneering Days*, p.69.

26. E.g. April and June 1911.

27. Tape-recorded reminiscences of Archie Henry in possession of John Foster, Department of Politics, Strathclyde University.

28. Walton Newbold thought that it was a 'brilliant' speech by Regan which caused the I.L.P. to adopt the outrightly pacifist 'Bermondsey resolution' in 1917 (though he wrongly gives the date as 1915). Newbold Papers, Manchester University Library.

29. Kirkwood, *My Life of Revolt*, p.86.

30. Gallacher, *Revolt*, p.27.

31. Kirkwood, *My Life of Revolt*, p.168.

32. Murphy, *New Horizons*, p.44.

33. Kendall, *Revolutionary Movement*, p.348, quoting *Justice*, December 1915.

34. Gallacher, *Last Memoirs*, p.73.

35. E.g. Kendall, *Revolutionary Movement*; J. Broom, *John MacLean* (Loanhead, Lothian, MacDonald Publishers, 1973); N. Milton, *John MacLean* (London, Pluto Press, 1973); McShane, *No Mean Fighter*.

36. *Forward*, 25 August 1917.

37. Preserved in MacLean Papers; another copy in Highton Papers.

38. Kirkwood's son claimed that Gallacher, when challenged by David Kirkwood, did not know that Marx had written more than one book.

39. Bell, *Pioneering Days*, p.55.

40. Ibid., p.56.

41. E.g. G. Monies, reviewing Kendall's *Revolutionary Movement* . . . in *Scottish Labour History Society Journal*, 1, 1969, p.26; Hugh MacDiarmid, Introduction to Broom, *MacLean*, 12.

42. J. Paterson to Llewellyn Smith, 17 January 1916. *BCM*, III, 16.

43. From one of the hundreds of unsorted, unnumbered sheets of autobiography in the Walton Newbold Papers, Manchester University Library.

44. Gallacher, *Revolt*, pp.58-62; cf. Kendall, *Revolutionary Movement*, pp.119 and 356; McShane, *No Mean Fighter*, pp.77-8.

45. See Ch. 6. The article was probably by William Regan, who was not a revolutionary but a Catholic pacifist. McShane, *No Mean Fighter*, p.80.

46. Statement of John MacLean at his trial, 10 November 1915. MacLean Papers, File 2.

47. Trial of John MacLean, April 1916. Defence Statement. MacLean Papers, File 2.

48. Ibid.

49. McShane, *No Mean Fighter*, p.103.

50. E.g. *TCM*, 4 and 5 April 1916; appeal of George Barnes to Imperial War Cabinet, 28 November 1918, CAB 23/42.

51. Kendall, *Revolutionary Movement*, p.114.

52. Milton, *John MacLean*, p.69.

53. Broom, *John MacLean*, 70; Kendall, *Revolutionary Movement*, 122.

54. Though when not upset or suspicious he was obviously a delightful man with a fine sense of humour, and devoted to his family though incapable of providing for them. For the vexed question of whether he suffered from paranoid delusions, see Ch. 12.

55. 'Notes from Intelligence Officer Glasgow to Lt.Col. Levita, General Staff, Scottish Command: Particulars of *Vanguard*'. MUN 5/70, filed with papers on the suppression of the *Forward*. Quotations from *Vanguard* in the file display total opposition to dilution.

56. *Worker*, 8 January 1916.

57. Ibid.

58. *Forward*, 29 December 1917, p.3.

59. See D. M. Chewter, 'History of the Socialist Labour Party of Great Britain from 1902 to 1921 with special reference to the development of its ideas', Oxford B.Litt thesis 1965, esp. p.90.

60. Murphy, *New Horizons*, p.47.

61. *Sheffield Daily Independent*, 1 May 1917. Hyman (thesis, p.235) quotes the poem; his guess of 'bloody' to fill the gap in the second line may or may not satisfy readers.

Chapter 10

1. Gallacher, *Revolt*, p.140.

2. Ibid., p.141.

3. Ibid., p.179; Hinton, *First Shop Stewards' Movement*, p.257.

4. I.e., Executive.

5. *TCM*, December 1918.

6. STUC *Annual Report*, 1918, pp.44-5.

7. *TCM*, 13 March 1918; STUC *Report*, 1918, p.53. Emanuel Shinwell moved the Trades Council resolution, though he does not seem to have supported it himself.

8. STUC *Report*, 1919, p.41.

9. Ibid., p.42.

10. STUC: Minutes of the Parliamentary Committee (hereafter 'STUC Minutes'), 16 November 1918. In STUC offices.

11. STUC *Report* 1919, p.42.

12. A.S.E. *Monthly Journal*, December 1918, p.17.

13. Ibid., p.18.

14. Ibid., August 1917, p.4. Bunton did not approve of his successor: 'Personally he [Bunton] was in sympathy with the movement for a 40-hours week . . . What he objected to was the everlasting attempts to kick over the traces, thereby fostering revolutionary methods', Interview, *Glasgow Herald*, 23 January 1919, p.5.

15. A.S.E. *Monthly Journal*, January 1918, p.4.

16. See Ch. 2. One veteran of the strike says that 'Harry Hopkins was a very popular figure. But when you've said that, you've said the lot'. Tape-recorded reminiscences of Tom Scollan, in possession of John Foster, Strathclyde University.

17. A.S.E: statement on behalf of the suspended District Committee, sent to the Executive with an appeal for reinstatement. Probably February 1919. Eight pages, duplicated; in Highton Papers. Hereafter 'D.C. Statement'. Quoted at p.2.

18. Ibid.

19. Ibid., pp.2-3.

20. 'The Shorter (?) Working Week'. Quoted in D. S. Morton, 'The 40 Hours Strike: an Historic Survey of the First General Strike in Scotland', Clydebank branch S.L.P. (1919), p.3. Morton was one of the secretaries of the strike committee; later a Labour councillor in Stockport. I am very grateful to Walter Kendall, who lent me a copy of this rare pamphlet.

21. D.C. Statement, p.3.

22. A.S.E. *Monthly Journal*, January 1919, p.9.

23. Ibid., p.20.

24. Glasgow Trades Council *Annual Report*, 1919, p.8.

25. D.C. Statement; Glasgow Trades Council *Annual Report*, 1919; STUC ditto; tape-recorded reminiscences of Finlay Hart, Foster collection.

26. Ben Shaw (its secretary), speaking at 1919 STUC: STUC *Annual Report* 1919, p.110.

27. *Forward*, 11 January 1919, p.1.

28. STUC *Annual Report* 1919, p.43.

29. *TCM*, 15 January 1919.

30. STUC Minutes, 18 January 1919.

31. Ibid.

32. Ibid., 22 January 1919. This source estimates that 400-500 delegates attended; Morton, '40 Hours Strike', p.4, estimates 800.

33. STUC Minutes, 22 January 1919.

34. Glasgow Trades Council *Annual Report*, 1919, p.9.

35. STUC Minutes, 22 January 1919.

36. Ibid.

37. Ibid., 24 January 1919.

38. STUC *Annual Report*, 1919, p.44.

39. D.C. Statement, pp.4-5.

40. Bell, *Pioneering Days*, p.163.

41. D.C. Statement, p.6.

42. A.S.E. *Monthly Journal*, February 1919, p.21.

43. Ibid., pp.22-3.

44. *Forward*, 25 January 1919, p.2. These were unions whose leaders happened to be prominent in the STUC or the Glasgow Trades Council (Joseph Houghton of the Dock Labourers; Hugh Lyon of the Scottish Horse; James Kiddie of the N.U.R.; George Kerr of the M.E.A.)

45. D.C. Statement, p.2.

46. Morton, '40 Hours Strike', pp.6-7.

47. *TCM*, 12 February 1919.

48. Ibid.

49. Quoted by Morton, '40 Hours Strike', p.3.
50. *Glasgow Herald*, 28 January 1919, p.6.
51. McShane, *No Mean Fighter*, p.103.

Chapter 11

1. *Glasgow Herald*, 25 January 1919, p.5.
2. *Daily Record*, 24 January 1919, p.1; cf. also 25 January, p.9.
3. *Daily Record*, 3 February 1919, p.1. The next day, though on p.1, it admitted that 'Yesterday the start was, to be frank, an indifferent one'.
4. *Glasgow Herald*, 28 January 1919, p.5 and 29 January, p.7.
5. *Glasgow Herald*, 27 January 1919, p.8. The 'official assurance', from the manager of the Corporation Tramways, appears in an adjoining column.
6. *Glasgow Herald*, 28 January 1919, p.5.
7. Morton, *40 Hours Strike*, p.6.
8. *Glasgow Herald*, 29 January 1919, p.7.
9. *Glasgow Herald*, 28 January 1919, p.5.
10. *Glasgow Herald*, 30 January 1919, p.6.
11. Ibid.
12. Ibid.
13. *Glasgow Herald*, 3 February 1919, p.6; *Strike Bulletin*, 1 February 1919, p.2. This and many other contemporary documents are reproduced in H. McShane (intro.), *Glasgow 1919* (Glasgow, Molendinar Press, 1974).
14. *Glasgow Herald*, 30 January 1919, p.6. Middlemas *(Clydesiders, p.93)* wrongly attributes Shinwell's phrase to Kirkwood.
15. Acting Prime Minister, as Lloyd George was at Versailles.
16. *Glasgow Herald*, 30 January 1919, p.6.
17. Ibid.
18. Evidence of Lieut. Gray, Central District, Glasgow City Police. *Glasgow Herald*, 8 April 1919, p.7.
19. *Glasgow Herald*, 9 April 1919.
20. *Glasgow Herald*, 10 April 1919, p.8.
21. War Cabinet no. 522, 30 January 1919. CAB 23/9.
22. Report by the Minister of Labour, War Cabinet no.521, 28 January 1919. CAB 23/9.
23. War Cabinet no. 522, 30 January 1919. CAB 23/9.
24. Ibid.
25. Of Lanarkshire.
26. War Cabinet no. 522, as before.
27. It was to comprise the Secretary for Scotland (chairman), the Lord Advocate, the Minister of Labour and the Director of Personal Services, War Office. No record of its meetings seems to have survived; they are not in CAB 27 along with other Cabinet Committees.
28. War Cabinet, 522, as above.
29. *Glasgow Herald*, 1 February 1919, p.5.
30. This account of Bloody Friday is compiled from *Glasgow Herald, Daily Record,*

and *Strike Bulletin,* all 1 February 1919; *Daily News,* 3 February 1919; *Forward* and *Glasgow Observer,* 8 February 1919; Morton, *40 Hours Strike,* pp.8-9.

31. *Glasgow Herald,* 1 February 1919, p.5.
32. Shinwell, *Conflict without Malice,* p.63.
33. War Cabinet no. 523, 31 January 1919. CAB 23/9.
34. He recommended deportation under Regulations 14 and 42. Possibly the Cabinet decided that this would involve memories of 1916 that were better left dormant.
35. *Glasgow Herald,* 31 January 1919. Leader, p.6.
36. *Glasgow Herald,* 7 February 1919, p.7.
37. Ibid., also *Daily Record,* 7 February 1919, p.2.
38. *Glasgow Herald,* 3 February 1919, p.8.
39. Ibid., 4 February 1919, p.5; *Daily Record,* 4 February 1919, p.1.
40. *Glasgow Herald,* 5 February 1919, p.8.
41. Ibid., 6 February 1919, p.5.
42. Ibid., 3 February 1919, p.8.
43. *Strike Bulletin,* 11 February 1919.
44. *Strike Bulletin,* 12 February 1919; *Forward,* 15 February 1919.
45. The deputation had seen William Adamson, then leader of the Labour Party; C. W. Bowerman, Secretary of the T.U.C.; and Sir David Shackleton, a former Labour M.P. and by 1919 Permanent Secretary at the Ministry of Labour.
46. STUC Minutes, 8 February 1919.
47. Ibid., 15 February 1919.
48. *TCM,* 12 March 1919.
49. Clyde Workers' Defence Committee papers, Mitchell Library, Glasgow.
50. A BSP propagandist.
51. James Murray, J. MacArtney, N. Oliver, Robert Loudon, David Mackenzie and Neil Alexander.
52. *Glasgow Herald,* 18 April 1919, p.8.
53. Ibid.
54. Ibid., 19 April 1919, p.4.
55. Scott Dickson.
56. *Glasgow Herald,* 19 April 1919, p.4.
57. *Forward,* 26 April 1919; cf. also STUC *Report* 1919, p.63.
58. *Forward,* 3 May 1919. In *Last Memoirs* (p.124), Gallacher says that one jury-man kept a diary of the case 'in which he tells how he argued and argued to get an acquittal for Manny and me'. No doubt this man formed the minority of one, and he may have been the *Forward's* source.
59. *Glasgow Herald,* 19 April 1919, p.4. The appeal was dismissed.
60. STUC *Report,* 1919, p.72.
61. Ibid., p.68.
62. Ibid.
63. *Glasgow Herald,* 29 January 1919, p.7.
64. Edinburgh Trades Council, *Annual Report* 1919, p.9.
65. Press report pasted in to STUC Minutes, 23 August 1919.
66. STUC Minutes, 3 October 1919.
67. STUC Minutes, 14 September 1920.

68. *TCM:* Industrial Committee, 14 May 1919. Cf. also full Council, 7 May: 'Mr. Marchbanks N.U.R. moved that this [Council] give no countenance to any letter that proposed drastic action . . . he did not believe the workers would stop work . . . He did not want to see any fiasco now'.

69. *TCM:* Industrial Committee, 14 May 1919.

70. 9 & 10 Geo. V, Ch. 42. It received the Royal Assent on 15 August 1919.

71. D.C. Statement, pp. 5-6.

72. *Glasgow Herald,* 19 April 1919. Middlemas *(Clydesiders,* p.96) garbles it.

73. *Glasgow Herald,* 18 April 1919.

74. *Glasgow Herald,* 1 February 1919, p.5.

75. *Daily News,* 3 February 1919; cf. also *Manchester Guardian,* same date.

76. Evidence of Alexander McKendrick, Officer of the Juvenile Delinquency Board. *Glasgow Herald,* 12 April 1919.

77. *Glasgow Herald,* 11 April 1919, p.9.

78. *Glasgow Herald,* 18 April 1919, p.5.

79. *Forward,* 19 April 1919.

80. Among miscellaneous papers relating to the trial in the Mitchell Library is a drawing of George Square headed 'The Lord Advocate v. Shinwell and Others', and signed by Robert C. Boyce, C.E., 144 St. Vincent Street, Glasgow. This confirms that there were tramlines along the north, south, and west, *but not east,* sides of the Square.

81. *Glasgow Herald,* 23 January 1919, p.5.

82. Shinwell, *Conflict without Malice,* p.61.

83. *Daily Record,* 30 January 1919, p.1.

84. Gallacher, *Last Memoirs,* pp.123-4. In *Revolt,* pp.223-4, Gallacher accuses Shinwell, without naming him, of offering 'romantic and dangerous suggestions . . . which would have ended everything in a medley of confusion and disorder'. Cf. also Bell, *Pioneering Days,* p.166, where he says 'the law of libel forbids' him from naming names.

85. Bell, *Pioneering Days,* p.166.

86. *Glasgow Herald,* 28 January 1919, p.5.

87. To contemporaries it seemed that 'In consequence of the conflict with authority that occurred on Friday, troops . . . have been drafted into the city' *(Glasgow Herald,* 3 February 1919, p.7). But the troops were already on their way before the riot, in consequence of the decision of the Cabinet on 30 January.

88. Gallacher, *Revolt,* p.221.

89. Ibid., pp.233-4.

90. *Daily Record,* 1 February 1919.

91. *Glasgow Herald,* 1 February 1919.

92. Ibid.

93. McShane, *No Mean Fighter,* p.108.

94. *Daily News,* 3 February 1919.

95. Headline in *Glasgow Observer,* 8 February 1919.

96. E.g. W. Ferguson, *Scotland: 1689 to the Present* (Edinburgh, Oliver & Boyd, 1968), p.361.

97. Stress in original.

98. 'Fortnightly Report on Revolutionary Organisations in the United Kingdom and Morale in Foreign Countries', 2 December 1918. Cabinet paper GT 6425. CAB 24/71.

For the quality and sophistication of Thomson's information, cf. (from his report on 21 October 1918, GT 6079, CAB 24/67): 'An exact translation of the word *Bolshevik* is, I am told, *out-and-outer'.

99. B. H. Thomson, *Queer People* (London, Hodder & Stoughton, 1922), p.276. For more evidence of Cabinet panic between 1919 and 1921, see Jones, *Whitehall Diary*, I, entries for 8 February 1919, 2 February 1920 ('Bonar Law so often referred to the stockbrokers as a loyal and fighting class until [sic] one felt that potential battalions of stockbrokers were to be found in every town'), 4 and 5 April 1921.

100. *Glasgow Herald*, 21 January 1919, p.7; 3 February 1919, p.8.

Chapter 12

1. A. Marwick, 'The I.L.P. 1918-32', Oxford University B.Litt thesis, 1960, pp.35, 118; R. E. Dowse, *Left in the Centre* (London, Longman, 1966), pp.38-9.

2. *Forward*, 10 January 1920, pp.6-7.

3. *Forward*, 10 April 1920.

4. *TCM*, 1 December 1920.

5. *TCM*, 23 February 1921.

6. STUC *Annual Report* 1921, p.100.

7. *Forward*, 30 April 1921, p.4.

8. See J. Paton, *Left Turn!* (London, Secker & Warburg, 1936), pp.78-83.

9. *Forward*, 8 January 1921, p.5.

10. Paton, *Left Turn!*, p.86.

11. *Forward*, 9 April 1921, p.7.

12. *TCM*, 6 July 1921.

13. STUC *Annual Report* 1922, p.29.

14. *TCM*, 23 August 1922.

15. *TCM*, 6 September 1922; 27 September 1922.

16. Kendall, *Revolutionary Movement*, p.314; Chewter thesis, pp.205-61.

17. L. J. MacFarlane, *The British Communist Party: its origin and development until 1929* (London, MacGibbon & Kee, 1966), p.69.

18. E.g. by H. Pelling, *The British Communist Party* (London, A. & C. Black, 1958), esp. pp.15-17.

19. MacFarlane, *Communist Party*, p.28.

20. Gallacher, *Revolt*, pp.262-3. Gallacher's savage attack on Clark here probably reflects the dislike of the ex-B.S.P. leadership for the ex-S.L.P. leadership it supplanted when the party was 'Bolshevised' in 1922-3.

21. MacFarlane, *Communist Party*, p.83. Cf. also R. Martin, *Communism and the British Trade Unions 1924-33* (Oxford, Clarendon Press, 1969), p.29.

22. MacFarlane, *Communist Party*, p.89.

23. L. Chester, S. Fay and H. Young, *The Zinoviev Letter* (London, Heinemann, 1967).

24. The Unemployed Committee was MacLean's committee, of which the communist Peter Kerrigan was a member.

25. *TCM*, 5 October 1921.

26. *Forward*, 15 October 1921. Cf. also *TCM*, 12 October 1921.

27. Martin, *Communism*, Ch. 8 *passim*; McShane, *No Mean Fighter*, Chs. 10-12.

28. Taped reminiscences of Tom Scollan. Foster collection.

29. Gallacher, *Last Memoirs*, p.163.

30. Gallacher, *Revolt*, pp. 214-5.

31. Gallacher, *Last Memoirs*, p.118.

32. Gallacher, *Revolt*, p.216.

33. Kendall, *Revolutionary Movement*, pp.284-5. Broom, *John Maclean* and Milton, *John Maclean* both take the same line.

34. In P. Berresford Ellis and S. Mac A'Ghobhainn, *The Scottish Insurrection of 1820* (London, Gollancz, 1970), Introduction, pp.15-16.

35. 'Gey ill to thole': 'very hard to put up with'.

36. Obituary in *Forward*, 8 December 1923.

37. MacLean Papers, File 1, *passim*.

38. MacLean to his wife, from Peterhead Prison, 22 May 1917. MacLean Papers.

39. War Cabinet no. 364, 12 March 1918. CAB 23/5.

40. Ibid.

41. Trial of John MacLean 1918. Transcript in MacLean papers. MacLean's speech from the dock is reprinted in e.g. Bell, *John Maclean*, pp.157-70; J. MacLean (ed. N. Milton), *In the Rapids of Revolution* (London, Allison & Busby, 1978), pp.100-114.

42. Not William Gallacher, the revolutionary. Papers which confused the two were liable to be threatened with libel actions.

43. MacLean to his wife, 15 May 1918. MacLean Papers. Cf. also press cutting, undated, in MacLean Papers.

44. Protest circular by Mrs. MacLean, 9 November 1918. MacLean Papers.

45. Ibid.

46. MacDonald to Munro, 5 July 1918. MacLean Papers.

47. MacDonald to Mrs MacLean, n.d. MacLean Papers.

48. Hogge to Mrs. MacLean, n.d. MacLean Papers.

49. Munro to J. S. Middleton, 13 November 1918. MacLean Papers.

50. 'The case of John Maclean'. Cabinet paper no. GT 6379, 26 November 1918. CAB 24/70.

51. Ibid.

52. Imperial War Cabinet no. 39, 28 November 1918. CAB 23/42.

53. War Cabinet no. 508, 29 November 1918. CAB 23/8. Cf. also memo by Munro to the Imperial War Cabinet, GT 6499, 17 December 1918. CAB 24/71.

54. Gallacher to J. Broom, 14 June 1962. MacLean Papers.

55. McShane, *No Mean Fighter*, p.100.

56. Bell, *John Maclean*, p.79.

57. Thomson, 'Fortnightly Report', unnumbered, 13 January 1919. GT 6654. CAB 24/73.

58. 'Fortnightly Report' no. 31, 28 January 1919. GT 6713. CAB 24/74.

59. Scottish Record Office, '1918-22 Peace Propaganda', H.H. 31/34. Quoted in G. R. Rubin, 'A Note on the Scottish Office Reaction to John Maclean's Drugging Allegation Made at the High Court, Edinburgh, 1918', *Scottish Labour History Society Journal* 14, 1980, pp.40-5.

60. *Forward*, 22 March 1919, p.2.

61. Gallacher, *Revolt*, p.215.

62. Ibid., p.216.

63. *Daily Record*, 27 December 1920, quoted in Kendall, *Revolutionary Movement*, p.429.

64. 'John Maclean's Electioneer', 1922. MacLean Papers.

65. *Socialist*, 21 May 1921; MacLean, *Rapids of Revolution*, p.229.

66. *Co-operative News*, 8 December 1923.

67. *Scottish Co-operator*, December 1923.

68. *Forward*, 8 December 1923.

69. V. I. Lenin, *Left-wing Communism - an Infantile Disorder* (London, Popular Edition 1920), p.61.

70. Gallacher, *Revolt*, p.253.

71. *Vanguard*, November 1920, p.5. Quoted in part by Kendall, *Revolutionary Movement*, pp.286-7.

72. From about 1919 to 1923, MacLean was separated from his wife and daughters. They had been reconciled for only a few days when he died.

73. John MacLean to Jean and Nan MacLean, 23 December 1922. MacLean Papers.

74. *Vanguard*, December 1920, p.7.

75. The minute book of its Townhead Branch (MacLean Papers) peters out inconclusively in 1926.

76. Kendall, *Revolutionary Movement*, p.288.

77. Bell, *John Maclean*, p.118; MacShane, *No Mean Fighter*, p.140.

78. Bell, *John Maclean*, p.82.

79. *Forward*, 18 May 1918. 'Socialist War Points', p.1.

80. E.g. Barnes and Edwin Montagu. I.W.C. no. 39, 28 November 1918. CAB 23/42.

81. *Forward*, 5 June 1920.

82. Bell, *John Maclean*, p.103.

83. N. Nicolson, *Lord of the Isles* (London, Weidenfeld & Nicolson, 1960).

84. MacLean, *Rapids of Revolution*, p.223; cf. also p.168.

85. MacLean, *Rapids of Revolution*, p.204.

86. Bell, *John Maclean*, p.95.

87. Words put into the mouth of the hero of *No Mean City*, by A. McArthur and H. Kingsley Long (London, Corgi Books ed., 1957, p.181). First published in 1935. McArthur was a Gorbals baker who committed suicide soon after writing *No Mean City*.

Chapter 13

1. *Forward*, 14 and 21 December 1918.

2. *Glasgow Observer*, 21 December 1918, p.3.

3. *Glasgow Herald*, 16 December 1918, p.7.

4. *Glasgow Herald*, 30 December 1918.

5. Ibid.

6. *Forward*, 21 December 1918, p.1.

7. For arguments about the effect of the Representation of the People Act 1918 on the Labour vote nationwide, see N. Blewett, 'The Franchise in the United Kingdom, 1885-1918', *Past and Present*, *31*, 1965, pp.27-56; M. D. Pugh, *Electoral Reform in War and Peace* (London, Routledge, 1978); H. Matthew, R. McKibbin and J. Kay, 'The

franchise factor in the rise of the Labour Party', *English Historical Review*, 91, 1976, pp.723-52; P. Clarke, 'Liberals, Labour and the franchise', *English Historical Review*, 92, 1977, pp.582-90.

8. *Glasgow Herald*, 16 December 1918, p.7.

9. Taylor, *English History*, 39. Perhaps, once the recruits had gone, there were fewer pro-war workers left in Glasgow than elsewhere.

10. Middlemas, *Clydesiders*, esp. p.83.

11. *Forward*, 30 March 1918, p.1.

12. *Glasgow Herald*, 30 December 1918.

13. *Forward*, 12 May 1915, p.2.

14. *Forward*, 19 September 1914, p.2. Taylor died in 1916.

15. J. Scanlon, *Decline and Fall of the Labour Party* (London, Peter Davis, 1932), p.9. Scanlon had been the plater whose helper Maxton was.

16. Interview, ISMcL with J. H. Dollan, 1970.

17. STUC *Annual Report* 1919, p.30.

18. For a justification of this procedure see I. S. McLean, 'The problem of proportionate swing', *Political Studies*, 21, 1973, pp.57-63; I. S. McLean, 'Oxford and Bridgwater', in C. Cook and J. Ramsden, eds., *By-elections in British Politics* (London, Macmillan, 1973), pp.140-64, esp. pp.141-2.

19. But see S. Pollard, *A History of Labour in Sheffield* (Liverpool, Liverpool University Press, 1959); H. K. Hawson, *Sheffield: growth of a city 1893-1926* (Sheffield, J. W. Northend, 1968); and W. Hampton, *Democracy and Community* (London, Oxford University Press, 1970).

20. *Forward*, 14 June 1919, p.7.

21. Ibid., 12 July 1919, p.5; 19 July 1919, p.5.

22. Results:

	1918	%		1919	%
Co. U.	9359	50.9	Lab.	13135	68.8
Lab.	9027	49.8	Co. L.	5967	31.2
maj.	332	1.8		7168	37.6
Turnout:		69.2			71.9

23. M. Cowling, *The Impact of Labour 1920-4* (Cambridge, Cambridge University Press, 1971), p.1. Spen Valley polled on December 20, but the result was not announced until January 3rd.

24. In the Paisley by-election (12th February 1920) there was a 10% swing from Independent Liberal to Labour although Asquith himself was the Liberal candidate.

25. *Forward*, 15 November 1919, pp.2, 6.

26. In the two largest movements in modern times, the Scottish National Party made a net gain of 103 seats in 1968 and Labour made a net gain of 120 in 1971. *The Scotsman*, 8 May 1968 and 6 May 1971.

27. *Forward*, 25 September 1920.

28. Headline in *Forward*, 13 November 1920, p.1.

29. *Forward*, 13 November 1920. The calculation is not necessarily trustworthy, because Labour did not always fight all three seats in each ward, nor did its opponents. But these were in fact the seats won by Labour in 1922, plus Cathcart (a freak result depending on an even split between a Coalition Liberal and Conservative).

30. *Forward*, 13 November 1920, pp.6-7.

31. *Forward*, 22 October 1921, p.3.
32. *Forward*, 21 November 1921, p.2.
33. *Glasgow Herald*, 9 November 1922, p.6.
34. Of the total electorate in these 24 wards, not of the votes cast.
35. Calculated from figures in *Glasgow Herald*, *loc. cit.* The source lumps together Labour and Communist votes, but this does not seriously distort the figures, because the only Communist to poll well was John MacLean (Kinning Park), where in 1922 he was not opposed by Labour.
36. Result:

	Lab.	9137	34.0%
	N.Lib.	9104	33.8%
	Con.	8661	32.2%

Cathcart went Conservative in 1923; Labour did not regain it until James Maxton's nephew won in 1979.
37. Paton, *Left Turn!*, pp.98-9.
38. Marwick thesis, p.40.
39. *Forward*, 15 October 1921, p.5.
40. *Forward*, 5 November 1921, p.4.
41. *Forward*, 25 November, 1922, p.5.
42. See, e.g., Cowling, *Impact of Labour*, p.35.
43. Paton, *Left Turn!*, p.105.
44. *Forward*, 8 October 1921, p.3.
45. *Report of the Royal Commission on the Housing of the Industrial Population of Scotland, Rural and Urban*. Cd 8731, 1918.
46. Cd 8731, paras. 12-16.
47. Cd 8731, paras. 233-4.
48. Cd 8731, para. 402.
49. Cd 8731, para. 1944A.
50. The Majority and the Minority did not differ on the facts, but only on the Minority's refusal to consider state provision of housing as a remedy.
51. Cd 8731, Minority Report, para. 50.
52. Ibid., para. 51.
53. Ibid., para. 53.
54. Although the Commission reported in 1917, all the evidence drawn on in the preceding paragraphs is from before 1914.
55. 9 & 10 Geo. V, Ch. 7.
56. Report by Lord Hunter, paras. 9, 24, 30, 32. Included in memo from Addison to the Home Affairs Committee of the Cabinet (GT 6836: CAB 24/75) approved on 21 February 1919 (Home Affairs Committee no.20: CAB 26/1.)
57. K. and J. Morgan, *Portrait of a Progressive: the political career of Christopher, Viscount Addison* (Oxford, Clarendon Press, 1980), pp.96-101.
58. 10 & 11 Geo. V, Ch. 17.
59. Ibid., section 2(1)d.
60. Speech in Glasgow Corporation, reported in *Forward*, 9 August 1919, p.4.
61. Cd 8731, para. 2242.
62. 'In Bermondsey did Addison / An Artisan's Abode Foresee / While Alf, the sacred Harmsworth, wrote / In reams too numerous to quote / Against the E.P.D.' — G. D. H. Cole (ed.), *The Bolo Book* (London, 1921), p.24. See also P. Abrams, 'The

failure of social reform 1918-20', *Past and Present*, 29, 1963, pp.43-64; S. Armitage, *The Politics of Decontrol of Industry* (London, Weidenfeld & Nicolson, 1969); Morgan and Morgan, *Portrait of a Progressive*, pp.106-113, 141-7.

63. The following, from the Home Affairs Committee's discussion on the 1919 rent act, should not be lost to posterity:
'Sir A. C. Geddes asked why there was a shortage of houses. Dr. Addison replied that the chief reason was that none had been built for five years'. CAB 26/1.

64. *Forward*, 10 January 1920, p.1.

65. *Forward*, 1 May 1920, p.7.

66. *Forward*, 29 May 1920, p.4.

67. *H.C. Debs.*, 129, 2285.

68. *Forward*, 3 July 1920, p.7.

69. STUC *Annual Report*, 1921, p.22.

70. Later M.P. from Newport (1929-31) and Motherwell (1935-45) and a leading right-wing member of the Labour Party N.E.C.

71. *Forward*, 7 August 1920, pp.4. and 8.

72. *Forward*, 11 September 1920, p.4.

73. *Forward*, 3 July 1920, p.1.

74. *Forward*, 10 July 1920, p.8.

75. *Forward*, 31 July 1920, p.8.

76. *H.C. Debs.*, 129, 2238.

77. Quoted in T. N. Graham, *Willie Graham* (London, Hutchinson, 1948), p.93.

78. *H.C. Debs.*, 130, 1797.

79. *Forward*, 31 July 1920, p.8.

80. Quoted by Sheriff MacPhail, Dumbarton Sheriff Court. *Scottish Law Reporter*, vol. LIX, p.462.

81. Ibid., p.464.

82. 'Notice of removal' being the Scots equivalent of English 'Notice to quit'.

83. *Scottish Law Reporter*, vol. LIX, p.580. The anomaly was removed by the Rent Restriction (Notice of Increase) Act 1923, which laid down that 'notice of intention to increase rent shall have effect as if it were a notice to terminate the tenancy'.

84. *Glasgow Herald*, 4 November 1922, pp.3, 8.

85. *Forward*, 11 November 1922. The claim in the last sentence was suspect.

86. Quoted in *Glasgow Herald*, 6 November 1922, p.6.

87. *Glasgow Herald*, 7 November 1922, p.3.

88. Ibid., 10 November 1922, p.11. This was rather hard on the Coalition M.P. for Tradeston, who was a housing reformer and co-sponsored with William Graham some amendments to the 1920 Act.

89. *Glasgow Herald*, 11 November 1922, p.12.

90. *Forward*, 25 November 1922, p.5.

Chapter 14

1. Taped reminiscences, Foster collection. Mr. McShane added, 'This was something John Saville couldnae understand'.

2. There is an excellent portrayal of railway life in Springburn before 1914 in J. Thomas, *The Springburn Story* (Dawlish, David & Charles, 1964).

3. The *Glasgow Herald* had sneered at 'journal addressed . . . to a class which can read and write . . . [but not] think or reason'.

4. *Forward*, 28 August 1915, p.1.

5. *Forward*, 10 November 1917, p.2.

6. *Forward*, 31 December 1921, p.1.

7. *Forward*, 12 November 1921, p.2.

8. For more about residuals analysis, see I. Crewe and C. Payne, 'Analysing the Census data', in D. Butler and M. Pinto-Duschinsky, *The British General Election of 1970* (London, Macmillan, 1971) pp.416-36; I. Crewe and C. Payne, 'Another Game with Nature: an ecological regression model of the British 2-party vote ratio in 1970', *British Journal of Political Science*, 6, 1976, pp.43-81.

9. *Glasgow Herald*, 8 November 1922, p.5.

10. Figures from *The Catholic Directory for the Clergy and Laity in Scotland*, 94th Annual Volume, 1922.

11. Ibid.

12. McShane, taped reminiscences.

13. See his leaders in *Forward* on, e.g., 29 November 1919 and 9 October 1920.

14. *Forward*, 2 October 1920, p.7.

15. STUC *Annual Report* 1920, p.90.

16. *TCM*, 8 October 1919.

17. STUC *Annual Report* 1921, pp.93-4.

18. *Forward*, 30 April 1921, p.4.

19. *Forward*, 10 January 1920, pp.6-7; 7 January 1922, p.7.

20. *Forward*, 1 October 1921, p.4.

21. Ibid.

22. *Forward*, 20 November 1920, p.5.

23. *Forward*, 13 November 1920, p.1.

24. *Forward*, 20 November 1920, p.5.

25. *Glasgow Observer*, 30 October 1920, p.7.

26. *Forward*, 8 October 1921.

27. *Glasgow Observer*, 30 October 1920, p.7.

28. *Forward*, 13 November 1920, pp.6-7.

29. *Forward*, 12 November 1921, p.2.

30. *Glasgow Herald*, 27 October 1921, p.8.

31. Ibid.

32. *Glasgow Observer*, 5 November 1921, p.3.

33. *Glasgow Herald*, 2 November 1922, p.3.

34. *Glasgow Observer*, 4 November 1922, p.3.

35. *Irish Weekly* (Belfast), 11 November 1922, p.7.

36. T. Brennan, *Reshaping a City* (Glasgow, Grant, 1959), p.126.

37. Johnston, *Memories*; Brotherstone, 'Suppression of the *Forward*', p.8.

38. See letter by Charles Diamond to *Pall Mall Gazette*, quoted by *Glasgow Observer*, 7 January 1910, p.12.

39. E.g. Middlemas, *Clydesiders*, pp.37-40.

40. *Newspaper Press Directory*, 73rd Annual Issue, London 1918. The *Forward* had no sports (and no advertisements for alcoholic drink).

41. J. Handley, *The Irish in Modern Scotland* (Cork, Cork University Press, 1947),

p.227.

42. For information in this paragraph I am grateful to the staff of the *Scottish Catholic Herald* (successor to the *Glasgow Observer*), especially John Cooney.

43. A. McBride, 'Can the Labour Party Capture the Glasgow Town Council?', *Forward*, 17 March 1917. Middlemas *(Clydesiders*, p.24) wrongly claims that the I.L.P. won ten out of 75 seats in 1898.

44. Under Ferguson, a Protestant, who was none the less for many years a patron of the U.I.L. in Glasgow (see Handley, *Irish in Modern Scotland*, pp. 269-90), and Bailie P. O'Hare, who tried unsuccessfully to return to council in 1913 with Labour help. *Glasgow Observer*, 1 and 8 November 1913.

45. *Glasgow Observer*, 31 October 1908.

46. Ibid., 2 November 1907, p.5.

47. *Glasgow Star*, 7 January 1910, p.12.

48. He had 'made himself the catspaw of the Temperance caucus on the Corporation'. *Glasgow Star*, 27 January 1906.

49. *Glasgow Star*, October 1909, p.8.

50. *Glasgow Observer*, 6 November 1909, p.3.

51. The annual municipal election article was usually headed, 'Glasgow Municipal Elections/The *Observer* Ticket'.

52. *Glasgow Observer*, 29 October 1910.

53. Ibid., 5 November 1910, p.3.

54. Ibid., 4 November 1911, p.3.

55. Ibid., 2 November 1912, p.3; cf. also *Glasgow Star*, 1 November 1912, p.9.

56. *Glasgow Observer*, 9 November 1912, p.3.

57. Ibid., 1 November 1913, p.3. On the 8th it noted that the 'Labour Party had furnished a contingent of willing workers' for ex-Bailie O'Hare.

58. Ibid., 31 October 1914, p.3, and 7 November 1914, pp.7 and 8.

59. Ibid., 25 October 1919, p.3.

60. Ibid., 1 November 1919, p.3.

61. Ibid., 30 October 1920, p.3. But the earlier objections to Shinwell had vanished: 'Shinwell is . . . particularly sound on Irish matters and should have every Irish vote'.

62. Ibid., 29 October 1921.

63. Ibid., 4 November 1922.

64. 'The Education (Scotland) Bill 1917', Cabinet memo by R. Munro, 24 November 1917. Scottish Record Office ED 14/120. Circulated in revised version: GT 2818.

65. 14 December 1917, War Cabinet 298/1. Copy minute in ED 14/120.

66. Press-cuttings from *Glasgow Observer*, 6 April 1918, in S.E.D. files. ED 14/100.

67. Cuttings from *Glasgow Observer*, 18 May and 8 June 1918, in S.E.D. files. Endorsed 'Seen by the Secretary'. ED 14/100.

68. *Glasgow Observer*, 2 November 1918, p.6.

69. 8 & 9 Geo. V. Ch. 48, Sect. 18, subsects (1) and (3).

70. W. M. Haddow, *My Seventy Years* (Glasgow, R. Gibson & Sons, 1943), pp.86-7.

71. Ibid., Chs. 9 to 11.

72. *Forward*, 12 April 1919, p.5.

73. Report of a meeting of the Good Government League, *Glasgow Herald*, 22 October 1921, p.10.

74. *Glasgow Herald*, 2 June 1922.

75. He held no formal position, but his article in *Forward*, 25 November 1922, on the General Election, shows that by then at least he ran the machine.

76. See *Glasgow Observer*, 6 November 1920; *Glasgow Star*, 11 November 1922.

77. Handley's pioneering work, published as long ago as 1947, is an exception which has still not been followed up.

78. *Glasgow Observer*, 6 January 1906, p.5.

79. Ibid.

80. Handley, *Irish in Modern Scotland*, p.290.

81. *Glasgow Observer*, 15 January 1910, p.5.

82. Ibid., leader, p.9.

83. Ibid., 5 February 1910, p.9.

84. Ibid., 3 December 1910, p.3.

85. Handley, *Irish in Modern Scotland*, p.276.

86. Ibid., 285, quoting *Glasgow Observer*, date not given.

87. Ibid.

88. *Glasgow Observer*, 22 January 1910, p.6; cf. *Evening Times* (Glasgow), 14 January 1910, p.5.

89. *Glasgow Observer*, 22 January 1910, p.9: same comment also printed in *Glasgow Star*, 21 January 1910, p.3.

90. *H.C. Debs.*, 82, 940.

91. F. S. L. Lyons, *John Dillon* (London, Routledge 1968), Ch. 13.

92. 'A Survey and some Counsel by C.D.' *Glasgow Observer*, 26 October 1918, p.3.

93. *Glasgow Observer*, 1 June 1918.

94. Ibid., 2 November 1918, p.6.

95. *Glasgow Herald*, 7 December 1918, p.5; 10 December 1918, p.5. The *Observer* did not even print the list.

96. Probably William Regan, possibly Wheatley.

97. *Forward*, 11 January 1919, p.2.

98. Govan, however, had a high proportion of Catholic baptisms, though it is never thought of as a centre of the Irish machine.

99. *Glasgow Observer*, 23 November 1918, p.6.

100. Ibid., 7 December 1918, p.3.

101. Including its own.

102. *Glasgow Observer*, 4 January 1919, p.6.

103. Except in Liverpool, where the Irish were not integrated into the British party system until the 1930s.

104. Johnston, in *Forward*, 6 May 1916, p.1.

105. 'Catholic Socialist Notes', in *Forward*, 28 October 1916 and 4 November 1916. There are other attacks on Sinn Fein on 2 December 1916, p.1; 20 January 1917, p.4; 20 October 1917, p.1.

106. *Forward*, 13 April 1918, p.2.

107. Ibid., 14 September 1918, p.3.

108. *Glasgow Observer*, 28 December 1918, p.3.

109. Handley, *Irish in Modern Scotland*, p.283.

110. See above, n. 33.

111. *Glasgow Observer*, 4 November 1922, p.3.

112. Ibid., 7 October 1922, p.8.
113. See the tributes on his retirement, *Glasgow Observer*, 2 December 1922, p.13.
114. George Hardie, half-brother of Keir Hardie and later M.P. for Springburn.
115. *Glasgow Observer*, 4 November 1911, p.3. Stewart and Campbell were both elected.
116. Ibid., 6 November 1920.
117. Ibid., 30 October 1920, p.3.
118. Mile-End, the other Catholic but deviantly pro-Labour ward, is harder to explain. Perhaps the Labour strength among Parkhead and other heavy engineering employees obscured any opposite tendency among the Catholic unskilled. One Labour candidate in 1920 was an Episcopal clergyman whose service on the School Board probably met with Catholic approval.
119. See, e.g., *Scotsman*, 18 January 1910; Glasgow *Evening Times*, 9 December 1918, where improbably high estimates of the Irish vote are given, ranging from 12,000 in Bridgeton and elsewhere to 3,000 in Cathcart and Hillhead.
120. *Evening Times*, 28 October 1920, p.3, reporting statement of the Vigilance Committee of the Loyal Orange Lodge of Scotland.

Chapter 15

1. *Forward*, 25 November 1922.
2. *H.C. Debs.*, 159, 133-6. Wheatley, Shinwell, Johnston, George Hardie, Muir, Maclean, E. D. Morel and Joseph Sullivan also spoke.
3. Though Newbold returned in 1929 as an orthodox Labour member and created no stir.
4. See, e.g., L. McNeill Weir in *Forward*, 2 December 1922.
5. Shinwell, *Conflict Without Malice*, p.83; cf. also P. Snowden, *An Auto-biography* (2 vols., London, Ivor Nicholson & Watson Ltd, 1934), vol. II, p.573; D. Marquand, *Ramsay MacDonald* (London, Jonathan Cape, 1977), p.286.
6. B. Webb, *Diaries 1912-24*, ed. M. Cole (London, Longman, 1952), p.230; Snowden *Autobiography*, II, p.574. Kirkwood, *My Life of Revolt*, pp.195-8; G. McAllister, *James Maxton: the portrait of a rebel* (London, John Murray, 1935), pp. 106-9.
7. Marquand, *MacDonald*, pp.273-4.
8. MacDonald's diary, 1 May 1923. Public Record Office: McDonald Papers PRO 30/69/1753. MacDonald's executors have asked that all references to his diary be made subject to MacDonald's own disclaimer pasted into it: it was meant as 'notes to guide and revive memory as regard happenings' and was not to be published in full.
9. *H.C. Debs.*, 165, 2377-2406.
10. *Times*, 28 June 1923; MacDonald to Clifford Allen, 1 September 1923. Both as quoted in Middlemas, *The Clydesiders*, pp.130-1.
11. The Speaker more or less admitted what he had done. *H.C. Debs.*, 173, 871; Jones, *Whitehall Diary*, I, p.279.
12. *H.C. Debs.*, 173, 1341-2. MacDonald had moved on to other concerns since his first political job as secretary to the Scottish Home Rule Association in 1888.
13. *H.C. Debs.*, 173, 792.
14. Government of Scotland Bill, 1924. Copy in MacDonald Papers, PRO 30/69/59.

15. Ibid. Underlined in MacDonald's copy.
16. *H.C. Debs.*, 215, 996-9.
17. See also M. Keating and D. Bleiman, *Labour and Scottish Nationalism* (London, Macmillan, 1979), Ch. 3.
18. B. Webb, *Diaries 1924-32* (ed. M. Cole, London, Longman, 1956), p.54
19. PRO 30/69/1753. The list is not dated, but from internal evidence it almost certainly dates from 1929, not 1924.
20. Snowden, *Autobiography*, II, p.759; Marquand, *MacDonald*, p.492.
21. Middlemas, *Clydesiders*, pp.237-8.
22. Ibid., pp.244-5.
23. Quoted in McAllister, *Maxton*, p.187.
24. Middlemas, *Clydesiders*, pp. 129-30, 279.
25. Kirkwood, *My Life of Revolt*, p.v.
26. Kirkwood, as quoted in *Forward*, 1 May 1926.
27. Quoted in McAllister, *Maxton*, p.209.
28. *H.C. Debs.*, 159, 100.
29. *H.C. Debs.*, 163, 322-335.
30. MacDonald's diary 9 Dec. 1923, PRO/30/69/1753.
31. Both letters quoted in Middlemas, *Clydesiders*, pp.135 and 139.
32. Jones, *Whitehall Diary*, I, p.266; cf. Middlemas, *Clydesiders*, pp.139-40.
33. MacDonald's diary, 24 January 1924, PRO/30/69/1753.
34. MacDonald to King George V, (?) 29 Feb. 1924, quoted in Marquand, *MacDonald*, p.321; Webb, *Diaries 1924-32*, p.11.
35. CAB 23/47. Cabinet 11 (24), 8 February 1924.
36. CAB 24/165, CP 114 (24) 18 February; *H.C. Debs.*, 170; 335-349.
37. CAB 24/165, CP 173 (24) 11 March.
38. Ibid.
39. Out of government: speech at Poplar, 2 June 1925, quoted in N. Branson, *Poplarism 1919-25* (London, Lawrence & Wishart, 1979), p.215. In government: CAB 23/47. Appendix to Conclusions of Cabinet 11 (24), 5 February.
40. CAB 24/165, CP 125 (24) 19 February; CAB 23/47, Cabinet 16 (24). 21 February; *H.C. Debs.*, 169, 2240.
41. CAB 23/47; Cabinet 17 (24), 28 February.
42. Wheatley to MacDonald, 7 March 1924, endorsed with MacDonald's comments. PRO 30/69/211.
43. CAB 24/116, CP 212 (24); Sir Maurice Hankey to MacDonald, 3 April 1924. PRO 30/69/13.
44. CAB 24/166; CP 212 (24).
45. *H.C. Debs.*, 171, 2197-2262, esp. at 2206 (Neville Chamberlain) and 2237 (Sir John Simon).
46. CAB 24/166: CP 245 (24) 6 April; *H.C. Debs.*, 171, 2257-8.
47. The Cabinet, anticipating that it would lose, had already decided that the vote would 'not be taken as a question of confidence'. Cabinet 25 (24). 7 April CAB 23/47. See also *H.C. Debs.*, 172, 87-149, 243-50; R. Lyman, *The First Labour Government*, (London, Chapman & Hall, 1957) pp.122-9.
48. Hankey to MacDonald, 3 April 1924, PRO 30/69/13.

49. Lyman, *First Labour Government*, p.129; Middlemas, *Clydesiders*, pp.152-5; Marquand, *MacDonald*, p.324.

50. Webb, *Diaries 1924-32*, p.19.

51. Reply to Deputation from the smaller local authorities, 26 May 1924, HLG 29/130.

52. Memo from Treasury, Ministry of Health, and Scottish Office ? March 1924. In MacDonald papers PRO 30/69/13; Notes of a Meeting at No. 10, 6 April 1924 CAB 23/47.

53. Webb, *Diaries 1924-32*, 19. After writing these paragraphs I discovered that Emanuel Shinwell makes the same judgment: E. Shinwell, *I've Lived Through It All* (London, Gollancz, 1973), p.72.

54. Report of deputation from the smaller local authorities, HLG 29/130.

55. CAB 23/47, CP 89 (24), reproduced as appendices to conclusions of Cabinet 11 (24) 8 February.

56. CAB 24/165, CP 197 (24) 19 March. See also CAB 23/47, Cabinet 19 (24), 7 March and Cabinet 22 (24), 26 March; CAB 24/165, CP 135 (24).

57. As Parliamentary Under-Secretary of Health for Scotland, Stewart seems to have functioned much more as Wheatley's deputy than as Adamson's. Stewart, unlike Adamson, was a member of the Cabinet Committee on Unemployment & Housing, CAB 7 (24), CAB 23/47.

58. *Forward*, 16 Feb. 1924 and 15 March 1924.

59. Webb, *Diaries 1924-32*, p.31.

60. Jones, *Whitehall Diary*, I, pp.270, 274.

61. J. S. Rowett, 'The Local Government Policies of the Labour Governments of 1924 and 1929-31', paper for SSRC Urban Politics/History Seminar, York 1980; CAB 165/24, CP 122 (24), 'Poor Law Relief to Strikers', rejected in CAB 23/47, Cabinet 15 (24) of 20 February.

62. Rowett, 'Local Government Policies', p.6.

Chapter 16

1. Supply and Transport Committee memo. Dated 2 June 1920. CAB 27/82. In April 1926, though, 'only' Greenwich, Lincoln and Merthyr obstructed Government plans to set up local Voluntary Service Committees. CAB 27/260. CP 163 (26).

2. For this incident, see C. Oakley, *The Last Tram* (Glasgow Corporation Transport Department, 1962), pp.74-80; corrected by I. S. McLean and J. C. Gordon, 'P. J. Dollan, James Dalrymple, and Glasgow's tramways 1926-9: a study in political and administrative change', paper presented to SSRC Urban Studies Conference, York 1981.

3. *Forward*, 13 November 1920; 25 November 1922.

4. *Forward*, 7 July 1928, 'Why I disagree with Maxton' by PJD.

5. I.L.P. councillors lingered on, usually unopposed by Labour, in Shettleston and Parkhead wards, but the I.L.P. got derisory votes elsewhere. The last I.L.P. councillors disappeared in 1949.

6. For details with local voting statistics, see I. S. MacLean, 'The Rise and Fall of the S.N.P.', *Political Studies* XVIII, 3, 1970, pp.357-372.

7. See e.g. K. Newton, *Second City Politics* (Oxford, Clarendon Press, 1976); A.

Sutcliffe and R. Smith, *Birmingham 1939-70* (London, Oxford University Press, 1972); W. Hampton, *Democracy and Community* (London, Oxford University Press, 1970), [Sheffield]; R. Baxter, 'The Liverpool Labour Party 1918-63', Oxford University D.Phil. thesis, 1970.

8. *Forward*, 6 January 1923. The programme included Bennet's *All Creatures Now* and Wibye's *Seek Sweet Content*.

9. *Forward*, 21 October 1939.

10. *Glasgow Observer*, 22 and 29 October 1927. The *Observer* asked its readers to 'vote for no candidate who will not pledge himself against' accepting the paper.

11. Cllr. John Mains, quoted in *Glasgow Herald*, 16 March 1970.

12. See I. Budge, J. Brand, M. Margolis and A. Smith, *Political Stratification and Democracy* (London, Macmillan, 1972), Chs. 3 & 5; J. Brand, 'Councillors, Activists, and Electors: Democratic Relationships in Scottish Cities', in S. C. Patterson and J. Wahlke, eds., *Comparative Legislative Behaviour: Frontiers of Research* (N.Y., Wiley, 1972), pp.235-266.

13. The table shows the correlation at its lowest for 1931 ($r = +0.78975$). The reason may be technical. The 1921 and 1931 Censuses have no direct measure of class. So we have used housing density as a surrogate measure. But in 1931, relatively low-density council house building had already started. So DENSITY is a poorer surrogate for class than in 1921 or 1911. We do not use it at all for 1961-71.

14. This remains the case even if R.C. RATE 1 is added to the regression equation *before* PROTRANG.

15. McLean, 'Rise and Fall of the S.N.P.', p.367.

16. *Glasgow Observer*, 27 October and 3 November 1928.

17. *Glasgow Observer*, 29 October 1932.

18. *Scotsman*, 4 May 1966 and 3 May 1967 ('Butler' swing calculated by author); interview, I. S. McLean with Henry Dutch, 9 February 1976; *Scotsman*, 17 March 1970.

19. 'Labour wash their hands of "policy" decision on R.C. schools', *Scotsman*, 17 March 1970.

20. Ibid. Soon afterwards, the Scottish Conference of the Labour Party threw out a resolution calling for immediate integration — 'it could be embarrassing in relation to an election'. *Scotsman*, 4 April 1970.

21. Figures compiled from *Glasgow Corporation Housing Department: Review of Operations 1919-47*, Glasgow (1947).

22. Sir Patrick Abercrombie and R. H. Matthew, *The Clyde Valley Regional Plan 1946* (London, H.M.S.O., 1949), p.176.

23. W. J. Reader, *Architect of Air Power* (London, Collins, 1968), pp.117-125; *Forward*, 2 January 1926, 6 February, 1926, 12 March 1927.

24. *Scotland's Older Houses: Report by a Sub-committee of the Scottish Housing Advisory Committee* (Chairman J. B. Cullingworth) (Edinburgh, H.M.S.O., 1967), Paras. 63, 64, 167. Emphasis in original. Hereafter cited as *Cullingworth Report*.

25. *Cullingworth Report*, para. 181. This paragraph does not specify Glasgow, but Table C on p.89 makes it clear that it was one of the authorities in Cullingworth's sights with its 'Improvement Rate' of one grant per 1000 houses.

26. Cabinet 34 (24) 27 May 1924. CAB 23/48.

27. Another Housing (Scotland) Act in 1935 defined 'overcrowding' and offered

subsidies to building programmes which relieved it; the first post-1945 Act was the Housing (Repairs and Rents) (Scotland) Act 1954, which required authorities to submit clearance programmes. By 1967 Glasgow had demolished only 32,000 dwellings. *Cullingworth Report*, paras. 27, 29, 33.

28. T. Brennan, *Reshaping a City* (Glasgow, Grant, 1959), pp. 38, 171.

29. Ibid., p.177.

30. R. Smith, in A. Sutcliffe, ed., *Multi-Storey Living: The British Working-Class Experience* (London, Croom Helm, 1974), Ch. 8 *passim*, esp. p.226.

31. *Cullingworth Report*, para.107.

32. Smith, in Sutcliffe, ed., *Multi-Storey Living*, p.219: cf. also D. Niven, *The Development of Housing in Scotland* (London, Croom Helm, 1979), Ch. 1.

33. Abercrombie, *The Clyde Valley Plan*, p.321.

34. Ibid., p.138.

35. Ibid., p.133.

36. Clyde Valley Regional Planning Advisory Committee, *Report to the Constituent Local Authorities*, [Hamilton] 1947, Appendix 1, pp.10-17; Smith, in Sutcliffe, ed., *Multi-Storey Living*, p.223.

37. Brennan, *Reshaping a City*, p.26 ('Unfortunately, at this time these were problems of inter-departmental co-operation in the City administration'); Abercrombie, *Clyde Valley Plan*, p.176, n.2.

38. R. Smith, 'The Origins of Scottish New Towns Policy and the Founding of East Kilbride', *Public Administration* 52, 2, 1974, pp.143-159; P. M. Jackson, 'Local Authority Public Expenditure: A Case-Study of Glasgow', Ph.D. thesis, Stirling University, 1975, pp.4,6.

39. Smith, in Sutcliffe, ed., *Multi-Storey Living*, p.225.

40. *Glasgow Herald*, 18 April 1962.

41. Interviews, I. S. McLean with the late Hugh McCalman, 19 March 1970; J. C. Gordon and I. S. McLean with Dame Jean Roberts, 16 June 1977; Smith, 'Origins of Scottish New Towns Policy'; *Glasgow Herald*, 21 March 1947, 29 October 1947.

42. Budge *et al*, *Political Stratification*, p.92.

43. Some landmarks in this mountain-range of writing are P. Bachrach and M. S. Baratz, 'Two Faces of Power', *American Political Science Review* 56, 1962, pp.947-52; M. Crenson, *The Unpolitics of Air Pollution* (Baltimore, Md, Johns Hopkins University Press, 1971); S. Lukes, *Power: a radical view* (London, Macmillan, 1975).

44. For a slightly more optimistic review of the same events see S. G. Checkland, *The Upas Tree* (Glasgow, University of Glasgow Press, 1976), Chs. V-VIII.

Conclusion.

1. Interview, ISMcL with the late Rt. Hon. Arthur Woodburn, 19 February 1970.

2. Printed in *Glasgow Herald*, 8 November 1922, p.8. See also Hawson, *Sheffield: The Growth of a City*, esp. p.295.

3. Anon., *The Scottish Socialists: a gallery of contemporary portraits* (London, Faber & Faber, 1931), pp.211-3. The author was Thomas Henderson, Labour M.P. for Tradeston.

Bibliography

This bibliography is arranged in the following sections:

I. Public Records
II. Other unpublished materials
III. Contemporary Government publications
IV. Periodicals
V. Interviews
VI. Unpublished theses
VII. Published works used as primary sources
VIII. Other works cited
IX. Bibliographies and handlists

I. Public Records

A. Public Record Office.
Cabinet papers 1914-24. CAB 1, CAB 23, CAB 24, CAB 37, CAB 41.
Cabinet papers 1914–24. CAB 1, CAB 23, CAB 24, CAB 37, CAB 7.
Records of the Ministry of Munitions. Historical records collected under the class mark MUN 5.
Records of the Ministry of Housing and Local Government; files concerning rent control, 1915-1923. HLG 41. Files on Housing Act 1924. HLG 29.

B. Scottish Record Office.
Scottish Office: general wartime policy, 1914-1918. HH 31.
Scottish Office: housing policy, 1912-1920. DD6.
Scotch Education Department: education policy and the 1918 Education Act. ED 7, ED 14.

II. Other unpublished materials

Addison Papers. Bodleian Library, Oxford.
Aldred Papers, Baillie's Institution, Glasgow.
Beveridge Collection on Munitions, British Library of Political and Economic Science. (This collection, which is separate from the rest of the Beveridge papers, consists of papers made up into ten folio volumes during Beveridge's lifetime. References in the text, where it is cited as 'B.C.M.', are to volume number, then to piece number, then to page in the volume.)

Clyde Workers' Defence Committee: miscellaneous papers and legal correspondence. Mitchell Library, Glasgow.

P. J. Dollan: unpublished reminiscences (c. 1880-1920). In the possession of Mr. J. Dollan.

Dollan-Gibson-Broady Collection: Glasgow University Library. (This collection was made by Mr. M. Broady and donated to the Library. It consists, *inter alia*, of ephemera, especially election addresses, of P. J. Dollan and other Glasgow politicians, Labour, I.L.P., and Progressive.)

Edinburgh Trades Council: Minutes: in the offices of the Council, Albany Street, Edinburgh 3. Seen by courtesy of Mr. John Henry, then secretary of the Council, 1970.

Glasgow Central Labour Party: Minutes. Mitchell Library, Glasgow.

Glasgow I.L.P. Federation Executive: Minutes. Mitchell Library, Glasgow.

Glasgow Trades Council: Minutes (including Industrial Committee and Executive Committee). Mitchell Library, Glasgow. Cited as *T.C.M.*

Highton Collection, Glasgow University Archives. (This small collection consists of letters, pamphlets, and other material which once belonged to Herbert Highton, sometime chairman of the Glasgow Trades Council, and which was used by Scott and Cunnison for their book (see Section VII).)

Independent Labour Party: Minutes of the National Administrative Council. Microfilm copy from Hull University Library.

Lloyd George Papers, consulted when at Beaverbrook Library, London. Now in House of Lords.

Ramsay MacDonald Papers. Public Record Office, Kew.

MacLean Papers, National Library of Scotland. MS Acc. 4251.

J. T. Walton Newbold Papers, Manchester University Library.

Scottish Trades Union Congress: Minutes of the Parliamentary Committee (1914-22). In the Congress office, Woodlands Terrace, Glasgow. Seen, 1970, by courtesy of Mr. James Jack, then General Secretary of the Congress. Cited as S.T.U.C. Minutes.

Smillie Papers: miscellanea bought by Nuffield College Library, Oxford, from the estate of Robert Smillie.

Papers of the late Bailie James Welsh, in the possession of Mr. David Welsh.

III. Contemporary Government publications

Clyde Munition Workers Enquiry, *Report*. (Cd 8136, 1915.) (Members, Balfour and Macassey.)

Royal Commission on the Housing of the Industrial Population of Scotland, Rural and Urban. *Report*; Minority Report. (Cd 8731, 1917; chairman Ballantyne.)

Commission of Enquiry into Industrial Unrest; *Report of Commissioners for Scotland*. (Cd 2669, 1917.) (Chairman Fyfe.)

History of the Ministry of Munitions. (12 vols. in parts, n.d.) Vols. I, II, IV, VI. Cited as H.M.M.

IV. Periodicals

Amalgamated Society of Engineers: *Monthly Record* (later *Monthly Journal and Report*)

The Bailie
Catholic Directory for the Clergy and Laity in Scotland
Co-operative News
Daily News
Daily Record and Mail (Glasgow)
Edinburgh Trades Council, Annual Reports. (In Council offices)
Evening Times (Glasgow)
Forward
Glasgow Herald
Glasgow Observer
Glasgow Star & Examiner
Glasgow Trades Council, Annual Reports. (Mitchell Library, Glasgow)
Parliamentary Debates, (Commons), Fifth Series
Irish Weekly (Belfast)
Labour Party: Annual Conference Reports
Newspaper Press Directory
Proceedings of the Institution of Mechanical Engineers
Scottish Co-operator
Scottish Law Reporter
Sheffield Daily Independent
Socialist (journal of the Socialist Labour Party)
Strike Bulletin (1919)
Scottish Trades Union Congress: Annual Report. (In Congress offices)
Scotsman
Vanguard
Worker (journal of the C.W.C.)
Willing's Press Guide and Advertiser's Directory and Handbook

V. Interviews

Janey Buchan
T. W. Burt
Neil Carmichael, M.P.
James Dollan
Henry Dutch
Peter Gemmill
Robert Gray
@ Finlay Hart
@ Archie Henry
The 2nd Lord Kirkwood
Hugh McCalman
@ Henry McShane
John Mains
Dame Jean Roberts
Sir William Robieson
A. R. Rollin
@ Tom Scollan
Frank Semple

Rt. Hon. John Wheatley
Rt. Hon. Arthur Woodburn
@ Tape-recorded reminiscences in the possession of Mr. John Foster, Department of Politics, University of Strathclyde.

VI. Unpublished theses

R. Baxter. *The Liverpool Labour Party, 1918-63.* Oxford, D.Phil., 1970

D. M. Chewter. *History of the Socialist Labour Party of Great Britain from 1902 to 1921, with special reference to the development of its ideas.* Oxford, B.Litt., 1965.

S. Cooper. *John Wheatley: a study in Labour history.* Glasgow, Ph.D., 1973.

M. K. Edwards. *The provision of community facilities in Drumchapel.* Glasgow University Dept. of Town Planning, Diploma thesis, 1970.

J. Hinton. *Rank and File Militancy in the British Engineering Industry, 1914-18.* London, Ph.D., 1969.

R. Hyman. *The Workers' Union, 1898-1929.* Oxford, D.Phil., 1968.

P. M. Jackson. *Local Authority Public Expenditure; a case-study of Glasgow.* Stirling, Ph.D., 1975.

I. S. McLean. *The Labour Movement in Clydeside Politics, 1914-22.* Oxford, D.Phil., 1971.

R. Martin. *The National Minority Movement.* Oxford, D.Phil., 1964.

A. Marwick. *The I.L.P., 1918-1932.* Oxford, B.Litt., 1960.

D. W. Urwin. *Politics and the Development of the Unionist Party in Scotland.* Manchester, M.A. (Econ.), 1963.

H. R. Vernon. *The Socialist Labour Party and the Working-class Movement on the Clyde, 1903-1921.* Leeds, M.Phil., 1967.

VII. Published works used as primary sources

Sir Patrick Abercrombie and R. H. Matthew. *The Clyde Valley Regional Plan 1946.* London, H.M.S.O., 1949.

C. Addison. *Politics from Within.* 2 vols., London, Herbert Jenkins, 1924.

C. Addison. *Four and a Half Years.* 2 vols., London, Hutchinson, 1934.

Lord Askwith. *Industrial Problems and Disputes.* London, John Murray, 1920.

Amalgamated Society of Engineers. *The Treasury Agreement (1915).* (Cole Collection, Nuffield College Library, Oxford.)

G. N. Barnes. *From Workshop to War Cabinet.* London, Herbert Jenkins, 1923.

T. Bell. *Pioneering Days.* London, Lawrence & Wishart, 1941.

T. Bell. *John MacLean: A Fighter for Freedom.* Glasgow, Communist Party Scottish Committee, 1944.

W. Beveridge. *Power and Influence.* London, Hodder & Stoughton, 1953.

A. L. Bowley. *Prices and Wages in the United Kingdom, 1914-20.* Oxford, 1921. (Economic & Social History of the War. British Series.)

G. D. H. Cole. *Labour in Wartime.* London, G. Bell & Sons, 1915.

G. D. H. Cole. *Workshop Organisation.* Oxford, 1923. (Economic & Social History of the War. British Series.)

G. D. H. Cole. *Trade Unionism and Munitions.* Oxford, 1923. (Economic & Social History of the War. British Series.)

E. T. Cook. *The Press in Wartime*. London, Macmillan, 1920.

Clyde Valley Planning Advisory Committee. *Report to the Constituent Local Authorities* (Hamilton), 1947.

J. Denvir. *The Irish in Britain*. London, Kegan, Paul, Trench & Tubner, 1892.

P. J. Dollan. *The Clyde Rent War*. Glasgow, 1925.

W. Gallacher. *Revolt on the Clyde*. London, Lawrence & Wishart, 1936.

W. Gallacher & J. Paton. *Towards Industrial Democracy*. Paisley (1920).

D. Lloyd George. *War Memoirs*. 2 vol. edition, London, Odhams, 1938.

Glasgow Corporation Housing Department. *Review of Operations 1919-47*. Glasgow, Glasgow Corporation, 1947.

T. H. Graham. *Willie Graham*. London, Hutchinson (1948).

W. M. Haddow. *My Seventy Years*. Glasgow, R. Gibson & Sons, 1943.

Anon. (T. Henderson). *The Scottish Socialists: a gallery of contemporary portraits*. London, Faber & Faber, 1931.

F. W. Hirst. The Policy of the Engineers. *Economic Journal*, 1898.

T. Johnston. *Memories*. London, Collins, 1952.

T. Jones. *Whitehall Diary*, vol. I, 1916-25 (ed. Middlemas). London, Oxford University Press, 1969.

P. U. Kellog & A. Gleason. *British Labor and the War*. New York, Boni & Livewright, 1919.

ed. A. W. Kirkcaldy. *Labour, Finance, and the War*. London, British Association, 1916.

D. Kirkwood. *To the Manchester Labour Conference*. (Glasgow) 1917.

Labour Party. *Report of a special committee appointed by the Annual Conference of the Party held at Manchester in January 1917 to inquire into and Report upon the circumstances which resulted in the Deportation in March 1916 of David Kirkwood and other workmen employed in Munition Factories in the Clyde District*. London, Labour Party (1918).

J. Leatham. *Glasgow in the Limelight: Why did the Second City 'go Labour'?* Turriff, Deveron Press, 1924.

J. Lee. *Tomorrow is a New Day*. London, Cresset Press, 1939.

V. I. Lenin. *Left-wing Communism — An Infantile Disorder*. (London, Communist Party of Great Britain, 1920 ed.)

G. McAllister. *James Maxton, Portrait of a Rebel*. London, John Murray, 1935.

A. McArthur & H. Kingsley Long. *No Mean City*. (London, Corgi Books, 1957 ed.)

(Sir) L. Macassey. *Labour Policy, False and True*. London, Thornton Butterworth Ltd., 1922.

J. McGovern. *Neither Fear nor Favour*. London, Blandford Press, 1960.

J. MacLean (ed. N. Milton). *In the Rapids of Revolution*. London, Allison & Busby, 1978.

Lord MacMillan. *A Man of Law's Tale*. London, MacMillan, 1952.

H. McShane (intro.). *Glasgow 1919*. Glasgow, Molendinar Press, 1974.

H. McShane & J. Smith. *Harry McShane: No Mean Fighter*. London, Pluto Press, 1978.

D. S. Morton. *The 40 Hours Strike: An Historic Survey of the first General Strike in Scotland*. Clydebank, 1919.

J. T. Murphy. *Preparing for Power*. London, Jonathan Cape, 1934.

J. T. Murphy. *New Horizons*. London, John Lane, 1941.

W. Orton. *Labour in Transition*. London, P. Allan & Co., 1921.

J. Paton. *Proletarian Pilgrimage*. London, Routledge, 1935.

J. Paton. *Left Turn!* London, Secker & Warburg, 1936.

J. Scanlon. *Decline and Fall of the Labour Party*. London, Peter Davis (1932).

W. R. Scott & J. Cunnison. *Industries of the Clyde Valley during the War*. Oxford, Economic & Social History of the War, British Series, 1924.

E. Shinwell. *Conflict without Malice*. London, Odhams, 1955.

E. Shinwell. *I've lived through it All*. London, Gollancz, 1973.

P. (Viscount) Snowden. *An Autobiography* (2 vols.). London, Ivor Nicholson & Watson Ltd., 1934.

F. Stevenson. *Lloyd George — a Diary* (ed. A. J. P. Taylor). London, Hutchinson, 1971.

W. Stewart. *J. Keir Hardie: A Biography*. London, I.L.P., 1921.

(Sir) B. H. Thomson. *Queer People*. London, Hodder & Stoughton, 1922.

(Sir) B. H. Thomson. *The Story of Scotland Yard*. London, Grayson & Grayson, 1935.

B. Webb. *Diaries 1912-24* (ed. M. Cole). London, Longman, 1952.

B. Webb. *Diaries 1924-32* (ed. M. Cole). London, Longman, 1956.

E. Wertheimer. *Portrait of the Labour Party*. London, Putnam, 1929.

ed. T. Wilson. *The Political Diaries of C. P. Scott, 1911-1928*. London, Collins, 1970.

VIII. Other works cited

P. Abrams. 'The Failure of Social Reform, 1918-20', *Past and Present*, 24, 1963, pp. 43-64.

S. Armitage. *The Politics of Decontrol of Industry*. London, Weidenfeld & Nicolson, 1969.

R. P. Arnot. *The Scottish Miners*. London, Allen & Unwin, 1955.

P. Bachrach and M. Baratz. 'Two faces of power', *American Political Science Review*, 56, 1962, pp. 947-52.

R. N. W. Blake. *The Unknown Prime Minister: The Life and Times of Andrew Bonar Law 1858-1923*. London, Eyre & Spottiswoode, 1955.

N. Blewett. 'The Franchise in Britain 1885-1915', *Past and Present*, 32, 1965, pp. 27-56.

J. Brand. 'Councillors, Activists and Electors: Democratic relationships in Scottish cities', in S. C. Paterson and J. Wahlke, eds., *Comparative Legislative Behavior: Frontiers of Research* (New York, Wiley, 1972), pp. 235-66.

N. Branson. *Poplarism 1919-25*. London, Lawrence & Wishart, 1979.

C. Brogan. *The Glasgow Story*. London, Frederick Muller, 1952.

J. Broom. *John Maclean*. Loanhead, Lothian, Macdonald Publishers, 1973.

T. Brotherstone. 'The Suppression of the "Forward".' *Scottish Labour History Society Journal*, 1, 1969, pp. 5-23.

J. Buchan. *The Four Adventures of Richard Hannay*. London, Hodder & Stoughton, 1930.

I. Budge, J. Brand, M. Margolis and A. Smith. *Political Stratification and Democracy*. London, Macmillan, 1972.

D. Butler and M. Pinto-Duschinsky. *The British General Election of 1970*. London, Macmillan, 1971.

D. Butler and A. Sloman. *British Political Facts, 1900-79*. London, Macmillan, 1980.

S. G. Checkland. *The Upas Tree: Glasgow, 1875-1975*. Glasgow, Glasgow University Press, 1976.

L. Chester, S. Fay and H. Young. *The Zinoviev Letter*. London, Heinemann, 1967.

S. B. Chrimes, ed. *The General Election in Glasgow, February 1950*. Glasgow, Jackson, Son & Co., 1950.

P. F. Clarke. 'Liberals, Labour, and the Franchise', *English Historical Review*, 92, 1977, pp. 582-90.

H. A. Clegg, A. Fox and A. F. Thompson. *A History of British Trade Unions since 1889*. Vol. I, 1889-1910. Oxford, Clarendon Press, 1964.

N. Collins. 'Social background and motivation of councillors': a paper for the Robinson Committee. Birmingham University, INLOGOV, 1977.

C. Coote. *A Companion of Honour*. London, Collins, 1965.

M. Cowling. *The Impact of Labour, 1920-1924*. Cambridge, Cambridge University Press, 1971.

F. W. S. Craig. *British Parliamentary Election Results, 1918-1949*. Glasgow, Political Reference Publications, 1969.

F. W. S. Craig. *British Parliamentary Election Statistics, 1918-1968*. Glasgow, Political Reference Publications, 1968.

M. Crenson. *The Unpolitics of Air Pollution*. Baltimore, Md, Johns Hopkins University Press, 1971.

I. Crewe and C. Payne. 'Another Game with Nature: an ecological regression model of the British two-party vote ratio in 1970', *British Journal of Political Science*, 6, 1976, pp. 43-81.

D. Crow. *A Man of Push and Go: The Life of George Macaulay Booth*. London, Hart-Davis, 1965.

J. Cunnison and J. Gilfillan, eds. *The Third Statistical Account of Scotland: Glasgow*. Glasgow, Collins, 1958.

R. E. Dowse. *Left in the Centre: The Independent Labour Party, 1893-1940*. London, Longmans, 1966.

P. Berresford Ellis and S. Mac A'Ghobhainn. *The Scottish Insurrection of 1820*. London, Gollancz, 1970.

Department of Employment. *British Labour Statistics: Historical Abstract, 1886-1968*. H.M.S.O., 1971.

D. Englander. 'Landlord and Tenant in Urban Scotland: the background to the Clyde rent strikes, 1915', *Scottish Labour History Society Journal*, 15, 1981, pp. 4-14.

A. McL. Ewing. *The History of the Glasgow Herald, 1783-1948*. Privately printed (Glasgow, *Glasgow Herald*, 1949).

W. Ferguson. *Scotland, 1689 to the Present*. Edinburgh, Oliver & Boyd, 1968.

Anon. *The Glasgow Herald, 1783-1958*. Glasgow, *Glasgow Herald*, 1958.

R. Gregory. *The Miners in British Politics*. London, Oxford University Press, 1968.

J. E. Handley. *The Irish in Modern Scotland*. Cork, Cork University Press, 1947.

H. J. Hanham. *Scottish Nationalism*. London, Faber & Faber, 1969.

W. Hampton. *Democracy and Community*. London, Oxford University Press, 1970.

J. Harris. *William Beveridge: a biography*. Oxford, Clarendon Press, 1977.

H. K. Hawson. *Sheffield: The Growth of a City, 1893-1926*. Sheffield, J. W. Northend, 1968.

G. C. L. Hazlehurst. *Politicians at War, July 1914-May 1915. A Prologue to the Triumph of Lloyd George.* London, Jonathan Cape, 1971.

E. J. Hobsbawm. *Labouring Men.* London, Weidenfeld & Nicolson, 1964.

J. Hinton. 'The Clyde Workers' Committee and the Dilution Struggle', in A. Briggs and J. Saville, eds., *Essays in Labour History, 1886-1923* (London, Macmillan, 1971), pp. 152-184.

J. Hinton. 'The Suppression of the *Forward* — a Note', *Scottish Labour History Society Journal,* 7, 1973, pp. 4-9.

J. Hinton. *The First Shop Stewards' Movement.* London, Allen & Unwin, 1973.

E. Hughes. *Keir Hardie.* London, Allen & Unwin, 1956.

J. Hume and M. Moss. *Beardmore: the history of a Scottish industrial giant.* London, Heinemann, 1979.

R. Jenkins. *Asquith.* London, Collins, 1964.

J. B. Jefferys. *The Story of the Engineers, 1800-1945.* London, Lawrence & Wishart (1945).

M. Keating and D. Bleiman. *Labour and Scottish Nationalism.* London, Macmillan, 1979.

J. G. Kellas. *Modern Scotland: The Nation since 1870.* London, Pall Mall, 1968.

J. Kellett. *Glasgow: A Concise History.* London, Blond, 1967.

W. F. H. Kendall. *The Revolutionary Movement in Britain, 1900-21.* London, Weidenfeld & Nicolson, 1969.

S. Lukes. *Power: a radical view.* London, Macmillan, 1975.

R. Lyman. *The First Labour Government, 1924.* London, Chapman & Hall, 1957.

F. S. L. Lyons. *John Dillon.* London, Routledge, 1968.

L. J. MacFarlane. *The British Communist Party: Its Origin and Development until 1929.* London, MacGibbon & Kee, 1966.

I. S. McLean. 'The Rise and Fall of the SNP', *Political Studies,* 18, 1970, pp. 357-72.

I. S. McLean. 'The Ministry of Munitions, the Clyde Workers' Committee and the suppression of the *Forward:* an alternative view', *Scottish Labour History Society Journal,* 6, 1972, pp. 3-25.

I. S. McLean. 'The problem of proportionate swing', *Political Studies,* 21, 1973, pp. 57-63.

I. S. McLean. 'Oxford and Bridgwater', in C. Cook and J. Ramsden, eds., *By-elections in British Politics* (London, Macmillan, 1973), pp. 140-64.

I. S. McLean. 'Red Clydeside, 1915-19', in R. Quinault and J. Stevenson, eds., *Popular Protest and Public Order* (London, Allen & Unwin, 1974), pp. 215-42.

I. S. McLean and J. C. Gordon. 'P. J. Dollan, James Dalrymple, and Glasgow's tramways 1926-9: a study in political and administrative change', paper presented to SSRC Urban Studies Conference, York, 1981.

J. McNair. *James Maxton, Beloved Rebel.* London, Allen & Unwin, 1955.

D. Marquand. *Ramsay MacDonald.* London, Jonathan Cape, 1977.

R. Martin. *Communism and the British Trade Unions, 1924-33.* Oxford, Clarendon Press, 1969.

A. Marwick. *The Deluge.* London, Bodley Head, 1965.

W. H. Marwick. *A Short History of Labour in Scotland.* Edinburgh, W. R. Chambers, 1967.

H. Matthew, R. McKibbin and J. Kay. 'The franchise factor in the rise of the Labour Party', *English Historical Review*, 91, 1976, pp. 723-52.

J. Melling. 'The Glasgow Rent Strike and Clydeside Labour — some problems of interpretation', *Scottish Labour History Society Journal*, 13, 1979, pp. 39-44.

R. K. Middlemas. *The Clydesiders: a left-wing struggle for Parliamentary Power*. London, Hutchinson, 1965.

R. Miller and J. Tivy, eds., *The Glasgow Region*. Glasgow, Glasgow University for the British Association, 1958.

Sir D. Milne. *The Scottish Office*. London, Allen & Unwin, 1957.

N. Milton. *John Maclean*. London, Pluto Press, 1973.

R. Mitchison. *A History of Scotland*. London, Methuen, 1970.

K. and J. Morgan. *Portrait of a Progressive: the political career of Christopher, Viscount Addison*. Oxford, Clarendon Press, 1980.

C. L. Mowat. *Britain Between the Wars*. London, Methuen, 1955.

K. Newton. *Second City Politics*. Oxford, Clarendon Press, 1976.

N. Nicolson. *Lord of the Isles*. London, Weidenfeld & Nicolson, 1960.

N. Nie, C. H. Hull, J. G. Jenkins, K. Steinbrenner and D. Bent. *SPSS Handbook* (2nd ed.). New York, McGraw-Hill, 1975.

D. Niven. *The Development of Housing in Scotland*. London, Croom Helm, 1979.

C. A. Oakley. *The Second City*. Glasgow, Blackie & Son Ltd., 1946.

C. A. Oakley. *The Last Tram*. Glasgow, Glasgow Corporation Transport Dept., 1962.

H. M. Pelling. *The British Communist Party*. London, A. & C. Black, 1958.

S. Pollard. *A History of Labour in Sheffield*. Liverpool, Liverpool University Press, 1959.

B. Pribicevic. *The Shop Stewards' Movement and Workers' Control*. Oxford, Blackwell, 1959.

M. D. Pugh. *Electoral Reform in War and Peace*. London, Routledge, 1978.

W. J. Reader. *Architect of Air Power*. London, Collins, 1968.

J. S. Rowett. 'The Local Government Policies of the Labour Governments of 1924 and 1929-31', paper presented to SSRC Urban Studies Conference, York, 1981.

G. R. Rubin. 'A Note on the Scottish Office Reaction to John Maclean's Drugging Allegations made at the High Court, Edinburgh, 1918', *Scottish Labour History Society Journal*, 14, 1980, pp. 40-5.

Scottish Development Department. *Scotland's Older Houses*: Report of a Subcommittee of the Scottish Housing Advisory Committee, submitted to the Secretary of State (chairman Cullingworth) (H.M.S.O., 1967).

J. A. Smith. *John Buchan*. London, Hart-Davis, 1965.

R. Smith. 'The Origins of Scottish New Towns policy and the founding of East Kilbride', *Public Administration* 52, 1974, pp. 143-59.

R. Smith. 'The politics of an overspill policy: Glasgow, Cumbernauld and the Housing and Town Development (Scotland) Act', *Public Administration* 55, 1977, pp. 79-94.

A. Sutcliffe, ed. *Multi-storey living: the British working-class experience*. London, Croom Helm, 1974.

A. Sutcliffe and R. Smith. *Birmingham, 1939-70*. London, Oxford University Press, 1972.

A. J. P. Taylor. *Politics in Wartime*. London, Hamish Hamilton, 1964.

A. J. P. Taylor. *English History, 1914-45*. Oxford, Clarendon Press, 1965.

J. Thomas. *The Springburn Story.* Dawlish, David & Charles, 1964.

C. J. Wrigley. *David Lloyd George and the British Labour Movement.* Hassocks, Sussex, Harvester Press, 1976.

IX. Bibliographies and handlists

C. Cook and others. *Sources in British political history, 1900-51,* 5 vols., London, Macmillan, for the British Library of Political and Economic Science, 1975-8.

C. Hazlehurst and C. Woodland. *A guide to the papers of British Cabinet Ministers, 1900-51.* London, Royal Historical Society, 1974.

I. MacDougall. *Interim Bibliography of the Scottish Working Class Movement.* Edinburgh, Scottish Labour History Society, 1965. Now superseded by I. MacDougall, *A Catalogue of some Labour Records in Scotland and some Scots records outside Scotland* (Edinburgh, Scottish Labour History Society, 1978): a stupendous work hiding behind a ridiculously modest title.

C. L. Mowat. *Great Britain since 1914.* London, Hodder & Stoughton, 1971.

Public Record Office: *Guide to the Public Record Office.* London, H.M.S.O., 1969.

Public Record Office Handbooks (all published London, H.M.S.O.):

List of Cabinet Papers, 1860-1914.	1964.
Classes of Departmental Records for 1906-39.	1966.
List of Cabinet Papers, 1915 and 1916.	1966.
Records of the Cabinet Office to 1922.	1966.

Index